HAP

Also by Thomas M. Coffey

Agony at Easter: The 1916 Irish Uprising
Imperial Tragedy
Lion by the Tail
The Long Thirst: Prohibition in America
Decision over Schweinfurt

HAP

MILITARY AVIATOR

THE STORY OF THE U.S. AIR FORCE
AND THE MAN WHO BUILT IT
GENERAL HENRY H. "HAP" ARNOLD

THOMAS M. COFFEY

THE VIKING PRESS
NEW YORK

Published simultaneously in Canada by
Penguin Books Canada Limited

LIBRARY OF CONGRESS CATALOGING IN PUBLICATION DATA
Coffey, Thomas M.
HAP : the story of the U.S. Air Force and the man
who built it, General Henry "Hap " Arnold.
Includes bibliographical references and index.
1. Arnold, Henry Harley, 1886–1950.   2. United
States. Air Force—Biography.   3. Generals—United
States—Biography.   4. Aeronautics, Military—United
States—History.   I. Title.
UG626.2.A76C63   1982   358.4'0092'4   81-69928
ISBN 0-670-36069-4   AACR2

Grateful acknowledgment is made to Harper and Row, Publish-
ers, Inc., for permission to reprint selections from *Global Mission*
by H. H. Arnold. Copyright 1949 by H. H. Arnold. Copyright
renewed 1977 by Eleanor P. Arnold.

The ornament used throughout the book is the military aviator
golden eagle badge. The photographs are from the collection of
Col. William Bruce Arnold, Ret.

Printed in the United States of America
Set in Baskerville

CONTENTS

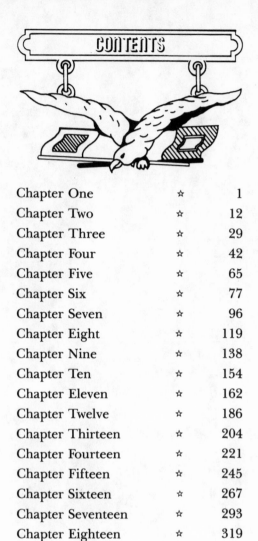

Photographs follow page 203.

HAP

CHAPTER I

O n January 13, 1950, retired General of the Air Force Henry Harley
"Hap" Arnold, finding it difficult to complete an article on military
aviation for the *Encyclopaedia Britannica,* sent a telegram to the *Britannica*
from his modest ranch house in the Valley of the Moon, near Sonoma,
California. The telegram was characteristically impatient. It was also
tragically prophetic: "Help. Have been working on rewrites for *Britannica* and am all at sea. . . . What's the score before I strike out and the
game is called on account of darkness? . . . Am I on the right track?" [1]

At that time, General Arnold had already suffered five heart attacks
serious enough to require hospitalization. No one knew how many lesser
attacks he had failed to report. His wife was now so concerned about his
condition that she didn't like to leave him home alone. When she had to
do so, she would ask Bruce Simmons, who had been his driver during
active-duty days, to look in on him. [2] Simmons now lived just down the
hill from the Arnolds and helped out on the little forty-acre "ranch"
they had bought for their retirement years. The young master sergeant
and the five-star general had developed a firm attachment to each other
in the ten years since Simmons had become Arnold's driver. When
Arnold retired in 1946, as one of only four permanent five-star generals
in the nation's history, he had invited Simmons to come with him to
California and Simmons had gladly accepted. Occasionally they would
have a falling-out owing to Arnold's well-known impatience, but he
would make it up to Simmons a day or two later by taking him to Sonoma
and buying him pastries at the bakery there. Since Simmons was as
concerned as Mrs. Arnold about the general's health, he willingly looked
in on him when she was away, but he had learned he must do it subtly.
One day, shortly before Christmas of 1949, he had gone up to the house
in her absence while Arnold was taking a nap. Tiptoeing into the
semidarkened bedroom, he had been alarmed because he could see no
sign that the general was breathing. He had moved closer, bent over the
bed, and looked directly down into the general's face.

Arnold opened his eyes and roared, "What the hell do you want?"

Simmons jumped in fright and Arnold, laughing, said, "You thought I was gone, didn't you?"

He had known for some time he might go at any moment—each new attack further weakened the tissues of his heart—yet he seldom talked about the prospect of death, and he refused to sit still in an effort to preserve his strength. He had said one day to his son, Bruce, "It's hell to be sick. They want to keep me alive by wrapping me in cotton and placing me in a glass case, but I'll be goddamned if I'll let them." [3] He continued his writing and he continued as best he could to look after his property. The day after his telegram to the *Britannica*, he walked down the hill to Simmons's house to outline the work he planned for the next morning. The two of them would go into a fairly level part of the hilly land where something needed to be done.

"What time?" Simmons asked.

"About six or six-thirty."

"My God, General, tomorrow's Sunday. Can't we wait till eight or eight-thirty?"

No. General Arnold was not accustomed to starting any day that late. But this time the question was to become moot. Early the next morning he awoke and said something to his wife, who was still half asleep. A few minutes later he was dead at the age of sixty-four.

During forty-one years of active service in the U.S. Army and Air Force, he had compiled a record unparalleled in military history. Universally acknowledged as the father of the modern American Air Force, he had taken charge of the then Army Air Corps in 1938, when it was a puny collection of twenty thousand men and a few hundred less-than-battleworthy planes. By 1944, under the whip of his compelling, relentless, and often unreasonable dynamism, it had grown into an organization of 2.4 million men and eighty thousand aircraft. Never before or since has a military machine of such size and technical complexity been created in so short a period. At the height of World War II, Arnold commanded the largest, mightiest air force the world had ever seen and perhaps will ever see. When his B-29s dropped the atomic bombs on Japan in 1945, the U.S. Air Force dominated the entire world.

In the process of building this gigantic and unprecedented air fleet, Arnold had spent several billions of American taxpayers' dollars. But when he died in 1950, his entire personal estate amounted to only two $10,000 insurance policies and his "ranch," for which he had paid $7,500. His widow had the right to a federal pension of $75 per month. [4]

People who knew "Hap" Arnold weren't surprised that he died virtually broke. Money had never attracted him. Airplanes were his obsession. The Wright brothers had taught him to fly in 1911, and he was the holder of U.S. Army Pilot's License Number Two. He spent more than half his life fighting for the development of air power and air transportation. But on many occasions throughout his active years, it seemed unlikely that he would even complete a full Air Corps career, let alone play such a pivotal role in the development of air power and air transport. Arnold was an incurable maverick who never hesitated to act on his own initiative or take positions that infuriated his superiors. Time after time he found himself in deep trouble.

January 1917—The Signal Corps Aviation School at Rockwell Field, North Island, San Diego. Captain Arnold was the school's supply officer when, on January 10, two men, Lt. Col. Harry G. Bishop and Lt. W. A. Robertson, took off from the field and disappeared. At nine o'clock the next morning when there was still no word from the lost fliers, Capt. H. A. Dargue, the officer in charge of training, went to the base secretary, Maj. Frank Lahm, who had authorized the flight, to suggest that they send out search planes. Lahm vetoed the idea then and renewed the veto again at noon. Later in the day, base commander Col. W. A. Glassford also declined the suggestion.[5]

By this time the matter was causing agitation on the base, especially among the young fliers, who could imagine themselves crashing in the desert without hope that anyone would come looking for them. Arnold openly sided with Dargue against Major Lahm and Colonel Glassford. When Lahm denied that he had even authorized the flight, intimating that it was Dargue who had approved it, Arnold stepped forward and swore he had seen Lahm's signature on the permit.[6]

Despite the protests of Dargue, Arnold, and other young fliers, one day followed another without any move to send planes in search of the lost men. Not until January 16, six days after their disappearance, did planes finally take off to look for them.

For three days, the planes from San Diego, plus several people on the ground, criss-crossed northern Mexico in an effort to find the two lost fliers.[7] One of the search planes, it was later learned, came within a few miles of their plane, which was downed near the head of the Gulf of California. By the third day of the desert search, nine days after the men had disappeared, the rescue team had all but abandoned hope. Then suddenly they came upon the fliers, still alive but barely so.

When the full scope of their ordeal became known—an ordeal which might have been shortened if the search had begun immediately —unrest intensified among the young fliers and students at the San Diego Aviation School. Arnold and Dargue incited further unrest by demanding an Army investigation of the matter. They succeeded, in a manner of speaking, but theirs was a Pyrrhic victory. Long before the investigation (which was inconclusive) had even begun, Colonel Glassford made sure that both men were elsewhere. At the end of January, Arnold was transferred to Panama.[8] At the moment, his career in the air did not look propitious.

February 1926—Washington, D.C. Major Arnold was now stationed at Air Service headquarters in the Munitions Building as chief of the information division. It was not as prestigious a job as it might appear. The Air Service in 1926 was a depressed and almost insignificant branch of the Army. The previous October, Arnold had stated to a presidential fact-finding board that the entire effective force of the service at that moment was only thirty-five planes. This testimony came just before the court-martial of Arnold's friend Brig. Gen. Billy Mitchell, who for several years had led the campaign to establish an enlarged air force, separate from the Army. An assertive and sometimes abrasive man, Mitchell had been dismissed as assistant chief of the Air Service in April 1925 for criticizing the Army General Staff's laggard aviation policies, and had been indicted five months later when he publicly accused both the Army and Navy staffs of "incompetency, criminal negligence and almost treasonable administration of the national defense."

Arnold had testified at Mitchell's court-martial, supporting him warmly though he and some of his colleagues had been warned by superiors that they would damage their own military careers by doing so. When Mitchell was convicted, on December 17, 1925, for "making statements to the prejudice of good order and military discipline," the future of men like Hap Arnold and others who had supported him, as well as the future of air power in America, looked bleak. The decision so depressed Arnold that he considered leaving the Army to take a job as president of the newly formed Pan American Airways.[9] While this possibility was pending, however, he continued to campaign for a stronger air force. Even after Mitchell had been suspended, and the General Staff had pointedly forbidden the young air zealots to pursue their public agitation, Arnold, with several associates, kept up a steady, surreptitious flow of air-power propaganda to friendly congressmen and newsmen.[10] These associates included Maj. Millard F. "Miff" Harmon, Capt. Ira C. Eaker, Lt. David Lingle, and, not surprisingly, Maj. H. A. "Bert" Dargue, the same man with whom Arnold had teamed, to their mutual detriment, nine years earlier in San Diego. (Partly through Arnold's efforts, Dargue had been reinstated in the Air Service.)

In early February 1926, when War Department officials noticed that the cry for more air power was continuing unabated in the press, and when it became apparent that congressmen were still being bombarded with letters in favor of a separate air force, Secretary of War Dwight F. Davis ordered the chief of the Air Service, Maj. Gen. Mason M. Patrick, to conduct an investigation and find out who the agitators were. The investigation didn't take long: Patrick knew the men behind the mailings because until the Mitchell trial he had been abetting them. It was imperative now that he take some action, at least against the principal offenders, who were Arnold and Dargue.

Patrick was reluctant to punish Dargue, who had been his personal pilot and was one of his most reliable aides, but he wasn't at all hesitant about punishing Arnold, with whom he had never been on friendly terms. One day in 1925, he had become so angry at his information officer that he had thrown a paperweight at him.[11] General Patrick now called Arnold into his office to announce to him that as a result of his attempts at "influencing legislation in a manner forbidden by regulations and otherwise decidedly objectionable,"[12] he had two choices. "You can resign from the Army," Patrick said, "or you can take a court-martial."

Both choices seemed inordinately severe. After recovering from his surprise, Arnold said, "How long do I have to decide?"

Now it was Patrick's turn to be surprised. Resignation from the Army would seem infinitely preferable to a trial that was certain to establish his guilt and entail dismissal from the Army as well as public disgrace. Still, he had given the unmanageable major a choice. "You have twenty-four hours," he said.

Arnold went back to his office, called his wife, and asked her to meet him in the Ellipse, near Constitution Avenue.[13] When she arrived, they sat down on a park bench, despite the February cold, and he told her about Patrick's ultimatum.

"What do you think I should do?" he asked.

Eleanor Arnold was not a timid woman. She remembered that two years earlier, when they were stationed in San Diego, General Patrick had asked her husband to try to influence a California congressman in favor of a bill the Air Service wanted.

"Well, Hap," she reminded him, "they told you to do that once."
"I know it."

"I don't think you did anything wrong," she said, after they had talked awhile, "and you're not going to leave the service with a chip on your shoulder. I think you should ask for a court-martial."

As he listened to her, his mood brightened. Finally he said, "I was hoping you'd say all that. I wanted to hear you say it."

When he returned to Patrick's office the next day and announced he had chosen the court-martial, the Air Service chief had a problem for which he was not prepared. In any court-martial of Arnold, Patrick's own lobbying activity, and his tolerance of his whole staff's activities for some time, would almost certainly be discussed. Furthermore, after all the bad publicity the Army had received during the Mitchell trial, it was doubtful that the General Staff would appreciate another one like it. Was Arnold certain, Patrick asked, that he perferred a court-martial, considering all its implications for the service and for his family? Yes, Arnold was certain.

In that case, General Patrick told Arnold, he would take the matter up with higher authorities, and meanwhile, he was dismissed.

A few days later, Arnold was again summoned to Patrick's office. This time, the chief of the Air Service was more relaxed—almost jocular.

"In your opinion," he asked disarmingly, "What's the worst facility we have in the entire Air Service?"

"Oh, there's no doubt about that," Arnold said. "It has to be Fort Riley, Kansas."

General Patrick said, "Good. You are now the commanding officer of an observation squadron there."[14]

March 10, 1933—At 5:55 p.m., Colonel Arnold, now commanding officer at March Field near Riverside, California, felt the earth tremble beneath his feet, then begin to sway in what was obviously a major earthquake. Despite the intensity of the quake, it was quickly apparent that the March Field facilities had suffered no significant damage. Within the next hour, however, radio newscasters said the quake had wreaked havoc in several neighboring southern California cities, including Los Angeles, and had devastated Long Beach, where sixty-five people were reported dead, at least one thousand injured, and countless thousands homeless. Hundreds of buildings had collapsed and hundreds more were in danger of following them.[15]

Fires were raging throughout the Long Beach business area,

prompting the fire department to estimate (erroneously, as it turned out) that the death toll might reach five hundred. All hospitals were full and one of them had laid out its patients on the lawn because the front wall of the building had collapsed. Thousands of bewildered people were milling aimlessly in the streets. Other thousands were jamming the highways north toward Los Angeles, like refugees evicted by war. The work of fire fighters was impeded by the fact that the quake had broken many water mains, sending geysers as high as seven stories into the air and diminishing pressure. In addition, each new shock damaged more buildings, dislodged more heavy debris, and filled the air with huge chunks of flying masonry, creating new waves of panic and inflicting added injuries upon the people in the streets.

When Arnold heard these reports, he canceled a practice mission scheduled that night by one of the bomb groups stationed at March. Then he put in a call for Col. Charles H. Hilton, commander of Fort MacArthur, a coast artillery base that guarded the harbors at Long Beach and San Pedro.[16] Colonel Hilton, a man several years older than Arnold and very much senior in rank, was also the designated officer in charge of any emergency measures that might be necessary in case of a Los Angeles area disaster. But this evening Hilton was not in when Arnold called. He was on a trip, but no one at Fort MacArthur could say exactly where he had gone or when he would return. Arnold decided to take independent action. It was not a difficult decision for him to make. Time after time during his career he had ignored Army regulations and acted on his own initiative. Time after time he had also been disciplined for it, but the Army hadn't yet broken him of the habit.

Unable to reach Colonel Hilton at Fort MacArthur, he put in a call for one of his pilots, Capt. Ira Eaker, who was on detached duty in Los Angeles,[17] improving his military prospects by studying for a degree at the University of Southern California. When Arnold called he was in his apartment near the campus, about twenty miles from Long Beach.

"Can you get away right now," Arnold asked, "and go down to Long Beach?"

The "right now" was superfluous, as Eaker was well aware. Whenever Arnold wanted anything done, he wanted it done "right now." Eaker assured him he could go immediately.

"Talk to the mayor and chief of police," Arnold said. "Find out what we can do to help."

Despite traffic congestion caused by the northward flow of refugees from the continuing quakes, Eaker was in Long Beach within the hour, making his way to City Hall through the milling crowds of homeless, bewildered people who filled the streets. After conferring with harried city officials, he called Arnold.

"What they need most," Eaker said, "are more tents, blankets, and field kitchens."

Already the Navy and the California National Guard had swung into action, providing men, equipment, and food. Marines and sailors were patrolling the Long Beach streets. While Fort MacArthur had sent no equipment, perhaps because no one there considered himself authorized to expend government property, the base had sent fifty enlisted men and seven officers to the Long Beach Armory for relief duty.[18]

Arnold, at March Field, didn't concern himself with authorization to expend government property. He simply organized a convoy of trucks, backed them up to the quartermaster depot, and loaded them with food, Army field kitchens, tents, blankets, anything that might be useful. One of his staff officers, familiar with Army regulations, and seeing the kitchens on the truck, said to him, "You can't send those things down there. It's not your job." It was the responsibility, he pointed out, of the commanding officer at Fort MacArthur.

"To hell with that," Arnold said. "Those people need food."[19] Before the night was over, the trucks were on their way to Long Beach.

As the days passed and Long Beach began to recover, the need for help from the armed services diminished. Arnold was able to discontinue his Air Corps contributions, put the matter from his mind, and go on to other work. But not for long. He soon received a call from Gen. Malin Craig, at that time commander of the Army's Ninth Corps Area, which included the entire West Coast. Craig called to reprimand him and to inform him he was under investigation once more for a possible court-martial—a result of his activities after the Long Beach earthquake.[20] This time he was accused of giving away government property without the authorization of Colonel Hilton, the Fort MacArthur commander and the designated disaster officer for the southern California area.

March 1940—For more than seven months after Adolf Hitler's invasion of Poland had launched what was destined to become World War II, there was almost no activity on the western front except for an occasional "wake-up" gun-burst from the French dug in behind their "impregnable" Maginot Line, answered by a burst or two from the Germans dug in behind their "impregnable" Siegfried Line. But nobody, not even the dull, timid, foolish men governing France and

England, believed that the winter lull would continue into spring and summer.

In America, Hap Arnold, now a major general and Chief of the Army Air Corps, contemplated this situation with the knowledge that his organization might be called upon soon to provide air defense for the United States, and he had only a pathetic skeleton force of untried planes with which to do it. Since becoming chief in September 1938, he had discovered that to build the Air Corps into the fighting force that might one day be needed, he had to overcome resistance not only from America's politically powerful isolationists, who opposed defense spending because they were against involvement in any "foreign war," but also from some of the country's interventionists, who approved of defense spending but believed that half or more of the nation's meager aircraft production should be sent to the now desperate French and British.

Arnold, though sympathetic to the French and British, was charged first and foremost with the responsibility of building an American air force. Even if every plane built in 1939 and 1940 by every American aircraft company were at his disposal, he would not have enough to train the crews and create the operational units he was likely to need. He was prepared to cope with the opposition of the isolationists. In that struggle, President Franklin D. Roosevelt, his commander-in-chief, was with him all the way. But he hadn't yet figured out how to deal with the interventionists, who wanted to send away more planes than he could spare, because in that struggle Roosevelt was with him only a small part of the way. And the leader of these interventionists was one of the most powerful men in Roosevelt's cabinet—Henry Morgenthau, the secretary of the treasury.

Morgenthau had interested himself in the plight of France and England because of his deep and well-founded concern about Hitler's regime. After the Munich pact of September 1938, in which British Prime Minister Neville Chamberlain donated Czechoslovakia to Hitler, Morgenthau and Roosevelt agreed that there was no time to lose in helping to rearm America's apparent allies. But they found the secretary of war, Harry H. Woodring, less than enthusiastic. Woodring was basically an isolationist. Morgenthau, determined to circumvent Woodring, had suggested to the president that the Treasury Department might properly supervise the sale of arms to foreign nations since such a sale would involve large exchanges of currency. Roosevelt, reluctant at that moment to infuriate isolationists by replacing Woodring, had acceded to Morgenthau's suggestion.[21]

The result had been a tug-of-war for planes between the War

Department and Arnold on one side, Morgenthau and our beleaguered European allies on the other. It was a struggle that had continued through 1939 and was reaching a peak when, on March 5, 1940, Arnold was called to testify at a secret meeting of the House Military Affairs Committee.[22] He was soon to realize that there is no such thing as a secret meeting of congressmen.

Arnold told the committee, in confidence, that the Air Corps was paying too much for its airplanes. The cost of 2,100 planes ordered during the corps' expansion program, he said, had exceeded original estimates by $20 million. This was due, he said, not only to a rise in cost of materials, but to the large orders placed with American aircraft companies by the British and French. The American companies, he indicated, were giving preference to the orders of the Allies because they didn't want to lose their business.

Arnold's secret testimony soon reached the White House, and President Roosevelt reacted quickly. On the afternoon of March 12, he summoned to his office the War, Navy, and Treasury secretaries and their assistants, plus the Army and Navy air chiefs, General Arnold and Admiral John Towers.

The president began by addressing himself to the need for cooperation and coordination between all the members of his government in arranging foreign sales of aircraft and arms. He then moved on to the need for caution in answering questions before congressional committees. He wasn't happy, he said, with the way some people had been testifying before Congress—in particular, some War Department people.

At this point he looked directly at Arnold. If certain chiefs could not take care of themselves as witnesses before committees, he said, it might be necessary to send the second or third in command up the hill to testify.

Then, staring coldly at Arnold, he issued a threat that could not be misunderstood. As for officers who refused to "play ball" with the administration, there was a place where they might be sent, and it was called Guam.[23] Arnold had finally managed to infuriate his highest possible superior, the commander-in-chief. Though he was not fired, it was several months before the president again allowed him in the White House.

Arnold was a man who seemed to seek out trouble and to work best under pressure. As a boy he had learned to cope with the requirements of a father more demanding even than he himself would later become. Indeed it was because of his father's expectations rather than his own that he accepted his appointment to the Military Academy. And once he was securely in the Army, where he no longer had to cope with his father's pressure, he began to supply his own, creating it for himself by his refusal to accept conventional military wisdom. He was headstrong, often tactless, scornful of slow, conservative Army methods, critical of superiors, single-mindedly relentless in pushing his own beliefs, and impatient with those who failed to share his vision. Yet despite all this, he rose through the officer ranks as the years passed until, in September 1938, he became chief of the Air Corps. To the surprise of many military men, including Arnold himself, the Army establishment proved itself sufficiently flexible and tolerant of his independence to advance him to the top.

How did he manage to climb so high? He must have been doing something right. Even the more conservative Army generals, many of whom had been involved in restraining or chastising him from time to time, would concede that much. Though he might defy them, he was able to make them admire him. Though he sometimes ignored their discipline, he knew how to maintain discipline among those he commanded. Tough, impatient, and exacting with the men who worked under him, he nevertheless managed to command their respect and even, to an amazing degree, their affection. Almost puritanically strict, he could also be boyish, fun-loving, and engaging. Single-minded and unswerving in his aims, he could be flexible in achieving them. At all times practical, he cherished an imaginative vision of air power and air transportation that seemed, to most of his contemporaries, beyond the realm of possibility. While he often ignored Army procedures and was considered an abysmal administrator, he was unequalled in his ability to get things done. The contradictions within his commodious personality seemed often to make him uncomfortable, yet he was able to reconcile those contradictions and to exercise his unique abilities within the Army establishment, which he so often criticized and defied.

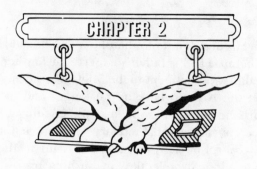

In the summer of 1893, when Henry Arnold was seven years old, Dr. Herbert A. Arnold, his father, sent him out to work, for room and board but no pay, on a farm near their home in Ardmore, Pennsylvania, a few miles west of Philadelphia.[1] To Dr. Arnold it was reasonable and proper that a seven-year-old boy should be put to work, not only to keep him out of mischief but to instill in him a sense of responsibility. Dr. Arnold's own father, Thomas Arnold, a nailer by trade at the Hooven Nail Works in the Montgomery County seat of Norristown,[2] had put him to work at that age. Though Thomas Arnold had disassociated himself from the Mennonite Church of the Brethren, which had been the family's religious affiliation for two centuries, he had not abandoned all of the Mennonite tenets, one of which was that everyone should learn, at an early age, to work. He had, however, abandoned another tenet of the Mennonites at that time—that six or seven years of education were enough for anybody because no more than that was necessary to make a man a good farmer. Herbert, Thomas's son, attended the Norristown public schools and was graduated from the high school there in 1873. When he expressed a desire to study medicine, his father did not discourage him. Since it was customary at that time and place to begin such study under the tutelage of an established physician, he apprenticed himself to Dr. Joseph K. Weaver of Norristown, then completed his studies at Jefferson Medical College, from which he was graduated in 1878. After practicing for a year in Evansburg, he opened an office at Gladwyne, where he also bought a farm, and where Henry Harley Arnold was born on June 25, 1886.

Henry was the third child and second son in a family of five children. Because Dr. Arnold, like his father, retained many strict Mennonite standards despite his conversion to the Baptist faith, his house was not a free-and-easy, fun-filled place for his growing children. At all times a stern, exacting man, he strenuously disapproved of any kind of play, either for children or adults, nor did he suffer jokes or lighthearted banter. The main purpose of life was salvation, and the road to salvation was work, of which he demanded as much from himself as from others. His first child, Elizabeth, who was four years older than his first son, Thomas, and six years older than Henry, had the job of watching over the boys and restraining their high spirits, which she did with efficiency and some degree of officiousness. (She handled her assignment so zealously, in fact, that as the boys grew older she became protective, especially of Henry, to the point of being almost possessive, a circumstance from which he constantly struggled to free himself.[3])

In 1890, Dr. Arnold moved his family from the farm to a house in Ardmore, but he did not sever his association with the Pennsylvania Dutch farmers in the area. Each morning at five he would harness his horse, climb into his buggy, and begin his rounds of the farms in his territory, riding the back roads hour after hour to treat his patients, mostly Mennonites, who respected his medical skills even though, following his father's example, he had rejected their religion. At five in the evening, twelve hours after leaving home, he would return to the plain dinner his wife, Louise, had ready for him, then hurry into his crowded waiting room to treat more patients until eleven or even midnight.

The good doctor's only concession to the human need for pleasure came on Sundays, after the entire family returned home from the three-hour service at the Baptist Church in Ardmore. The Arnolds' Sunday dinner was always a wholesome feast. But even that provided no more than a circumscribed pleasure for the children, who were allowed to speak (after carefully laying down knife and fork) only when their father addressed them directly; and perhaps even less pleasure for his wife, since he refused to eat what he called store-bought food. She had to churn the butter, bake the bread, and each autumn preserve a winter's-worth of vegetables from the garden she had to cultivate. Until her sons were old enough, she also had to chop the wood for her iron cook stove.

Mrs. Louise Arnold, who came from a neighboring Gladwyne farm family, the Harleys (which accounts for young Henry's middle name), was also a product of the Mennonites. Her parents were still members of the Church of the Brethren (sometimes known as "Dunkards" or "Dunkers" because they practiced baptism by immersion), but were less exacting in their beliefs than the Arnolds. They had even allowed their daughter to seek an education, making her one of the first "Dunker" girls ever to go to high school. Unlike her husband, but very much like her second son, whom she sometimes called "Sunny" because of his cheerful disposition and sometimes "Harley" in honor of her own family, she was fun-loving and prone to laughter. As young Henry grew and began taking exception to his father's views, she often agreed with him, but not to the extent of directly challenging her husband. Though no longer a Mennonite (having followed him into the Baptist fold), she was still too steeped in the Mennonite tradition to assert herself against him. A Pennsylvania Dutch husband governed his household even more absolutely than other husbands did in the male-dominated nineteenth century. Mrs. Arnold waited on the doctor constantly, taking care of his every need, without winning or even expecting any more than an infrequent sign of appreciation. He was not the kind of man who would talk sweetly to her, help her into the buggy, or hold her chair when she sat down. Yet he was capable of making an occasional remark that showed his feeling for her. Tired from his long day's work, he would tell her how he looked forward to the time when just the two of them could sit in front of the fire together and talk.[4] Despite his austere nature, there is every indication that she dearly loved him.

The first Mennonite settlement in America, at Germantown, which is now a part of Philadelphia, was founded in 1683, but it was not until 1740 that Mennonites (including Henry Arnold's great-great-great-grandfather John Arnold) began to reach America in significant numbers, after the early settlers sent back word to Europe that a man named William Penn, a Quaker, was founding a colony where religious freedom would be upheld and war denounced. This was exciting news to the German Mennonites of the upper Rhine valley. Since the Reformation, they had been victims of so many wars and so much persecution that they had compiled a chronicle, "The Book of Martyrs," which told one gruesome story after another about the deprivations, tortures, and brutal murders members of their faith had suffered.

In America, where they soon became known as the Pennsylvania Dutch, they prospered by working hard and helping each other. They got along especially well with the Quakers, who respected them for their industry and agreed with their pacifism. But it was the question of pacifism that first threatened the solidarity of the American Mennonites. When the quarrel between the thirteen colonies and the English mother country began to intensify, the Mennonites naturally sided with their fellow colonists. And when the Revolutionary War began, some of them were so enthusiastically anti-British that they broke their vows never to bear arms.

Among those Mennonites who joined the Revolutionary Army were seven of Henry Arnold's direct ancestors—three on his father's side and four on his mother's. It was not surprising, therefore, that in the Civil War, his grandfather Thomas Arnold fought with the Union forces at Gettysburg. And when the Spanish-American War began, his father joined as surgeon of the Pennsylvania Cavalry, taking part in the invasion of Puerto Rico in July 1898. By the time he mustered out of service, in November 1898, Dr. Herbert Arnold was so enamored of the military life that he immediately joined the Pennsylvania National Guard, in which he served with extraordinary distinction as a reserve medical officer until his retirement in 1922. His work in improving the National Guard's sanitary system included the introduction of locked water barrels, kitchen garbage incinerators, and rigid sanitary inspections, all of which measures, new at the time, were subsequently adopted by the regular army.

Dr. Arnold's love of military life naturally and predictably carried over into his home life, and he governed his own house as if it were an army barracks.[5] Discipline was so rigidly maintained that Henry Arnold, though he later proved the strength of his character, did not seriously challenge his father's authority until after he had grown up and begun to establish his own authority in the Army. As a boy, Henry was mischievous and venturesome, and an indifferent scholar; even the fear of his father failed to make him diligent in elementary and high school. But in his teens, he accepted the parental dictum that he would attend Bucknell College and become a Baptist minister as willingly as his older brother Tom was apparently accepting his destiny to be a West Point cadet and Army officer. Dr. Arnold, because of his military record and his acquaintance with the local congressman, Irving P. Wanger of Norristown, was able to assure Tom that he would have an excellent chance of winning an appointment to the Military Academy if he did well in the entrance examination, which was to be held in the spring of 1903. Meanwhile, Tom was allowed to enroll at Penn State, where he showed an immediate interest in electrical engineering.

It was not until just before the date of the West Point examination that Tom informed his father he had no intention of taking it.[6] Having made that declaration, he then astonished the entire family by braving his father's fury and maintaining his resolve to continue his studies at Penn State. Dr. Arnold's wrath could not shake his oldest son's resolve. Finally, humiliated by the first defeat he had ever experienced within his own family, Dr. Arnold turned to his second son, Henry. One of his sons, he announced, was going to take that examination. Since the two youngest, Clifford and Price, were not yet eligible, there was no one but Henry. Though Tom, at nineteen and already in college, was old enough to consider himself a man and therefore qualified to defy his father, Henry, at seventeen, was not.

On the day of the examination, he was there with pen in hand, and to the amazement of everyone concerned, including himself and his high school principal, who had scoffed at the notion that Henry might be admitted to the Military Academy, he came in second. He had done remarkably well for a high-spirited youngster who had always seemed allergic to books, well enough, in fact, to frighten him with the hitherto unthinkable notion that he might actually have to go to the academy. But he was soon relieved of that fear when he learned that only one appointment was to be granted and it would go to the man who had come in first.

Quite contentedly, Henry Arnold resumed his plans for Bucknell and the Baptist ministry, but once again his fate took an unexpected turn. The young man who had won the appointment announced, the evening he was to leave for West Point, that he was married. Since a married cadet in those days was no more admissible than a black cadet, he was automatically eliminated and Arnold, on July 27, 1903, one month after his seventeenth birthday, found himself, to his bewilderment, in a plebe's uniform at West Point.

It was then that he first demonstrated the adaptability that was to become an extremely useful characteristic throughout his military career. As one of the youngest members of the plebe class (many candidates at that time prepared themselves by taking a year or two of college work elsewhere), he was confronted by a way of life that differed vastly from all of his previous experience. For a boy barely seventeen who had seldom spent a night away from his mother, the plebe routine at West Point in 1903 could be a formidable test of endurance, tenacity, and resilience.

When Arnold arrived (as one of twenty-five delayed applicants who were called "Juliettes" because they reported in July), he found the academy compound almost deserted.[7] The bulk of the cadet corps was at "summer encampment," a kind of tent city on the academy reservation to the east of the tactical field. Only a skeleton force of tactical officers, enlisted men, and upperclassmen was on hand to greet the twenty-five new "beasts," as plebes were called. A cadet corporal (a yearling, or third classman, who had been a plebe himself just a month earlier) lined them up in a small squad, then barked at them to button their coats, straighten their ties, stand erect, get their shoulders back, drag in their chins.

Singling out one man after another, he would say, "What's your name, mister?"

"Shaughnessy."

"Shaughnessy what, mister? Shaughnessy Smith? Or Shaughnessy, sir?"

When that man had learned his lesson, the cadet corporal would move on to another. "Where are you from, mister?"

"Pennsylvania."

"Pennsylvania what, mister? Pennsylvania Dutch? Or Pennsylvania, sir? Now where are you from?"

When they finally learned to say "sir," they were marched off to the cadet store, where enlisted clerks, after looking down their noses just cynically enough to suggest their insolence, loaded each of them, as if they were not only beasts but beasts of burden, with a mattress, sheets, blankets, coverlet, portable wash basin, and water dipper, all of which they were then required to balance on their heads while double-timing back to their new, bare rooms. If one of them stumbled and fell, he was ordered to "get up in double time." Having been given two or three minutes to deposit these items and perhaps meet their new roommates, they had to turn out again, in double time, and run back to the cadet store for a load of such incidentals as toothbrush and -paste, shoe-blacking, canvas belts, dress hats. After one more footrace back to their rooms with these things, they ran to the quartermaster depot, where they were hastily measured and given their basic beast uniforms—a pair of light gray flannel trousers, black shoes, a cap, a campaign hat, and a woolen shirt so heavy it would not allow them for a moment to be unaware of the summer heat.

On their next double-time trip, this time to the ordnance depot, they were loaded down with rifles, bayonets, and trenching tools, and sent running back to their rooms. But not to rest—as soon as they had changed to their uniforms, they were ready for several hours of drill. Since it was their first day, their officers gave them a break. They were allowed to drill without their rifles.

After three weeks at this pace, the new group of beasts, finally beginning to look like soldiers, was marched off to the summer encampment, where Arnold was assigned to Company F and did a lot more drilling—about four hours each day. This left plenty of time for the plebes to be ragged and braced back by upperclassmen. Though hazing had been outlawed two years earlier, after it resulted in the death of a cadet, there were still plenty of ways in which upperclassmen could make life miserable for plebes, who were not even allowed to address them without first asking permission.

On August 31, the entire cadet corps, which numbered about five hundred at that time, broke camp, returned to barracks, and began the academic year, preparing for classroom recital the next day. By this time, the plebes, their feet toughened and all their excess weight lost on the drill field, were expected to know the black book of regulations by rote—they could earn demerits for even the slightest lapse of memory. They had better also know the guard manual, because henceforth they had to take their turns at twenty-four-hour guard duty. And on Sunday, their day of rest, they had to report for compulsory chapel, which, if they were Protestants, like Henry Arnold, meant they had to sit through an Episcopal service no matter what other denomination they might actually profess.

Though the Sunday chapel rule may have seemed rigid (especially in a secular army), it was counterbalanced in 1903 by the relaxation of another equally strict regulation—the ban on the use of tobacco. One evening at retreat the cadets received an order from the adjutant saying pipes and cigars (but no cigarettes) would thenceforth be permitted in the dormitories during release from quarters. As soon as they were dismissed and broke ranks, they let loose a rousing cheer. And anyone visiting their dormitories that night would quickly understand why the rule had been relaxed. Most of them already had pipes and tobacco hidden in their lockers. The commandant, aware that many of them were sneaking smokes, thus violating cadet regulations, had apparently decided the rule was easier to eliminate than their smoking habits.

For Arnold, the permission to smoke was a boon he could relish more than his companions because even before arriving at the academy he had been forbidden to use tobacco.[8] His father considered smoking only slightly less evil than drinking. As the academic year progressed into fall and winter, Arnold began to settle naturally into the West Point plebe routine, thanks to a comforting discovery. The cadet discipline, which most of the plebes found painfully rigid, was not as severe as the rules in his father's house. Life at West Point gave him, in fact, a sense of freedom he had never known, and he quickly put that freedom to use by shirking his studies, though not so prodigally as to get him into academic trouble. He passed his semiannual examinations just before Christmas because he knew that if he were to fail even one of them, he might be dismissed from the academy and sent home to face his father's fuming indignation.

While Arnold was studying for these semiannual examinations during his plebe year, an event was taking place at Kitty Hawk, North

Carolina, that would profoundly affect his future. It was there on December 17, 1903, that the brothers Wright, Orville and Wilbur, became the first ever to get an airplane off the ground. But like almost everyone else in the world, Arnold remained either unaware of this feat or indifferent to it at the time. What is more remarkable is that four years later, when Arnold graduated from West Point, he hadn't yet heard of the Wright brothers or their historic flight.[9] The only notice he took during his West Point years of mankind's early attempts to conquer the air was a casual observation of a balloon ascension from the academy ground in February 1906. Describing this flight in a letter to his mother, he made it obvious that he didn't take it very seriously. "I don't know why [the balloonist] selected this place for his ascension but he did. The balloon was about 25 feet in diameter, almost a sphere. He inflated it with illuminating gas. After going up he went due north and was still going north the last I saw of him."[10]

Arnold probably would have paid little attention to airplanes even if he had known about them, because he had developed a new interest —horses. While he worked hard enough on his mathematics, French, surveying, bridge-building, military problems, and other subjects to get by, placing himself securely in the unnoticeable academic middle of his class, he devoted much of his energy to riding because he had fixedly decided to become a Cavalry officer. It was his dream of the Cavalry, he later admitted, that dominated his life as a cadet. "That was why we were here! It was what we lived for—our whole future!"[11]

To any young American soldier at the turn of the twentieth century, the Cavalry was still the most glamorous outfit in the world. Galloping charges against bloodthirsty Indians were not just the stuff of penny dreadfuls. They were the core of firsthand stories which older cavalrymen still told, with gruesome and highly colored details, to the young cadets. "When we speculated on the stations we would draw," Arnold recalled, "we were not always sure whether the ones we named were inside now peaceful Indian reservations or on the frontier, but it didn't seem to make much difference. We rode. We thought about horses all the time. We knew the name of every Cavalry hero; and outside of drill, on our own time, we tried to emulate and beat every riding stunt on record. We jumped and mounted over two other horses to a third, rode in pyramids, schooled our horses at high jumping, and a hundred other things. And in between mounts we cussed and swaggered, and even occasionally chewed surreptitiously, as Cavalry troopers were supposed to do."

As for the chewing, there was more than one time when Arnold wished he hadn't. He had first decided to try it after he saw his Cavalry instructor put a wad of tobacco between tongue and cheek.[12] He could see that it was a manly thing to do. He'd have to learn to do it when he graduated and joined his Cavalry unit, so why wait? The taste was bitter but like other men he could get accustomed to it. And he did, to such an extent that during a track meet against the hated Naval Academy, he put a slug of tobacco in his mouth before getting on his mark for a half-mile race. Toward the end of the race, gasping for breath, he inadvertently swallowed the tobacco, some of which went down the wrong way. Collapsing on the ground, he went into a spasm and had to be removed to the infirmary, where he was treated for an apparent heart attack. He recovered quickly and was about to tell the medical officer what had actually happened when he decided he had better keep his mouth shut. A real cavalryman wouldn't swallow his tobacco.

On the athletic fields at West Point Arnold distinguished himself just about as much as he did in the classrooms. Even without a slug of tobacco in his mouth, he was not exceptionally fast. But his five-foot-eleven-inch, 185-pound frame gave him enough strength to compete in the shotput at some of the interclass track meets. And his willingness to absorb punishment earned him a place as a substitute fullback and halfback on the academy football squad. In a letter to his mother in the autumn of 1905, he described exactly what football meant to him.

"Today I played on the scrub against the varsity," he wrote. "I tell you the life of a man on the scrub is no cinch. He is used for a dummy. If the varsity wants to try a new play, they use the scrub to see if it is a success, and so it goes. The scrub gets battered and bumped and cussed out and everything else coming just because they are not as good as the varsity. I don't want you to think I am knocking or have the blues for I am not knocking and haven't the blues but I just feel like writing for the top of my head is full of bumps the size of hens' eggs."[13]

Football wasn't quite the game for him, but he soon found the sport he could love, and it was, not surprisingly, polo. Each summer the academy organized a squad and Arnold was one of its most enthusiastic members. He was not destined to be remembered at the academy for his athletic skills, however, any more than for his scholarship. What his classmates remembered best about him was the inordinate amount of mischief he perpetrated. Free at last from the restrictions his stern father had laid upon him, he seemed to explode in an adolescent frenzy of high jinks, as if there were an imp inside him that he had to release before he could get on with the business of becoming a man.

Much of this mischief arose from the activities of a secret nocturnal cadet society called the "Black Hand," of which Arnold was a founding member.[14] Despite its chilling name, the Black Hand had no sinister motives, no subversive or perverse ideology. It was simply a vehicle for boyish pranks, often led by Arnold, and it was tolerated by West Point authorities for the same reason adolescent Halloween pranks used to be tolerated by the public at large, before the modern, namby-pamby trick-or-treat vogue was adopted. It gave the boys a chance to work off their high spirits and even their hostilities, if any, without causing more than minor damage. Much of the fun for the academy Black Hand members arose simply from the audacity of being out of their bunks without authorization in the middle of the night. That in itself was a triumph over the established authority, and the triumph was even more delicious if it was certifiable in the light of day by some tangible sign of mischief accomplished. The moonlight cavorting of the Black Handers often came to nothing more, therefore, than a restless prowl in search of windows to be soaped, garbage cans to be overturned, or buggies to be upended. Occasionally, however, the boys would come up with a stunt slightly more imaginative.

Like all soldiers, Arnold and his buddies hated reveille, especially since it came at 5:00 a.m., forcing them out of bed and into their uniforms for a bone-chilling outdoor trek to the bathhouse-latrine, which was across the quad from their barracks. (Not until 1907 did West Point dormitories have indoor plumbing facilities.) One night the Black Handers devised a way to get back at reveille, at least symbolically. By huff and by puff they hauled the reveille cannon up the barracks stairs and managed to get it out onto the roof, sitting astride the apex. Not only did they shut it up for at least one morning, they left it on ignominious display so that the entire cadet corps could look up gratefully the next day and see how it had been silenced. This project was unusual for the Blank Handers because it was, essentially, an antinoise prank; ordinarily their pranks were pronoise, since it was often the noise they made that won them the attention they sought.

On another occasion Arnold came up with a devilish scheme that was not soon forgotten. He and his friends lugged a dozen or so huge cannonballs to the top of the dormitory stairway, then released them all at once, racing down ahead of them so that they would be in their bunks when everyone else was awakened by the heavy racket of those menacing missiles, descending a step at a time. Arnold, being not quite as fast as some of his friends, was almost caught during this escapade. And in his last year at West Point, two months before his graduation, he actually was caught during the Black Hand's most spectacular stunt, but this was such a glorious piece of mischief he was almost proud to have it pinned upon him.

One day, when they were at liberty from the post, the Black Handers found a shop where they could buy fireworks. Pooling their funds, they bought almost the entire stock—if a thing was worth doing, it was worth doing well. On the appointed night, having planned and timed their operation with all the precision and coordination of a military attack, they let loose such a varied and deafening series of salvos from every corner of the grounds that, in Arnold's words, "bugles blew, sirens sounded, officers and men tumbled from their beds, the whole reservation was alive."

The climax of the fiery bombardment, ignited by Arnold himself on the roof of his barracks, was an elaborate pinwheel display that spelled out "1907—Never Again!" What the "Never Again" was supposed to mean not even Arnold seemed to know—perhaps it was a confection someone had ordered from the fireworks dealer, then rejected. In any case, for Arnold it meant he would never again be involved in a stunt like this; when he put his match to the display it lit up the whole roof, and there he was, as he later recalled, "silhouetted against the light of my own handiwork, in full view of the entire corps."

He won for his enterprise on this occasion not just the applause of his peers but also a swift response from his superiors. He was assigned to several weeks of solitary confinement on the top floor of the barracks, allowed out only to attend classes and to walk endless tours of the quad, in full uniform with a rifle on his shoulder. This was doubly embarrassing because, owing to circumstances for which his father was responsible, a very pretty young lady from back home in Ardmore was just then making plans to come and visit him. Her name was Eleanor Pool and that was almost as much as Arnold knew about her. She was not his girl friend. He had no girl friends. In fact, though their families were acquainted, and he had seen her a few times, he had never met her.[15] The Pools were bankers, members of the Ardmore gentry, as it were, and owners of a large Tudor-style house, with tennis court, in the best part of town. Since Herbert Arnold was the most respected physician in the area, he was their family doctor, but he was not part of their social milieu. There were some aspects of the Pools' way of life that he could hardly view with approval. Sidney Pool was the kind of jovial, convivial businessman who liked to gather his friends around him, tell some stories, have some fun. He made no secret of the fact that he liked an occasional drink. What was worse, so did his wife, Annie, who could be charged with the additional sin of having sung in operas during her earlier years. But despite such flaws, they were people of quality and high standing in the community, and it seemed to Dr. Arnold that their comely young daughter Eleanor would be quite suitable for his son Henry, who was about to achieve the socially acceptable status of an Army officer.

One day in March 1907, when Dr. Arnold was treating Eleanor Pool for a spring head cold, he decided the time was ripe for his son to meet her.[16] As he left the house, he casually mentioned to her mother that his own daughter, Betty, was planning a trip to West Point to visit Henry. Would Eleanor like to go along? The outing would be good for her, help her fight off her cold. Eleanor's mother thought it an excellent idea, and so did Eleanor herself. The plans were set and one weekend in April, Eleanor Pool, chaperoned by Betty Arnold, who was seven years her senior, made her first trip to the academy. After a train trip to New York, they boarded a small, rinky-dink trolley that tootled up the right bank of the Hudson to the little station just below the West Point plateau. From there they rode up the hill in a horse-drawn hack to the only available lodging, the always-crowded West Point Hotel near Trophy Point. A small building, reputed once to have been General Washington's head-quarters, it became each weekend a swarming hive of young ladies, all from proper families and all well chaperoned, who were there to dance with their cadet friends at the academy hops or go walking around the grounds with them during the precious few hours the cadets had free.

Whether Arnold was eagerly anticipating Eleanor Pool's visit has never been recorded. He was attracted to women, like most young men, yet he was inordinately awkward and shy around them, partly because his country background had not taught him many of the social graces.[17] He didn't know how to approach a girl, make small talk, or strike up a friendship with her. With boys it was easy. All you had to do was shake hands, slap them on the back, argue with them and maybe out-shout them if they disagreed with you. But girls had to be treated according to a set of rules he had never learned—except for the etiquette the academy had imposed on him, he could rely only on country manners, polite but hardly polished. A simple pastime like dancing, for example, was so far beyond his competence that he never attended a hop until his senior year, and then only once—not because he shared his father's view of dancing as a moral danger, but simply because dancing was so foreign to his family's way of life and he knew so little about it that he was embarrassed even to try it.

It was not until Betty Arnold and Eleanor Pool, having settled themselves into their tiny hotel rooms, went forth to meet Betty's brother that they learned of his incarceration. The news was no doubt a greater shock to Betty than to Eleanor, who could see immediately that if she didn't meet one cadet, she would meet another. At the age of twenty, and having already traveled in Europe, she was well aware that men found her attractive, and besides, she couldn't fail to notice that here at West Point there were several hundred available young men for only a few available women. As for Henry Arnold's mischief, she came from a family that was amused by slightly unconventional behavior, whereas Betty, steeped in the Arnold tradition of rectitude, disapproved of even slightly improper conduct.

Prevented from meeting this brother she loved so much, Betty decided she would at least try to see him. If they were to appear in front of his barracks, one of his fellow cadets would surely tell him to come to the window of his top floor "cell." It was thus that Henry Arnold and Eleanor Pool first surveyed each other. He could see that she was a very pretty blue-eyed blonde. Petite and slender, she had a quick smile and darting eyes which seemed to take in her entire surroundings at a glance. She, on the other hand, could see nothing but his face in the window, a handsome face with an engaging smile that made him look effervescently cheerful. (She did not then know that this smile was an almost permanent feature of his face.) Since they were unable to converse, their only communication was a fleeting exchange of hand-waves, after which Eleanor and Betty moved on into the West Point weekend social whirl. Before long, Eleanor did indeed meet another cadet, who became her escort at a house party that evening. Henry Arnold, if not forgotten, had been quickly relegated to the back of her mind, perhaps to the relief of Betty Arnold, who was never enthusiastic about the possibility that some other girl would try to take her young brother away from her.

Despite his long punishment, Arnold was permitted one important pleasure as his graduation from West Point approached. He was allowed, like his classmates, to order his officer uniforms. And like his closest companions, who had decided nothing but the Cavalry would satisfy them, he ordered his trousers "not with the prescribed stripe of an inch and a quarter, but with one inch and a half wide, to stress the glorious Cavalry Yellow."[18]

By graduation week in June 1907, he had not only completed his punishment for moonlight fireworks, but also achieved the one honor for which he had striven wholeheartedly during his years at West Point. He had developed such skill in horsemanship that he was named to the graduation riding exhibition team. All the afternoons of equestrian drilling and horse training had paid off and his selection to the Cavalry was now beyond doubt.

As the summer green enveloped the plain above the Hudson, and the upperclassmen, with their struggle behind them and graduation almost upon them, succumbed to a mood of euphoric anticipation, it began to look as if Arnold would actually complete his cadet days without managing to get into any more trouble. One of the first features of graduation week was the graduation ride. Proud relatives, friends, and sweethearts of the cadets filled the riding hall to see it. The members of the exhibition team stood at attention beside their horses in the corridor leading from the stable to the hall. In only a few minutes they would ride their handsome mounts into the hall, circle the arena, and begin their precise, difficult program. But first there was one more short ceremony to endure—an inspection by Capt. F. C. Marshall, the senior Cavalry instructor, who was also a stickler for proper form. As he walked at his slow, stiff, erect pace along the line of cadets and horses, he noticed a great lump in the cheek of Cadet Arnold, who was otherwise impeccable in uniform and bearing.

The captain stopped and took a closer look at him. "Mr. Arnold," he said (cadets and lieutenants were so addressed in those days), "you have a chew of tobacco in your mouth. Spit it out, sir."

Arnold, after first obeying the order, could not resist what he thought would be taken as a joking remark. "Sir," he said, "I thought all good cavalrymen chewed tobacco."

Perhaps another Cavalry officer might have smiled and moved on, but not Captain Marshall. "Mr. Arnold," he said, "you're impertinent."[19]

The graduation ride went off without a flaw and this whole minuscule incident had been all but forgotten the next day when the delinquency list (or "skin list," as the cadets called it) came out with Arnold's name at the top. For having a "chew of tobacco in mouth at Cavalry drill" and for "impertinent reply to tactical officer when reproved for same," he was sentenced "to be confined to area barracks and gymnasium, and to walk the area during all recreation periods until graduation," which was still four days away.

Having spent so much of his four years at West Point walking punishment tours, Arnold was hardly surprised that he should spend his last four days doing so. He did graduate without further incident, however, and returned home to Ardmore on leave, allowing his proud father to show him off to acquaintances, and waiting for his Cavalry commission to arrive in the mail.

He was sitting with his mother at breakfast one morning, his father having gone off on his daily round of house calls, when the envelope arrived from the War Department. Though he had been eagerly awaiting it, he was now, suddenly, too much a man of the world to be anything but casual about it. As he later recalled, he "tossed it to her gaily without looking at it. Does a World Champion Rider, after all, carefully inspect the inscription on his trophy when they hand it to him?"[20]

Since he already knew what was in the envelope, he paid scant attention as his mother opened it, extracted the letter, and began to read. When she raised her eyes from the page, she looked straight at her son.

"You'd better read this, Harley," she said.

He took it from her and, still without any sense of alarm, ran his eye down the page until he came to the words: "Henry H. Arnold, 2nd Lieutenant of Infantry."

His glamorous equestrian world suddenly collapsed. The Cavalry-striped trousers, the prancing horses, the Kiplingesque charges against savage Indians, began to fade from his mind's eye and dissolve into the distance. Was it the tobacco in his cheek the day of the graduation riding exhibition that had cost him his coveted and presumably well-earned Cavalry assignment? He would never find out. But there is little reason to assume he was passed over because of such a minor infraction when the Cavalry had so many important reasons to reject him. He had not been a distinguished cadet. An academic rating in the sixties out of a class of 110 was hardly an indication of brilliance. His selection as a member of the graduation riding team was a trifling honor when balanced against the glaring fact that he had failed ever to become a cadet officer. His only claim to leadership was his dubious distinction as an organizer of the infamous Black Hand and its frequent mischief. His popularity with other cadets was a mark in his favor but not a sign of unusual ability. On the basis of his military record to date, the Army could hardly regard him as a promising officer with the potential for one day assuming high command. On the other hand, there was no reason to believe he would be an incompetent officer. While his accomplishments were minor, so were the peccadilloes that had so often got him into trouble. And he had, at least, completed the rigorous course at West Point. The Army had a place for officers like him, but it was not in the elite, high-riding Cavalry. It was in the mud-slogging, footsore Infantry.

Arnold was not, however, in any mood to accept that place. So violent and persuasive was his sense of outrage at being passed over that he managed to convince even his father that he had been treated unfairly. And his father was not the kind of man who would accept injustice without a fight, nor was he lacking in political influence. His friendship with Congressman Irving Wanger had helped get his son into West Point four years earlier. And he was also well acquainted with Pennsylvania's powerful Senator Boies Penrose, the tough, ruthless boss of the Republican machine that ran Philadelphia. Neither of these politicians would ignore the plea of an offended father and highly respected doctor who had the ear of so many hundreds of Pennsylvania Dutch farmers.

Penrose and Wanger, both of whom happened to be at home when Dr. Arnold petitioned them, were so accommodating as to accompany the West Point graduate on the train to Washington in the hope of interceding personally for him with the Army's adjutant general. On the way, young Henry gave them such an earful of indignation that even he wondered later if they didn't regret "their agreeable willingness to oblige my ex-Cavalry father." After listening to him about as far as Havre de Grace, they exchanged glances, then persuaded him that he should let them go first to the War Department and join them there at ten-thirty the next morning.

When he arrived, he found that they had already talked to the adjutant general. Nevertheless, this worthy officer, Maj. Gen. Fred C. Ainsworth, in whom Arnold could see little more than unbending pomposity, began lecturing him about his station in life. He must not forget that he was now a second lieutenant in the Army, which meant he was at the very bottom of the commissioned ranks, and that he would have to do what everyone in the Army, including himself, the adjutant general, had to do—namely to obey orders from higher authority and accept whatever assignments he was given.

Arnold's reply to this must have made the adjutant general wonder what West Point was teaching its cadets about respect for rank. "No, sir!" the young graduate said, still furious at what he considered the most grievous hurt ever inflicted upon him. "No, sir! I am not a second lieutenant in the United States Army. I haven't accepted my commission yet."

In those days there was no legal requirement that a West Point graduate spend a specified period of time in the Army, and it was beginning to appear that Arnold was not destined to do so, that if he didn't get out, the adjutant general might at any moment invite him out. Before this could happen, Senator Penrose took the young man firmly by the arm, ushered him from the office, and told him to wait in the hall.

After Penrose and Wanger had spoken privately to the adjutant general, Arnold was ushered back into the room and had to listen again, this time more thoughtfully, to the same speech he had heard a few minutes earlier. To make himself unmistakably clear, the adjutant general added that only Secretary of War William Howard Taft had the power to change this assignment to the Infantry, and the secretary was at present on a trip to the Philippine Islands. However, if Arnold had any preference in Infantry stations, perhaps something could be done about that.

Infantry stations! Arnold suddenly realized he couldn't name any Infantry stations. He could, of course, name such installations as Forts Wingate, Custer, Apache, Crook, and Riley, since they were Cavalry stations. Infantry! They constituted the bulk of the Army. Surely he could think of a few of their stations. Yet his Cavalry-laden mind refused to come forth with any. Where was it the secretary of war had gone? To the Philippines? Maybe if he could be sent there and get to talk to him, a transfer to the Cavalry would still be possible.

"I would like," he blurted out, "to go to the Philippines."

The adjutant general, who had clung steadfastly to his duty despite the implied pressure of a visit from two such powerful politicians, must have been pleased by this sudden invitation to send the obstreperous Mr. Arnold so far away. Showing what Arnold later described as remarkable forbearance, he said, "I think that can be arranged." Then with a nod he quickly dismissed the young man before he had time to change his mind.

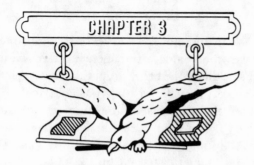

CHAPTER 3

The American Army in the early part of this century maintained such a leisurely pace that it was not until September 14, 1907, that Arnold and several other recently graduated second lieutenants en route to the Philippines were required to report at their port of embarkation, San Francisco. And when they arrived there, they found themselves too early. No transport vessels would be going to Manila until November.

"Meanwhile you will be on duty here," the adjutant general at the Presidio informed them. Then he added with a smile, "Your duties will consist of having a good time in San Francisco and letting me know your address. Good day, gentlemen."[1]

Though San Francisco in 1907, still recovering from the earthquake and fire of 1906, looked ramshackle and half-built, and though it was not the wide-open city it is today, it had enough attractions to keep a young second lieutenant entertained. Its restaurants were already famous. One could sail on the bay or take excursions into the surrounding countryside. Arnold still loved horses, and there were plenty of places to ride. There were also in San Francisco at that time plenty of brothels and houses of assignation offering their temptations to unattached men, but the best of these a young officer couldn't afford, and the others he couldn't afford to be seen in. There is no indication that Arnold ever was seen in any of them. He hadn't overcome his adolescent clumsiness and puritanical stiffness around women, and he still remembered fondly Miss Eleanor Pool, the Ardmore girl who had waved at him in his top-floor window when he was confined to barracks at West Point the previous April. During his summer leave he had even seen her at a party in Ardmore, but he had never brought himself to tell her how attractive he found her, or even to invite her out for an ice-cream soda and a walk in the park.[2]

On November 5, the new "shavetails" embarked for the Philippines on the transport *Buford*, a remodeled cattle boat, "very narrow in the beam and as rough as a ship could be."[3] It steamed out of San Francisco harbor directly into six days of a Pacific storm, during which Arnold was one of the few who did not get seasick. He was already, however, beginning to develop his famous impatience. After two days at sea, he wrote in his diary: "Still on the briny deep. Can't even get sick to vary the monotony."[4] The north Pacific weather was cold as well as rough, but that didn't bother the young second lieutenants because they were wearing their heavy winter uniforms, having accepted the advice of some returning Philippine veterans who told them to wait and buy their summer outfits in Manila, where Chinese tailors made them very cheaply.[5] Arnold welcomed this advice because, while he had millions of dollars in his charge, he was almost broke. This bit of irony arose from the fact that, before sailing, he had been assigned to assure the safe passage of several boxes of cash belonging to the Philippine government. These sentry-guarded funds, nearby and yet untouchable, heightened his awareness of how little he had in his pocket. His San Francisco sojourn had left him so close to insolvency he would need the money saved during this month of enforced thrift aboard ship to pay for the uniforms when he got them.

The combination of his lack and surfeit of funds prevented him from enjoying the ship's one-and-a-half-day layover in Honolulu. He had heard so many stories about the likelihood that the Philippine money would be stolen before he could deliver it that he hardly dared let it out of his sight. And the eighty-degree Hawaiian temperature, reaching him through his winter O.D.s, stifled whatever pleasure he could hope to glean when he wasn't worrying about the money.

As the Buford, after leaving Honolulu, sailed closer and closer to the Equator, Arnold's woolen uniform, the only one he had to wear, became "a torture of hot scratchiness" to him and to those of his companions who had taken the same advice about buying their summer outfits in Manila. The ship docked in Manila on the night of December 6, but Arnold, convinced that robbers lay in wait to steal the Philippine government money if he left it, remained aboard until next morning, December 7, when he got his first glimpse of the city. It was little more than a glimpse. Within minutes after the big cash boxes were unloaded, they began to disappear.

"On the strange, babbling pier," he later recalled, "carabao carts, driven by the most villainous men I had ever seen, were waiting. Before I could finish my halting instructions in West Point Spanish, the first Filipino driver suddenly started away with about ten of the money boxes. I started to run after him, but looked back, and the other money chests were being driven off in apparently different directions."[6] He was now in such a jam he forgot all about the sweat soaking his winter uniform.

In vain he chased after one cart, then another. Those water buffaloes were faster than he had imagined. Before he could even shout for the police, they had disappeared, in several directions, with his precious cargo. For much of the day he ran up and down Manila streets, wide and narrow, searching desperately for them. Finally, frightened and desolate, he made his way to the address where he had been told to deliver the money. How would he explain his dereliction? Those terrible stories about robbers had been right. He had been given sufficient warning. How could he have let them, in spite of that warning, snatch from him such a colossal amount of money? And then to make their getaway on buffalo-drawn carts! There could be no explanation. On his first assignment as an Army officer, he had allowed an apparently unarmed gang of nondescript thieves to take away from him millions of dollars in government money. And only now, several hours later, he was arriving to report it. What would the Philippine officials say? What would they do to him?

He was astonished to find, when he walked in and identified himself, that they simply smiled at him. The money? It has been delivered, every box of it, hours earlier. They gave him a receipt for it and thanked him. Gradually, as he stared at the receipt, he realized his good fortune and a sense of relief overcame him. But not for long. With his big problem solved, he became more aware than ever of the humid Philippine heat attacking him through his heavy woolen uniform.

Assigned to the 29th Infantry Division at Fort McKinley, he soon made it clear to friends that he didn't like the accommodations. With two West Point classmates, Lt. Benjamin Castle and Lt. Wiley Dawson, he moved into a large, two-story bachelor officers' quarters occupied by no one but themselves.[7] They hired a Chinese cook and Filipino houseboy, bought some bamboo furniture, scrounged some quartermaster beds, and settled down to a primitive existence. On a typical day they would arise at five a.m., eat breakfast, then go to their respective companies for close-order drill, target practice, swimming, wall-scaling, and so forth, from six to ten. After drill, they would do company paperwork until noon, then return to quarters for lunch and a siesta, which lasted until five, though it was sometimes cut short for the second lieutenants, who had to be reminded occasionally that they were in the Army.

After siesta came the traditional Army social ritual of paying courtesy calls, dressed up in white uniforms. When a new officer arrived on a post, he had to call on each of his colleagues, one after another, and leave his card. Within ten days, these officers had to return his call and leave their cards. The trick, of course, in which both the caller and the callee conspired, was to visit other officers when they were out, since the card-leaving was sufficient in itself to fulfill the ritual obligation.

Though it was an easy life it had several drawbacks, the most depressing of which were the tedious sameness of the days and the lack of any function except constant readiness. The Army at that time was not encouraging new ideas or experiments. The good soldier was not one who looked for new ways to do things. His best chance to distinguish himself was to do things well the old way. It was frustrating, therefore, to restless young lieutenants like Arnold who had supposed that their lives as officers would be filled with innovations and adventures. Only by reminding each other of the rumors of impending Japanese attacks on the islands could they make their drills and maneuvers seem important. They did, of course, have other distractions. Since there were no screens on the windows, great armadas of mosquitoes were able to fly through all the buildings, diving onto any morsel of human flesh they might find exposed; and red ants marched in massed formations, also in quest of human flesh, so that a man soon learned to place each leg of his bed in a can of kerosine. Then there were the cockroaches, almost big enough to fight the mice, and even more difficult to eliminate. And there was the humidity-spawned mold, which quickly rotted leather and fabrics unless they were aired in the sun every day—if there was any sun. In the spring, around the beginning of March, came the rainy season and sheets of water poured down all day, every day, for at least two months.

Arnold found the social obligations of his station more difficult to bear than any of these physical inconveniences. He could quickly adapt himself to discomfort, but the courtesy calls were an embarrassment to him. The story of his Cavalry charge into the office of the adjutant general in Washington the previous summer had been leaked to some of the Army and Navy service journals,[8] and the presumption of a newly graduated second lieutenant who would try to dictate the branch in which he would serve was a source of amusement to most of the officers who read or heard about it. But few of Arnold's regimental colleagues in the 29th were even slightly amused. They were proud Infantry officers and carried a special scorn for the Cavalry, perhaps because they resented the snobbery of the horsemen and the extra stipend handed to them each month in the form of "mounted pay." To these officers Arnold's passionate effort to get into the Cavalry was an insult to the Infantry. Though he tried tactfully to get them to accept him, he did not completely succeed, perhaps because tact was not one of his more noticeable virtues, and he was still unable to disguise the hope that he would eventually become a Cavalry officer.

To Lt. Ben Castle, one of the men with whom he shared quarters, it was obvious that while Arnold performed his duties well enough, "his heart was not in the Infantry. He didn't want to be an Infantry officer. That's all there was to it." He didn't mind expeditions into the field despite the jungle hardships. What he hated was the garrison life at Fort McKinley. Besides all the call-paying and card-leaving, there was the obligation to attend stuffy formal dinners and Saturday night dances, and sometimes to escort senior officers' daughters. The islands were such notorious marrying grounds for the daughters of colonels and generals that a junior officer had to be nimble if he wanted to avoid their snares. Arnold wasn't comfortable around these girls and he wasn't interested in marrying any of them. Yet he was noticeably handsome and he had that perpetual smile, which was as charming to women as it was disarming to men. Any day, without warning, some colonel's daughter might come down with an infatuation for him and ask her daddy to help get him for her. To save himself from such a possible fate, it would be sensible to find a means of escape from Fort McKinley, and eventually he did.

When an opportunity came to join a military mapping detail under Capt. Arthur S. Cowan of the Signal Corps, Arnold quickly seized it. The duty promised to be only temporary and the Signal Corps had none of the glamor of the Cavalry, but at least it was one tentative step away from the Infantry. His well-known dislike of the Infantry may even have been what got him the assignment. Lt. Col. Charles E. Nathan, his commanding officer, could have offered it to any of the lieutenants. Many of them would have considered it an experience potentially valuable to their careers. Yet the old colonel, without mentioning it to anyone else, simply called Arnold over to him and said, "There's a chance here for a second lieutenant to go on mapping duty."[9] Arnold was so excited by the prospect he wasted no time wondering whether the colonel was taking advantage of an opportunity to get rid of him.

Captain Cowan's group was engaged in mapping the entire island of Luzon. They moved from one campsite to another in the "bosky" (as the jungle was called), hacking their way through the dense, tangled vegetation, breathing the thick, wet, heavy air, and living in tents. They would place a triangulation point on the highest possible ground, survey and map the terrain around it, then hack their way to the next hilltop and begin again.

After several months of this rugged detail, Arnold was as lean and hard as he had ever been. He was also, though perhaps not consciously, beginning to accept some of the values his father had preached to him since earliest childhood. During that mapping expedition on Luzon, he threw himself completely into his work for the first time in his life. And after the task of mapping the Luzon Valley was completed, Captain Cowan retained him for the task of mapping Corregidor Island, which the Army already envisioned as an impregnable stronghold guarding Manila Bay.

During his two years in the Philippines, Arnold never did return to his regiment, nor did he abandon his attempts to separate himself from it permanently. While he derived great satisfaction from his mapping work, admitting that it made his Philippine duty "unexpectedly exciting," he still clung to his old Cavalry aspirations and kept spurring his father on to new efforts in the hope, however slim, of fulfilling them. Dr. Arnold, himself a Cavalry zealot, having once been attached to it, did not hesitate to call upon Army friends in his son's behalf. In late January 1909, when an old Cavalry associate, Charles M. Gandy, was promoted to lieutenant colonel, the doctor used the occasion to push the matter in a letter of congratulation. Colonel Gandy's reply was cordial but not very helpful. "I am glad your boy enjoys his service," he wrote on the eighth of February. "I am sorry that he did not get the Cavalry, since he wanted it and was entitled to it on his academic work, but he will undoubtedly get more promotion in the arm to which he was assigned. . . . If the boy still pines for the yellow stripe, he might be able to arrange a transfer later on."[10]

Two or three months after this latest rebuff by the Cavalry, Arnold received a cable which at least offered him the possibility of prolonging his absence from the Infantry. Early in 1909, the Signal Corps had ordered Captain Cowan to Washington. When he arrived there he found that his new duty was to recruit two second lieutenants for a new kind of military experience—flying. The corps had been assigned to look into the possibilities of the airplane partly because no other branch of the service wanted to be bothered with it, and partly because the only thing this strange plaything could conceivably do for an army was to deliver messages. Cowan, remembering Arnold's discontent and impressed by his hard work and resourcefulness, cabled him to ask if he would be interested. Arnold, by return cable, informed him that he would indeed be interested.[11] Actually, his interest in the matter was almost solely as a means of getting out of the Infantry; he had never even seen an airplane, and didn't much care whether he ever saw one. In any event, no further correspondence was forthcoming from Cowan.

In the summer of 1909, the 29th Infantry, having completed the usual two-year tour of duty in the Philippines, was reassigned to garrison duty on Governor's Island, just off the tip of Lower Manhattan. And Arnold, despite his efforts to escape the outfit, was sent along with it. He did, however, avoid traveling with it. Because he had been unable to spend much of his $128.32 monthly earnings ($116.66 base pay plus ten percent for foreign service) during his many months on mapping detail in the jungle, he had saved enough money to afford a leisurely trip back to New York the long way around the world, via Hong Kong, Singapore, Suez, Alexandria, Cairo, Genoa, Lucerne, and Paris.[12] It was not by accident that he planned to stop in Lucerne. He had heard from home that Mrs. Sidney Pool was spending the summer in a hotel on the lake with four of her children, including Eleanor.

On June 19, 1909, he boarded the S.S. *Grosse Kurfuerst* for the long voyage, during which he was to encounter, in addition to several British and German officers also returning home: an Italian count who hated America; two "red-light ladies" from Singapore who were prepared to love everybody; a Dutch father who watchfully made certain they didn't get around to loving his son; and a brother and sister so inseparable the ship's captain suspected them of being something else. For a young man still as unsophisticated as Arnold, it was an eye-opening trip, but he was less impressed by the civilians and their bizarre behavior than he was by the British and German officers, whose daily arguments, reflecting the polarization of attitudes in Europe, made him realize that the possibility of a great war was very real.

"Every time the British and German officers met in the ship's smoking room or on deck," he recalled, "little tensions would occur. The last few months had seen the Bosnia-Herzegovina ferment and other frictions enflaming the European crisis, with England and France tentatively engaged on the side of Russia against Germany and Austria-Hungary." The Germans would "bawl out toasts and songs" in the dining salon and the British would show their discomfort "because the 'bloody Germans' were making a scene." At night, when both sides would meet on deck, trying to escape the stifling heat of the staterooms, their arguments would become serious and ominous. "After two or three drinks, the Englishmen became as rude as the Germans. Everybody knew a war was coming and both British and German knew he couldn't lose it. Every phase of the thing was discussed and hashed over again, except the fact that the United States might be a factor. . . .

"To the barking of the German officers regarding the superior condition of their army, the British officers, exchanging smiles, would inquire ironically, 'What about the Royal Navy?' . . .

"The Germans would explode. 'The British Navy is only a big

bubble,' they would say. 'One prick and it was gone forever! All this silly English emphasis on sea power!' But I saw they had an uneasy belief in it."[13]

After leaving the S.S. *Grosse Kurfuerst* at Genoa, he went directly to Lucerne, where he made successful inquiries as to the exact whereabouts of the Pools. Reaching Mrs. Pool by telephone, he learned that her two daughters, Eleanor and Lois, were at that moment in town buying Alpine capes and stocks for a mountain-climbing endeavor, and that they would be returning home, across Lake Lucerne, on the 5:00 p.m. boat.[14].

When Arnold reached the dock he had no trouble finding Eleanor, whom he could never forget, but he was disappointed to discover that she didn't recognize him. "Here stood this skeleton in a grey suit," she later recalled. "He was nothing but bones. I didn't know him." After the West Point incident, when she waved at him in his upstairs window, she could recall having seen him only once, at a party in Ardmore that summer, "but he was very bashful and didn't dance," so he hadn't come close to exciting her interest. He was, however, a hometown boy, and her mother had invited him to come and stay a few days at their hotel. He and Eleanor spent the boat trip talking about Ardmore and piecing together their sparse recollections of each other. She didn't find him unattractive, and more important, her mother liked him, so his stay stretched into several days, then a week, then two weeks (he didn't have to report for duty at Governor's Island until October 22). He and Eleanor climbed mountains together and he talked to her about his jungle adventures in the Philippines. Like Othello, he was much more articulate when he talked about his experiences as a soldier than when he tried to make small talk. He was rough-hewn, unpolished, still boyish and impulsive, but intelligent, cheerful, and on closer inspection, really quite handsome. She was not displeased when her mother invited him to travel with them down the Rhine and return home with them by way of London. But before this expedition got under way, he received a frantic message from his sister, Betty, informing him that his father was so ill he might soon die. Knowing Betty and her eagerness to see him, he might have doubted the urgency, but he decided to go immediately to Cherbourg by way of Paris and catch the first steamer for home. He left Eleanor Pool with a heavy heart, not only because he would miss her company, but also because, before they parted, she told him something that saddened and disappointed him. She was already engaged, to another man. Perhaps he had no right to be disappointed. After all, he hardly knew her. Yet she had been in his mind for two years now, and he found it hard to face the apparent fact that he had not once been in hers during that entire time.

In Paris on his way home, he was walking along a street, enchanted by the magic of the place, its sights, sounds, and smells, when he heard the noise of an engine above and looked up to see "a queer contraption overhead."[15] This, he eventually learned, was "the flying machine in which Monsieur Louis Blériot had, on the 25th of July, only a few weeks previously, flown from Calais, across the English Channel, to Dover." Was it the kind of craft he himself would have had to learn to fly if Captain Cowan had secured his transfer to the Signal Corps? It didn't look very substantial, and filled him with no desire to fly. It did, however, casually raise in his mind the first thought he ever had about the future possibilities of aircraft. Now that one man had actually flown across the Channel, proving it could be accomplished, "what if a lot of men did it together at the same time? What happens then to England's Splendid Isolation," which all those British officers had mentioned nightly with such comfortable confidence during his trip from Hong Kong to Genoa?

When he reached Ardmore, he found that his father had, in fact, been quite ill but was on the way to recovery. Arnold spent a month at home, coping with the fuss his too-attentive sister made over him, brooding about his imminent return to his despised Infantry outfit, and convincing himself that the adventure in his life was at an end now that he had been assigned to Governor's Island. He expected his duty there to be "the dullest garrison job in the Army," and when he arrived in late October, he found that his expectations were almost certain to be fulfilled. He was back with the 29th Infantry, which had just arrived from the Philippines, and once again he was conducting close-order drill, paying calls, leaving cards, and attending stuffy dinners and dances. He might have imagined he was still at Fort McKinley except that Governor's Island was even less attractive to him. It was "so flat that it wasn't even fun to ride a horse on it, when a second lieutenant could get one, and the life there was flatter than the terrain."[16]

The closest he came to an "adventure" during his two years on Governor's Island was an almost catastrophic incident with a cannon.[17] On the roof of a building at old Fort Jay was a big gun, perhaps from Civil War days, quite useless except as a decoration. The commanding officer, having decided that it should be stored in the basement, assigned this unenviable job to Arnold, whose well-known disdain for the Infantry made him eligible for any unpleasant detail that might arise. He went through every available Army manual without finding a word about how to move a cannon from roof to basement. Though he did eventually discover that this gun had been moved up a steep ramp to the roof, he also discovered that the ramp was now a stairway, at the bottom of which was a mess hall. Having no other way to go, he put his crew to work rolling the heavy gun down the stairs. They managed quite efficiently until, at about midday, they came to the last flight. As they pointed the cannon down the stairs, they lost their hold, and the cannon went careening straight toward the mess hall, which was full of men eating their noon meal. There was nothing Arnold and his crew could do but shout useless warnings. The cannon crashed right into the mess hall and rolled all the way across it, but by some miracle, it chose a path between the tables, speeding past the startled men as they were lifting food to their mouths. None of the men was injured.

Governor's Island did have the advantage of being close to Manhattan, but there was no bridge or tunnel, and opportunities to get into the city were infrequent. When Arnold was given leave—at Christmas, 1909, for instance—he went home to Ardmore, but that was a limited pleasure for several reasons. He had now outgrown the stern, joyless regimen of his father's house. He liked to exercise his boyish exuberance, have some fun, even take a drink once in a while. He had reached the stage when he could express his opposition to his father's views, but he could not shake those views, and the tension between father and son was evident.[18] His trip home that Christmas was somewhat melancholy as well because it reminded him of his apparent failure with Eleanor Pool. Though she was in town, having returned from Europe, and though she seemed happy to see him, she was still engaged to someone else, and she was about to return to Europe for two years of study in Germany. He went back to Governor's Island in January 1910 with little expectation that he would ever see her again.

The flatness of the island terrain, about which he repeatedly complained, was the one thing that eventually helped relieve the tedium of his life there. Because it was so flat, Governor's Island became New York's first airport, attracting such pioneer aviators as Wilbur Wright and Glenn Curtiss.[19] Wright, who had just returned from Europe, where even King Edward had deigned to examine his machine, used the island as the base for his flight up the Hudson, around Grant's tomb, and back. Curtiss landed on the island at the end of his epic flight all the way from Albany with just one refueling stop. By this time, seven years after the invention of the airplane, aviation was causing considerable public excitement, and it was beginning to stir the imagination of Arnold, who had little else to occupy his restless mind. In the autumn, he and some friends went to Belmont Park on Long Island for the first international air meet ever held in America. There he became conscious of the airplane as something that might be more than a toy, and he began to follow, with more than passing interest, the exploits of intrepid aviators like Alberto Santos-Dumont, Walter Brookins, Arch Hoxey, Grahame White, Eugene Ely, and Charles Willard.

Both the Wright brothers and Curtiss were now manufacturing planes, and each had teams of daredevil fliers at the show, competing with foreign fliers in the performance of figure eights, tight turns, dives, and other marvels of what at that time was considered acrobatic flying. No one did anything so daring as a loop, roll, or chandelle—in the aircraft of 1910, such maneuvers could not even be conceived. These aviators hadn't yet learned to cope with stalls and spins. Brookins, only nineteen years old at the time, impressed Arnold by completing the quickest 360-degree turn ever recorded. Brookins also crashed that day in his Wright "speedster," but he walked away from the wreckage unharmed, making the airplane look like a much less dangerous conveyance that it actually was. On that score, Arnold was not deluded. One of his instructors at West Point, Thomas Selfridge, had become, in 1908, one of the first men ever to die in a crash of a heavier-than-air machine.

Arnold knew, of course, that the Army now had some interest in aviation. Captain Cowan's cable, asking him if he might like to become a flier, had apprised him of that. In 1907, the Signal Corps had established an Aviation Division, and for a while during his later months in the Philippines, Arnold had expected Cowan to arrange his transfer to it; but nothing had come of the matter, and despite Arnold's slowly developing interest in airplanes, he had little hope that he would ever fly one. Putting such a faint possibility almost though not quite from his mind, he decided to concentrate his energies on something just slightly more attainable—a promotion. He had been a second lieutenant for more than three years and in the ordinary course of events he would have to resign himself to that bottom rank for another three or four years, especially since he had not ingratiated himself with his Infantry superiors. Even though he had now abandoned all hope of getting into the Cavalry, he was still convinced he had to get out of the Infantry.

This was his mood when he discovered one day that the Ordnance Department had announced some vacancies and that the lowest rank in Ordnance was first lieutenant. Buoyed by this chance for immediate promotion, he began studying for the competitive examination that had been announced to fill the vacancies. It was certain to be a difficult test, and judging by his West Point academic record, his chances of passing it might seem slim, but Arnold was a more determined and serious young man now than he had been at West Point. He had never exerted himself there because he had never felt any need to do so. It was not that he lacked confidence in himself. On the contrary, his school problems had arisen partly because he had too much confidence: since he was certain he could earn top grades if he wished, he was under no compulsion to prove it. But he wanted the transfer to Ordnance and the accompanying promotion, and he felt certain he could win it, whatever competition he might encounter. This kind of self-assurance was a characteristic he would exhibit throughout his life. He would often be sluggish or indifferent about endeavors that didn't interest or challenge him, but if he truly wanted to do something, it was not easy to convince him it couldn't be done.

Perhaps for this reason he had not abandoned his interest in learning to fly. Though his exposure to flying had been minimal, it had impressed him more deeply than even he had realized. Because he had not been able to put airplanes out of his mind, he reacted quickly when, in the spring of 1911, he received an inkling that his Signal Corps possibilities, instituted by Captain Cowan more than two years earlier, were not dead. On April 7 he wrote, through channels, to the adjutant general in Washington:[20]

> Sir:
> I have the honor to request that I be detailed for aeronautical work with the Signal Corps.
> It is believed that my experience in topographical work will prove to be of value in that work. Attention is invited in this connection to letter from the Chief Engineer's Office, Philippine Division, commending me for work performed under his direction.

After dispatching this letter, he proceeded to take the Ordnance examination and was awaiting the result when he received an official letter from the War Department asking him if he would be willing to volunteer for training under the Wright brothers at Dayton, Ohio, as an airplane pilot.

There could be no doubt about his answer, but as a courtesy, he showed the letter to his commanding officer, who apparently thought he was seeking advice. The reaction was exactly what Arnold would expect from an Infantry officer. "Young man, I know of no better way for a person to commit suicide."

Arnold was aware by this time that air travel was unquestionably dangerous but it was also a marvelously adventurous challenge, and he was beginning to sense that for a man of vision it offered a future of unlimited possibilities. He invited no one else to advise him in the matter. He simply informed the War Department that he was ready, and about a week later he received his copy of Special Order 95, dated April 21, 1911, which said:

> The following named officers are detailed for aeronautical duty with the Signal Corps, and will proceed to Dayton, Ohio, for the purpose of undergoing a course of instruction in operating the Wright airplane:
>
> 2nd Lt. Henry H. Arnold, 29th Infantry
> 2nd Lt. Thomas DeW. Milling, 15th Cavalry

Though Milling was two years younger, Arnold had known him well at West Point, liked him, and thought him intelligent. But his willingness to leave the glamorous Cavalry for a chance to learn to fly amazed Arnold. If Arnold had been chosen for the Cavalry, it is doubtful he would have been willing to forsake it.

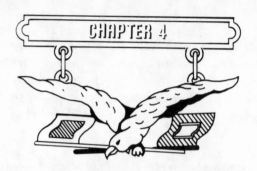

When Arnold and Milling arrived at Dayton in late April 1911, they found a quiet, sleepy, residential town of about 150,000 people, basically a horse-and-buggy town, on the edge of which those two stubborn brothers Orville and Wilbur Wright were trying, with their strange invention, to introduce the age of flight even before the automobile had been fully accepted. There were a few cars, of course, owned by the wealthy and venturesome, but there were no motorized taxis. To reach the Wright Aircraft factory by any conveyance more modern than a horse and buggy, young officers had to take a little Toonerville trolley, which was open in the rear.[1] At the factory, a small brick building, they were greeted by Orville Wright (Wilbur was then in France) and the manager, Frank Russell. It did not take long for these two to show the newcomers around the plant. They had only four rooms, in which they employed no more than twenty-five men. In the largest room, at the rear of the factory, they assembled their aircraft, two of which they were now manufacturing for the Army. These were to be the second and third planes ever purchased by the Army, which had bought its first plane from the Wright brothers in 1909. The year before that, in response to a Signal Corps call for bids, Orville Wright had brought a plane to Fort Myer, near Washington, for a demonstration, and it was during this demonstration that Lt. Thomas Selfridge, Wright's passenger, was killed, when some of the wing wires came loose and flew into the path of the propellor. It had taken Orville Wright several months to recover from his own injuries in the crash, but this had not discouraged him. In 1909, he and his brother had returned with another plane, the same catapult-launched model. This time their demonstration was so successful they had earned a $30,000 contract for the plane and the training of two officers to fly it. Since then, six officers—Lts. Frank Lahm, Frederic E. Humphries, Benjamin D. Foulois, Oliver A. Dickinson, and George E. M. Kelly, and Capt. Paul Beck—had undertaken flying lessons, though none had been certified as aircraft pilots.

The Signal Corps had ordered its second and third planes, new

Wright B-models, a month before Arnold and Milling arrived in Dayton, after Congress had finally appropriated $125,000 for a full-scale experiment in military aviation. Part of that money was earmarked for the purchase of the two planes and part of it would be used to give Arnold and Milling a complete training course in how to fly them. Arnold could now understand the curious two-year delay since he had informed Captain Cowan by cable from the Philippines of his willingness to learn to fly. Though the Signal Corps had organized its Aviation Service in 1907, it had taken four years before Congress was ready to accept the notion that the Army might need more than one airplane. But Congress was not alone in its reluctance to spend money on such an outlandish endeavor as flying. Most Army officers were certain they didn't need any airplanes.

Arnold was pleased to be reunited with Tommy Milling, an amiable, round-faced young man, two or three inches shorter and considerably lighter than Arnold, just as quick-witted but somewhat less dynamic. Like Arnold, he had been chosen for this duty by Captain Cowan, whom he came to know at Fort Leavenworth after Cowan's return from the Philippines. He had caught Cowan's attention because of his dashing style as a polo player and the fact that he rode around the base on a wild, outlaw horse. Athletic skill and courage seemed likely to be useful qualities in a flier. Since Arnold and Milling were two years apart at the Military Academy, they had not been pals, but they were destined now to be very close for at least the next two years, despite a certain element of competition between them. After their initial introduction to the Wright plant, they returned to Dayton, found a boardinghouse, and rented adjoining rooms.

Their training began with twelve-hour days of ground instruction at the factory, where they learned first how the Wright airplane was constructed and maintained. It was built around a light cypress frame and covered with canvas, which had to be stretched tight and then stiffened with a chemical paint. The control wires were exposed, and their tension could be tested only by strumming them like the strings of a guitar or a violin and listening for the proper sound. The plane's pair of side-by-side seats and the engine—just to the right of them—were also completely exposed to the elements. The two pusher-type propellors, located behind the double wings, were connected to the forty-horsepower, four-cylinder engine by bicycle chains, which Arnold scarcely trusted when he first saw them. (It was only natural that the Wrights should have thought of bicycle chains to drive their propellors, since they had begun their careers as bicycle builders.) Worse than that, in order to make the propellors rotate in opposite directions and thus balance the torque, the chain leading to one propellor had to be crossed like a figure eight.

Well, you can't cross a bicycle chain, Arnold said to himself when he saw it. It will break. It must break. Of all people on earth, two bicycle manufacturers ought to know that. Looking back years later, however, he had to acknowledge that he never heard of one of their crossed chains breaking.[2]

Arnold and Milling studied all this construction in minute detail, knowing that when the two new planes were delivered to the Army, they would be expected to teach mechanics how to maintain them. But the days they spent at the factory were not limited to learning how aircraft were built. In one room, the Wrights had balanced an older model plane between two sawhorses and converted it into a ground trainer to help their students (civilian as well as military) become thoroughly familiar with the controls, which were more complex than those in modern aircraft. Since the aileron had not been invented, lateral control of the plane was maintained by a slight warping or twisting of the wings. The stick that controlled warping, located between the two seats, also controlled the rudder. The pilot could make a right turn by pulling the warping lever back to lift the left wing, while simultaneously rotating the handgrip to the right for however many degrees of right rudder he might want. This was not a natural maneuver. Only by long drilling could a man learn it so well that it would be instinctual when he was actually flying a plane.[3] And it had to be instinctual because the balance of the early planes was too delicate to tolerate more than a minor mistake. On the outside of each seat was another, much simpler, stick, which controlled the elevator. Like the yoke in a modern plane, it put the craft into a climb by raising the nose when it was pulled back; it put the craft into a descent by lowering the nose when it was pushed forward. Few of the Wright students had trouble with the elevator controls, but no student could be trusted to fly alone until he had completely mastered the warp and rudder controls.

If any student should think flying looked safe and simple, the Wrights could point to two very recent tragedies, which proved the contrary. Two of the most skillful members of their barnstorming team, Ralph Johnstone and Arch Hoxey, known as the "Heavenly Twins" because of their aerial feats, had died in successive crashes within recent months at air shows in Denver and Los Angeles. Orville Wright, ordinarily a taciturn man, could become eloquent when he spoke to his fliers on the subject of safety. And if they seemed less than impressed, he could point ominously to the wagon that was parked just outside their cow-pasture airport at Simms Station on every morning they were scheduled to fly. The man in the wagon, Arnold later recalled, would wait until after the last flight was completed, then "untie his horses, turn them around, and, slowly shaking his head, solemnly drive back to Dayton. The man was the local undertaker."[4]

On May 3, Arnold and Milling took a nervous nine-mile ride on the interurban line from Dayton to Simms Station for their first flights. At one end of the old pasture was a thorn tree. At the other end was a wooden shed big enough to shelter the two planes available for instruction. Otherwise the field was bare. There were two experienced instructors on hand, one of them, Al Welsh, taking charge of Arnold, and the other, Cliff Turpin, taking charge of Milling. If the two fledglings were frightened, and they had good reason to be, they were not willing to admit it. In later life Arnold professed not to recall the details of his first flight, though it seems extraordinary that he could have forgotten any part of such a crucial incident in his life. When a man took off in an airplane in 1911, he was doing something only a few dozen people had done before him. And he was entrusting his life to a machine that was not much more trustworthy than a tiger.

What information we have about Arnold's first flight comes from his first log.[5] He and Welsh were aloft for seven minutes and the air was "rough"; Arnold did not touch the controls. During the next eleven days, he and Welsh flew together twenty-eight times for a total of three hours and forty-eight minutes, an average of eight minutes per flight. On the third flight he was allowed to put his "hand on elevator," and on the fourth, he "had charge of elevator part of time." Not until his ninth flight did he have charge of the warping lever part of the time. On the eleventh, he "handled levers nearly all of time." On the twelfth, he began learning to land the plane, and on the nineteenth flight, he "landed without assistance." From that flight onward, he was in charge of the aircraft. "I could fly! I was an aviator!" he later exclaimed.

He was ready at last to go up alone, but there was one irritating aspect to that. Tommy Milling had soloed a few days ahead of Arnold and considered himself slightly superior to Arnold as a "natural pilot," a phrase much in use before pilots began talking about "flying by the seat of the pants." For many years (even today in some circles), it was believed that a flier, like an athlete, had to have a certain instinct for the job, and that the best fliers were those with natural aptitude, those with so much affinity for the aircraft they could sense its moods and movements through the seat of their pants. Arnold never believed that, perhaps because he didn't consider himself a "seat of the pants" pilot.

"In that day, when there was none of our modern standardization of planes, controls or flying equipment," he recalled at the end of his career, "it was seldom the plane, or an unknown quantity in the air, but almost always the pilot, who was blamed for being in error. You had to believe that to keep up your morale. Even today, when the airplane is ninety per cent of flying, and the pilot less than ten percent, you will find young airmen who insist, 'Joe must have done something special [to account for his accident].' All this influenced the subsequent 'seat of the pants' flying tradition much longer than it should have."[6] (When Arnold said this, he had already proven that intelligence was more important to a flier than instinct by rapidly converting several hundred thousand young civilian groundlings into skillful military pilots during World War II.)

In any event, Milling did consider himself a "natural" pilot and derived some satisfaction from the fact that he soloed after only five days of training and one hour and fifty-four minutes in the air. He felt that Arnold, who wasn't ready until he had put in three hours and forty-eight minutes of flying time, "didn't like that at all."[7] Arnold might also have felt slighted when, after two days of flying, Orville Wright himself took an interest in Milling, going up with him five or six times in that first week, but never with Arnold. It was Wright who, on Friday of the first week, came to Milling and said, "Now you can go alone."[8]

After flying around uneventfully "for ten or fifteen minutes," Milling came back over the field and began spiraling down for his landing instead of making the usual long, straight approach. Wright, seeing this strange circular descent for perhaps the first time (it later became popular), rushed out onto the field, afraid his precocious student was about to crash. But when Milling landed safely, Wright became more than ever fascinated by his skills and thereafter "went flying with me nearly every day." Milling admired Orville Wright almost to the point of idolatry. "It was from him that I learned all of my flying," he later declared. "He was a great pilot, I think the greatest in the world."

Arnold's admiration for the Wright brothers seemed slightly less personal, more distant, but no less worshipful. On Sundays, the Wrights would invite both officers to dinner, and after stuffing themselves with food, the young men would sit transfixed, listening to the two brothers tell their story.

"They never took themselves half so seriously as we took them," Arnold observed. "Still, to Milling and me, sitting at their Sunday dinner table and listening to their quiet stories, what they had done was a miracle. . . . Without any formal scientific training whatsoever, two 'ordinary' Americans from an ordinary town in the state of Ohio had not only grasped and advanced the whole known science of aerodynamics —they had become its admitted masters."

On the days when the weather was too foul for anything but "hangar flying," the boys at Simms Station sat around trying to outdo each other with their harrowing tales of aerial adventure. "The best times of all," according to Arnold,

> were when the Wright brothers themselves joined us. There was a saying among early airmen that when the Wrights were on the ground—quiet Orville in his derby and business suit, the even gentler Wilbur in plain cap—you never recognized them, but when they were in the air, they could be spotted miles away.
>
> Their presence in the hangar always made the sessions different. Despite their mild, retiring way of listening until everyone else had made his speech . . . you always felt them there. They were usually so courteous, almost diffident, really. Wilbur, for example, often hesitated to give an opinion without first consulting the little black notebook of aeronautical data he always carried with him.
>
> Once, I remember well, a loud argument was in progress about just how the loop would be accomplished—a time we hoped was not far off. Opinions differed as to whether it would be done from "the inside" or "the outside"; as to just how the airplane would behave. The Wright brothers listened with interest, never saying a word. Then, as everyone was laying down the law about this or that approach, Wilbur quietly attracted our attention and pointed overhead. In the slightly windy air far above the top of the shed, a lark was fighting hard to fly straight upward, and as we watched, the bird struggled over on its back and curved down again, coming out in level flight from a crude but indisputable loop.[9]

An even more telling indication of the effect the Wrights had upon Hap Arnold was a remark he made in summing up his feelings about them. "More than anyone I have ever known or read about, the Wright brothers gave me the sense that nothing is impossible." In later years, when Arnold's Air Force subordinates were forced to cope with his stubborn insistence on this belief, they could have blamed the Wright brothers.

After their first solo flights, Arnold and Milling continued to practice almost daily for another six weeks, polishing their skills and convincing themselves that they now controlled the airplane instead of being controlled by it. Besides repeated takeoffs and landings, they tried tight turns, figure eights, climbs, dives, and all the other maneuvers about which they had heard the boys in the hangar brag. One day Arnold even tried racing his plane against the interurban electric train that ran past the field.[10] At about forty-five miles an hour, the train won. Now that he had mastered the mechanics of operating the aircraft, flying began to be fun, but he didn't mention that in his weekly reports. His May 20 letter to the chief of the Signal Corps, for example, indicates nothing but hard work:

> Sir:
> I have the honor to report the following progress, made in operating the Wright machine, during the week ending this date. I have taken the machine up by myself eleven times for a total time of one hour and forty minutes. During weather not suitable for flying I have been studying the construction of the machine.
> Very respectfully,
> Henry H. Arnold
> 2nd Lt., 29th Inf.

By mid-June, when they had completed their course of instruction under the Wright brothers, Milling and Arnold were the only two fully trained and qualified pilots in the Aviation Service. They had earned certificates, soon to be delivered, as U.S. Army Aviators Numbers One and Two, and, with about fifteen hours of experience in the air, they were ready to instruct others in the art of flying. On June 14, having sent one of the two new Wright B-model planes ahead of them, dismantled and packed in a boxcar, they reported at what was to become the first regular Army flying school and air base, near College Park, Maryland, about seven miles northeast of Washington. The Signal Corps was then in the process of taking over the thousand-acre site, a civilian "airfield" which adjoined the Baltimore & Ohio Railway yards on one side and a fish hatchery on another. The airplanes were to be housed in four wooden hangars which had already been built, while the fifteen enlisted men recently detailed to the Aviation Service were to live in tents. The officers were to find quarters for themselves in Washington, where they would perform administrative duties at Signal Corps headquarters when they were not flying. Arnold moved into an apartment house called the Toronto at 20th and P streets.[11]

Two Signal Corps officers, Capt. Charles DeForest Chandler, the designated commander of the school, and Lt. Roy Kirtland, his adjutant, were to be Arnold's and Milling's first students. Captain Chandler, whose only previous air experience was in balloons, had also been appointed chief of the Aviation Service. For two weeks, until the first plane arrived by freight train, there was little to do at College Park. When it did arrive, Arnold and Milling flipped a coin to decide who would be the first to fly it. Arnold won the toss, and after he proved in an uneventful flight that the plane was airworthy, he began instructing Chandler, on mornings and afternoons when the wind stayed below five miles per hour. A few days later the second plane arrived and Milling gave Kirtland his first lessons. Since both students were quick learners, the Army soon had four certified pilots. Toward the end of July, Capt. Paul Beck, who had been learning to fly a Curtiss plane at Fort Sam Houston in San Antonio, brought it to College Park, increasing the number of fliers to five.

By that time, the liveliest question at College Park was: What are we doing here? Though they had been told to fly, and to teach flying, they hadn't been told why. No one in the Army had explained their mission to them, perhaps because almost no one in the Army outside the Signal Corps believed they had a mission. Even within the Signal Corps few people considered the airplane more than a toy. At best it was seen only as an observation platform, somewhat superior to balloons because its speed and maneuverability made it less vulnerable to gunfire, but still limited by the problem of communications.

"Without radio air-to-ground communications," Arnold recalled, "the rapid delivery of intelligence still depended largely on horsemen. We, the airmen, were to jot down what we saw on brightly colored pieces of paper and drop the weighted paper to the ground, where a Cavalryman, galloping hell for leather, would pick it up and take it back to the Command Post."[12]

The young fliers at College Park were not satisfied with such a limited concept of their usefulness. If the War Department was unable to define their mission, they decided they had better define it for themselves. What they should do, they agreed, was to find ways of developing the airplane into a military weapon as best they could. To this end they kept flying "a bit higher or a bit farther" each day, and mounting new gadgets on their machines in an effort to increase their usefulness.

On July 1, Arnold piloted Milling all the way to the outskirts of Washington, about seven miles, and back. On July 7, Milling outdid him by flying Kirtland to Washington Barracks, a distance of eight miles. That same afternoon, Arnold, unable to cross the perimeter of the field because he was officer of the day, decided to get above it, and in the process established a military altitude record of 3,260 feet. On August 18, he broke that record by flying to a height of 4,167 feet.[13] That same month, however, he suffered his first mishap—a warning of more to come.

On what the Army announced as an unprecedented "long military cross-country flight," two crews—Arnold and Chandler in one Wright plane, Milling and Kirtland in the other—were to take off from College Park and land forty-two miles away near Frederick, Maryland, where the District of Columbia National Guard was holding its annual summer encampment. Milling and Kirtland didn't make it, but were forced instead to land near Kensington when their engine died, an all-too-common occurrence in early airplanes. Fortunately they were not injured.

Arnold and Chandler, taking off at 6:34 a.m. in the calm air of early morning, arrived over Camp Ordway, their destination, at 7:23, and made what they considered a routine landing. To the members of the National Guard and the people of Frederick, there was nothing routine about it. The whole town had declared a holiday in anticipation of this accomplishment. Spotters had been stationed along the route from College Park, and when the plane came into view, all of Frederick's factory whistles blew. For the entire day, Arnold and Chandler were treated like heroes. That afternoon, the mayor, in a civic ceremony, gave each of them an engraved cigarette case to commemorate the occasion.

It was late in the day when they took off for home, and that proved unfortunate. They ran into head winds and, with dusk approaching, they got lost. This was not surprising—in fact, it was remarkable that two men with no navigational training or practice, flying a plane that drifted like a straw in the wind, had found their way on the flight to Frederick. On the return flight, bewildered as to their location, they finally landed in a field to ask a farmer for directions. On takeoff they crashed, and though neither man was hurt, the plane was damaged, and so was Arnold's confidence. By now, the Army had suffered its second air casualty when Lt. George Kelly, learning to fly a Curtiss plane, died in a San Antonio crash on May 10. And so many civilian pilots had already been killed that anyone who flew was forced to wonder how long he could survive. The early planes were so flimsy and their engines so unreliable that the likelihood of an eventual crash was overwhelming.

Milling, on takeoff from College Park one day, had made his first turn and was approaching the fish hatchery just beyond the end of the field when "suddenly there was a connecting rod poking out through the cylinder at me." Since he wasn't high enough to turn and glide back to the field, he could do nothing but cut his engine and await the worst. On this occasion, however, the flimsiness of the plane worked to his advantage. Even with the pilot aboard, the Wright B-model weighed no more than eight hundred pounds. Looking down straight ahead of him, Milling noticed that on the fish hatchery property was a grove of young trees.

"I just brought her down and lifted the nose up and dropped it flat on the top of the trees," he recalled.

He was still in the plane when a detachment of men arrived from the field, each with a long pole in hand. "They went around and put the poles under the wings and balanced the tail and just walked out with it and let it down on the ground."[14]

By this time, Arnold and Milling had become minor celebrities around Washington. When Arnold reached his apartment near Dupont Circle after returning to town by train the night of his first mishap, he had to answer several phone calls from reporters who wanted to know whether "the big flight to Frederick" had been a success. Each time he and Milling went to a restaurant, their fellow diners would point them out with remarks like, "There they are. They're the ones." At the same time, the women they met seemed to find them increasingly attractive. Arnold gradually became accustomed to this without taking it too seriously. Still unpolished and not quite comfortable around women, he was nevertheless much less awkward and constricted than he had been, but he had not yet found a girl he liked as well as the cultured, wealthy, distant (in Germany), and unattainable Eleanor Pool.

While Arnold very definitely felt the glamour of being an aviator during visits to Washington restaurants, or at parties, or even in the Army and Navy Club, where his colleagues had grudgingly to acknowledge the public excitement the airplane was beginning to generate, he knew during the long hours he spent at College Park that flying itself offered no glamour—only hard work and danger so frequent that it demanded every possible measure of mental alertness and preventive care. The maintenance of the aircraft, in particular, was a matter that couldn't be taken for granted. He and Milling, unable to handle this themselves, realized that since their lives depended on the mechanics who did it, they had better make certain of their competence.[15]

Though the Signal Corps had been diligent in choosing the best possible mechanics for its Aviation Service, few of these men had even seen an airplane when they arrived at College Park. After long hours of discussion as to how they should be trained, Arnold and Milling decided to start them from scratch. Taking clear photographs of both the Wright and Curtiss planes, they labeled every part of each, including the most obvious. The photograph of the Wright plane, still extant, is amusing to a modern viewer because it included nomenclature now so obvious one can hardly imagine that as recently as 1911 it had to be explained: "Propellor," for instance; "Upper right wing," "Upper left wing," "Engine section," "Radiator," "Elevator," and "Rudder." Beginning with these photographs, Arnold and Milling developed, and then passed on to their mechanics, the Army's first system of aircraft nomenclature and maintenance.

Meanwhile a former Army officer named Riley E. Scott arrived on the scene with an invention he called a "bomb-dropper." It was the first bombsight, complete with a telescope to measure airspeed and a table to calculate corrections for wind direction and altitude. Scott worked his device by lying flat beside it on the lower wing and sighting through its telescope. Though Arnold wanted to help him test it, his weight at the time—a trim 160 pounds—was too much for the plane when it was also carrying Scott and his bombsight; it simply wouldn't get off the ground. Arnold agreed, though, that with the 125-pound Milling at the controls, the plane should at least be able to clear the field, so it was Milling who tested the first bombsight.

He and Scott proved conclusively to everyone at College Park that the invention was worthy of development, but no one at the War Department was interested in it. In 1912 Scott took his invention to France, where he won the Michelin Prize of $5,000 by first hitting a sixty-foot square twelve times out of fifteen from 650 feet, then a somewhat larger target eight times out of fifteen from 2,600 feet. Six years later during World War I, at a time when the United States hadn't yet developed a bombsight, Arnold learned that the Germans were using their version of Scott's invention against American troops.

Though the idea of firing a rifle from an airplane seems obvious now, it was not tried until 1910, when Lt. Jacob "Jake" Fickel, whom Arnold had known in the Philippines, persuaded Glenn Curtiss that it would be safe to let him take a few shots from a Curtiss plane with the manufacturer himself at the controls. In the late summer of 1911, during an air show at the Nassau Boulevard field on Long Island, Fickel repeated his feat with Arnold as his pilot. This time, in competition against the British team of T.O.M. Sopwith (later to become famous as a yacht and aircraft builder) and Malcolm Campbell (later to be knighted for his auto speed records), the Arnold-Fickel team won handily, thanks to Fickel's amazing skill in putting six bullets through a dinner plate on the ground from a moving plane 200 feet in the air. Once again, nobody at the War Department was interested.

In September 1911, Arnold climaxed an eventful summer by

becoming the first pilot ever to carry U.S. air mail.[16] He flew a small satchel of letters from the Nassau Boulevard field to Hempstead, Long Island, a distance of five miles. Two months later, to avoid the Washington winter, the entire College Park contingent, plus planes and equipment, moved in a nine-car train to Augusta, Georgia, where weather experts had promised them balmy southern air and satisfactory flying conditions in even the coldest months. No sooner had they arrived and pitched their tents than "a blizzard which would have done credit to Alaska descended on our camp. Icy winds howled, the tents were buried and collapsed, the four aircraft were knocked completely out of commission and had to be repaired."

In late January 1912, after the damage had been repaired, heavy rains began, followed by a Savannah River flood which made a lake of the landing field. Despite all this, they stayed in Augusta until April, and even got in some flying time between disasters. "We were more experienced now." Arnold recalled, "and flew in winds which were often stronger than those that had kept us on the ground in College Park." The winds were sometimes so strong that the Wright planes, at maximum airspeed (forty-five to fifty miles per hour), would be moving backward over the ground. This was even more dangerous for the Curtiss plane, which was woefully underpowered. Captain Beck, after watching Arnold and Milling take off one day in a virtual gale, decided he could do likewise in his Curtiss plane, and soon crashed into a tree. Beck had two serious crashes in Augusta, and while neither of these mishaps injured him, both served to enforce the generally held conviction that no pilot should make plans for a long life. And if Beck's accidents were not enough, there was also the case of Lt. Frank M. Kennedy, whom Beck was teaching to fly the Curtiss plane. In February at Augusta, Kennedy suffered a crash during which his head plowed a five-inch-deep furrow in the ground. His life was saved only because he was wearing a special new leather helmet, and perhaps also because the ground had been softened by the torrential rains. Kennedy recovered from his injuries and flew in balloons during World War I, but never again piloted an airplane.

In April 1912, the Signal Corps flying school moved back to Maryland and Arnold, after a short visit to Fort Leavenworth, followed his colleagues to College Park on May 12. On the first of June he broke his own altitude record by flying a Burgess-Wright airplane (built by the Burgess Company of Marblehead, Massachusetts, under license to use the Wright patents) to the astonishing height of 6,540 feet, an accomplishment that received nationwide publicity.

Eleanor Pool, still a student in Berlin, opened a letter from her parents shortly thereafter and found with it a *New York Times* clipping that announced Lt. Henry H. Arnold's marvelous contribution to the advancement of aviation.[17] She remembered him well, of course, from the exchange of hand-waves at West Point in 1907, their few awkward subsequent meetings at home in Ardmore, and the two pleasant weeks in the summer of 1909 when they hiked in the Swiss Alps. But she had never entertained any romantic feelings about him. Now she found herself thinking differently about him. Not only was he an aviator, which in 1912 was exciting enough in itself; he was suddenly a famous aviator, celebrated in *The New York Times*.

"I used to know that young man," she said proudly to several of her young women friends.

They scoffed and teased her. "You never saw him in your life," one of them said.

"I do know him," she insisted. But would she ever see him again? In the autumn she would be going home for good, her studies completed. Perhaps they would run into each other in Ardmore, though it would hardly mean anything even if they did; she was still engaged to another man.

In late June, Arnold, who was now the Air Service engineering officer, flew up to the Burgess plant in Marblehead with Kirtland to take delivery of the Army's first plane with propellor and engine in front.[18] It was called a "tractor" plane in those days because its engine pulled it instead of pushing it. This one featured a 70-horsepower Renault engine, in contrast to the 35- or 40-horsepower engine in the Wright B-models, and was equipped with floats for water takeoffs and landings. Arnold found it easy to fly after he accustomed himself to looking around and over that big engine in front of him. He quickly developed confidence in the plane, not only because it had been thoroughly tested by the Burgess Company pilots, whom he considered reliable, but also because it easily passed all the Army acceptance tests that he himself had conducted. He had no misgivings about the plane when he and Kirtland loaded it for what they hoped would be a nonstop flight from Salem, Massachusetts, to Bridgeport, Connecticut, where they were to demonstrate its capabilities in National Guard maneuvers. Their takeoff was smooth and routine, but as they flew south past Boston, ominous clouds gathered and rough weather closed in, forcing them to land at South Duxbury, near Plymouth. Early the next morning, after refilling the gas tanks and pumping the night's accumulation of water out of the floats, they taxied onto the bay, now glassy smooth, and turned into the gentle breeze to take off again for Bridgeport.

In retrospect, it appears that Arnold and Kirtland had too much faith in the plane. They were so sure of its lifting power that they had overloaded it with an anchor for water mooring, ropes, tools, and their own personal luggage, much of which they could have sent by land transport. The previous day, when they had taken off from Salem into a brisk wind, the plane had managed to lift this heavy load, but the wind was so gentle the next morning that they would need a long run to gain enough airspeed to lift them off the water—a longer run, as it happened, than Arnold had anticipated. "We managed to get airborne but were headed directly toward the steeples of the town. I tried to turn; the plane slipped, and we dropped into the water like a stone."

One of the floats broke off on contact and one of the wings crumpled. Though Kirtland was hardly injured, Arnold, after scrambling up onto the remaining wing, found that he had severely bitten his tongue, dislocated one thumb, and sustained several gashes, from which he was bleeding freely. He had little time to worry about these injuries, however. What was left of the plane was in such imminent danger of sinking that in order to balance it on the remaining float, he and Kirtland had to find just the right places to sit on the teeter-tottery wing. And by the time they did so, they discovered they were drifting out to sea.

A few minutes later they were heartened by the prospect of rescue when a sailboat came into view and approached them. There were two men on it and as they came nearer, Arnold, seeing their military uniforms, decided they were elderly Army veterans from the Soldiers' Home in Plymouth. Certain of rescue now, he began explaining to them the circumstances of his predicament and thanking them for coming out to help. Closer and closer they sailed, until their boat was almost close enough for Arnold to touch, but still they said nothing. Finally, without uttering a word to Arnold or Kirtland, they simply sailed around the plane and headed back to shore. It was some time later that a Coast Guard boat spotted the plane and came to pluck Arnold and Kirtland out of the sea. With their damaged aircraft on a tow rope behind them, they finally reached shore at the exact spot where, according to the monument in front of them, the Pilgrims had landed.

Although he continued flying in New York State and Connecticut National Guard maneuvers during the several weeks of his recovery, Arnold had a lot of time to think about the dangers of his new occupation. While the Army had been relatively fortunate up to 1912, suffering only two casualties (Selfridge and Kelly), civilian fliers were falling to their deaths in ever-increasing numbers. Then in June 1912, just two weeks after Wilbur Wright died of typhoid fever and two weeks before Arnold's crash into the sea, one of Wright's most dependable pilots and Arnold's original instructor, Al Welsh, had come to College Park from Dayton to work on the very problem that was soon to cause Arnold's crash—the problem of low aircraft load capacity. If airplanes were to have any military significance, they would have to be able to carry guns, bombs, radios, cameras, and perhaps other devices that hadn't yet been invented. Welsh had several ideas he wanted to test when he took off from the College Park field on the afternoon of June 12. The air was calm and he had with him as a passenger one of the school's newly trained pilots, Lt. Leighton W. Hazelhurst, Jr. After reaching a height of about two hundred feet, Welsh put the plane into a dive, apparently to gain airspeed before going into a long climb. It was a maneuver often practiced in those days, although a modern flier might wonder why—except in the case of certain acrobatic maneuvers that call for a quick burst of speed, the momentum gained in such a dive would hardly provide enough energy to compensate for the lack of altitude, and a dive from two hundred feet is always dangerous. Yet even the most skillful pilots didn't seem to know that in 1912. Welsh was able to pull the plane out of the dive before he reached the ground, but perhaps because he was carrying too much weight, he pulled it out too quickly. The frail craft simply couldn't take the strain. It crumpled and crashed, killing both men instantly.

Then on September 18, another day when the weather was fine, one of the school's most skillful graduates, Lt. Lewis C. Rockwell, took to the air with Corp. Frank S. Scott as his passenger. The men were to stage a flying exhibition for the benefit of the Army's acting chief signal officer, Col. George P. Scriven, who was visiting College Park to assess the progress of his young fledglings. Rockwell had completed his performance and was letting down to land in front of the hangar line when his engine suddenly roared as if the throttle had been pushed full forward (an unlikely possibility under the circumstances) and the plane plunged to earth at maximum speed, killing both Rockwell and Scott. This was only one of many accidents Arnold knew about but was unable to explain. It was beginning to look as if airplanes, like people, had minds of their own and were subject to similar self-destructive urges.

None of this had any apparent effect on Arnold's skill as a pilot or his enthusiasm for flying. He seemed able to suppress any misgivings about the fate that might await him if he continued to fly (misgivings held by most pilots of the time) by dreaming of the marvelous air age to which he was helping give birth. Already he was beginning to envision big, fast airplanes that would carry passengers from city to city and, in time of war, dominate the battlefields with bombs and machine guns. (Milling and Chandler, at College Park, had already experimented successfully with the famous aerial machine gun invented by Col. Isaac N. Lewis, and though the War Department rejected it—because Ordnance had already chosen the heavier Benet-Mercier model, ideal for ground operations, and saw no need to buy two kinds of machine guns—there was no doubt in Arnold's mind that such weapons would soon have to be mounted on planes.) His vision of the future of aviation as well as his accomplishments—especially in setting altitude records —had made him so prominent that first the press and then other air enthusiasts had begun to solicit his opinions.

One day in the summer of 1912, "a sharp-faced, eager young captain" attached to the General Staff came to see him. Though Arnold didn't know it at the time, this man had expressed in the *Cavalry Journal* in 1906 the outlandish opinion that during the years ahead, "conflicts no doubt will be carried out in the air, on the surface of the earth and water, and under the water." Despite such views he had become, at the age of thirty-two, the youngest officer ever appointed to the General Staff, because his abilities were undeniably extraordinary. He had just returned from Alaska, where he had supervised the construction of a telegraph network, but that was not the subject of his visit to Arnold. From Alaska he had made a short trip to Japan, where he had studied the Japanese army, to the extent that he was permitted, and had learned that the Japanese air force already had ten planes, which was more than the United States could boast. His experiences in Japan, plus his expectations about coming developments in aircraft capability, had prompted him to embark on research for a paper he intended to submit to the General Staff about the military future of aviation.

Since his visitor had never flown an airplane, Arnold may have been astonished by his presumption, but he was also impressed by his knowledge. The man wasn't really interested in carrying on a conversation. Mostly he expounded facts, opinions, and dreams about aviation, pausing only occasionally to ask for specific data, and before he was through, he had managed to create the impression that he, the groundling, was the true air expert, and that Arnold, the aviator, would do well to listen to him. Arnold did listen to him, and was destined to continue doing so for several years thereafter. His visitor that day was Capt. William Lendrum "Billy" Mitchell.

In the early morning hours of October 9, 1912, a hand-delivered letter from the General Staff to the Signal Corps Aviation School at College Park put Arnold and Milling to the most severe test they had yet faced in their nerve-straining careers as pilots. The letter presented them with an unprecedented problem and gave them no time to think about it:[19]

> Information has been received that a small force of troops is operating in Virginia, near Washington.
> You are directed to make an aeroplane reconnaissance of the triangle Rosslyn, Alexandria, Falls Church, departing and returning as soon as possible.
> Your flight must conform to the rules for the Mackay Trophy competition for 1912.
> A map of this district is furnished herewith for your information.

The Mackay Trophy was a new award for outstanding aerial accomplishment which was henceforth to be given annually by Clarence H. Mackay, the publisher of *Collier's* magazine. The difficulty of the challenge was increased by the fact that it was presented as if it were a military order, to be carried out immediately, as if the nation were at war and the troops in question threatened Washington. Arnold and Milling had to glance at the maps they were given and, without further preparation, scramble to their planes.

Milling took off first at 9:34 a.m., and Arnold two minutes later at 9:36.[20] After climbing to "a safe cross-country altitude," each in turn pointed his plane toward Washington with high hopes, since the air was relatively calm and the visibility good. But the smooth air over College Park proved to be misleading. Above Washington the air was so turbulent that Milling had scarcely enough strength to control his kitelike little aircraft. And then, in addition to the fear that he might lose control, he found himself overcome by airsickness. Convinced that there was no possibility of completing the required flight under these conditions, he turned and flew back to base, landing at 9:56 a.m., just twenty-two minutes after takeoff.

Arnold, passing over Washington two minutes after Milling, encountered the same gusty turbulence and was equally distressed by it. Perhaps because he was thirty-five pounds heavier and proportionately stronger, he was better able to control his craft, but not by much. He had to summon all his strength to maintain the plane's equilibrium and follow the required course, which took him first over Washington Barracks, then eastward toward Fort Myer in Virginia. He was close to Fort Myer when he managed to spot the small force of Cavalry troops on a country road beneath him, but he was so busy controlling the plane he didn't dare pick up the map in the seat beside him to pinpoint their location. Nearing exhaustion, he turned toward home and finally completed the forty-three-minute flight, landing at 10:19. By this time he was much too tired, however, to land in the precise spot designated by the judges. Feeling fortunate to be able to land at all, he brought the plane down 159 feet from the mark on the field.

When he emerged from his plane, "his appearance was that of physical exhaustion and nervousness." A half hour later, when he appeared before the panel of judges, he admitted he was still very tired, especially in the muscles of his arms.

Even though he was unable to pinpoint the location of the troops, there was no doubt that he had found them since the troops had seen him fly over their heads. For the first time in history, an airplane had proven its usefulness as a reconnaissance vehicle under operational conditions. The judges were so impressed they recommended Arnold for the highest honor he had yet received during his military career, the 1912 Mackay Trophy. It was the first Mackay Trophy ever awarded.

He had won it, however, at an incalculable cost to himself. He had always been aware of the element of risk in flying. Each time another flier crashed, his awareness of risk intensified. After he himself crashed into the Atlantic three months earlier, that awareness had become a constant burden to him, and the difficulty of completing the trophy competition flight added to the burden. Milling, a man of unquestionable courage, had turned back after eleven minutes in that turbulent air. Arnold had refused to turn back, and he could take satisfaction from this, especially when he faced the feeling from some quarters that Milling was the better pilot. But in completing the course, he had also intensified the nervous strain under which he was now living every day, and he could not help wondering how long he could continue to risk his life in these frail, capricious machines before reaching his limits.

Even the War Department seemed now to be impressed by the potential of the airplane, at least as a reconnaissance vehicle. Though the General Staff was still unable to envision it as an offensive weapon, a few of the top commanders, perhaps under the influence of young Captain Mitchell, were beginning to see that it was more than a toy. Cognizant of Arnold's trophy-winning feat but not of the nervous strain under which he and Milling were operating, the General Staff quickly sent them to Fort Riley, Kansas, for extensive reconnaissance maneuvers, which would soon bring Arnold to the most grievous and disruptive crisis he had yet been forced to face.

Ever since the invention of cannon shortly after the discovery of gunpowder in the fourteenth century, artillery commanders throughout the world had been plagued by their inability to aim these powerful weapons accurately. When a field piece was fired at close range against a fortress wall or a hillside, it was possible to see where a ball struck or a shell exploded, and, if it was off target, make corrections accordingly. But against an objective that was out of sight, or even in sight but several miles away, it was almost impossible to judge exactly where the projectile had landed and what corrections would be needed for the next salvo. To American artillery officers, therefore, the significance of Arnold's reconnaissance flight was obvious: if one could spot enemy troops from the air, one could also spot other targets and help direct gunfire against them. But only if there was a means of communication between the airplane pilot and the battery commander.

Thus when Arnold and Milling reached Fort Riley in late October, having traveled from College Park in a four-wheel-drive truck that was the only ground vehicle currently assigned to the Air Service, the mission facing them was to prove not only that they could pinpoint a shell-burst from an airplane but that they could in some way tell the battery where—farther or nearer, left or right—to place the next shell.

There were two possible ways to solve this communication problem. The first and probably most reliable way was the one they had already used—dropping their messages on yellow cards weighted by iron nuts for a mounted messenger to pick up and take to the battery. This was not a very rapid method and it depended on an accurate drop; if the wind carried the message card too far afield it might never be found. In an effort to make the method more precise, Milling and Arnold attached to each of their planes a stovepipe through which to drop the weighted card so it wouldn't be caught by the wing wires or bandied about by the prop wash.

The second possible method, one that Arnold intended to test, was the use of a "crude, one-way radio," air-to-ground only, and with a range of no more than fifteen miles. Though there was already much talk about the potential military uses of radio, it was not yet considered very reliable. Ground-to-air messages would be sent up from the battery by panel code, but nobody knew whether Arnold and Milling would be able to read and decipher them while at the same time spotting the artillery bursts and maintaining control of their aircraft.

Communication was not the most serious concern in the minds of Arnold and Milling as they prepared for the artillery-spotting test, however. They were more worried about the relatively new Wright C-model planes that they had sent to Kansas by freight train from College Park, and in which they planned to conduct their experiment. This model was a larger, military version of the Wright B, with a six-cylinder engine that developed about 55 horsepower and generated considerably more speed. The Wrights had begun building it during the winter of 1911–12 in response to the Army's call for a plane that could carry more weight. But similar as it was to the Wright B except in size, it was quite different in flying characteristics. Milling found that at top speed "the center of pressure would shift very quickly . . . which would pull it down into a stall." While it had not yet killed anyone, it had already begun to develop a bad reputation.

Though it was Milling who had turned back during the trophy competition flight, he seemed to feel, perhaps because he had never experienced a crash, that he was better able than Arnold to cope with the dangers of flying such an unstable machine. It was not that he was more optimistic. He, too, expected to be killed, but he seemed able usually to talk himself into a state of calm when faced with danger. Speaking of himself and other pilots in those early days, he once said, "Everybody expected to be killed. That's absolutely true. Good Lord, I don't know of anybody who didn't figure he'd be killed before he got through, and I still don't see how in the devil I wasn't, when I look back and see how close I came to being killed, so many times. But the reason you don't is, to begin with, you know how to fly. That's what Orville Wright always said. The second thing is, you don't panic. This thing about reliving your life, all that goof you hear—I don't think I've ever been cooler in my life than when I knew, by the Jesus God, there it is, I'm through. Well, if I'd panicked, I would have been through, but I said to myself, 'not till I see the last of it.' "[21]

Between October 28 and November 3, Arnold and Milling had to delay their Fort Riley experiment because of bad weather. On November 2, Arnold and a wireless operator made a thirty-three-minute flight to Ogden, six miles northeast of the post, but this flight was terminated because "the cold was intense" in their completely open and unprotected cockpit. On the third, Milling made two short flights despite a twenty-five-mile-per-hour wind, but both were aborted due to engine troubles. On the fourth, Arnold and Milling each made successful flights, Arnold sending radio signals and Milling, in another experiment, sending smoke signals back to earth.

On the fifth, they tried their revolutionary experiment in conjunction with actual artillery fire. By the time they finished, Arnold had faced a near-disaster so terrifying he decided to give up flying forever.[22]

Though the day was dark and cold, his Wright C-model plane was running smoothly when he took off from the Fort Riley parade ground with Lt. A.L.P. Sands of the Field Artillery as an observer/photographer. Flying over the artillery range on the big 52,000-acre base 140 miles west of Kansas City, Arnold located the target he had been told to find and radioed its position to the battery awaiting his message. Then, as prearranged, he flew to the rear of the battery and turned toward it. The artillery men fired their salvo just as his plane came overhead so that he could observe the burst of the shell and inform them how close they had come to the target.

Using Arnold's coded radio information, the artillery guns were placing their shells directly on target after four volleys. The experiment was a success. While not spectacular, it helped to prove something that few people were willing to concede in 1912—that there actually was a possible military use for airplanes.

The air was rough but the machine was "handling beautifully" as Arnold flew back toward the parade ground. Then suddenly, without warning, it went into a flat spin (perhaps caught by one of the mini-whirlwinds so frequent on the Kansas plains) and turned a complete circle, the diameter of which, Arnold estimated, was not much greater than the plane's width. It felt to him as if "some unseen force" had taken hold of the plane and twirled it. Before he had recovered from the flat spin, he found himself plummeting toward the earth from an altitude of 400 feet. As the ground kept rushing up at him, he glanced over his shoulder, thinking the propellor chain had broken. It hadn't. The controls were all intact. Lieutenant Sands, oblivious to their predicament, was trying to take pictures of a group of soldiers lined up at a pay window on the ground below.

Arnold was totally unprepared to cope with his plane's behavior. In 1912 it was generally supposed that Wright airplanes could not be brought out of a stall. Several pilots, some of whom Arnold knew, had died in the attempt. Though Orville Wright had, in fact, figured out how to do it, the news hadn't yet circulated. In desperation, Arnold did what he thought was most likely to save them. He hauled back on the elevator because, in ordinary circumstances, that was the natural way to return a plane to level flight. But if a plane gropes for level flight before it has built up sufficient airspeed to keep it airborne, it will simply go into another stall and fall off into another dive.

Each time Arnold pulled back the stick, his plane did exactly that. Within thirty seconds, plane and crew plunged more than 300 feet. During that precipitous drop, Arnold later reported, he "gave up everything as lost." But he continued to work the controls until suddenly —he never knew why—the plane came out of its spin. Either he had finally made the right move, pushing the elevator forward by inadvertence, or the plane itself, through the momentum of its dive, built up enough airspeed to bring the controls back into play, so that he was able to level off just as he was about to hit the ground. Cutting his engine, he landed in the nearest field.

When the plane rolled to a stop, he climbed down and said to his companion, "Come on, Sandy, let's walk over to the barracks." Apparently expecting to take off and fly back to the parade ground, Lieutenant Sands said, "Walk? Aren't we going to . . . ?" He stopped short when he saw the fear in Arnold's face.

Hearing footsteps, they turned to see the men from the pay line running toward them silently, as if expecting to find them dead.

Half an hour later at the barracks, Arnold, Sands, and their fellow officers began opening bottles of champagne. For the others it was a celebration of Arnold's successful demonstration and his amazing escape from what looked like certain death. But for Arnold it was something quite different; it was an attempt to control his shattered nerves. When Milling came in from his own flight, he found the party in full bloom. Champagne was "spread all over the table" and everybody seemed to be "trying to get happy." But Arnold was not succeeding. He was in the throes of a crisis that overtakes most pilots at some point in their careers. He was suffering from a severe case of F.O.F.—Fear of Flying.

He walked to Milling and said, "That's it. A man doesn't face death twice."

In one short afternoon, all of his enthusiasm for aviation had been wiped from his mind. He would be just as happy if he never saw another airplane.

The next day, in a report to his commanding officer, he wrote: "At the present time my nervous system is in such a condition that I will not get in any machine." The day after that, in another report, he added: "You know as well as I do that for the past year and a half I have been flying in almost any kind of weather and at almost any time. That being the case it would take some awful strain to put me out of commission the way this has." But there was no doubt in his mind that he was out of commission. "I cannot even look at a machine in the air," he admitted, "without feeling that some accident is going to happen to it."

He requested a twenty-day leave of absence in the hope that he could calm his nerves. By the first of December he was back in Washington, working at Signal Corps headquarters, his flying career apparently at an end.

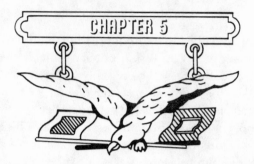

CHAPTER 5

I n the autumn of 1912, Eleanor Pool, having completed her studies in
Germany, returned to her parents' home in Ardmore, Pennsylvania,
not very excited by the prospect of living in Philadelphia after the gay
life she had enjoyed in Berlin. Besides studying music and English, she
had learned to speak French and Italian passably, and German so fluently
that she had earned a certificate to teach it to Germans. She was steeped
in European culture and had absorbed her share of European sophis-
tication. She had also found herself remarkably popular with European
men, several of whom had tried to sweep her off her feet. Like many
beautiful young American women of wealth, she had been welcomed
into the most exclusive social circles and had even danced with the Kaiser's son at the great Sans Souci Palace in Potsdam.[1]

One of her suitors, the latest of several whom she had rejected, was
a German officer who went so far as to book passage on the ship that
brought her home, and throughout the voyage continued to press her to
marry him. By this time, having met aboard ship a charming, much-
traveled Turkish businessman named Joseph Tarica, whose conversation
fascinated her, she found the German officer increasingly burdensome,
but she was unable to shake him. On the last night before reaching New
York, when she and Tarica were dining at the captain's table, the
German officer had burst into the room with a pistol in his hand and
more than a little alcohol in his system. Unless she agreed to marry him,
he announced, he would kill her, and then himself. Tarica had champi-
oned her magnificently, leaping to his feet and wresting the gun out of
the officer's hand. Though Tarica was an older man and had never
pretended to be a suitor, she would always remember this kind and
courtly gentleman who had been willing to risk his life for her.

Hap Arnold remained at Fort Riley with Milling, in the capacity of
supply officer, until the artillery-spotting experiment was completed at
the end of November 1912, but not once was he tempted to fly again. By
the time the two men returned to Washington it was evident that his

65

brush with death had filled him with more than temporary fear of flying. He had succumbed to a depressing phobia, which gave no indication that it might ever subside. He was not the first person to suffer such a trauma. The Air Service, aware of the mental strain of flying those unpredictable airplanes, took a fairly sympathetic view of grounded pilots, and Arnold, with his distinguished record and his comprehensive knowledge of aviation, was no exception. To make use of this knowledge, the Air Service put him behind a desk in Washington as an aide to Brig. Gen. George P. Scriven, now the chief signal officer. Arnold was thus placed in the ironic and anomalous position of being a recognized aviation expert who was afraid to get into an airplane.

He was not happy in his new job. It was difficult to remain in the one branch of service that reminded him daily of his phobia, and to face every day a group of associates who knew why he was now a desk officer, and who might therefore consider him a coward though they would not say so. More important, he would never find it easy to shake from his own mind a certain sense of cowardice—he was a soldier, and a soldier should not succumb to a fear of death. Milling had also experienced some close scrapes, but he had not succumbed. Not that Milling had said anything to make Arnold feel uncomfortable. He understood as well as any man the gripping fear that had forced Arnold to resign from the air. They were still friends, but their friendly rivalry as fliers was now at an end. While Arnold sat at his Washington desk, a member now of the "chairborne infantry," Milling took off for the Burgess plant in Marblehead to inspect some planes being built for the Army. Burgess asked him to fly one of his planes in an air meet at Boston. Milling did so, and won several events, including an all-day, 140-mile tristate race.

Shortly before Christmas, Arnold was granted the leave of absence he had requested in early November, and he went home to Ardmore to face his family and friends for the first time since losing his glamorous status as an aviator. His embarrassment was minimized by the fact that almost no one in his home town realized he had resigned from flying, and there is no indication that he spent much time telling people about it.

One pleasant surprise awaited him in Ardmore—Eleanor Pool, who obviously looked at him differently now. Was it simply because she saw him as an intrepid aviator, something he could no longer claim to be? When she told him how Tarica had stood up for her and how much she admired him for it, Arnold had to wonder whether he would have had the nerve to risk his life wresting the gun from the German officer as Tarica had done.

To Eleanor, Arnold was no longer the awkward boy he had been, but a man who had proven his courage and accomplished daring feats.[2] He had established records as a flier, he had even won an important trophy, and he still had that dazzling smile. He could hardly fail to notice that she now took a greater interest in him than she had before, and it rekindled in him his old flame for her.

Back in Washington after the holidays, sitting at a desk all day, he began to wonder whether even the Infantry might not be preferable. It would be better to be out of the Air Service entirely than to remain in it as a bureaucrat. At that early age he had already begun to hate administrative duties. Even letters from Orville Wright, whom he admired to the point of adulation, could give him no pleasure since they were all about airplanes: "The Light Scout machines are not at all difficult to handle; in fact I think it is the easiest machine that we build. Its high speed in landing is its only drawback. It is a very strong machine and has a larger factor of safety than any of the other models."[3] But it was a subject about which Arnold remained difficult to convince. Wright wrote of the C-model: "Referring to Paragraph No. 1, if the machines are supported by trestles at the last uprights of the wings, our Model 'C' will stand a test far in excess of the load that is required of it in flight. We have tested this machine with a total load, including weight of machine of 1960 pounds, without any sign of the spars or uprights bowing."[4] He didn't mention any signs of flat spins or unexplainable dives. It would take someone even more persuasive than his idol, Orville Wright, to sell Arnold on the safety features of the Wright C-model, the plane that had almost killed him.

Accidents and fatalities were now increasing at such an appalling rate that Congress, on March 2, 1913, passed a law establishing "flight pay" for military aviators—a stipend that would amount to an additional thirty-five percent of base pay. But one had to survive in order to collect it, and there was a pessimistic feeling among the thirty or so fliers in the Air Service that their current casualties, about twenty percent, would soon be as high as fifty percent. Though aviation had begun in America, the Western European nations had done much more to advance the art, and judging by casualty rates, the Europeans were building better planes than the Americans. In France, for instance, where there were already six hundred aviators, the death rate was one person for every 54,000 miles flown, while in America the rate was one for every 12,800 miles.[5] (Since Arnold, before grounding himself, had made more than one thousand flights at an average of at least twenty-five miles per flight, he had already beaten the statistics.) During the first eight months of 1913, the Signal Corps, under General Scriven's orders, recognized these circumstances and launched some corrective measures. The Air Service established more flying schools; it drew up requirements forcing American manufacturers to improve their planes if they wanted to do business with the Army; it began ordering planes with European engines, which were generally superior; and it installed radios, as well as rudimentary flight instruments, in the planes on hand. In addition to all this, Scriven himself learned to fly so he would better understand aviation needs.

While the outlook for Army aviation improved, however, Arnold's feeling about it remained dismal, and he made no effort to resume his flying career. His spirits were not lifted by an assignment he received in late spring to supervise the closing of the flying school at College Park. The winters in Maryland were not hospitable enough to make twelve-month flying practical there in open-cockpit planes. The new schools were being established in California and southern Texas, where the climate was milder. But Arnold had some fond memories of College Park, as well as some chilling ones, and the job of closing it was a constant reminder that he was also closing out his own flying career in a less-than-glorious way.

During May, while he was immersed in this unwelcome assignment, he received a visit in Washington from his sister, Betty, and Eleanor Pool, who had traveled to West Point together in 1907 at the suggestion of Arnold's father. Six years later, Dr. Arnold still thought the banker's daughter would be a good catch for his son. As the Pool family doctor, he was again treating Eleanor, this time for hay fever, from which she suffered chronically, and again he prescribed a trip to see his son as the best possible cure for her. He mentioned that his daughter, Betty, then in Richmond, was going to Washington to see her brother. It would do Eleanor a world of good, he suggested, to go along and keep Betty company. Eleanor, quite uninterested in his daughter but much more interested in his son now than she had been in 1907, agreed that it would be a pleasant change from her life in Ardmore.[6]

The unfortunate Betty was never asked if she would like company in Washington; she simply had to make the best of it, despite the fact that she was always less than eager to see other women take an interest in "Harley," as she still called him. Much to Arnold's embarrassment, she hadn't yet been able to relinquish her close attachment to him and her feeling that his welfare was her responsibility.

When Betty and Eleanor arrived, he fortunately had something more positive to report about his career than his retirement from flying—he had been promoted on April 10 to first lieutenant. As for his being grounded, he did not dwell on that, though he did tell them he was engaged in the task of closing College Park. Each morning he would take them out into the beautiful Maryland countryside in an Army automobile and, when they reached the field, leave them to amuse themselves while he went about his duties, which were not strenuous. Then after lunch they would drive back into the city and go to ball games. Eleanor could see that he was "very discouraged about the future of aviation," but she didn't seem to realize that much of his pessimism was a personal matter. It is possible that on this occasion he didn't even inform her that he was no longer a flier. In later life, she had the impression that he had done some flying at College Park while she was there. The record does not substantiate this. She also, in later life, believed that he had retired from flying after he became engaged to her because "they wouldn't allow the fliers to marry in those days." This suggests that he had spared her the details of his decision to quit flying.

Pessimistic though he was about flying, Arnold was still full of enthusiasm about Eleanor, who had often been in his thoughts during the last six years. Sensing her awakened interest in him, he felt encouraged to court her now, but with sister Betty in attendance, the courtship had to be circumspect. It would have been anyway. Arnold's background was much too proper and the customs of the times too rigid to permit even the most innocent of intimacies. Though he could see she was immensely intrigued by him, and she was telling herself he was "the most interesting man" she had ever met, not so much as a kiss passed between them as their days together continued. They talked about the Army and Army life, about aviation, about people back home in Ardmore, about the dangers of war in Europe, about baseball, about everything except the subject that interested them most—each other. He took her often to the Army and Navy Club for dinner, and sometimes they were able to steal moments, or even hours, away from Betty.

The Sunday morning before Betty and Eleanor were to catch a train back to Philadelphia, Arnold took Eleanor for a walk through the streets of Washington. Coming to the White House, they stopped and looked in at the grounds, but they weren't thinking about the lawns and trees, or the building itself, or the new president, Woodrow Wilson, who had moved in less than three months earlier. They were thinking of each other, how sad their parting would be, and how much they would miss each other.

Suddenly, without preamble, he turned to her and, in his quick manner of speaking, said, "Will you marry me?"

Up to this moment he had been so reticent, so inept at conveying his feelings, that his abrupt proposal flabbergasted her. It seemed to her it "came out of a clear sky." He still hadn't made his first attempt to kiss her. And he had not once told her he loved her. Yet she sensed that he truly did.

As soon as she got hold of her own feelings, she looked up at him (she was only five feet tall) and demurely said, "I think that would be a very good idea if you can take me with my hay fever."

Thereupon he solemnly took off his West Point class ring and slipped it onto her finger. Since it was much too big, she put it in her purse after a few moments. The two of them then went off, as if nothing had happened, to meet Betty for lunch, and not once during the lunch did either of them mention to her that they had become engaged.

Late in the afternoon, when the two young women were sitting side by side on the train to Philadelphia, Eleanor felt certain that Betty was uncomfortably aware something important had happened. Betty may even have noticed that her beloved Harley's class ring was missing from his finger. Without saying a word, she reached over, picked up Eleanor's purse, opened it, and looked inside. The ring was there. Betty knew now what had happened but she said nothing.

The following Sunday Arnold came to Philadelphia to ask Eleanor's father for her hand in marriage. In the morning, before that ritual was to take place, the two lovers were able to sneak away by themselves and, for the first time since openly acknowledging their love for each other, enjoy the pleasure of being alone together. They enjoyed it so much and were so reluctant to interrupt it that the dozen or so people anticipating Sunday dinner at the Pool home became quite hungry awaiting their arrival. One of the Pools' guests that day was Miss Ruth Harrison, who would quite coincidentally become, several years later, the wife of Arnold's close friend and subordinate Carl Spaatz, but who in 1913 was a school friend of Eleanor's younger sister, Lois.

"We waited and waited for Bee and a young man who was visiting her," Mrs. Spaatz later recalled. "But they didn't return so we finally sat down to eat."[7]

Eleanor's family and friends called her "Bee," short for "Beetle," a nickname her older brothers had given her when she was a little girl because, to stop her from tagging along with them wherever they went, they told her one day she would have to go home unless she was willing to bite in two a beetle they had caught. As the story was told in the Pool family, she had done so. She was not the kind of girl that boys could intimidate. Though she denied in later years that it had ever happened, she never lived down either the story or the nickname.[8]

Shortly after dinner was served, Bee finally walked in with a tall, blond young man and introduced him as Mr. Arnold. "He looked confused. He blushed. I thought he was charming," Mrs. Spaatz recalled.

After dinner, Bee's father, Sidney Pool, a cheerful, smiling man with no pretensions even though he was a highly respected banker, took young Mr. Arnold out onto the porch of the large, Victorian house for a conversation both had been anticipating since the previous Sunday when Bee returned from Washington.

Arnold, in his usual direct style, wasted no time getting to the point. "I'd like to ask you, sir, may I marry your daughter?"

"Bee can marry anyone she wants," her father replied, "as long as he's not a goddamned foreigner." It was an odd remark to come from a man with an English background who had sent his daughter to study in Europe, but it probably reflected, rather than intolerance of foreigners, a certain amount of concern about his daughter, who had been semi-engaged several times in the past, once to an Italian gentleman Mr. Pool could not abide.

Bee Pool's entry into Hap Arnold's life was a blessing to him in many respects, not the least of which was that it helped pull him out of the doldrums into which his retirement from flying had thrown him. Still unhappy as a desk officer in the Air Service, he now resolved to do something about it. The depth of his unhappiness can be measured by what he did; he applied for a return to the Infantry and reassignment to the Philippines, about as far away from airplanes as he could get. On July 14, 1913, his request for transfer "to a regiment serving in the Philippine Department" was turned down because there was no vacancy at the moment.[9] The rejection suggested, however, that his plea might be reconsidered if a vacancy did arise. Meanwhile, the Air Service assigned him to attend hearings at Hammondsport, New York (the birthplace of Glenn Curtiss), on the question of whether an airplane invented by Samuel Pierpont Langley of the Smithsonian Institution in 1903, at government expense, had actually gotten into the air. (The consensus was that it had failed and that the Wright brothers were the first ever to fly; in 1914, however, the Langley plane, with a larger engine, would manage to take off.) Since the Pool family summer home on Lake Ontario was near Hammondsport, Arnold's assignment to this hearing was so convenient for him it may not have come about by accident. Though he never liked administrative work, he had learned quickly how to get things done in the Army, and his combination of charm, directness, and persistence was difficult to resist. In any case, the Langley hearings gave him an opportunity to spend much of the summer just a few miles from his fiancée, and it is safe to say that Miss Bee Pool got more of his attention than Langley's unfortunate airplane. The wedding was set for September 10.

On August 16, by which time Arnold's Infantry assignment had come through, he was back in Washington to testify—together with General Scriven, Tommy Milling, Billy Mitchell, and several others—at a hearing of the House of Representatives Military Affairs Committee on the subject of aeronautics in the Army. Mitchell spoke just before Arnold and, as was his custom, delivered a long monologue. He was more than ever enthusiastic about flying, although he still hadn't done much of it.

When Arnold's turn came, he mentioned his status immediately. "I am to be relieved the first of September and will go back to join my regiment."[10]

"At your own request?" Chairman James Hay of Virginia asked.

"Yes, sir."

He then spoke at some length about the role of airplanes in the current Balkan war; the valiant efforts of the Signal Corps within the previous six months under Scriven to foster aviation in the Army; the high death rate among American fliers; his belief that while the airplane was invented in the United States, "then the country went to sleep and left France, Germany and England to develop it"; and his feeling that the Air Service should not yet become a separate, independent branch.

"Until it becomes better able to take care of itself," he said, "I think it would be far better with the Signal Corps. At the present time it is not able to take care of itself." (This was an issue destined to keep coming up for the next thirty-four years. Though Arnold eventually did as much as any man to make the separate U.S. Air Force a reality, he would often find himself in trouble during those years because his views, especially on the timing of the move, didn't always coincide with those of other air officers.)

In the midst of Arnold's testimony, Chairman Hay returned to his personal situation. "You say you have been relieved?"

"Yes, sir, upon my own request."

"And how long do officers generally stay in the Service?"

"That depends upon the temperament of the officer," Arnold replied. "Lt. Milling has been in the service for some time. He started at the same time I did, and it has not affected him as far as I can see, but his length of service has made him more cautious, that is all. Some other officers find that it gets on their nerves, and they become practically worthless as aviators."

"I suppose that after an officer loses his nerve he is worthless as an aviator," the chiarman said rather redundantly.

"Yes, sir. And he must quit or he will kill himself. He will probably kill himself and somebody else with him."

Arnold was speaking then in the presence of fellow officers who knew he was referring to himself though he didn't directly say so. The very fact that he addressed the subject was a measure of his sensitivity about it. Milling, in his testimony that day, said nothing about the dangers of flying. Thirty-four years later, when Arnold was writing his memoirs, he was still sensitive about his 1912 decision to quit flying.

"At this hearing, in answer to a question from the chairman," he wrote in his book, *Global Mission*, "I verified that I was about to be relieved from aviation duty, at my own request. Eleanor Pool and I intended to be married in September; and in those days, you didn't plan to continue flying after you were married—unless you were an optimist."[11] He seems to be suggesting there that he told the committee his marriage was the reason he quit flying. Actually he said no such thing at the hearing, which was attended by many people who knew otherwise. But one can easily understand that it was much less painful to him, and also quite flattering to her, to suggest that he had renounced flying not because of his fear of flying but because of his love for her. And once he had established that story in her mind, he was stuck with it for the rest of his life.

Dr. Arnold was delighted with his son's engagement to Sidney Pool's daughter (he may even have felt he had arranged it), and as near as anyone could see, so was Mrs. Arnold. No one asked her to express the opinions or attitudes of the Arnold family—her husband and her daughter performed that function adequately.

Betty Arnold visited Bee Pool shortly after the engagement announcement to set the bride-elect straight about one matter Betty deemed important.

"Now that you're going to be an Arnold," she proclaimed, "you'll have to join the Baptist Church."[12]

Bee was astonished by such presumption. Her father had belonged to the Church of England before coming to America, her mother was a Unitarian, and she considered herself a Quaker. She did not choose to be a Baptist, and when she didn't choose to do something, she could be as strong-minded as Betty. Trying to sound friendly and reasonable, she said, "Betty, I couldn't be true to myself if I became a Baptist."

"Well, every wife in the Arnold family becomes a Baptist," Betty insisted, ignoring the fact that the family itself had been Baptist for only two generations. "You've got to do it."

Besides feeling outraged, Bee felt hurt at being ordered about so peremptorily, but she could see no point in trying to convey that to Betty. Instead of continuing the argument, she simply waited until the next weekend when Hap came home. Though he had intended as a boy to become a Baptist minister, he no longer entertained strong religious feelings.

She told him what Betty had said and asked him, "Do you think I should become a Baptist?"

"Hell, no!" he exclaimed. "Will you tell me what that's got to do with us?" The wedding, he decided without consulting Betty, would be exactly where the Pools wanted it, at the First Unitarian Church in Philadelphia. Betty decided thereafter that she would not be a member of the wedding party. But in the days and weeks ahead, she changed her mind about that several times. As the wedding approached, no one was quite sure what she would do.

Her mother, on the other hand, tried in every possible way to help her prospective daughter-in-law, even going so far as to drop hints that her son didn't have to treat his bride the way his father treated her. Sidney Pool was a gentleman with courtly manners learned in an English boarding school, and after the Arnolds had visited the Pools, Mrs. Arnold grasped the opportunity to tell her son pointedly how pleasant it was to go there and have Mr. Pool show her so many courtesies. Unlike her husband, he thoughtfully opened doors for her, helped her into her chair, and even listened to her when she talked. Bee Pool took an immediate liking to Mrs. Arnold. She considered her "a serene, radiant woman, with a broad mind, in a family of narrow minds." Bee also felt that some of what her mother-in-law-to-be said to Hap seemed to rub off on him, though he remained thoughtless about the little niceties a woman might like.

On the day before the wedding, the Pools received a surprise visit from the Arnolds. Dr. Arnold had heard a rumor that Mr. Pool intended to serve liquor at the reception after the ceremony. Was that true?

Yes indeed, said Sidney Pool. He was planning a champagne supper.

But did he not know the Arnolds were teetotalers?

He knew that, to be sure. On the other hand, many of the guests were not. And anyone who didn't wish to drink could decline to do so. This was a wedding, his daughter's wedding, an occasion to celebrate. "No daughter of mine," he said, "is going to have a wedding at which there is no liquor."

She would either have her wedding without liquor, Dr. Arnold insisted, or she would have it without the Arnolds.

To break this impasse, Sidney Pool, the more flexible of the two men, finally relented and promised there would be no champagne at the champagne supper. He did not promise, however, that the entire celebration would be so abstemious.

With the liquor problem presumably settled, there were no more complications until Hap's sister, Betty, announced to the young couple that she intended to go with them to his next station, the Philippines, and keep house for them. Hap was not altogether unprepared for this. During his first tour of duty in the Philippines, Betty had offered to do likewise, but he had been able to put her off that time by telling her he had no house to keep; he was in the jungle on a mapping mission. This time, with a new bride, he would have to have a house, but he was sure Bee would be able to keep it nicely.

Betty was shocked when he declined her offer, so shocked that on the wedding day, an hour before Bee was to leave for the church, she received word that her soon-to-be sister-in-law had again changed her mind and decided once more she would not be a member of the wedding. Bee, who was getting to know Betty better every day, was less than totally upset by this news. She was surprised, though, when she arrived at the church and found that Betty, having changed her mind one last time, was there.

It was a big wedding with six bridesmaids, six groomsmen, a church full of people, and a nervous bridegroom. After the ceremony, which came off smoothly, Tommy Milling, the best man, and Lois Pool, the maid of honor, perpetrated a bit of harmless mischief by getting away to the reception in the bride's limousine, leaving the second best for Hap and Bee. Back at the Pool home, as the crowd began arriving for the reception, the younger and sportier gentlemen were discreetly informed that they could find something better than cake and lemonade upstairs in Sidney Pool's private sitting room. Pool had always kept a full cellar. He himself drank Scotch and water sparingly. His fun-loving wife, Annie, whom he called "Matie," drank gin, less sparingly but not excessively. And visitors were usually offered a wide choice. In his sitting room he had what was called in those days a "cellarette," a sizable piece of furniture that looked like a chest of drawers but was actually a liquor cabinet, complete with glassware and all the necessary implements. For the reception, this was well stocked, as was his bedroom. In his bathroom was the ice.

With so many people in the house it was easy at first for the young officers to slip away from the crowd and go upstairs for drinks. While the bride and groom were still in attendance, nobody seemed to notice. But after the rice-throwing ceremony was finished and Hap and Bee had left—for one night at the Bellevue-Stratford in Philadelphia, then a few days at Spring Lake, and a real honeymoon by ship to Panama—the frequency with which the men kept disappearing upstairs was hard to ignore, and so was the condition of some of them when they came back downstairs. Yet Dr. Arnold, who could be obtuse, failed to perceive that anything was amiss until Tommy Milling, who had spent most of his time upstairs, accidentally put his arm through a glass door. He was not badly hurt, but seeing him bleed, his companions didn't know that. When one of them ran downstairs and summoned Dr. Arnold, the whole liquorish plot was suddenly exposed. The resultant scene between Dr. Arnold and Sidney Pool put an end forever to friendly relations between the Arnolds and the Pools.

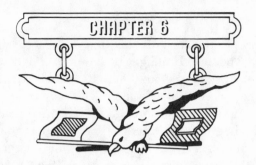

Once again Hap Arnold was in San Francisco on his way to the Philippines, and once again he was almost broke. This time he had with him a new bride, who was one of the reasons he was almost broke. The wedding ring had cost him $51, life insurance, $67; and after his Panama honeymoon, and then two months with the Ninth Infantry at Fort Thomas, Kentucky, there was her railroad fare all the way across the country to California. In 1913, the Army did not pay for transportation of wives. But Arnold didn't care about any of that. He wasn't even bothered by the fact that he had now returned to the Infantry. He was happier than he had ever been in his life, and his bride was the reason for that, too.

He was so intoxicated by his love for her that he had only one regret—that he couldn't buy her all the wonderful things they saw together in the San Francisco shop windows. They were staying at the inexpensive Stewart Hotel on Geary Street, and each day when they went out, they would pass, around the corner on Powell, a flower shop that featured exquisite violets. Bee loved violets and he knew it. As a wealthy man's daughter, she used to wear bunches of them back East. As a young lieutenant's wife she would have to get along without them. Yet every time they passed that flower shop on Powell Street, he was tempted to stop.

"Some day," he would say to her, fingering the remaining money in his pocket, "I'm going to buy you a bunch of violets."

On the day they sailed from San Francisco, shortly before Christmas, he finally decided he could splurge just this once. Taking her by the hand, he walked her boldly into the flower shop, picked out the prettiest bunch of violets, and handed them to her. Then taking a five-dollar gold piece from his pocket, he gave it to the clerk and prepared to walk out of the shop.

"Your change," the clerk said, and gave him back $4.75.

Arnold looked at the money, the man, and the violets. Was this all you had to pay for violets in California?

"Two bits," the man said.

Arnold was crestfallen. "All this time we've been going without violets," he said, "because I thought they were five dollars a bunch."[1]

After a one-day stop in Guam, where Bee caught her first glimpse of Oriental life, they reached Manila in mid-January and went directly to Fort McKinley. As soon as they arrived they realized their honeymoon was at an end. First, they were moved into quarters that they had to share with another officer, and with cockroaches so large Bee attacked one of them with a broom and failed to kill it. Two or three days later they were removed to another house, next door to a senior first lieutenant named George C. Marshall, who welcomed them very hospitably and invited them to dinner.[2] But just as prospects seemed to be brightening, Bee, who was now pregnant, went into the base hospital with painful complications. She eventually miscarried. About the time she became ill, Hap (whom she was now calling "Sunny" in deference to his mother's habit of doing so) was ordered into the field to take part in a major maneuver at Batangas, on the coast of Luzon, sixty miles south of Manila. For about two weeks, therefore, he was unable to be with her and comfort her, or even to find out exactly how well she was progressing.

The maneuver in which he took part turned out to be a significant one. It was to be an "invasion" of Luzon and a march on Manila by a "White Force" of 4,800 troops, which would be resisted by a "Brown Force" of 3,200 troops. The Whites, recruited from units in northern Luzon, were to travel to Batangas in ships and then storm ashore from a fleet of small boats. Lieutenant Marshall, who had already been an instructor at the Army's Command and General Staff School, was named adjutant to the White Force under an elderly colonel who was nearing retirement age. Before the "invasion" even began, the colonel was judged incapable of managing it. The same day, his chief of staff became ill and had to be removed to a Manila hospital. This left no one with enough information to command the operation except Marshall, a mere lieutenant. But the commanding general's representative with the White Force, a captain named Ewing E. Booth, believed Marshall equal to the task, so he was appointed to take charge of it.[3]

Arnold, worried about his wife, had difficulty focusing his mind on the maneuver. When he reached Batangas on January 23, 1914, the day after he left her in the Fort McKinley hospital, he wrote her immediately.

"My darling wife—I do hope that by this time you are feeling better. . . . I hated to leave you sick in bed worse than anything. So please get well for your own sake as well as mine."

The next day, after receiving a reassuring note from her, he wrote, "it came as an answer to many of my troubled thoughts. I do so hope that you continue to get better all the time and wish that I knew that you were out of bed now. I will not be able to stop worrying until I know that you have entirely recovered. I hope dearest that we never have to go through those troubles again. It caused me more serious thoughts than anything that has happened in the last 28 years of my life." Which was to say, his entire life. He did not, of course, mention what "those troubles" were, since they were "female troubles," to use the idiom of the day, and were not to be discussed explicitly. In all of Arnold's letters to his wife during this crisis, the exact nature of her illness was not once mentioned.

The following day, January 25, he was already impatient to receive another letter from her. "Even though I cannot hear from you I should just like to feel you are getting well. If I could only get some word before starting I should be satisfied."

He was referring to the start of the maneuver, the "invasion," which was already one day overdue. "Marshall has just arrived on the scene," he wrote. "He is just 24 hours late in arriving in spite of the fact that he assured us there would be no tie-up in the Quartermaster transportation. You remember he assured us of that when we were at his house for dinner."

These lines suggest that Arnold had already become impatient with Marshall, whom he had just met a few days earlier. Perhaps he was simply expressing his eagerness to get this maneuver finished so he could return to Bee. He didn't yet know about the high-level problems that had thrown Marshall into command of the whole operation. He didn't know either that a shortage of small boats would delay the landing operation until the twenty-ninth.

Day after day, his letters to Bee continued, each conveying a warm love and tenderness that Hap Arnold, burdened with the notion of his day that a man ought not be demonstrative, found difficult to convey in person. On January 31, he pleaded with her to write him again. "I do not know if you are still in bed, are getting better or worse, and it worries me very much."

By this time, the White Force, of which he was a part, had landed successfully and begun its advance northward toward Manila. "These maneuvers are getting more strenuous every day," he wrote Bee. "Some days it is just a long hike over the road but yesterday and today we had to get the enemy out of a position and so had to hike over ploughed ground, through sugar cane fields and bamboo thickets."

At one point on this march, Arnold and his company of Infantry came upon Lieutenant Marshall under the shade of a bamboo clump, dictating the order for "the attack that was to break through the defenders' lines" and make the entire maneuver a success. Arnold had now watched Marshall in action for a few days and his view of the man had already changed: "Marshall still holds the job as main guy for this detachment and tells the colonels where to take their regiments and what to do with them. However, everyone agrees that he has the ability to handle the situation so there is no hard feeling."[4]

On February 4, the maneuver was ended, and a few days later Arnold returned to Bee, who was well on the way to recovery. He was saddened to learn that the baby she had aborted would have been a boy, but he was delighted that Bee herself was as good as new. On February 10, they were able to follow a custom they had instituted the previous October—celebrating each monthly return of their wedding date.

Having watched George Marshall in action during the entire Batangas invasion maneuver, Arnold now entertained an awesome respect for him. "That man," he said to Bee, "will one day be the Army Chief of Staff."[5] In the years ahead, his admiration for Marshall would never diminish, nor was he the only person mightily impressed by this young lieutenant who had proved able to handle so complex a command situation. The news of that Batangas maneuver was to launch within the Army a legend about the ability and efficiency of George Marshall.

Arnold had been "at home" in Fort McKinley with his wife for only ten days when he was again ordered into the field on a maneuver to test the defenses of Corregidor, the now fortified island in Manila Bay. Bee, a bride for only five months, undoubtedly hated to see him leave her again, yet she could look forward to one compensation she would cherish the rest of her life—his almost daily letters. Arnold still had too much of his father in him to be able to show his love demonstratively in person, but his letters would always remain as proof that the love was there.

"I think I am getting more crazy about you every day," he wrote from Corregidor on February 19. "I know that I love you more: so please, dearest, be careful of yourself and take no chances. . . . It would put me out of commission permanently if anything serious ever happened to you. . . . Darling, I love you and want to see you more every minute I am away."

While he was away, Bee traveled to Batangas for a few days by the sea. On the twenty-third, he wrote to her there: "Darling I hope that you arrived at Batangas without any difficulty. Do you know that you are becoming more necessary to my peace of mind and in order to be happy I am much more dependent on you all the time? I think that I am increasing my capacity for loving, for otherwise I can't explain it. . . . I miss you terribly and I want to violate your new rule and make love with you on Monday, Tuesday and every other day. You dear girl, I love you more all the time and can hardly see how I will be able to wait until I see you."

By the twenty-sixth, his impatience to see her had almost reached its limits. "Darling I cannot seem to stand the separation this trip as well as formerly. It seems as if you have become dearer to me and more necessary in the last couple of weeks than in all of the time I have known you before. I am glad that I love you so much but sorry that it must be from a distance, temporarily at least."

Arnold's thoughts were so deeply concentrated on his wife during these two weeks away from her that he gave the maneuver itself only distracted attention. Yet at times, when the big guns around him began to fire their blank but noisy cartridges, he could hardly ignore it. On the night of the twenty-fourth, he was routed out of "bed"—the hard rock of Corregidor covered by just a blanket, under a shelter half—when the enemy fleet launched an attack on the island. "Search lights turned night into day, and guns were fired continuously. Red and green lights were sent up over various batteries showing that they had just opened or just ceased to fire. We were being bombarded by the enemy's fleet. The search lights picked them up about 10,000 yards out at sea. While all attention was being directed toward the hostile fleet, a small boat towing barges supposed to be loaded with troops sneaked around toward Manila. . . . That bunch escaped observation until it was almost past and then the lights that were turned upon it made even the port-holes visible. The Regimental Reserves were called out. All the boats disappeared, the firing stopped, the search lights were turned off one by one."[6]

It seemed, as he described it, that the defense of Corregidor had prevailed against the invaders, but there was an ominous aspect to this maneuver that he didn't mention in his letters, perhaps because he didn't learn of it until later. While the Corregidor guns were repelling the enemy fleet, an enemy Field Artillery captain named Harrison Hall had moved several big guns "by hand and mule, up to the supposedly impassable ridge on the north side of the entrance to Manila Bay. . . . Hall set his batteries up and actually fired on Corregidor, getting hits on its gun emplacements."[7] Unfortunately, his accomplishment failed to impress the U.S. Army until twenty-eight years later when the Japanese, playing for keeps, repeated it.

On his return to Bee at Fort McKinley, Arnold may very well have "violated" her "rule" by making love with her every day. In April she was pregnant for the second time, and this time without complications. The spring and summer of 1914 would have been a completely idyllic period for the Arnolds except for two disturbing circumstances. Capt. Charles Chandler, whom Hap had taught to fly at College Park, was now on Corregidor with a flying student of his own, Lt. H. A. "Bert" Dargue, and a new Army hydroplane. Chandler was a close friend now and Dargue was destined to become an even closer friend. The two of them spent a lot of time with the Arnolds, making a special point of being with them on the tenth of each month for the commemoration of their wedding.[8] They insisted that Hap come over to Corregidor for a look at their airplane, and eventually he did go over to see it, but he didn't fly in it. His airplane phobia had not abated.

In August, an even more disturbing event took place: war broke out in Europe; and while there was much talk about America staying out of it, everybody in the Army realized that before very long they might be firing real shells and bullets rather than the blanks they used in maneuvers.

Meanwhile, however, Army life in the Philippines was pleasant enough. The Arnolds now had a comfortable house (built on stilts as protection against the dampness), which was maintained by the Army, with a cook and houseboy to do most of the work. (They also had another offer from his sister, Betty, to come over and keep house for them now that Bee was going to have a child, but Hap was able to resist that.[9]) From September 12 to December 8 he served as quartermaster and mess officer for the Field Officers' Musketry School at McKinley, and also as range officer during machine-gun practice at Camp Stotsenburg, across the Pampanga River near Angeles. He liked the quartermaster job because it kept him busy, "but not that chow job." (The mess job is one that almost no officer wants.) Once again, however, Arnold demonstrated his surprising adaptability by performing both jobs so well as to earn a glowing commendation from his commanding officer.[10] He was often away from Bee during this time, but not for long periods. Whether he was with her or away from her, he worried more than she did about her condition.

"Now sweetheart," he wrote from Camp Stotsenburg on October 30, "I want you to remember everything that I told you—not to worry, lean over too much, carry anything heavy, open sewing machines." Two days later: "Remember, no hard work, lifting, excitement or worry. Lots of sleep, a lunch morning and afternoon." And on November 4: "What is this about your going to town? No more of that or you will be in disgrace . . . Autos O.K. Street cars never."

Bee gave birth on January 17, 1915, to a healthy baby girl, whom they named Lois Elizabeth in honor of her sister and his. Betty Arnold might be unhappy to learn that her name had come in second, but by this time her brother didn't much care how she felt. He was free of her at last.

While the Arnolds were in the Philippines, the anti-American insurrectionist movement there was simmering, but it scarcely touched their lives, except for one night when the bugles blew the call to arms and they were routed out of bed by a raid against the base. The men hurried to their battle stations while the women and children were herded into the streets in front of their houses, which were built of wood and thatch and would therefore be easy to burn. The rebellious Filipinos did burn some warehouses that night but didn't get near the quarters. Quiet was restored and everyone went back to sleep, only to be aroused again by another call to arms. This time, Arnold, suddenly awakened by the bugle call, confused it with the fire call, which sounded similar. Ruefully he looked at Bee and said, "Do I take a bucket, or a gun?"[11] He didn't need either—it was a false alarm. The revolutionists had returned to the hills. During all of his time in the islands, Arnold never did see one of them.

Early in 1915 the Arnolds were transferred to Batangas, where Hap was in charge of F Company in the Caribou Regiment of the 13th Infantry. They lived in tropical splendor on "a beautiful post overlooking the bay." They had a magnificent view, an excellent officers' club that held weekly hops (Bee had finally taught Hap to dance), and a beautiful baby with whom to share their love. They had many reasons to be happy, but unfortunately, Bee wasn't feeling well. Her weight had dropped to ninety-five pounds and she couldn't eat. One doctor said she had tuberculosis, another said it was dengue fever or malaria. Finally Hap sent her north to the Philippine summer capital, Baguio, in the mountains above Manila, hoping the cooler air would cure her. After a short time there, she became deathly ill, and one day she came out of a coma to find herself lying in a dugout canoe being paddled down river by an almost naked Filipino: it was the quickest way to get her to a hospital. When she got there her disease was diagnosed as an acute intestinal disorder. She was operated upon by a doctor she later described as a butcher, and though she eventually recovered, she was left with adhesions that caused her periodic distress for the rest of her life.[12]

In late January 1916, when Arnold had finished the usual two-year tour of duty in the islands, he was reassigned from the 13th Infantry back to the 3rd Infantry and sent home. It was a difficult two-month journey by way of China, with Bee ill most of the time in their tiny cabin. Fortunately, one of Hap's friends, Lt. Millard F. "Miff" Harmon, was on the same ship, and he became so infatuated with baby Lois that he would take her off their hands and wheel her around the decks for hours at a time while Hap tried to comfort her mother.[13]

When the ship reached Hawaii en route to San Francisco, a cablegram, through the adjutant general in Washington but actually from Maj. Billy Mitchell, was awaiting Hap. Mitchell had become the executive officer of the Air Service, which was now called the Aviation Section of the Signal Corps. His enthusiasm for aviation had finally expressed itself in something more than words. In addition to transferring to the Air Service, he had even learned to fly, during the winter of 1915–16, at his own expense. And as the war in Europe continued without any end in sight, he was determined to enlarge and improve the U.S. air arm so it would be ready if the country became involved.

Though Mitchell knew the circumstances of Arnold's resignation from flying, he was also familiar with Arnold's abilities and aerial accomplishments. Arnold was exactly the kind of officer the Aviation Section needed. It was about time he forgot his phobia and came back where he belonged. The Mitchell cablegram was double-edged. Would Arnold volunteer for duty in the Aviation Section? Or, if so detailed, would he object to it?

With some apprehension, Arnold sent a cable to Washington asking what that meant.

The return cable from Washington presented him with a Catch-22 choice: "If you apply for detail in the Aviation Section, Signal Corps, you will come in with the rank of captain. If not, you will be detailed and come in with the rank of first lieutenant."[14]

Bee's first reaction was, "Oh gracious, no!"[15] She couldn't imagine it. The glamour of flying no longer appealed to her. She knew now about the dangers and she didn't enjoy the prospect of Hap's returning to it. He was much more than a suitor now. He was her husband and the father of her child. All these considerations, together with her illness, put her "in a very bad state." But when she got hold of herself and stopped to think that Hap was a soldier as well as her husband, she realized he should do whatever he decided he had to do.

Though Arnold may not have realized it at the time, he was facing the most pivotal choice of his career. And it was, of course, a choice —despite the cablegram, he could have refused to return to aviation if he had insisted. But while he had enjoyed his two tours of duty in the islands, he still disliked the Infantry. What were his prospects if he were to remain in it? A few tours of duty at various camps in the United States. Close-order drill. Barracks inspections. Hikes and bivouacs. Maybe a march through Mexico in search of Pancho Villa. Then another two years in the islands, still as a first lieutenant. Now that he had started a family, he could use the extra money he would earn as a captain if he took Mitchell's offer. And he hadn't really lost his interest in airplanes —only in flying them. But would he have to fly? There were plenty of jobs for ground officers in the Aviation Section. And maybe it was time to rethink his fears about flying. The newer planes were vastly superior to that old Wright C in which he had almost killed himself three and a half years earlier.

After docking at San Francisco, Arnold took Bee and Lois to Watertown, New York, and reported to his new outfit, the 3rd Infantry, at Madison Barracks. He knew now what his choice would be. Two months later, at the end of May 1916, he reported to the Aviation Section's Rockwell Field, North Island, San Diego—but not as a flying officer. He was to be the supply officer for the new aviation school there. The field was named in honor of Lt. Lewis C. Rockwell, a classmate at West Point whom Arnold had inspired to fly, and who had died before Arnold's eyes in a 1912 crash at College Park. The Aviation Section had adopted a policy of naming its facilities after those of its fliers who had died in crashes. Arnold could reflect chillingly on the likelihood that there would now be an Arnold Field someplace if he hadn't managed to pull out of his dive the last time he flew a plane.

On the day Arnold received his orders to leave Madison Barracks for San Diego, the rest of his unit was ordered to the Mexican border. Bee, who had recovered her health after leaving the tropics, went down to see the troop train off for Texas because several of the officers on it were now her friends. She was standing beside the train, talking to the wives of some of these men, when one of them said to her, "Well, I'd rather see my husband go to the border than do what your husband's going to do."[16]

By this time, Bee was pregnant again, and she was still uncomfortable about the possibility that Hap might return to flying. Yet it didn't seem likely that a man with his restless energy would be content to be a supply officer. She was determined not to interfere.

There were twenty-three officers with Military Aviator or Junior Military Aviator ratings in San Diego when Arnold arrived, in addition to twenty-five students. One of the rated pilots, he was happy to learn, was his friend from the Philippines Bert Dargue, now also a captain, and officer in charge of training. Since Dargue and Arnold were renewing their friendship in an atmosphere dominated by airplanes, Arnold could not help feeling a certain pressure to return to flying. His retirement from the air, in the face of danger, had left a bitter sense of failure, which, for his own peace of mind, he ought to expunge. For more than four months he resisted the pressure to fly again, but eventually, whether or not he had to fly as a means of redeeming his self-respect was no longer the compelling question. Confronted every day by the sound of engines, the smell of the cockpit, the conversation of Dargue and the other pilots, he began to want to fly again. Most of the planes on the field were the new Curtiss JNs, the soon-to-be famous "Jennys," and they intrigued him. They had some weight and power and speed, unlike the flimsy kites he used to fly.

Finally, on October 18, he could resist the urge no longer. Just two weeks short of four years after the harrowing misadventure at Fort Riley, he took to the air again, as a passenger, on a twenty-minute flight above San Diego with Dargue as the pilot.[17] It was uneventful but apparently exhilarating. That afternoon, when he came home with Dargue from the field, Bee took one look at him and knew what had happened.

"Well, did you have a good trip today?" she asked.

He gave her a funny look, a mixture of sheepish pleasure at what he had done, amazement at being so easily found out, and concern about her reaction. "How did you know?" he asked.

"I've got awfully good eyes," she said, not bothering to tell him that the fair skin of his face was sunburned except for the area that would have been covered by goggles.

He made no attempt to deny it, though he admitted he would have preferred to withhold it from her because of her pregnancy. The notion that pregnant women were pitifully frail creatures was prevalent in those days.

"It's perfectly all right," she said. "If you want to do it, go ahead and do it. That's your life."[18]

Only those who were present would know whether there was any displeasure in her tone of voice. Bee Arnold was no more clever than her husband at hiding her true feelings. But however she may have felt at the time about his return to the air, she never threw it up to him later. "I felt when we went out there," she said in later years, "that Hap wouldn't be a supply officer very long."

But Arnold's return to the air was not just a simple matter of taking a twenty-minute flight as a passenger. His fear of flying was still strong. The difference was that now he had developed a determination to conquer it. Five days later he flew again as a passenger, and within the next month he went up seven more times, but always with someone else flying the airplane.

Finally, on November 26, he went up alone, for six minutes, which is about as long as it would take to circle the field and hurry right back in to land. But the next day he again flew alone, for eleven minutes; two days later, for sixteen minutes; and three days after that, on December 1, for nineteen minutes.

Though he was now pushing back his fear, he hadn't yet banished it completely. What he would have to do, he decided, was to take some positive, aggressive action against it. One day (probably December 16, 1916, when he flew for forty minutes, though the exact date is a matter of conjecture), he took off on a flight that was like no other he had ever attempted. He was determined to put himself through every dangerous maneuver man is capable of in an airplane.[19] He tried snap rolls, slow rolls, and loops. He stalled, he spinned, he flew upside down for as long as he could keep the wings balanced. He dove for the deck and buzzed the ground. He did everything his imagination could conceive to test the airplane's endurance, and, more important, his own endurance, and he found to his enormous relief that he could take as much punishment as the plane. After he landed that day he was able, for the first time in four years, to look at an airplane without fear. "When I'm going to die, I'm going to die," he decided. It was not up to him. But when his time did come, he would just as soon die flying as any other way.

By the sheer power of his will he had conquered his phobia, redeemed his self-respect, and renewed his courage. He seemed to have banished forever his fear of flying.

Arnold was not yet fully refledged when the unfortunate flight of Lt. Col. Harry G. Bishop and Lt. W.A. Robertson into the Mexican desert occurred on January 10, 1917, with results that threatened the careers of both Arnold and Bert Dargue. Colonel Bishop, a Field Artillery officer, had requested the use of a plane and pilot to take him on a flight the destination of which was unspecified. Maj. Frank Lahm, once Arnold's French instructor at West Point and currently the base secretary (the equivalent of adjutant) at Rockwell, had signed an authorization for the flight, leaving the destination blank. Dargue, as officer in charge of training, had gone to Lahm on January 6 to protest against the proposed excursion, pointing out in particular that if the destination remained unspecified, Colonel Bishop and his pilot would have a license to fly wherever they pleased, even as far away as San Francisco. Lahm acknowledged that this was true but made it clear that it was none of Dargue's business. Having received his instructions, he was expected to carry them out. Arnold, who happened to be in Lahm's office at the time on other business, heard this entire conversation. A few days later, out of curiosity, he asked Dargue to show him the permit for the flight. It was signed by Lahm.

On the tenth at 10:00 a.m., an hour and a half after Bishop and Robertson took off, Dargue, who still disapproved of the flight, went to the base commander, Col. W. A. Glassford, and pointed out that because Colonel Bishop would be using the plane all day on a joyride, five students would be deprived of instruction flights.

Glassford called in Lahm and asked whether either he (Glassford) or Lahm had signed the permit for the flight. Lahm said neither of them had signed it.

Though Lahm had become a major just a day or two earlier, Dargue—very much his junior and still only a captain—refused to be intimidated. He disclosed that he had in his possession the original permit for the flight, signed by Lahm.

None of this would have been important if Bishop and Robertson had not been lost for nine days. The matter might not have become important if Glassford and Lahm had agreed to an immediate search for them. But for six days they delayed beginning the search (perhaps they hoped the two would be found quickly, and didn't want to call attention to a flight they couldn't justify), and this became a cause célèbre among the pilots. Every flier on the base could imagine himself downed in the desert without anyone looking for him. Arnold quickly embraced the side of Dargue and the pilots, which was bound to be the losing side since Glassford and Lahm had the power of rank.

Though Bishop and Robertson were finally found, near the head of the Gulf of California, Arnold and Dargue by that time were destined to be reassigned as soon as Colonel Glassford could arrange it. And when they both subsequently testified to Army investigators about the matter, they were signing their own tickets to exile. Dargue was sent back to the Coast Artillery, where he had served previously; Arnold was sent to Panama, ostensibly to organize an air squadron there but more likely, as he later acknowledged, because "my superiors wished to get me as far away from San Diego as possible."[20]

On January 29, 1917, the day before his departure,[21] Bee gave birth to their first son, prematurely, after a seven-month pregnancy; but it was not easy to celebrate his arrival in view of her delicate condition and Hap's imminent exile to Panama. Since Bee hadn't yet fully recovered from her first sojourn in the tropics, it seemed foolish to take her to Panama with two tiny children. Hap left her in the hospital at Coronado while he went off to Panama by way of Washington and New York. Before he left, they decided to name the new baby Henry H. Arnold, Jr.

When Arnold reached Panama, his new commanding officer, Maj. Gen. Clarence Edwards, greeted him with the news that his efficiency report from San Diego was "awful."

"May I see it?" Arnold asked.

The general declined. "It's so rotten," he said, "it makes you stink."

Edwards seemed sympathetic, however, and Arnold attacked his new assignment with such enthusiasm one might have thought it was the achievement of a lifelong ambition. "This job," he had written to Bee after being briefed in Washington, "is the biggest one I have ever had, or expected to have for years to come."[22] He also noted in another letter to her, "There was a lot of objection [in Washington] to my being detailed as a squadron commander. . . . I stand in well with some and not so well with others."[23]

His new job turned out to be neither the best nor the easiest he ever had. With the Kaiser's submarines strewing British and French ships along the ocean floor from the North Atlantic to the Caribbean, and now sinking American ships as well, President Wilson was edging ever closer to a declaration of war against Germany. Under these circumstances, a very real danger to the Panama Canal seemed imminent, and the Army's air arm was determined to prove useful in helping the Navy protect it. Before anything else could be done, all parties with an interest in the defense of Panama had to agree on the location of the new aero squadron, which was to be sent down as soon as Arnold could build facilities for it. The Navy, the Signal Corps, and the Coast Artillery had each selected an ideal site, but none of these sites was near the others. Arnold himself then selected a site, but no one would approve it. In the face of this deadlock, General Edwards told him to go back to Washington and get it settled by the War Department.

Arnold was on a ship bound for New York when, on April 6, 1917, the news came that the United States had declared war on Germany. He hurried to Washington and shortly after arriving there learned he would not be returning to Panama. He didn't mind that. He also learned he wouldn't be going to France, and this he did mind. After those four years when he was afraid to fly, he was eager to prove, against the Germans, that his courage had returned. But alas for him, he had turned up in the wrong place at the wrong time. Because of the frenzied activity that accompanied America's entry into the war, the Signal Corps Aviation Section was desperate for qualified officers at headquarters in Washington. On April 17 he was placed on temporary duty there, and on May 25, he was put in charge of the Information Division.[24] He continued to ask for duty in France but nobody was listening.

On April 17, the day his orders came through detailing him to Washington, he happened to be in Philadelphia to greet Bee and the children, who had just arrived from San Diego. She was feeling somewhat better now—much better when she learned that her husband was to be stationed in Washington rather than Panama or on the western front. She went to Washington a few days later and rented a large, fully furnished house near Dupont Circle, with servants' quarters, a library, butler's pantry, and nine bedrooms.[25] For a man who was at that moment making $340 a month, it was expensive—$65 a month—but it was worth it.

In June the Army put him on permanent duty in Washington and, as if in answer to his concern about paying $65 a month for that mansion, raised his salary by making him a temporary major. Then on August 5, he became a temporary full colonel, the youngest full colonel in the Army at that time. When he and Bee looked at those eagles on his shoulders, they seemed unreal. Thirty-one-year-olds just didn't become colonels in those days. At first, he later recalled, he used to take back streets to his office, "imagining that people would be looking at me incredulously."

Again he asked for a transfer to France. The Army's answer to that came August 15 and explained why those eagles had been pinned on his shoulders. With Brig. Gen. Billy Mitchell already in Europe, and Brig. Gen. (Temporary) Benjamin Foulois, Mitchell's rival star in the Aviation Section, on his way to Europe, there were very few experienced air officers to run the shop in Washington. Arnold was therefore relieved of his duties as information officer and named executive officer of the entire Signal Corps Air Division.

At the time the United States entered the war, the total strength of the Air Division was 52 officers and 1100 men, plus 200 civilian mechanics. Of the 55 planes on hand, Arnold considered 51 obsolete and 4 obsolescent.[26] None were combat planes. None had usable machine guns mounted on them. The United States didn't own a single bomber, nor did it own a bombsight, although, as we have seen, an American, Riley Scott, had invented the bombsight most of the European nations were using. Despite the fact that German and Allied planes had been fighting each other and bombing each other's lines for almost three years, the Army General Staff still considered the airplane useful only for reconnaissance.

A few days after the United States declared war on Germany, Billy Mitchell, stationed in France, decided the best way to awaken the American Army to its air needs would be "to get the French government to exert pressure on ours." Accordingly, he inspired a May 24, 1917, telegram from French Premier Alexandre Ribot to President Wilson, outlining the French estimate of American air requirements on the western front. By the spring of 1918, Ribot asserted, the United States should have sent (in conjunction with land operations) 4500 airplanes, 5000 pilots, and 50,000 mechanics with all necessary support personnel and material. Earlier, on May 1, the French had already disclosed confidentially that the Germans held air superiority over the front. They would not be knocked out of the air by anything less than heroic efforts.

The American air planners, including Arnold, were heartened by the Ribot telegram. Here at least was a concrete goal, put forward by a nation with three years of experience fighting the Germans. The French estimate would have to be taken seriously, and it was—by the White House, the Joint Army and Navy Technical Board, and by Secretary of War Newton D. Baker and Secretary of the Navy Josephus Daniels, all of whom approved it within three days. But when the Aviation Section prepared a bill for Congress that would implement this plan—a bill calling for procurement of 22,600 airplanes of all kinds, with the men and supplies needed to keep them in the air—the Army General Staff was appalled. Pared to its minimum the estimated cost would be $639 million. Up to 1917, the General Staff had appropriated a total of only $900,000 for its air arm since the invention of the airplane. In June 1917, two months after the nation went to war, Congress had passed a bill authorizing the Signal Corps to develop 16 airplane reconnaissance squadrons and 16 balloon companies (but no bombers or fighters) at a cost of $43 million: the General Staff had considered that an excessive expenditure just for aircraft. Faced with a proposal to spend another $639 million for planes, the General Staff was so stunned it refused to take any action whatsoever.

Finally, on July 4, 1917, Secretary of War Baker, ignoring the General Staff, took the matter into his own hands and submitted the bill to Congress, which passed it in twelve days, still without the approval of the General Staff.

From that day forward, Arnold was intricately involved in all the steps necessary to convert this money into an effective air force—the development and procurement of qualified aircraft; the construction of schools, fields, and other facilities; and the recruitment and training of personnel. It was an experience he would find immensely valuable two decades later, but at the time he was not successful. Because of continuing shortages, lack of precedent, limited priorities, competition with other elements of the war effort, ignorance about aircraft in the auto industry, which undertook to build most of the planes, and other factors, political and military, the American Army air arm never did become an effective fighting force during the First World War. And this was unfortunate because in the climactic months of the war, the Allied armies badly needed air support. Toward the end of 1917 and in early 1918, the military collapse of Russia allowed Germany to transfer hundreds of thousands of troops from the eastern to the western front for what the Kaiser envisaged as his final, victorious push. His armies were now so strong in the west that he had good reason to be confident. On March 22, 1918, he began the Somme River offensive, which very nearly split the French and British forces.

When German troops reached the Somme (on the twenty-third) they were able to bombard Paris, only seventy-five miles away, with their gigantic "Big Bertha" gun. On April 9, when the Somme offensive was finally stalled after a thirty-mile gain, the Kaiser launched the Lys offensive, followed by the Aisne, the Noyon-Montdidier, and finally the Marne. During each of these drives, and until they were finally stopped in the Second Battle of the Marne, the Germans came perilously close to breakthroughs that would have defeated the Allies. An effective American air arm could have done much to relieve the German pressure in these offensives.

The American failure to build and send more than a token air force to Europe was a continuing source of such bitter frustration to Arnold that his characteristic impatience, with which only his close associates had been familiar, now became famous throughout the Air Service and among those civilians involved in aircraft production. From late 1917 onward he made several inspection trips to Detroit and other auto centers that were supposedly becoming aircraft centers. With each trip his impatience grew. Automotive engineers and executives, despite all his arguments, couldn't seem to get it into their heads that an airplane was a creature quite different from a car. Nor did they share his feeling of urgency. He would return to Washington from these trips and in ever-growing exasperation, after arguing all day with production experts like Howard Coffin, director of the Bureau of Aircraft Production, and J. G. Vincent of the Packard Company, invite them to his home at night so he could continue the argument.[27] But as a colonel in a small branch of the Signal Corps, he had neither the power nor the prestige to win such arguments. By Armistice Day, November 11, 1918, the United States had only 2,768 fully trained pilots and observers on the western front, and most of them were flying British or French planes. Though some American-designed planes reached Europe, very few flew in combat.

Arnold's administrative involvement in the attempt to create an air force left him with much insight as to what should and should not be done if the country ever again had to build a large air force in a hurry, but it also imposed on him a double frustration. He had long ago learned to hate all desk jobs. He despised this one because it was part of an enterprise that was falling far short of expectations, and because it continued to prevent him from going into combat overseas.

By 1918, many of his friends were in France. Billy Mitchell, after a power struggle with Benny Foulois, had been placed in charge of all Air Service units at the front under Gen. John J. Pershing, while Foulois had been sent to the rear in charge of flying schools and services of supply. (Disgusted at their inability to get along with each other, Pershing had placed a brigadier general from the Corps of Engineers, Mason M. Patrick, above both of them.) Col. Tommy Milling was in command of all First Army air units, and Col. Frank Lahm, whom Arnold considered more of an acquaintance than a friend after the San Diego incident, was in command of all Second Army air units. Col. John Paeglow, whom Arnold had known in the Philippines, was in command of all American observation balloons. If these men could get to France, why shouldn't he? Hadn't he served long enough behind a desk?

On May 21, 1918, his hopes fell when he was named assistant director of military aeronautics, a position which made him the number two man in the Air Service's Washington headquarters. It was a title that gave him added power, but that seemed at the same time to nail him to his Washington chair. And he was desperate to get to France at that time because "I was convinced that without combat experience, my future in the air arm was limited."[28]

He soon found out, however, that his new position gave him one advantage he hadn't counted on—mobility. He was now high enough in the Air Service to go where he pleased as long as he could justify it. There was only one place he wanted to go, and finally, in September 1918, he came up with a good enough excuse.

A year earlier, in the fall of 1917, the Air Service, working with the Sperry Company and Charles F. Kettering's Delco Corporation, had invented and successfully tested two pilotless airplanes. Under Kettering's ingenious direction, these were soon converted into flying bombs, thereafter called "bugs," which were, in effect, the forerunners of the German World War II buzz bombs. Empty, the bug weighed only 300 pounds, but it could carry a 300-pound bomb load a significant distance across enemy lines. It would be cheap to manufacture and it was easy to launch from a simple track. Though early tests had gone awry, its development was far enough along, in the summer of 1918, to justify telling Pershing about its availability.[29]

In September, when Pershing informed Washington that he was interested in the bug, Arnold realized he had just received his ticket to France. Instead of sending someone else, he would go himself and brief the Supreme American Commander about the promising new invention. His third child and second son, William Bruce Arnold, had been born July 17 without complications, and Bee was comfortably situated in their Dupont Circle mansion. Though she did have some difficulties, she was obviously capable of handling them. Little three-year-old Lois, for instance, was a source of concern. She had begun to show aggressive hostility toward her tiny brother, Hank, going so far as to drop a heavy iron engine into his crib one day.[30] Fortunately it had missed him. It was hard to believe she had done it purposely, yet Bee was worried about her and had begun watching her more closely. A few days before Hap was to leave for Europe, Lois also came down with influenza, but Bee assured him the child would be all right. She would have been happier to have him stay with her, yet she understood his compulsion to go and she had no intention of trying to stop him.[31]

The troopship on which Arnold sailed, the S.S. *Olympia*, was to leave New York on October 17 but he arrived there several days early to make sure he wouldn't miss it.[32] On the thirteenth he was introduced to a young flier he was destined to see much more of: Maj. Carl "Tooey" Spatz (later changed to Spaatz as a guide to pronunciation), who had just returned from France after shooting down two German planes. On the fourteenth, Arnold went to the theater, ran into Spatz again and met Mrs. Spatz, whom he had seen once before, at the Pool home in Ardmore, when she was a schoolgirl named Ruth Harrison and he was a young swain in the process of becoming engaged. After the theater, he returned to the Biltmore and got to bed early, about 11:30, feeling fine.

He awoke at 9:00 a.m. on the fifteenth with a headache, a cough, and pains throughout his body. Since New York was then in the throes of a virulent influenza epidemic (which would eventually sweep the country and kill almost a million people), his symptoms caused him some concern, but he began taking aspirin and as the day wore on, he gradually felt better. That night, the cough and the aches returned. The next day he felt "pretty bad," and the following day, the seventeenth, he felt rotten as he boarded the *Olympia*. For the entire seven-day crossing he was in bed with fever and chest pains. When the ship docked at Southampton the night of the twenty-fourth at ten, an ambulance was waiting in the drizzle to take him to a troop hospital at Hersey Castle, ten miles away. It was beginning to look as though fate had decided he should never get to the western front.

On November 1 he talked his way out of the hospital in spite of some lingering symptoms in his chest and went directly to London en route to Paris. There were rumors of peace when he arrived in France and he wondered if he could possibly reach the front before the fighting stopped—he wanted at least to be able to say he had been there. On the tenth, he arranged to fly over the lines, but the weather was so foul that all planes were grounded. In his diary he wrote: "It looks as if I will go down in history as a desk soldier."

On November 11, a British colonel agreed to drive him to the front. They headed east at 9:00 a.m. and passed through the ruins of Verdun to the Argonne Forest, where they encountered the 103rd U.S. Infantry. Hap Arnold was at the front at last, right in the midst of the fighting, with guns exploding all around him—but the guns were firing in celebration, rather than anger. The hour of the cease-fire, 11:00 a.m., had arrived. Arnold has just missed World War I.

When Hap Arnold returned from France on December 21, 1918, he found that his most cherished hope had come true, in a manner of speaking, a year and a half late: he was no longer to be a desk officer in Washington. Now that the war was over, he was finally going to get his chance to take command of troops, 8,000 of them, plus 375 officers, and several squadrons of aircraft, at Rockwell Field in San Diego. But for what purpose? Demobilization. With the war at an end, the American public was eager to get the boys out of uniform and back home. Arnold's principal job in San Diego was to shrink his command by discharging as many men as possible as quickly as possible.

To aid him in this task, Maj. Carl "Tooey" Spaatz, whom he had met briefly in New York on the way to Europe, was assigned as his executive officer. A tall, square-jawed Texan whom neither of them had ever met before, 1st Lt. Ira C. Eaker, previously the assistant adjutant at Rockwell, was to become their adjutant shortly after Arnold arrived. Eaker had joined the Infantry as an R.O.T.C. second lieutenant when the United States entered the war, and had then been recruited into the Air Service for flight training, which he had completed in October 1918. Limited as he was in experience, Eaker viewed with awe men like Spaatz, who had actually shot down German planes, and like Arnold, who had been assistant director of the entire Air Service. When Eaker met Colonel Arnold, he decided he was looking at the most handsome Army officer he had ever seen, with the possible exception of General Pershing. "He was six feet tall, erect, wore his uniform with pride and grace," Eaker later recalled. "His instant trademark was a quick, engaging smile, but he possessed a reserve and dignity of bearing which did not encourage familiarity."[1]

The war years in Washington, although frustrating to Arnold, had accustomed him to authority, and had given him a sense of confidence in his own ideas. So many things he favored had worked and so many things he disapproved of had failed, especially in the field of aircraft development, that he saw no reason to be timid about his ideas. On his trip to France, he had even gone so far as to tell the commanding general what was wrong with his air installations at the front. He had developed a manner that asserted command. Without being autocratic, he spoke positively, as if he expected to be heard and heeded. The officers around him seemed to dance attendance upon him, doing his bidding.

Aircraft manufacturer Donald Douglas (at that time an employee of Glenn Martin) was in the lobby of Dayton's Miami Hotel one evening in early 1919 when "here comes this great big chap, with a bunch of aides running around him, flinging out orders right and left."[2]

Douglas said to someone nearby, "Who's that?"

"That's Colonel Arnold. He's just come back from the western front."

Douglas was impressed. "We'd seen a hell of a lot of fliers, but they were all boys," he later recalled. "Here was a man."

Eaker had intended to help the demobilization along by demobilizing himself, but after seeing Arnold and Spaatz in action, he decided to stay in the service. It seemed to him that "these two were going places and this would be a good team to join." There is a touch of irony in Eaker's decision, because Arnold himself was then so discouraged he was tempted to leave the Army.[3] He was still bitter about the fact that he hadn't been allowed to get to the front during the war, and he was fully convinced that only the men who had seen action would move ahead in the Air Service. He already had some evidence of this in the fact that he had been summarily dismissed from headquarters now that the combat veterans were returning to fill the best jobs.[4]

He was concerned not only about his own future but about the future of aviation, to which he had rededicated himself completely since his return to flying status in 1916. This rededication had approached the intensity of a born-again conversion. For the first time in his life, Arnold had found a cause to which he could give himself completely. But now that he had adopted that cause, it seemed to him that a lot of other people who should be embracing it were abandoning it. The war had proven to everybody, presumably even to the Army General Staff, that the airplane was more important as an offensive and defensive weapon than it was as a reconnaissance implement. Apparently recognizing this fact, the General Staff, in May 1918, had separated the Aviation Section from the Signal Corps and changed its name once more, calling it the Air Service of the National Army. Changing the name of the Army's air arm was a favorite sport of generals in the early years of aviation. By 1918, it had been known as the Air Service, the Air Division, the Aeronautical Division, the Airplane Division, the Air Service Division, and the Aviation Section. But none of the changes up to May 1918 had been substantive. They were simply the results of organizational reshuffling within the Signal Corps. The detachment of the air arm from the Signal Corps in May 1918, however, apparently represented a significant step forward, acknowledging the vital importance of aircraft and creating a separate Air Service. By this time, its size had escalated to more than 150,000 men, and though that was because of the war, it seemed inevitable that even when the war ended, the Air Service would assume a place in the new Army almost equal to that of the Infantry. It would certainly end up ahead of the Cavalry, which tanks and trucks, as well as airplanes, had made indisputably obsolete.

The demobilization orders handed down shortly after the armistice made it obvious that the men who governed the Army did not share these assumptions. While they didn't relegate the Air Service to its previous insignificant status, neither did they take into account its glaring need for technological development. These men were unaccustomed to thinking in terms of military technology. The Infantry and Cavalry didn't depend on technology; they depended on men and horses, and by God, men and horses didn't change. That was the trouble with the airplane—you couldn't count on it. As soon as you developed a good one and spent several million dollars getting it into production, somebody else came along with a better one. That was no way to run an army. So the General Staff, with the cooperation of a peace-minded Congress, pencilled in an Air Service budget that virtually eliminated the possibility of any important aircraft advances for years to come. The hope of developing more powerful engines, for example, was immediately squelched. Why? Because the Air Service now had on hand several thousand "Liberty" engines, manufactured during the war but never used. Though they were already obsolete militarily, they were not to be wasted. Empty your plate, the Air Service was told, before you ask for more.

It is easy to imagine how this kind of thinking affected a man like Arnold, whose vision of aviation's future was now so grandiose that even the farthest horizon could not contain it. He had been somewhat disturbed when Pershing, at the front, made Billy Mitchell subordinate to Brig. Gen. Mason Patrick of the Corps of Engineers, who had never flown an airplane. But that could be explained on the basis of personality. Mitchell was so aggressive he could be hard to take. Yet his concepts and his strategies were so brilliant that, by war's end, even the French and British acknowledged him as the greatest of air generals. It was he, more than any other man, who had opened the eyes of the world to the powers of the airplane.

"The air offensive which Mitchell laid on in the Meuse–Argonne in September [1918]" Arnold believed,

> was the greatest thing of its kind seen in the war, although the Germans had done it on a smaller scale. Billy himself had tried it on about one-fifteenth of the scale in the July fighting on the Marne. But the air attack that he launched as part of the American advance in the Meuse–Argonne between September 12th and 16th, 1918, was the first massed air striking power ever seen. Until then, the air fighting had been chiefly between individual pilots. With his mind full of what stronger, more coordinated numbers might have accomplished around Château-Thierry in July—with the successful bombing of the enemy supply center at Fere-en-Tardenois as an encouragement—he sold Pershing and the Allied High Command on the idea, and early in August began assembling a force of 1,500 combat planes—American, French, British, Italian, Belgian, Portuguese—every kind he could get his hands on. When the American ground forces—400,000 strong—struck, Mitchell struck ahead of them through the air.[5]

Mitchell's success during the war was so impressive that when Arnold went to France in 1918 and listened to him expound his ideas, "I realized . . . the Air Service needed Billy back home, fast, and with every argument I could muster I tried to convince him of this fact."[6]

Though reluctant to relinquish the adulation Europeans were heaping upon him, Mitchell eventually returned home on February 17, 1919, expecting to be named chief of the Air Service. But meanwhile, in December 1918, the General Staff had presented that post to another ground soldier, Maj. Gen. C. T. Menoher of the Infantry, and he intended to keep it, leaving Mitchell with a very subordinate role as his assistant. It might be argued that this was Mitchell's own fault, that if he had wanted the job he should have hurried home to fight for it, as Arnold had advised. But the General Staff knew all there was to know about Mitchell, whether he was at home or in Europe, and the fact that they chose someone else was interpreted as a sign that they didn't share his ideas and wanted to keep him as much as possible out of power and out of the public eye.

Arnold, who had been disappointed to see Mitchell passed over, was dismayed to see the chief's job go to another man who was "without any aviation experience or qualifications."[7] Menoher's appointment, combined with the drastic cutbacks in Air Service personnel and budget, deepened his pessimism about the future of Army aviation.

His pessimism increased his impatience, and he didn't hesitate to display his short temper in front of any superiors he considered responsible for the plight of the Air Service. He didn't even spare the secretary of war, Newton D. Baker, who came to San Diego in early 1919 on an inspection tour, one purpose of which was to impress upon all military commanders that they had to stop spending money now that the war had ended. He told Arnold, while they were driving around Rockwell Field, that he must cut the base budget to a bare, subsistence minimum. Arnold bridled at this. Perhaps he was already angry in anticipation of what Baker would order him to do. As they passed a group of barracks under construction, he pointed out that they were actually complete except for the roofs. Surely Baker didn't mean that such projects, in which a lot of money and effort had been spent, should be allowed to go to waste. Surely he didn't mean that these barracks, for instance, should be left without roofs?

As it happened, that was exactly what Baker meant. Construction was to stop immediately. In Arnold's opinion such a policy was absurd, and he didn't hesitate to say so in strong words. Lieutenant Eaker, who was in the back seat listening to this, was astonished to hear a temporary colonel talking so testily to the secretary of war.[8]

Eaker and Spaatz weren't the only men Arnold commanded at Rockwell who were to become his lifelong friends. One day, early in the year, Eaker came into Arnold's office and said, "Colonel, there's a man down at Ream Field [an auxiliary training facility south of San Diego near the Mexican border] whose conduct has been so bad it requires your personal attention."

The name of this bad fellow was 2nd Lt. James H. Doolittle. Sitting in front of the hangar the previous day, he had turned to another pilot, pointed to a plane practicing takeoffs and landings, and said, "I'll bet you five bucks I can sit on his landing gear while he lands."

Having made the bet, he invited himself along as a passenger the next time the plane took off, and when it was airborne, he astonished the pilot by climbing out onto the lower wing, then beneath it, onto the crossbar between the fixed wheels. The pilot, after pleading with him in vain over the engine noise to get back in the cockpit, finally brought the plane in and landed it. Doolittle then walked calmly over to the spectators who had gathered and said to the man who had taken his bet, "Give me my five dollars." When Arnold heard this story, he grounded Doolittle for a month, but he didn't forget him.[9]

One thing Arnold appreciated about his job at Rockwell Field was that it allowed him to fly more frequently than he was able to when in

Washington. As assistant director of the Air Service during the war, he did have a personal plane assigned to him—a speedy, French-built LePere—but he was so busy in headquarters he was able to use it only on inspection trips. He was allowed to take it with him when he transferred to San Diego, and he was happy about that because it was a much "hotter" airplane than the DeHavilland DH-4s and Curtiss JNs (Jennys) that everyone else at Rockwell had to fly. Though the DH-4s had been effective during the war, they were now obsolete. The LePere was a streamlined craft, more advanced than the DH, more powerful, and about ten miles an hour faster. Arnold, who was feeling increasingly comfortable about flying, used his LePere at every opportunity, to the envy of all the other pilots on the base.

One day, in the early summer of 1919, when he was landing the LePere at Rockwell, he lost control of it and crashed. He was thrown forward by the impact but was held by his safety belt, which probably saved his life.[10] However, he suffered internal abdominal injuries and even after he was healed physically, at least outwardly, his stomach continued to cause him distress.

In June 1919, with the demobilization at Rockwell Field virtually complete, Arnold was transferred to San Francisco as the air officer for the Army's Ninth Corps Area, where his principal job was to take charge of Army flying on the West Coast and to keep the commanding general, Hunter Liggett, informed about air matters. Since little was left of the Air Service, it wasn't a difficult job. Arnold's office was in the Santa Fe Building downtown, and because there were no quarters available at the Presidio, he found a house across the bay in Berkeley for Bee and the three children. Lois was now four; Hank, three; and the baby, William Bruce, a year old.

With all of his excess energy to spend and very little to spend it on, Arnold quickly became restless. Two or three weeks after his arrival at his new post, he began, on his own initiative, to organize an aerial forest fire patrol. Painfully conscious of how puny the Air Service had become, he believed the best way to build its stature was to make the public aware of it by beginning what he called "a new pattern of national usefulness in peace time." The U.S. Forestry Service was delighted with the idea, and Arnold was soon making regular flights over the forests of the Far West from the Cascades and the Olympic Mountains, down past the Sierra Nevada and the coast ranges as far as the Sierra Madre. Besides being useful in spotting fires, the patrol provided good training for his pilots. It was such a success that the Army continued it for several years, after which the Forestry Service itself maintained it.

While Arnold was launching his forest patrol, Billy Mitchell, back in Washington, was instigating a variety of other projects with the same general purpose—to gain attention and support for the Air Service. Though he was not in charge of the Air Service, he had the public thinking so. He was aviation's foremost spokesman, and when he wasn't talking about it, he was doing something about it. One of the things he did was to set up a border patrol to help the Immigration Service guard against illegal entry, especially from Mexico. Since Arnold's part in this job was to patrol the whole California–Mexico border as well as the entire Pacific coast, he soon had enough work to keep him busy. On July 4, after learning that Mitchell was at El Paso inspecting the Texas end of the patrol, he flew down from San Francisco to see the now famous flying general for the first time since both had returned from Europe.

Arnold found Mitchell a changed man. "He was sharper, more alert than ever." At the same time he had developed "an undercurrent of angry impatience" with people who were impeding the progress of aviation, especially people in the military. He was bitterly convinced that the growth of aviation was being blocked deliberately by battleship advocates and other enemies of air power. These included a lot of entrenched Army generals, but it was primarily the Navy that he railed against, the entrenched admirals who were "unable to face the fact that sea power was done for." He had worked out a program to prove to them what the airplane could do. His border patrol and Arnold's forest fire patrol were part of that program. He also planned a transcontinental air race, a flight to Alaska by a large formation of planes, and after that, a mass flight around the world. But above all, he was pursuing a campaign to make the Navy cooperate in a test that would prove whether or not airplanes could sink battleships. Among the captured German ships in the Navy's possession was a big, modern superdreadnaught, the *Ostfriesland*. Since it would never be used for any other purpose, Mitchell wanted the Navy to offer it, in a controlled experiment, as a target for aerial bombs. He flatly promised that, contrary to all naval doctrine, bombs would sink it.

The Navy, unwilling to entertain such a challenge to the omnipotence of its own cherished battleships, was refusing to cooperate. Adm. William S. Benson, chief of naval operations, went on record that summer with the declaration, "I cannot conceive of any use the fleet will ever have for aircraft."[11]

Later that summer, on August 1, Benson went to far as to promulgate a secret order which said: "In accordance with the policy of the

Navy Department of merging aviation activities with those of other naval activities, the Aviation Division of this office will be abolished." Mitchell obtained that order before it became public and, using it without referring to it, declared at a September hearing of the U.S. Senate Military Affairs Committee: ". . . in this country, our army aviation is shot to pieces and our naval aviation does not exist as an arm, under the new organization; . . . they have stopped having a separate bureau for aviation and have distributed those duties among six or seven different departments."

His remarks became a source of embarrassment to Assistant Secretary of the Navy Franklin D. Roosevelt, who apparently hadn't been informed of Benson's reorganization plan. When Roosevelt testified on September 12, he ridiculed, with his characteristic aplomb, Mitchell's presumption in delving into naval matters. "Of course," he said, "that shows General Mitchell knew absolutely nothing about the organization of the Navy Department."

Unfortunately, Mitchell had in hand that day a copy of Benson's order, which he read to the committee, perhaps unwisely. But Roosevelt, unlike his boss, Navy Secretary Josephus Daniels, and most of the admirals, was not an enemy of aviation. He testified that while he saw aviation in 1919 as an adjunct to the use of surface vessels, "in the future aviation may make surface ships practically impossible to be used as an arm."

In embarrassing Roosevelt, Mitchell was repeating a mistake he had often made, which was to lump everybody in the Navy together and assume that there were no champions of aviation among them. This was not so. Admirals William S. Sims, W. F. Fullam, and Bradley Fiske, among others, were as enthusiastic about air power as Mitchell himself. They were not as publicly outspoken about it as Mitchell, but they were carrying the banner within the Navy as ardently as he carried it in the Army. When he attacked the Navy en masse, he made it look as if the campaign for air power were simply an Army vs. Navy struggle. Mitchell was undoubtedly air power's most brilliant advocate. He envisioned almost everything that happened twenty years later During World War II, including the ascendancy of the aircraft carrier over the battleship, the ascendancy of land-based aircraft over aircraft carriers, the use of huge bombing armadas to attack the enemy homeland, and even the use of parachute troops behind enemy lines. But his propensity for contention and his intolerence of stupidity were so keen that he often made enemies when he tried to make converts.

☆ ☆ ☆

By the summer of 1920, Arnold had fitted himself smoothly into the Army organization in San Francisco. He had an enviable command, which offered opportunities for initiative within the confines of its limited budget. He got along well with General Liggett, a friend for several years, who had commanded the First Army in France, and was "very friendly toward aviation." He again had Maj. Carl "Tooey" Spaatz with him as his executive officer, which meant he didn't have to worry much about administrative work, which he hated. That left him plenty of time to fly from base to base, up and down the coast, inspecting his fire patrol and border patrol pilots. He also had more time for his growing family, because he no longer had to commute to Berkeley. At the beginning of the year he had been able to move his office into the crowded Presidio and secure family quarters there—"small quarters but very nice," as Bee described them. She was happy to be living within the city, on one of the Army's most beautiful facilities, and the social life was pleasantly active. The children were healthy and Arnold, as a colonel, was even making enough money to support them without scrimping. His income during 1919, including flight pay, had to come to $8,980, a handsome sum in those days.

He had reason to be a happy man, but he was not. Besides being deeply dissatisfied with the condition of the Air Service, to which he was now completely dedicated, he was concerned about himself. Since his crash in San Diego the previous year, he had suffered recurring stomach pains, which he thought were the result of the internal injuries he had sustained. And as if this was not providing him with enough discomfort, he learned that on June 30, he would revert from his wartime rank as a colonel to his permanent rank of captain, with a commensurate drop in salary. He also learned that Major Spaatz, by law, could not be dropped to his previous rank because he had earned his majority in action at the front.

Life in the postwar Army, it seemed to Arnold, was developing exactly as he had expected: those who had fought in France were getting preference, perhaps deservedly, over those who had remained at home behind desks. Once more his bitterness at not being sent to France welled up in him. But he was determined not to show his feelings to Spaatz, whom he liked and admired.

On the morning of July 1, Arnold arrived at headquarters early, wearing captain's bars, and switched his office and Spaatz's. When Major Spaatz came in, Captain Arnold stood and saluted.

"What the hell is this all about?" Spaatz exclaimed.

"Law is law," Arnold said. "You're in command now and you can't change it."[12]

Spaatz stared at him long enough to realize he was serious, then turned and walked out of the room. A few minutes later he returned and said, "Well, everything's fixed up."

Rather than take Arnold's job away from him, he had gone in to General Liggett and arranged a transfer for himself to Mather Field, near Sacramento. It was a gesture Arnold would never forget. (Arnold, incidentally, was promoted to major the next day, but Spaatz would still have outranked him, as the senior major, if he had stayed in San Francisco.)

Despite Spaatz's generosity, the incident did nothing to alleviate Arnold's stomach pains. Finally he put himself in the infirmary, where he was told that his malady had nothing to do with the internal injuries he had suffered. The doctors were convinced he had ulcers, an ailment thought at the time to be caused by worry. They told him he would have to stop eating meat, stop drinking alcoholic beverages, and start taking some white powders, which they didn't identify. They also said he would have to stay in the hospital for a while under observation. He accepted three of these four. For two years he ate no meat. For many years he virtually gave up drinking, despite the temptations of the Prohibition era. And he took his white powders faithfully. But as for sitting in the hospital under observation, that wasn't Hap's style. After a few days he simply put on his uniform and walked out. Though the treatment and the rest were helpful, they did not eliminate his ulcers. When he resumed flying, his stomach was soon bothering him again. And a year later, in the summer of 1921, he was back in the hospital for a short stay, which he terminated because Bee was about to have her fourth child. It was a boy and they called him John, the name of Hap's great-great-great-grandfather who came to America from Europe in 1740.

Because of Bee's pregnancy that spring, Hap had declined Billy Mitchell's offer to attend the Army War College, an important step forward for young officers. Perhaps he'd have another chance later. Meanwhile, he was getting along well enough in San Francisco, except for his ulcers. His new son, John, was a happy, healthy, beautiful baby who seldom cried. John had very white skin like his father, rosy cheeks, blue eyes, and curly blond hair. "But since he couldn't talk or run or play, he was just an oddity to me," his older brother Billy Bruce later recalled. "I certainly didn't expect him. One day he was just there, and accepted by everyone as a little brother."

Arnold's home life throughout this period was quite serene. The California climate relieved Bee's recurring hay fever and she was generally in good health. Their three older children, Lois, Hank, and Billy Bruce, were full of life. Hap used to sit on the porch of their Presidio quarters in the evening and watch them play. They liked to show off in front of him, putting tin cans on their heads and shouting "Happy Hooligan!" in imitation of one of the popular children's comics of the day. Hap was beginning to be weight-conscious because, while he had given up drinking, he hadn't given up sweet desserts. If the kids wanted jam or jelly on their bread, they soon learned to grab it quickly because they knew that when he said "Pass the jam," he was capable of upending the jar.

In the evening, he and Bee would play cribbage, or, if friends came over, they might all sit on the front porch and sing songs. This could be painful to the friends and the neighbors because, while Hap loved to sing, he couldn't carry a tune. "There's a Long, Long Trail A-winding" was one of the songs he most often abused. When Tooey Spaatz came to visit from Sacramento, the two of them would play chess. Though Spaatz would probably have preferred poker, which was his favorite game, he couldn't get Arnold interested in it.

The friendship between these two men deepened each time they saw each other. One night when Spaatz was in town, Arnold threw a party for him, arranging in advance to have it end with a surprise. Though Prohibition was now two years old, there was no shortage of liquor in San Francisco, or in Arnold's quarters. He was an enthusiastic host and despite his own abstinence enjoyed mixing drinks for friends. The night of the Spaatz party he mixed a lot of drinks for a lot of friends, and as the early morning hours approached, almost everyone was feeling mellow. It was then that he pulled a surprise on Tooey. A man pounded on the front door, announced himself as a Prohibition agent, and demanded entrance. Spaatz leaped to his feet and, while everyone in on the joke was laughing, ran for the kitchen. But as soon as the joke was over, Arnold found out it had been on himself rather than Spaatz. Tooey had destroyed the evidence of drinking by pouring the liquor down the sink. And it was Arnold's liquor.[13]

Both Spaatz and Arnold were frustrated in those years by the circumstances that kept them in California while the important action in the campaign for air power was elsewhere. In the summer of 1921, Mitchell had finally goaded the Navy into an aerial bomb exercise and had impressed everybody but the ruling admirals when his bombers, on July 21, sank the German battleship *Ostfriesland* in twenty-one minutes. Arnold and Spaatz could hardly match that accomplishment, but they did what they could, even though it was sometimes silly, to win publicity and attention for aviation. In April 1922, for instance, Arnold got involved in an argument that had started in the San Francisco press as to whether a pigeon or an airplane could carry a message faster. It was not quite as outlandish an argument as it might seem today. The Signal Corps still used pigeons extensively because the early radios were limited in range, and pigeons, unlike airplanes, could home into the exact destination for which a message was intended. Arnold "accepted the challenge for the airplane," and soon found himself flying to Portland with a large box full of trained Signal Corps birds, some with "distinguished combat records" in the World War. The race was to be from Portland to San Francisco, and the governor of Oregon, Ben Olcott, was to accompany Arnold as a passenger.

On the morning the race began, the pigeons were ceremoniously released as Arnold and the governor dashed to their plane. But it was cold, and as they tried to start the engine, they could see the pigeons disappearing southward. Forty-five minutes later, when the engine finally turned over, Arnold had to play catch-up, which didn't look easy inasmuch as he would have to make two or three refueling stops.

When he and the governor reached Medford, Oregon, they were told about pigeon sightings as far south as Red Bluff. Meanwhile, in San Francisco, it was a field day for the bookies, who mingled with the crowds on Market Street, following the race through telegraphic bulletins. As reports arrived of Arnold's delays and the numerous pigeon sightings closer and closer to San Francisco, people began putting their money on the birds.

Arnold at this time was almost ready to concede the race, and when he landed at Crissy Field, seven and a half hours after takeoff from Portland, he fully expected to be greeted as the loser. But to everyone's surprise, no pigeons had yet arrived. All those seen near San Francisco had apparently been local birds, flying merely for the fun of it. Not until forty-eight hours later did the Signal Corps birds reach their home coops.[14]

Three months later, on a flight in his aging and somewhat battered LePere from San Francisco to March Field near Riverside, seventy-five miles east of Los Angeles, Arnold had an experience that did not help his ulcer condition. As he was crossing the Tehachapi Pass, he "felt a bad jolt and noticed that the control wires to the tail surface had tightened." When he looked around he could see nothing wrong, which was somewhat reassuring since he had no choice but to continue—he was above the mountains, where he couldn't land, and he had no parachute (the Air Service had not yet decreed that parachutes be available on all flights).

Reaching the Mojave Desert and flying over it at 7,000 feet, he was beginning to regain some confidence in the airplane when "I felt a draft. I looked down and saw the bottom of the LePere's wooden fuselage had cracked wide open and apparently was opening more."[15]

Though he could have found level ground in the desert on which to make a forced landing, he chose to continue, but "very carefully, taking no liberties" with the plane, and landing at March Field "as if [it] were loaded with eggs." He didn't learn how close he had come to death until he pushed the throttle forward to taxi the plane to the hangar.

"The tail skid held fast, the engine kept on going, and the fuselage split in half directly under my feet. I had flown that old LePere all the way from Tehachapi Pass to March Field with nothing holding the fuselage together but the control wires."

Arnold in his memoirs was almost cryptic about the aftermath of this incident. He wrote simply: ". . . its effect on me became manifest in the fall of 1922, and after a tour in the hospital I was relieved as Western Air Officer and sent to Rockwell Field, San Diego, as Commanding Officer."

His stay at Letterman Hospital was ostensibly due to another ulcer flareup. In an August 23, 1922, letter from the hospital to his father, he wrote: "I still have another week in bed from next Sunday. Then I have an X-ray taken, and based on the X-ray pictures, the medicos make up their minds as to whether or not *they* think I should be operated on." By underlining the word "they," he let his father know that he didn't think an operation was what he needed. Arnold's own words, in both his memoirs and this letter, make it clear that he was suffering from more than ulcers. Toward the end of the letter to his father he wrote: "My old stomach now seems to be working all right. . . . It is really the first time since my attack two years ago that I have been able to forget that I had a stomach. . . . Hence if present indications mean anything I will be able to return to duty as soon as I can recover from my six weeks in bed. The surprise to me of the whole thing is the marvelous results obtained from just a few weeks rest and diet. I would never have thought it was possible."

His father was sufficiently concerned about his condition that fall to pay him a visit in San Francisco. Since Hap and Bee were already packing to leave for San Diego when they learned that he was coming, the prospect of his arrival caused some consternation in the Arnold household.

"The furniture will be gone," Bee reminded Hap. "We'll all be on Army cots for the last five days here."[16]

"We'll put him in the post guesthouse for a few days," Hap suggested, "and then he can travel to San Diego with us."

That plan did not appeal to Bee. "I can see your father on the train with our kids," she said. "He has the patience of an angry wasp anyway, and by the time Bunky [Hank] gets trainsick and John needs a change and Billy Bruce and Lois have their first fight, he'll be ready to start his lecture on child behavior. Then you'll sound off, and before you know it, there'll be the worst train disaster since the wreck of old ninety-seven."

Hap solved the problem by taking his father and Lois to San Diego on the night boat, and Bee and the boys followed by train. The elderly Dr. Arnold was sometimes difficult to endure, but his son was nevertheless fortunate to have him around on one occasion at San Diego. Arnold had always enjoyed working with wood and had developed a certain skill as a cabinetmaker. To brighten their Rockwell quarters, he decided to build a flower box. One Sunday afternoon he went to the base woodworking shop with his father and his son Henry. He was cutting some boards with a band saw when his left hand slipped and before he could pull it back, he had sliced the ends off his middle, index, and fourth fingers. While he howled in pain, old Dr. Arnold calmly picked up the three nubs and wrapped them in his handkerchief. Then he bundled Hap into the car, drove him to the base hospital, and stitched the three finger ends back into place. Arnold's left hand was gnarled thereafter, and the injured fingers were twisted, but they were usable.[17]

Arnold's job at Rockwell was so undemanding he must have felt the Air Service had put him out to pasture, and indeed it may be that someone in Washington had decided he needed a rest after his sojourn in the hospital. The field was no longer a busy flying school and air base. It functioned now mostly as an air depot, with only a handful of enlisted men and nine officers supervising the work of eight hundred civilians. Once the daily routine was established and his methods accepted, Arnold had little to do except to make certain his work standards were maintained. He had little reason to fly because his command was limited to this one small facility; there were no others to visit and inspect, except perhaps Ream Field, a few miles south of San Diego. But he continued his flying anyway, to keep up his efficiency. Rockwell was then such a sleepy base that when he returned from a flying trip, he felt free to buzz his own house to let his wife and family know he was home.

He had more time than ever to spend with his family and to pursue other interests. There was a lot of wildlife in the hills and deserts around San Diego and Arnold, who loved animals, used to come home with live rabbits, ducks, mules, even stray dogs. One day he arrived with a bobcat on a chain. To make a pond for the ducks, he dug up one of the walkways in the back yard. The mules came from friends in the 11th Cavalry, who roped them near the Mexican border and brought them up to San Diego. Having acquired two of them, "Big Red" and "Big Blue," Arnold had a cart built with four Jenny airplane wheels, four seats, a dashboard in front, and a long platform in the rear. One Sunday early in 1923, he took the family and a crowd of neighboring children for a ride in the cart out on a dirt road between Coronado and the North Island Naval Base. Bee, wearing high heels and a white dress, sat in front with him while Bruce and Lois sat in the rear with the rest of the kids hanging on behind. Suddenly, an animal—no one can remember what it was—darted out onto the road and frightened the mules into a runaway gallop, which Arnold, pulling the reins with all his strength, could not control.

One after another, the kids bailed out from the rear as the speed increased, but there was no escape for Bee, in her high heels, or eight-year-old Lois in her Sunday dress. Arnold had to find a way to stop the mules. Finally he handed Bee the reins, stepped over the dashboard onto the tongue of the cart, and "tightroped" his way along the tongue between the rampaging mules until he was able to grab their bits and yank them to a stop.[18] It was the first and last time the Arnolds went riding on their mule cart.

Lois at the age of eight was a beautiful but not altogether happy child, and her imagination sometimes created problems for the Arnolds. She had apparently either seen or heard about a child being baptized, and she decided one day to go into the business of selling baptisms to the other children on the base for a nickel apiece. The first person she practiced on was five-year-old Bruce, who suspected nothing until she intoned "I now christen you Billy Bruce Arnold" and dumped a bucket of water on his head. While he went crying into the house, Lois went forth, with Hank tagging along, in search of kids who would be willing to buy her nickel baptism. Before she got very far, the Protestant chaplain on the base heard about her enterprise from his little daughter, who had become one of her customers. He hurried to the commanding officer's quarters to remonstrate with Mrs. Arnold.

Bee, at the moment of his arrival, was comforting the dampened Bruce by encouraging him to play with his popgun. "But remember to point it up in the air," she cautioned. "That cork could put someone's eye out."

When she answered her doorbell and found the chaplain standing there, she invited him in for a cup of coffee, but he declined. "I'd like to take a minute to discuss your children with you," he said.

"My God! What have they done now?" she asked.

"Nothing serious. It's just that, well, did you know that they were going around the neighborhood offering to baptize other children for a nickel? My little girl happened to have a nickel and she came in drenched."

Just as Bee opened her mouth to say, "I can't believe it!" they heard the noise of Bruce's popgun in the dining room. "Billy Bruce!" she called. "Where are you aiming that gun?"

He entered the living room, pointing the gun heavenward as he had been told, and said, "I'm just taking a shot at Jesus."

The chaplain, without trying to hide his feelings, said, "Good day, Mrs. Arnold, I see you have your hands full," and turned to walk down from the porch.

As he did so, his commanding officer, Major Arnold, passed him on the walk and exchanged salutes with him. Then, running up the stairs toward Bee, he shouted in his usual loud voice (which was getting louder all the time because the years of flying had damaged his hearing), "What the hell is the chaplain doing here?"

The chaplain stopped in his tracks, looked back to let the Arnolds know he had heard that, too, and hurried away.[19]

The summer of 1923 was a tragic one for the Arnold family. First Billy Bruce contracted scarlet fever and was admitted to the base hospital in critical condition. Then baby John developed acute appendicitis just as his father was busy preparing for a visit to San Diego by Gen. John J. Pershing, Army chief of staff at the time. On July 30, while Bruce lay near death in one room of the hospital, two-year-old John died in another room as a result of a ruptured appendix.[20] The following day, Arnold had to greet the chief of staff and show him around the base as if it were a day like any other day.

Pershing stayed only one day so the Arnolds were soon left with their grief at the loss of John and their concern about Bruce. Gradually, Bruce began to improve and by the end of summer, despite their loss, the Arnold family was living normally again.

In 1923, California was not yet an aviation center. The important action was taking place, or at least being instituted, back East. On May 6, for instance, Lts. O. G. Kelly and John A. Macready took off from Mitchel Field, New York, and made the first nonstop transcontinental flight, landing before Arnold's eyes at Rockwell Field twenty-six hours and fifty minutes later. On August 22 in Dayton, Lt. H. R. Harris became the first man to fly the gigantic six-engine Barling bomber, which had been built at Billy Mitchell's insistence and was supposed to be able to carry a load of five tons, with a cruising radius of one thousand miles. (The largest airplane ever built in the United States up to that time, it was expected to prove every claim Mitchell was making for the airplane as an offensive weapon.) And on September 5, Mitchell put more fear into the Navy when his bombers, in another controlled test, sank the obsolete American battleships *Virginia* and *New Jersey*. While all of this was happening, Arnold's only accomplishment in the beleaguered cause of air power was to encourage two of his younger officers, Capt. Lowell Smith and Lt. J. P. Richter, in the first successful demonstration of refueling in flight, an exercise that later proved useful in extending the range of planes on long missions.

Late in the year Arnold "managed to get back east" for a short time and found Billy Mitchell "down in the dumps" despite his public popularity and his many accomplishments. He had reasons to be discontented. In 1921, General Pershing had bypassed him once more, after the resignation of General Menoher, to appoint Gen. Mason Patrick as chief of the Air Service, and Patrick was still in command. Part of Patrick's job, as he and Mitchell both knew, was to control the exuberant, impatient, unorthodox champion of air power, who sometimes hurt his cause as much with his outbursts as he helped it with his achievements. The Navy was not Mitchell's only enemy. Many of the governing Army generals also disliked him, and a lot of congressmen were tired of his harangues. He needed someone to moderate him, and Patrick might have been able to fulfill that function if Mitchell had been willing to listen to him, but Mitchell interpreted resistance to his ideas as proof that his opponents were stupid, stubborn, and stultified, their minds enmired in the nineteenth century. He may have been right, but these were the men he was trying to persuade, and it's difficult to persuade a man by telling him he's stupid.

"Air power doesn't seem to be getting anywhere at all," he said to Arnold. A few new planes, like the Barling bomber, were being built, but there was no organized program of aircraft research and development, no encouragement to aircraft manufacturers, and Congress, under the apparent influence of the Navy and the Army General Staff, was providing very little money even for piecemeal development. Nor was there any hope of help from the White House. Partly due to the vehemence of Mitchell's statements, air power had a new enemy there in the person of President Calvin Coolidge, who had taken office on August 3, 1923, after the death of President Warren G. Harding. The aggressive, bellicose General Mitchell was not Coolidge's kind of guy.

How deeply was Arnold affected by his friendship with Mitchell, his conversations with him, and his observation of his methods? There is no doubt that like most of the younger officers in the Air Service, he was profoundly influenced by Mitchell's ideas. As for Mitchell's methods, Arnold was often critical of them and tried to reason with him about his impatience and his demands for quick results. Yet Arnold himself was perhaps more impatient than Mitchell. Aircraft builder Donald Douglas has noted one striking similarity in their methods: "One Saturday I was in the hangar," he recalled,

> and in came Mitchell . . . .This was the first time I had ever met him. I, of course, was impressed. He had the well known characteristic that anything you showed him and boasted about, he would agree it was fine, but it had to be better. . . . He was that sort of chap. In that respect he was very much like Hap.
>
> Mitchell must have influenced Arnold's thinking to a great degree, as far as I can see, because they did both have that characteristic. [Hap] was a great fellow for getting people to think further ahead. This was what he did in the war, you know. He'd come out suddenly and call the industry leaders together. We'd be feeling pretty happy and contented with what we were doing, and Hap would say, "Well, this is fine, you're doing all right, but you've got to do better. We've got to have a bomber that's a hundred miles an hour faster. We've got to have a bomber that's got a thousand miles more range."[21]

One young officer, after meeting Arnold for the first time, said to a friend, "He operates at two thousand RPMs while everyone else is at one thousand."[22] The same was true of Mitchell, which might account partly for the affinity between them. Both men were often frustrated because others were unable to think and act as quickly as they did, and both frequently found themselves in trouble as a result of their impatience with superiors. Mitchell's troubles eventually ended his career, whereas Arnold continued to survive his troubles. Why? Perhaps it was because Arnold learned from observing Mitchell one thing Mitchell never seemed to learn—how far he dared go in defiance of his superiors.

Arnold later recalled saying to Mitchell: "Billy, take it easy. We need you. Don't throw everything away just to beat out some guy who doesn't understand. Air power is coming. Calm down, Billy. Get a balance wheel in your office. Let him look over some of the things you write before you put them out. Stop saying all those things about the independent air arm that are driving these old Army and Navy people crazy."

But to this warning, Mitchell replied, "When senior officers won't see facts, something unorthodox, perhaps an explosion is necessary. I'm doing it for the good of the [Service], . . . for the good of you fellows. I can afford to do it. You can't."

In the spring of 1924, General Patrick, whom Arnold had never considered a friend, informed him he would remain at his backwater San Diego post for at least one more year, and Arnold could only interpret this as a sign that he was not on Patrick's list of officers marked for advancement. During Arnold's trip to Europe in 1918, Patrick, then air chief at the front, had made the mistake of asking him for his "most critical reactions" to the air installations he had seen. And Arnold had made the mistake of giving him his most critical reactions, for which, he was convinced, Patrick had never forgiven him. But in August 1924, Arnold was surprised to find in the mail an order transferring him to Washington as a student at the Army Industrial College. Arnold never did find out who arranged this—it could have been Mitchell. It seemed unlikely that Patrick had suddenly decided to bring him in out of the California sun.

Arnold's move from San Diego to Washington was complicated by more family problems. He and Bee were both worried about Lois, who, at the age of nine, had begun making up stories about herself which went beyond childhood fantasy and indicated a certain reluctance to accept reality.

Then in May, Bee herself had developed intestinal complications, which could have originated with her surgery in the Philippines nine years earlier. Not fully confident in Army doctors as a result of that experience as well as what she considered the unnecessary death of her baby John at the Rockwell base hospital, she decided to go home to

Ardmore for consultations with Hap's father, whose professional skills she respected very highly even though she found his personality difficult. He recommended a private hospital in Philadelphia, and there she underwent more surgery in June.[23] She was still at her parents' Ardmore home, slowly recuperating, when Hap was ordered to Washington. Though his sister, Betty, volunteered to go to San Diego, ship their belongings east, and bring back the children, Bee would not permit it. "I just wasn't having anyone else pack up my household goods and my personal things, or take my children anyplace," she later recalled. In particular, she wasn't having Betty Arnold do it. She hadn't yet forgotten the problems Betty created for her before, during, and after her wedding in 1913. So Bee dragged herself out of bed, took a train across the country to San Diego, did her own packing and shipping, and then, with the children, returned in early September to Ardmore, since Hap hadn't yet been able to find a house for them in Washington.

Understandably in poor spirits after such an arduous journey, she began to imagine Hap having a good time, living a gay bachelor's life in Washington, while she, not yet fully recovered, had been forced to struggle with all that packing, plus the long journey with the three children. Shortly after her arrival in Ardmore she wrote him a mildly accusing letter in this vein, which he answered urgently, by return mail, on September 9: "Your letter received and most welcome—except when you suggest my being a bachelor in Washington. Nothing to that stuff. If I could get the house now, I would beg, borrow or steal the time off and go up to Philadelphia and bring you down here tonight. Washington at best is a nightmare and without you it is H—l. I need you, want you, look forward to seeing you soon. I love you. Hence, prepare for the worst—a trip down here as soon as we can find a place to hang our hats. . . ."

But the next day was September 10, their eleventh wedding anniversary, and like a lot of men who have been married that long, he forgot it. Undoubtedly he still loved her, as she loved him, but it would have been more than remarkable if their ardor had been as intense then as in those early days of marriage when they celebrated their wedding date monthly.

In a letter to her on the tenth, he began: "It has to be admitted that I overlooked this day, but it also must be admitted that I sent you a wire before I got back to the [Army and Navy] Club and found yours waiting for me. However, this d_____ town will make me forget that I am human if I stay here long enough. I am glad to be able to report to you that I think you are a wonderful wife even though we have been married eleven years today. I still have the same love and admiration for you that

I had when we were married, even though you do stick your curlers in my face at three a.m. I miss you dreadfully and more every day. If this keeps up I will hire [rooms in] the Willard [Hotel] and tell the creditors to go jump in the creek."

Thanks to her extended illness, John's illness and death, and his own drop in rank, Arnold was again strapped for money. And since he no longer held a command, as he had in San Diego, and therefore had no Army transportation available to him, he was forced to buy an automobile. It was a Nash, "with bumpers, motor meter, mirror, trunk on the back and everything." Well, not quite everything. It had "no balloon tires or four wheel brakes." But it carried a heavy load of debt. After arranging to finance it, he went off with his friend Maj. Jake Fickel, whom he had first met in the Philippines, to celebrate. They played nine holes on the municipal golf links at a cost of fifteen cents each.

A few days later, Arnold rented a row house at 3710 Fulton Street and moved the family down from Ardmore. It was a small house and everyone hated it. Bee, who was still conscious of having grown up in graceful luxury as the town banker's daughter, would have like something less modest, and the kids, too, found it confining.

Lois by this time had begun to develop an antipathy toward her mother that was worrisome because it seemed to exceed the bounds of childish petulance. One day, after Bee had taken her to the theater to see *Madame Butterfly*, she announced that she was no longer deceived by the family version of her birth. She knew now that her apparent mother was not her actual mother; her true mother was a Philippine chieftain's daughter, a beautiful princess named Mara, who had saved the life of Hap Arnold (whom Lois quite significantly did not deny as her true father), nursed him back to health, and had become the mother of his child. Later, after a short period in the United States during which he was married, he returned to the Philippines with his bride, and together they found Mara with little Lois, whom they bought from the native princess for ten pesos.

Lois told this story whenever an occasion arose, not always in the same detail, but she would always end on a note of mock magnanimity: "Mother [meaning Bee] has always treated me as one of her own children, but they still, to this day, deny the story."[24]

It is not unusual for children to imagine that they are actually princes or princesses, separated by some strange or tragic circumstance from their royal parents, and that these parents will one day come to claim them and take them back to some far-off land; but it is unusual, and somewhat alarming, for a child to believe this literally, as Lois seems to have done. Such a child today, in a family of substance, would probably receive psychiatric treatment, but in the 1920s, psychiatry was not as accepted, nor was treatment as available, as it is today. So Lois continued constructing her own reality, rejecting her mother as she increasingly idealized her father, while both of her parents continued to hope she would grow out of this disturbing phase.

At the Army Industrial College, Arnold became almost as much a teacher as a student because during the war he had gained extensive knowledge and experience in the subject he was now studying—the Army's relationship with the manufacturers who produced Army materiel. To the surprise of no one who knew him, he was soon involved in another dispute. Army policy in 1924, as in 1917–18, was to rely on the automobile companies as prime contractors for the manufacture of military aircraft. But Arnold remembered what a fiasco this arrangement had created during the war, and he said so. He was convinced that no car-maker "could take the plans for an airplane from an aircraft manufacturer and, without knowing anything about the techniques or employment of aircraft metals, or the small tolerances and other difficulties, build airplanes in quantity without unnecessary loss of time or long periods of schooling for metal-men." He argued his case so persuasively that, at least within the Industrial College, the notion of developing aircraft companies for mass production of planes began to take root. It was a concept Arnold was to foster fifteen years later when once again the Army needed a lot of planes in a hurry and it was his responsibility to procure them.

In December he finished the Industrial College course and was granted a leave. He and Bee took the kids to Ardmore for Christmas, where Bee and Lois stayed with the Pools while Hap and the two boys stayed with the Arnolds. The boys would rather have been at the other house. Dr. Arnold was so formidable looking, with his bushy white eyebrows and his bristly white mustache, that he "could frighten children just by looking at them."[25] And his house was so quiet, so orderly that no child would be comfortable playing in it, even though Hap's mother did her best to make them feel at home. She baked marvelous German Christmas cookies, made toys for them out of wooden match boxes, and even wrote stories for them, which she bound in colored paper covers. They loved her, but they were frustrated by the realization of how much fun Lois must be having at the Pool house, which was "big enough to allow you to get into all kinds of things without being caught," and was filled with music, laughter, good cheer, friendly, drinking adults, and a gigantic Christmas tree lit by real candles.

The constraint between the families and the somber mood in his father's house affected Hap as much as the boys since he, too, liked to laugh and sing and had almost as much of the boy in him as they did. He could take only so much of his father without exploding. Fortunately, he and the boys were able to get away from the Arnold house and go to the Pools for Christmas Eve, and the next morning all was right with the world because Santa Claus had brought each of the kids—except Hap—a Flexible Flyer sled.

Back in Washington, in early January, he was surprised to find himself stationed in General Patrick's office as chief of Air Service information. Again he didn't know whether Patrick, the Air Service Chief, or Billy Mitchell, his deputy, was responsible for giving him the assignment. But he knew which man he'd be working hardest to help. Arnold was now ready to go all the way with Mitchell in his struggle for air power.

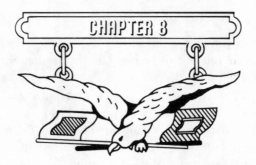

Arnold began his new job as the Air Service public information chief at a time when a new airplane-battleship controversy was exploding in the press, and he wasted no time leaping into it. In late 1924, the Navy had held secret bombing tests on the battleship *Washington,* a modern vessel that had to be scrapped by international agreement under the terms of an armament limitation treaty. Naval publicity men, without disclosing the outcome of those tests, had leaked rumors that the *Washington*'s hull, made of a new kind of steel armor, had easily withstood two one-ton aerial bombs dropped on it and finally had to be sunk by the big guns of the battleship *Texas.*

Arnold was able to ascertain from air power advocates within the Navy that the facts in the case were quite different. Two dummy sand-filled projectiles had been dropped on the *Washington* from four thousand feet, but no bombs had been dropped, and therefore no airplane-battleship confrontation had taken place during the destruction of the vessel, which had actually been sent to the bottom by a combination of depth charges and naval gunfire.

The Navy campaign to make it look otherwise had been effective, however, and before Arnold had even assumed his new job officially, he found himself trying to sweep away the rumors that Navy publicity men had planted in the press. Typical of Arnold's method and the work he would be doing as the top Air Service publicity man was a letter he sent on January 23, 1925, to E. N. Gott of the Boeing Company in Seattle, protesting against a cartoon in the Seattle *Times* that suggested that "after four days of futile bombing by airplanes, the battleship *Washington* was sunk by torpedoes, mines and fourteen-inch guns, and accordingly, an airplane as an offensive weapon against battleships is ineffective."

After insisting that this was not true, Arnold asked Gott "as a friend of the Air Service [more important, one of its contractors, though Arnold didn't mention that] and as a true citizen of Seattle to correct his mis-statement." It was utterly ridiculous, he insisted, to suggest that a battleship could survive an air attack. "The Air Service has claimed, still claims and has proven and is still willing to prove openly that any naval vessel afloat can be put out of action, whether under way or standing still, by airplanes."

When Billy Mitchell first made this claim it had sounded like an idle boast, but by 1925, the Air Service had proved its point. In retrospect it seems astonishing that the Navy continued building battleships even up to 1945, after nearly all the German and Japanese battleships had been destroyed by airplanes, many of them by the Navy's own planes. It was fortunate for the admirals during World War II that the Japanese didn't have enough air power to get at the American battleships that remained after Pearl Harbor. Japanese pilots proved in Hawaii, and even more convincingly in Malaya two months later (by destroying Britain's *Prince of Wales* and *Repulse*), that they could sink battleships as easily as could any other pilots. If they hadn't run out of aircraft carriers and planes, America's entire battle fleet would probably have suffered the same fate as theirs. The fact that, as late as 1945, the admirals hadn't acknowledged the vulnerability of their proud warships indicates how far from acknowledging it they were in 1925, and how difficult a job people like Mitchell and Arnold had in trying to persuade them.

Mitchell's strident impatience made the job even more difficult, to be sure. By 1925, the country was in an uproar over his battle with the Navy, his battle with the conservative Army generals, and his battle with his civilian boss, John W. Weeks, secretary of war in Coolidge's cabinet. Weeks, whose views reflected those of Coolidge, discounted Mitchell's assessment of air power. He wanted to keep peace with the Navy. After many attempts to silence Mitchell, he became exasperated beyond measure by Mitchell's remarks to the press and before the Congressional Select Committee of Inquiry into Operations of the United States Air Services. Finally, with White House approval, he decided to demote and banish the stormy nuisance. On March 6, 1925, Mitchell was relieved as assistant chief of the Air Service, demoted to the rank of colonel, and assigned as air officer at Fort Sam Houston in San Antonio.

General Patrick's position as Air Service chief was renewed at the same time, not because his views differed from those of Mitchell, but because he played within the Army rules. While he may not have liked Mitchell, Patrick often supported him, and when Secretary Weeks was pressing for Mitchell's dismissal, Patrick suggested that instead of being fired, the man should be "admonished by the War Department for his attitude and his methods,"[1] and told to stop using immoderate language.

For Hap Arnold, the removal of Mitchell was an irreparable loss because, even though Patrick was a staunch supporter of air power, he didn't seem to be a very effective one. And in any case, Arnold simply didn't like him, nor was he alone in that feeling. Partly because Patrick had the position many people thought Mitchell should occupy, he was unpopular with a sizable number of younger officers, and sometimes the butt of their jokes. He wore a toupee, which was a mistake on two counts, first of all because it fooled no one, and second because, as a flier, he was in constant danger of losing it, either to the wind or to prop-wash. One day while he was reviewing troops, the inevitable happened. A nearby airplane turned to taxi onto the runway and its prop-wash carried away his hairpiece as if it were a feather in a storm. By the time one of the enlisted men had retrieved it and brought it back dangling from two fingers as if it were a dead mouse, the story of Patrick's flying wig was already on the wing.[2]

He was also a rather unsociable man and a solitary drinker. His personal pilot, Capt. St. Clair Streett, an outstanding flier who had been very close to Mitchell, used to complain that Patrick would get liquor prescriptions from his doctor "for medicinal purposes" (the only way he could get it legally during Prohibition), then make Streett go to the drugstore to have the prescription filled, but never offer him a drink.

Arnold and Patrick had no such reasons for disliking each other. They simply couldn't get along, a fact that became obvious at the time of Mitchell's dismissal. Arnold arranged a farewell luncheon for his deposed friend at the Racquet Club in Washington, and apparently as an afterthought, to accommodate people who didn't get to the luncheon, a less formal barbecue party that night. Patrick attended the luncheon, thus openly emphasizing his sympathy for Mitchell, and that afternoon, Arnold went into his office to make sure he was included in the barbecue party.

"Sir," he said, "We're having . . ."

"Yes, yes, I know," Patrick said impatiently. It was a phrase he often used with subordinates who interrupted him when he was preoccupied.

"And we would like . . ."

"Yes, I know, I know," he said, still not listening.

"We would like, sir . . ."

"All right, I know. I know," the general cried out impatiently.

Maybe he does know, Arnold thought to himself. Maybe someone else had already invited him. Without chancing another outburst, Arnold left the room.

The next morning, Patrick summoned him to his office "in a wrath, and demanded to know why he had not been invited" to the evening party.

Finally, when he ran out of breath, Arnold managed to say, "Sir . . ."

"Yes, yes, I know!" Patrick shouted, and stopping short, picked up a paperweight from his desk and threw it at Arnold.[3]

It is possible that despite such incidents General Patrick liked Arnold better than Arnold liked him. Capt. Ira Eaker, who was an aide to Patrick at the time, got the impression from him that he actually admired Arnold, considered him a "bright, able officer and was completely satisfied with the work he was doing."[4] If it had been otherwise, Patrick would quickly have sent him elsewhere. But Arnold, who did not share Eaker's insight into Patrick's attitudes, was becoming discouraged again and once more considered resigning from the service.

This time he had a plan for getting ahead in civilian life. As Air Service information officer, he had been reading reports from the U.S. military attaché in Colombia about a German airline called SCADTA (Sociedad Colombo-Alemana de Transportes Aéreos), which was operating between Bogotá and Barranquilla. The line was already flying "far too close to the Panama Canal" when Arnold learned that its manager, a man named Dr. Peter Paul von Bauer, intended to lengthen his route through Panama and Central America to Cuba and the United States. Arnold decided, from a military point of view, that this should not be allowed. It was U.S. military doctrine at the time that no foreign power, especially one of our recent enemies, should have air rights over the Canal.

After consultations in the War Department, he went to Postmaster General Harry S. New and asked him what he would do if von Bauer applied for authority to carry mail between the United States and Colombia. New said that under the law he would have to grant the franchise "unless there was some other line, preferably an American line, that could perform the service."

An electric bulb immediately lit up in Arnold's head. Before the day was done, he, Tooey Spaatz, and another friend, Maj. Jack Jouett, were sketching in routes and rates for an airline of their own, which they would call Pan American. When a fourth friend, a former naval officer named John Montgomery, tried out the idea on some New York financial interests and received an enthusiastic response, Arnold went back to Postmaster General New with the good news in time to block von Bauer's mail franchise application.

By the end of summer 1925, plans for the formation of Pan American Airways were so far advanced that Arnold had decided

definitely to resign from the Army and become a part of the venture.
There was talk of his being the company's president, but that hadn't yet
been decided by the financiers who were now in control of it. And before
it could be decided, a chain of events began which was to alter the plans
of Arnold and his friends.

On the morning of September 4, the Navy dirigible *Shenandoah* was
caught in a storm over Ohio and torn into three parts, killing fourteen
members of the crew. It was a tragic accident but hardly an event of
national military significance until Col. Billy Mitchell, exiled in San
Antonio, heard about it. As fast as he could get hold of pen and paper,
he fired off a provocative 6,000-word statement to the press declaring
that such accidents were "the direct results of incompetency, criminal
negligence and almost treasonable administration of the national defense by the War and Navy Departments."

He had gone further now than the military establishment could
allow and he was removed from duty pending preparation of court-
martial proceedings against him. Quickly he began sending a stream of
letters and telegrams to Arnold asking him to function as his liaison man
and outlining the documents he planned to use in defense of himself
and the air-power cause.

Meanwhile, in October, Mitchell, Patrick, and Arnold were all
called to testify before a fact-finding group headed by New York banker
Dwight W. Morrow. It was a blue-ribbon panel appointed by President
Coolidge, ostensibly to make recommendations about national aviation
and air-power policy, but air enthusiasts viewed it with suspicion because
no one could imagine Coolidge taking any action that would foster air
power. Patrick testified in favor of creating an air corps within the Army.
Mitchell advocated an altogether separate air force, a position Arnold
had taken several years earlier. But Mitchell's testimony was hardly
helpful to his cause. He insisted on reading long passages from a book
he had written, *Winged Defense,* until everyone in the room was bored
and even friends like Arnold lost patience with him. "Come on, Billy,
put down that damned book," Arnold breathed to himself as Mitchell
droned on endlessly. "Answer their questions and step down."

When Arnold himself testified before the board on October 16, he
created considerably more excitement and controversy because he had
arranged a startling aerial display to accompany his remarks.[5] Adjutant
General Robert C. Davis and Assistant Chief of Staff Fox Conner, two
long-time skeptics about air power, had just finished speaking out
against any change in the organization of the Air Service or any

increased appropriation for it when a thunderous roar of aircraft engines overhead shook the hearing room in the House of Representatives Office Building.

Moments later, Major Arnold took the witness chair, and exclaimed, "Gentlemen, you have just heard the noise of the entire air force of the United States. Thirty-five planes. That's all."

Chairman Morrow, when he recovered from his surprise, began bombarding Arnold with questions. "Do you mean to say those thirty-five planes are all we have in the United States?"

"It is the entire air force of the Army," Arnold declared.

"But does it include the Navy?"

"Oh, no. Just the Army. But that is all we have for land defense." Arnold then explained that General Patrick had ordered an assembly of all available airworthy planes to take part in maneuvers at Mitchel and Langley fields. "Those thirty-five planes are all that we could get together in the whole United States," he said. "It is everything we had in pursuit, observation and combat. Just think of it, gentlemen. There are ten bombardment, twelve attack and thirteen pursuit planes, and that is all. We thought we were going to have forty-five, but couldn't get them. If anything happened to the country tomorrow, that is all we would have for defense."

Morrow, still skeptical, finally forced Arnold to admit he was exaggerating slightly, but he didn't shake the dramatic impact of Arnold's assertion. "Do you mean to say," Morrow persisted, "this is all you could get together for this particular demonstration, or all you could get together if Washington were attacked by an enemy?"

"It is all we could get together in a short space of time," Arnold admitted. "Of course, we have some more planes but they are in use at the training fields and schools. These thirty-five planes represent our actual air force, which would be called upon in case of attack."

"What you mean to say, then, is that the air force is scattered throughout the country instead of being concentrated under the chief of the Air Service?"

"Exactly."

"Then you don't wish to be quoted in tomorrow's papers as saying that the United States has only thirty-five planes?"

"I would not like to tell how many planes we have," Arnold said, "but we have been trying for five years to build up an air force, and you heard it all this afternoon—thirty-five planes."

The public was quite impressed by Arnold's alarming testimony and his pathetic aerial display, but President Coolidge was not. He happened to be ill that day, and apparently the thirty-five planes also flew over or near the White House, disturbing his nap. When General Patrick heard about the president's displeasure, he denied that he had ever authorized the stunt, but since he took no disciplinary action against Arnold, the truth of the matter was left in doubt. The only thing certain about the whole incident is that it annoyed an already unfriendly president, failed to help the Air Service, embarrassed General Patrick, and cooled even further the already chilly relations between him and Arnold.

As Mitchell's court-martial approached, not only the Army but the entire country was in an uproar about it and most of the officers in the Air Service angrily rallied around him. Support for him in the Air Service was not unanimous, however. Men like Col. Benjamin Foulois, who had always disliked him, could hardly be expected to embrace him now, expecially since he was patently guilty of the breach of discipline with which he was being charged. And General Patrick, who was concerned about what would happen to some of his young officers if they were unable to control their tempers, urged caution upon them.[6] One day when Arnold, Spaatz, and Eaker were in his office discussing the pending trial, Patrick warned them that they would be jeopardizing their own careers if they went overboard in defense of Mitchell. All three ignored his advice. Arnold and Spaatz testified for Mitchell. Eaker was an assistant defense counsel. But a sizable segment of officers did follow the lead of Patrick and Foulois, causing a subtle division of airmen for several years thereafter—those who supported Mitchell and those who did not.

The outcome of the trial was a foregone conclusion. Despite the efforts of Mitchell and his supporters to make air power the issue, the thirteen generals (including Douglas MacArthur) who judged him took into consideration only his evident insubordination, and on that issue found him guilty on December 17, 1925, suspending him from all military duties and forcing his resignation from the Army.

"Billy had it coming," Arnold later admitted, "but at the time we didn't think these things out. As the testimony of any of us who were called to the trial shows, the whole Air Service was angry."[7]

As for Arnold, his anger manifested itself in his continuing campaign for Billy Mitchell and air power from within General Patrick's headquarters. It was this refusal even to lower the key of the campaign that set the stage for his 1926 transfer into exile at Fort Riley, Kansas. Not the least bit intimidated by what had happened to Mitchell, he persisted, with the help of staff colleagues like Millard F. "Miff" Harmon, Ira Eaker, David Lingle, and H. A. "Bert" Dargue, in feeding air power propaganda to friendly newsmen and radio commentators.[8] Though the General Staff had ordered all of the air zealots to cease their public agitation, General Patrick himself, whose belief in air power remained steadfast despite his restraint during the Mitchell trial, seemed sympathetic to these young men on his staff who refused to surrender. They didn't tell him openly what they were doing, to be sure, but neither did they conceal their activities from him, which explained why he felt no need to investigate when Secretary of War Dwight F. Davis ordered him, in early February, to find out who in his office was leaking anti-Navy and anti–General Staff information to certain congressmen, newsmen, and a Philadelphia radio commentator. He knew the chief culprits were Arnold and Dargue. And if he had to sacrifice one of them, he was hardly likely to choose Dargue, a very able officer whom he liked personally. It would be Arnold, whom he cordially disliked.

When Patrick called Arnold in to give him a choice between a court-martial and resignation from the service, he undoubtedly expected Arnold to choose the latter. He may even have known that Arnold, for some time, had been planning to resign as soon as Pan American Airways got off the ground. But he miscalculated Arnold's probable reaction. Arnold subscribed staunchly to the dictum that a man must never abandon a fortress under siege, and he perceived the Air Service as being woefully besieged. He may also have perceived, more cynically, that the army could not afford another trial like the Mitchell fiasco. In any case, it didn't take him long to decide that he would ask for the court-martial. And he must have derived considerable satisfaction from watching Patrick's jaw drop when he returned to the general's office the next day and announced, "I'll take the court." He could not have imagined, however, that Patrick would be so diabolical as to send him to that desolate installation Fort Riley, the scene of his near-crash in 1912, the most traumatic experience of his military career.

Despite any satisfaction he may have derived from facing this new adversity squarely, Arnold and his family now found themselves in difficult times. On February 17, 1926, Patrick held a press conference at which he condemned the action of certain men in his office who, "entirely without his knowledge, and through mistaken zeal," had endeavored to influence legislation in what he regarded as an improper manner. His investigation disclosed, he said, that only two officers were involved. "Both of them will be reprimanded," he announced, "and one of them, no longer wanted in my office, will be sent to another station."

Everyone in Washington and everyone in the Army knew, as fast as the word could travel, that the unwanted officer was Arnold. Not only was he ordered to Fort Riley, he was ordered to report there immediately. Though his Air Service friends were mostly sympathetic, the aura of disgrace hung heavily over him, and Bee was so unhappy she could scarcely conceal it. Lois, Bruce, and Hank were sitting in their classrooms at the John Eaton School when their mother suddenly appeared, took them by the hand, one after another, put them in the family Nash, and drove them home.

"We're leaving Washington," she said.[9] But she didn't explain why.

When they got home they were further bewildered to find their father sitting on the floor in front of a bookcase, sorting out books, and singing in his off-key baritone, "Some of these days, you're gonna miss me, honey." It seemed to Bruce that for the first time in months he was really happy. He was getting out of Washington.

Within thirty-six hours, the Arnolds were completely packed, furniture and all. Bee took the children to Ardmore overnight while Hap cleared up his remaining affairs in Washington. It was the only time Hank had ever seen his mother cry.

On the train from Philadelphia west, the children could hear their parents talking guardedly. "They tried to disguise their conversation to fool us," Bruce later recalled, "but we weren't idiots. Before we were halfway across Missouri, we all knew that Pop had been kicked out of Washington in disgrace, and was never to return."[10]

By this time, Hap had decided the best way to handle the situation was to tell the kids openly what they had better expect. The sons of those Fort Riley cavalrymen were likely to be laying for Bruce and Hank, whom the family still called Bunky. "Now look here," he said to them, "when we get to Fort Riley, those Cavalry boys are going to jump on you because your father has had some trouble. But whatever happens, you take it on the chin. I want you to prove you're good Air Service boys."

They arrived at the Fort Riley railway station on a cold and sleeting February afternoon expecting a reception to match the weather, especially since the commanding officer there was Gen. Ewing E. Booth, "a stern old Cavalryman" who had been one of the judges during Mitchell's court-martial. But when they got off the train they found a savior awaiting them in the person of Capt. Fabian Pratt, the flight surgeon for the 16th Observation Squadron, which Arnold had been assigned to command. He had arranged for the Arnolds' quarters, a big, old stone house with a large porch, and even provided a hot meal. Pratt did everything possible to make them comfortable, but there was one thing he couldn't do—he couldn't make the courtesy call that was expected of every newly arrived officer at the home of the commanding general. That was a duty to which neither Hap nor Bee looked forward.

As they stepped up onto the porch of General Booth's house they could see him, through the front window, playing cards with several other officers. The living room was full of people and the Arnolds were acutely uncomfortable as they entered, but when Booth saw who had arrived, he came forward immediately, shook Hap's hand, and put an arm around his shoulder.

"Arnold, I'm glad to see you," he said. "I'm proud to have you in this command." Then, in a voice loud enough for all of his guests to hear, he added: "I know why you're here, my boy. And as long as you're here you can write and say any damned thing you want. All I ask is that you let me see it first."

The general had spoken and everyone at Fort Riley soon heard the echo. When the Arnolds went to the officers' mess the next night (it took a few days to set up housekeeping), a young captain came forward and said, "We'd love to have you sit at our table." Everyone treated them well. They were provided with horses and invited to join the Hunt Club. Suddenly Fort Riley didn't look so bad after all.

The squadron Arnold commanded was equipped with five DH-4s, now pitifully obsolete, and eight officers to fly them, plus eight or ten equally obsolete Jennys for training reserve officers in summer camps. With this tiny unit he was supposed to furnish aerial observation for all the Cavalry and Infantry outfits in the Seventh Corps Area, which included seven midwestern states. He was also expected to be the senior air instructor at the Fort Riley Cavalry School, through which almost all the promising Cavalry officers had to pass on their way to the higher ranks. Lacking the planes and men to perform these functions, Arnold was in an excellent position to sit out his exile doing nothing, but within a short time, he seems to have forgotten he was in exile. He began to like Fort Riley. He saw there a chance to deliver the air-power message to the very men the air-power advocates needed to reach but had not been reaching—future ground force generals.

Shortly after his arrival he managed to scrounge several more planes, newer and better than any in the squadron. Then he sold General Booth on the idea that all these officers studying at the Cavalry School should take indoctrination courses in aerial observation, which would include actual flight practice, so they would understand how useful the airplane could be to ground forces. Booth was so enthusiastic he made the course a part of the school curriculum.

One night when the entire family was asleep (Arnold usually retired early because he arose early) the telephone rang. The house had only one phone and it was downstairs. Arnold, stumbling down to it in the dark, banged his toe on a newel post. As usual, his anger flared, and he was hopping from foot to foot, cussing himself and the newel post, when he picked up the receiver.

On the other end was Juan Trippe in New York, the prime mover in the formation of Pan American Airways, which was now a reality. Would Arnold accept an offer to become its president, Trippe asked.

He had caught Arnold at precisely the wrong moment. Still preoccupied with his aching toe, he shouted "No, goddamnit!" and hung up.[11] All thought of resigning his commission was now gone. He had too many things to do in the Air Service, too many ideas to test.

Soon he was conducting maneuvers to find out how the Cavalry could best cope with enemy air attacks, how fast the horsemen would have to get off the road and seek cover when enemy strafers were approaching. And he was trying out new tactical procedures with his own airmen, seeking new ways for planes to help ground troops. General Booth was so pleased that at the end of the year, on December 17, 1926, he wrote an extraordinary commendation for the Air Service major who had come to him the previous February in disgrace:

> He is a hard worker, enthusiastic, and his judgement is sound. His recommendations are generally exceptionally worthy of consideration. . . . The progress in training between the Air Corps and the other combat units of this post has been of exceptional value and is improving all the time. His method of instruction and training of observers, ninety of whom are taking the course here, is especially good. In fact, I cannot conceive of a more desirable condition existing than does exist here between Major Arnold and his unit and the other units in this post.
> I shall be very sorry to see Major Arnold leave the post but feel that his excellent service here entitles him to as favorable a recommendation as I can give him.

At that time, General Patrick was still the chief of the Air Service and there was no indication that Arnold was about to leave Fort Riley, nor was there any indication that he wanted to leave. He was popular with everyone there except, perhaps, his own two sons. He liked to give airplane rides to the kids on the base, but for some reason Hank and Bruce did not understand and were disinclined to forgive, he never gave them a ride. He was also beginning to show, in his methods of disciplining them, that he hadn't abandoned or overcome all of his father's Victorian attitudes. At the end of each afternoon, whatever they might be doing or wherever they might be playing, they had to be back home, with at least one foot on the steps of the front porch, within fifteen minutes after the retreat gun sounded on the base. If not, they were solidly spanked despite Bee's continuing disapproval.[12]

"You strike that child and I'm leaving!" she would cry, whereupon he would quickly administer another whop, but she would never get around to leaving. Bruce grew to hate the odor of Dyanshine because when his father spanked them he would hold them over his knee, where they inhaled the Dyanshine with which he polished his Sam Browne belt.[13] At that age, Bruce was already in awe of his father. He accepted his authority but was not at ease when they were together. Though he didn't know why, he was never quite convinced that his father loved him.

Such spankings were not, of course, a daily occurrence, and Arnold was probably no more severe with his sons than the average man of his time. It was an even more common supposition then than now that you had to be hard on a boy if you wanted to make a man of him, and it was not surprising that Arnold should subscribe to such a theory since his own father had sent him to work on a farm when he was seven years old. But while he had no apparent doubts about how to raise the boys, he was obviously baffled by Lois, perhaps because he didn't understand little girls any better than he understood grown women, with whom he still often seemed overly respectful, awkward, and ill-at-ease. His method of handling his fanciful and increasingly difficult daughter was to indulge her, except for occasional outbursts of exasperation, even while worrying about her. But his indulgence may have compounded her problems by encouraging her to turn to him for love, and away from her mother, who was left with the onerous task of keeping her under control.

None of these family difficulties seemed insurmountable at the time, nor did they disturb unduly the fabric of Arnold's daily life at Fort Riley. The shortage of money was always a more immediate problem: by payday he was usually broke. As soon as he received his pay he would gather the family and drive to the nearest town, Junction City, where he would go from shop to shop paying all the debts he had accumulated. From Junction City they would drive the seventy miles to Kansas City, where they did the bulk of their shopping because the prices were lower and the selection greater. When all the shopping was done, Arnold would count the money in his pocket and decide, yes, they did have enough left to afford dinner at Wolfermans'.

For a short period during their stay at Riley those dinners at Wolfermans' were especially welcome events because Bee was forced temporarily to do the cooking at home herself, and there was common agreement within the family that she had no business in the kitchen. She had very little experience as a cook and didn't want any more. Shortly after their arrival the Arnolds had hired the wife of a sergeant, a young woman who could cook acceptably, was quite reliable, and was also fairly attractive.

One morning Hap came down to breakfast at his usual time, six-thirty, and found her nowhere in sight. In addition, the house was frigid—which wasn't the cook's fault. They had hired a striker to stoke the furnace and, to make sure he would be there to do so, had built a cozy room for him in the basement. When Arnold went down to find out why there was no heat in the house, he also found out why there was no breakfast on the table. The cook and the striker were naked together on his bed, obviously unconcerned either about food or about the chilliness of the air around them.[14]

Here was an aspect of life that Arnold had never known how to confront. The very mention of sex embarrassed him. Though his language was often profane, it was seldom earthy or obscene. He had been taught as a boy that bodily functions were unmentionable, and he was so uncomfortable mentioning them that he would usually resort to euphemisms when forced to do so.

As soon as he saw the striker intimately engaged with the cook, he retreated hastily, leaving them with a bare minimum of words, to wit: "I'll deal with you later." He was still muttering to himself in the kitchen when Bee came down for breakfast.

"All I want in the morning is a couple of eggs and a glass of milk," he said to her, "and what do I get? The house is cold, there's no breakfast, and I find the cook and striker fornicating in the basement."

"You find them what!" exclaimed Bee, as much astonished to hear him mention it as she was to learn that they were doing it.

"Fornicating!" he repeated. "I can't get any breakfast around here because of the goddamned fornication!"

From the kitchen door came the question, "What's fornication?" and the two parents turned to find all three of their children listening.

Fornication was an offense Arnold found too embarrassing to tolerate. He dismissed both of the fornicators, but he soon realized it wouldn't be easy to replace the cook, because good ones were hard to find on the base. While he launched his search, Bee had to fill in, and after eating her cooking for just a short time, he hastened in his efforts to get someone else. When he revealed his problem to several Cavalry officers at the mess hall, one of them, Maj. Alexander M. Milton (whose son, Theodore R. Milton, would one day become an Air Force four-star general), mentioned that he was about to be transferred and would be forced to give up an outstanding striker-cook combination, a Ninth Cavalry soldier and his wife.

When Arnold went home and told Bee they were about to hire the couple who worked for the Miltons, she said, "You mean Maggie and Cheatham?"

"Yes," he said. "What's wrong with them?"

"Nothing's wrong," she said, an expression of delight spreading over her face. "Maggie is just the best cook on the post."

The arrival of Maggie Cheatham was an event of great significance in the Arnold household. She was, as Col. Bruce Arnold later described her, a tall, stately woman who carried herself with dignity and a certain poised assurance that made everyone treat her with deference. "It wasn't long before she became a real member of the family for, besides being the cook, she dispensed justice, delivered punishment, gave ready advice to children and grown-ups alike; in short, she took charge."

Bruce, who was in second grade when the Arnolds arrived at Fort Riley, soon began to fall behind in his reading ability, possibly because the phonetic teaching methods at the school there were so different from the flash-card method at the John Eaton School in Washington. When school closed in June, he came home with a note from his teacher mentioning his deficiency and suggesting extra summer reading.[15] Bee, in alarm, rushed out and bought him some boys' adventure books, hoping they would intrigue him. But he was growing up in the midst of real Infantry and Cavalry units. He didn't want to spend his summer reading about a bunch of kids searching for a valley of diamonds when he could be watching real soldiers or riding after them on a real horse.

Having failed in several attempts to get him absorbed in the books, Bee said to Hap one day, "I guess you can't make a boy read if he doesn't want to."

She knew her husband well enough to realize she had used the magic word. As several of his subordinates had already learned, "can't" was a word that made him spring into action.

"The hell you can't," he said. "Billy Bruce, come here and bring that book."

He stared open-mouthed as Bruce stumbled through a page or so, then grabbed the book and began reading it himself. "Christ!" he cried.

"Who in hell would write stuff like that? No wonder the kid can't read. Bee, get rid of this goddamned trash."

Turning to his son he said, "I'll tell you what I'll do. I'll write you a book about real people who did real things. And it'll be a hell of a lot better than that junk."

When Arnold decided to do something, he never decided to do it the next day. That very moment he went into his study and began work on a children's book—the first of a series—whose hero was a pioneer airman named, not surprisingly, Bill Bruce.

At about this time, the early summer of 1926, Bee became pregnant again, and on February 24, 1927, she gave birth to another healthy baby boy. They named him David Lee, and he slipped into the family without causing any noticeable fuss among the other three children.

In the early summer of 1927, Arnold was called upon to satisfy an old adversary, President Coolidge, who had decided to vacation in the Black Hills of South Dakota and wanted his mail flown to him there by the Army Air Service so that it would be on his desk every Tuesday and Thursday morning. Since South Dakota was in the Seventh Corps Area, the responsibility fell upon Arnold. His pilots were to fly the presidential packet from North Platte, Nebraska, to Rapid City on those two mornings each week, and no excuse would be accepted if they didn't get there—Coolidge was very demanding about his mail. Arnold was summoned to two meetings where this was impressed upon him. At the second of these meetings, the postmaster general himself, Harry New, told him that whatever happened, come rain, sleet, snow, or high wind, the president's mail had to get through.

It was an assignment that required some imaginative thought because, as Arnold knew, the weather in the Black Hills was often treacherous. He was certain that on some days it would be either impossible or too dangerous to fly. If he didn't want any of his pilots killed, what was he to do?

The only solution he could devise would take some arranging and if it was discovered the consequences would be serious, but it was a chance he would have to take. He assigned reliable men to the mail-lift operation and instructed them carefully. On each flight they divided the presidential mail into two packages. When these packages reached Rapid City, one of them would be held back by the ground crew so they would have something to deliver on the following mail day even if it was impossible to fly that day. This meant the president got half of his mail late, but since Coolidge, during his five years in office, was hardly ever

known to get any urgent mail, no one knew the difference. At least *he*
didn't know the difference. All he knew was that he had mail on his desk
every Tuesday and Thursday, which was apparently enough to make
him happy. The following year, 1928, he returned to the Seventh Corps
Area for a vacation in the north woods of Wisconsin, where Arnold
repeated his trick so successfully that on November 28, 1928, he won a
commendation from the assistant secretary of war.[16]

In May 1927, after arranging the first Coolidge mail lift, Arnold and
the rest of his squadron flew to Fort Sam Houston, San Antonio, for a
war game maneuver. This led to the end of his exile because it brought
him to the favorable attention of General James E. Fechet, who was
replacing General Patrick as Air Service chief. When Arnold arrived in
Texas with his observation planes, Fechet—a big, bluff, hearty man,
friendly but tough and demanding—was angry because the bombers
assigned to take part in the exercise hadn't yet appeared. They had
stayed an extra day in Okalahoma City for no explainable reason, and by
the time they reached Fort Sill, Oklahoma, a storm was rising with winds
at gale force. Fechet appointed Arnold to get those bombers to San
Antonio. Despite the wind, he did so, with the loss of no lives and only
one plane (which ran into a hangar in Dallas while trying to turn
around).

Fechet made no effort to conceal his pleasure at Arnold's accomplishment. "I thought that I was through," Arnold wrote to Bee from
San Antonio on May 11, "but not so." With Patrick retiring and Fechet
taking charge in Washington, he felt he again had an opportunity to
move ahead.

With Fechet came a new name for the Air Service. It was now the
Army Air Corps. In June, Arnold was invited to Wright Field in Dayton
for an Air Corps board hearing, and while there, he made a concession
to his father's religious and fraternal sensibilities. He joined the Dayton
chapter of the Masons. But he was never a deeply religious man, and his
Masonic affiliation could hardly be considered an important factor in his
life or his career.

From Dayton he returned to Fort Riley and, while waiting for some
new development in his career, resumed writing his Bill Bruce stories
for boys. It was fortunate that he did so because, while he earned a total
of only $1,200 for the books, it proved sufficient to pay for mastoid
surgery, which David Lee had to have in March 1928. Bee took the baby
to Kansas City for this operation and on March 31, while she was gone,
Arnold said to Hank and Bruce, "You sit down and write to your
mother." The results were succinct:

Dear Mother,
Thank you for the belt and the necktie. The trees are getting little leaves on them. I hope David is getting along all right. The Shoefelts have already moved. And they have a dog.

Yours truly,
Bill.

Dear Mom,
Dad said you had a cold. Is David getting better? Chaplin [sic] Moon's funeral was yesterday and all the scouts were there. We got the shot today and I have a headache. Thank you for the belt and the necktie. The Rameys are going to move into the Shufelts house on April 7th.

Yours truly,
Henry.

P.S. Bring David home someday.

David's operation was successful and Bee did indeed bring him home. The two older boys were both healthy and growing apace. Eleven-year-old Hank was almost five feet tall and weighed eighty-six pounds, according to a school physical examination that fall. Ten-year-old Billy Bruce was four feet seven and weighed eighty-two pounds. Best of all, both of them had excellent hearing and 20/20 vision, ideal for future Air Corps pilots.

While Arnold carried on his work at Fort Riley, hopefully awaiting some new and exciting development, there was activity brewing elsewhere concerning him. Several years earlier he had applied for admission to the Command and General Staff School at Fort Leavenworth, Kansas, which could open the road to high Army rank. While General Patrick was Air Service chief, there was no likelihood that that application would be forwarded favorably. And even if it were to reach the commandant at Leavenworth it would not be received favorably because that commandant was General Edward L. King, another of the judges at the Billy Mitchell trial. He disapproved not only of the air-power campaign, but also of Hap Arnold personally.

General Fechet knew how Patrick and King felt about Arnold, but he had a different opinion, especially after observing his work during the 1927 San Antonio war maneuver. In the summer of 1928, when an officer scheduled to enroll at Leavenworth died, Fechet appealed to Maj. Gen. Charles P. Summerall, the chief of staff, and Trubee Davison, the assistant secretary of war, on Arnold's behalf. All three agreed that Arnold should get a chance at the vacancy. When Summerall wired King asking for his approval of the assignment, King replied that he didn't want Arnold, but if he did come he would be accepted. Then in a private letter to Fechet, King wrote that if Arnold came to Leavenworth as a student he would be "crucified." If his purpose was to deter Arnold, King had chosen the wrong strategy. Arnold leaped at the chance to attend the Command and General Staff School.

He did not find his year there an altogether pleasant or stimulating experience, however. General King, a hero in the World War, was a martinet who applied his discipline not only to his officer students but to their children as well. It was difficult for the kids to make a move without coming up against one of his regulations. There were rules about where families could or couldn't go, and when they could or couldn't go there. He even had a regulation that said children were to be kept quiet and off the streets after six o'clock every evening.

As for the curriculum he supervised, it would have been good preparation for the Civil War, and Arnold didn't hesitate to say so. He came home to their half-duplex quarters one night, after a long, boring day in the classroom, and said to Bee, "Well, we fought the Battle of Gettysburg again today, and guess who won. Right. Meade did it again, but think what Lee could have done with just one Wright airplane."[17] Though he was appalled to find the school ignoring the possible uses of the airplane, he studied diligently and did well even in Cavalry problems. He amazed some of the Cavalry officers by suffering through a long ride they didn't think he could endure. But despite his diligence, he had his problems with King, just as the tough old general had predicted.

Arnold and the other Air Corps officers at the school wanted time to fly so they could at least earn their flight pay. King, who scarcely believed in flying, couldn't be expected to believe in flight pay, which he and his Cavalry colleagues were not eligible to earn. Yet he couldn't actually prevent the pilots from flying, so he simply made it as difficult as possible. On one occasion, after an airman crashed a plane into the Missouri River, the general called all the air officers into his office and told them they didn't know how to fly. Then he proceeded to give them a lecture on the subject.

When he finally dismissed them, Arnold, before he was out of earshot, said to his colleagues in his usual loud voice, "That guy doesn't know a damned thing about flying."

King, hearing him, came running out after him and grabbed him by his Sam Browne belt.

"You take that back," he demanded.

"No, sir, you don't know anything about flying," Arnold repeated, "and you can't tell these men how to fly."[18]

King also called him on the carpet one day for buzzing his own quarters to let Bee know he was back from a flight and was coming in to land, but despite King's harassment, or perhaps because of it, Arnold passed all of his courses with high marks and was ready to graduate in June 1929. Before leaving, he couldn't resist one last jab at the general. He wrote his final paper on the subject of how air operations should be taught at the Command and General Staff School.

On graduation day, all the Arnolds were up early, and all of them were happy. Hap's mood had been improving each day as his time of departure from Leavenworth approached, and the children felt the same way. The family furniture was already on its way to their next post, the Fairfield Air Depot near Dayton, but there was still work to be done—last-minute packing, making an inventory of the government property in the house, and turning it in to the supply sergeant. Bee was engaged in such details when Hap left for the graduation ceremony at the Riding Hall.

Two hours later, Lt. Orval Cook, an Air Corps officer who was visiting Fort Leavenworth and had met the Arnolds socially, drove past the Riding Hall and noticed the Arnold automobile parked near the front entrance with the motor running.[19] Bee Arnold was in the driver's seat surrounded by children, dogs, and suitcases. Cook was puzzled because he was aware that her husband was at that moment taking part in the ceremony and receiving his certificate inside the hall. Why wasn't she proudly attending like all the other wives of graduates?

He pulled up beside the Arnold car and said to her, "Mrs. Arnold, are you having trouble?"

She shook her head. "No."

He was still puzzled. "Can I help you in any way?"

"Not at all," she said. "It's just that Hap told me to be out here with all the children and the dogs in the car and have the engine running so he could get out of this goddamned place just as fast as possible."

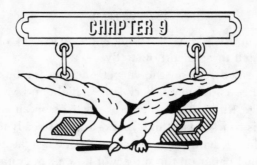

The Fairfield Air Depot, which later became Patterson Field, located fifteen miles from Dayton, was not yet a large facility when Arnold became its commander in July 1929. Its main function was the repair and overhaul of aircraft engines and other instruments, an indispensable activity but one that did not fascinate Arnold when he arrived there. Like most officers, he would have preferred to command an operational unit, yet he was not in a mood to complain. He had at least been brought back from exile. He might have a future in the Air Corps after all. General Fechet seemed to like him, and he now had two close friends, Spaatz and Eaker, in Fechet's office.

Dayton also brought mixed memories to his mind, because it was here that he had learned to fly the Wright airplanes that had almost killed him in 1912. With Hank and Bruce at his heels, he went one day to visit the old Wright flying field and hangar at Simms Station, the scene of his first flights. The little shedlike hangar was still there, the door held shut by a rusty padlock, which he easily broke. Inside there was only one reminder of his scary days with the Wright brothers—a long, thin pole to which a faded, mildewed piece of red cloth was attached. It was the signal flag the Wrights had waved whenever they wanted their fliers to come in and land. Bruce found it hard to believe that "this old man who was my father [he was only forty-three] was once a young lieutenant flying an ancient pusher [a plane with rear propellors] while the inventors of the airplane stood and watched and corrected him."[1]

Noting the decrepit condition of the hangar, Arnold sent carpenters to repair it, and requested that the government preserve it as a historic landmark. (It stands now in the Air Force Museum at Dayton.)

At the same time, Arnold was equally determined to destroy another relic of early aviation, the Barling bomber, that huge, underpowered, and badly designed plane built at the behest of Billy Mitchell between 1919 and 1923 for the purpose of proving his arguments about the irresistible power of large, long-range aircraft. Its World War Liberty engines, used because Congress refused to appropriate funds for the development of larger ones, were so inadequate that although the plane was able to fly in the fairly flat vicinity of Dayton, it didn't have enough power even to clear the Appalachian Mountains on an attempted flight to Washington.

While walking through a warehouse at the depot one day, Arnold spotted the disassembled corpse of the Barling, the only one ever built, and was so chagrined at the memory of its failure, at the embarrassment it had caused Mitchell and all the air-power advocates, that he couldn't stand even to look at it.

A few weeks later, lunching at home, he said to his family, "It's now twelve-twenty-five. At twelve-thirty, there's going to be a big fire on this base."

He was precisely correct. At twelve-thirty, great tongues of flame arose from the base dump and the Barling bomber was quickly consumed. At least it would not survive physically to mock Mitchell, Arnold, and the other air zealots who had clamored for it. The day Arnold discovered it in the warehouse he had asked why it hadn't been destroyed. He was told that every time its destruction was proposed, Washington vetoed the suggestion. Arnold knew how to get around that. He renewed the request, calling the plane simply "one heavy bomber" and not mentioning that it was the Barling. Permission to demolish "one heavy bomber" was quickly forthcoming.[2]

The facility he was now in charge of was actually "a hodge-podge of ancient hangars connected by old roads that wound through fields of wild wheat and other tall grasses." On the flight line, at the foot of a low plateau, there was a row of modern hangars. Atop the plateau was the family housing area, composed mostly of refurbished World War barracks. Fortunately for Arnold, the commanding officer's home was much more substantial. A several-times-remodeled two-story farmhouse, it had glassed-in porches on both floors, three large bedrooms, a high-ceilinged living room, and a big, country-style kitchen, where Maggie held sway. In all directions there was a feeling of space, with idyllic rural landscapes to contemplate. The Arnold family was soon quite happy there, and the house was usually full of people, many of them Arnold's old friends in transit—Spaatz, Eaker, Jake Fickel, and Bert Dargue. Even General Fechet himself stayed with them when he visited Dayton. Orville Wright occasionally came for Sunday dinner, just as Arnold used to go to the Wright home for Sunday dinner when the two brothers were teaching him to fly. Hank and Bruce liked the quiet, dignified old man but they were slightly ill at ease about his white mustache. It made him look too much like stern old Grandad Arnold. They were aware of his historic significance, and they listened silently when he sat in the living room talking to their parents. The subject was usually airplanes, and there was one thing Wright used to say that Hap Arnold, being a military aviator, must have found provocative. The old inventor "thought it a tragedy that his invention had become a devastating war instrument with the potential of killing thousands of innocent noncombatants."

In October 1929, the New York stock market crash shook the country, and though it didn't create immediate, nationwide economic disaster, it worried Bee because her father was a banker (First National Bank of Ardmore) and the collapse of stock values did not bode well for any business, including the banking business. While there was no apparent reason for alarm, there was reason for concern. As Christmas approached that year, most Americans were uneasy, but the Arnolds, aside from their slight worries about Bee's father, did not share the common concern. Living within the bosom of the Army, they could hardly imagine economic disaster. Hap's salary would come every month, whatever happened. They had special funds set aside in their bank for the education of the children. They had even managed to get out of debt and establish for themselves a modest savings account.

The rural setting of their farmhouse was ideally picturesque for Christmas, and Christmas was a feast that brought out the child in Hap Arnold. True to his German family tradition, he re-created the whole Nativity scene each year, using cookies that he shaped and baked himself.[3] It was a task for which he had to set aside a whole day, usually the Saturday before Christmas, when all of his children and many of their friends could take part in the fun. He would first cut out cardboard models of all the Nativity figures, human and animal. When these forms were converted into cookies and given time to cool, the children, under his guidance, would decorate them with icing. Each year he would include in the scene at least one challenging and apparently incongruous figure, like a rearing horse. "During a miracle," he would tell the kids, "a horse wouldn't stand still."

Less than a month after Christmas, on January 18, 1930, Hap received bad news. His mother had died. He hurried to Ardmore for the funeral and found his father prostrate with grief. Old Dr. Arnold, who had never been able to express his feelings for his wife while she was alive, displayed them pathetically now. "Father has been getting better," Hap wrote to Bee, who had stayed home with the children. "He was up a short time [yesterday]. He tries to be brave and stand up under the strain but it comes mighty hard. He will have to do a lot of readjusting."[4]

One disturbing sign of the times struck Hap while he was comforting his father. His brother Price arrived for his mother's funeral by bus because he couldn't afford train fare.

In April 1930, Arnold took charge of logistics for a 250-plane Air Corps mass maneuver at Sacramento, California, and he did the job so well he won the same assignment the following year, when a similar maneuver was held at Dayton with nearly 700 airplanes. On April 17, 1930, during the California maneuver, he was involved in a minor accident while taxiing out for a takeoff in an 0-32 observation plane at Crissy Field. Forced to swerve away from another plane and partially blinded by the dust it had kicked up, he ran into a 25,000-gallon gas tank, which should not have been that close to the runway.[5] The accident report assigned him only a small degree of blame, noting at the same time that he was a "superior" pilot, both in skill and judgment. He was flying frequently now, with no indication that he still suffered from his old fears; this mishap in San Francisco seems to have had no adverse effect upon him.

By 1930, aircraft design and performance were improving rapidly. Charles A. Lindbergh's successful flight across the Atlantic Ocean in 1927 probably did more to stimulate aviation than all of Billy Mitchell's preachments. But it was not until 1930 that aircraft wheels were first equipped with brakes. Adjustable-pitch propellors soon appeared, as well as metal fuselages and wings. Cockpits were beginning to fill up with sophisticated instruments, which allowed Jimmy Doolittle to make the first blind takeoff and blind landing. The first 200-mile-per-hour bomber—the twin-engined Martin B-10—was on the drawing boards. The Air Corps, though its appropriations were still meager, was getting help from the civilian air industry, reaping the benefits of technological advances developed by the aircraft companies for the growing airlines.

There were 1,000 commercial airports in the United States by 1929, and 1,200 more were under construction. The government had designated 25,000 miles of airways, mostly for airline use, and the aircraft industry was producing more than 7,000 planes per year. Though the passenger airlines were still dependent on government mail contracts for most of their income, dozens were operating, and as civilian travel increased, so did the demand for larger, safer, longer-range planes.

Arnold, observing all this and grasping its military significance, became increasingly absorbed in the research and development work being done at nearby Wright Field, where he took on an additional job as executive officer of the air materiel division in July 1930. His immediate reaction to the technological progress he saw was predictable. He was impatient for faster progress. Why couldn't everyone get his job done more quickly? Why wasn't somebody trying this or that? But there were people around him who felt that his impatience was sometimes misdirected.

Capt. Orval Cook, who had met Arnold at Fort Leavenworth and was now chief of the propellor division at Wright Field, was occasionally the target of that impatience and he didn't like it. Arnold, he said, "came by my desk practically every morning to ask me about things. We were doing a lot of research, development and testing. It took time but he wanted it done now. And because of that characteristic, he sometimes had people going down unproductive paths, wasting their time and the time of others."[6]

Maj. Grandison Gardner, assistant commandant of the Air Corps Engineering School at Wright Field in those days, was an admirer of Arnold's, but sometimes had similar reservations about him. After the two men had a minor run-in about the delivery of a new airplane, Gardner said to a friend, "Arnold has a reputation for making quick decisions. If he wouldn't make them quite so quick, maybe he'd make more of them right."[7] Only time would tell whether his average was high enough to justify his hurry-up methods.

Arnold's two boys were now old enough to get into substantial mischief, and Hank, especially, had a penchant for inadvertent misadventure. He and a friend were pursuing a hobby of saving insignias, which they cut out of the fabric fuselages of derelict, abandoned airplanes. One day they saw a National Guard insignia they didn't have and proceeded to cut it away with their jackknives, only to find that the plane in which they had left a gaping hole was still operational. They immediately hid the insignia in a culvert and said nothing about it. When Arnold was told that someone had cut the insignia out of a National Guard plane, he was quite sure who had done it, because he was aware of Hank's hobby. But he was also convinced Hank hadn't done it knowingly, and he was always quite tolerant of mischief, perhaps because he was so mischievous himself. He simply said to Hank, "Got any new insignia lately?"[8] And when the boy confessed, he made no fuss about it.

On another occasion, Hank was playing in the cockpit of a derelict plane that was still parked on the flight line. Without knowing what he was doing, he jettisoned a flood of gasoline from the plane's tanks onto the concrete. At dinner that night, his father said, "Some damned fool dumped a tankful of gas on the flight line today."

He looked directly at Hank, who kept his eyes down and said nothing.

"Probably a good thing," Arnold said at last. "If they had put that plane on the scrap heap with eleven hundred gallons of gas in it, we'd have had a hell of an explosion."

But while Hank's scrapes usually arose from boyish curiosity, Lois's waywardness was becoming a cause for deep concern. Her temper was violent; when she went into a tantrum she lost all self-control, and since she was now a budding woman, she was big enough to be dangerous. One night when the Arnolds were away, she got into an argument at the dinner table with Hank and Bruce. If their father had been there he would undoubtedly have stopped it quickly—he tolerated no nonsense at the table. But perhaps because of the rigid restraints upon them when he was present, his children would sometimes cut loose and become astonishingly wild when he was absent. One of them on this occasion threw a wet paper napkin, whereupon all of them began throwing wet napkins, followed by glasses of water and eventually a whole pitcher of water.

By this time Lois was so furious she was beyond reason. Grabbing a carving knife, she took a wild swipe at Hank and cut through the sleeve of his coat, miraculously missing his arm. Then she turned upon Bruce and brought the knife down at him from above. He held up a fork in self-defense, and by another amazing stroke of luck, the knife blade came down between the tines.[9]

The 1931 maneuvers at Dayton were the largest the Air Corps had ever held, and Arnold, responsible as he was for all the supplies and accommodations needed by 700 planes and 1,400 men, learned an eye-opening lesson about the task the Air Corps would face if the nation ever again became involved in a war. In addition to furnishing gas, oil, food, and medical care, he had to prepare the necessary airdromes; provide aircraft parking space, maintenance shops, spare parts, and mechanics; find sleeping and mess facilities in every location at which planes would be landing; and supervise the construction of a whole communications network. Because of the size of the maneuver, he had also to spread these facilities throughout central Ohio. "That gave us some idea," he said later, "of the area we must contemplate using in time of war when we talked of concentrating a thousand or two thousand airplanes."

This maneuver brought Arnold more than satisfaction for the job he had done. One of the observers was General King, his nemesis at Fort Leavenworth. When the exercise was finished, King sought out Arnold, and congratulated him for the way he had handled the G-4 assignment. He added that he had even appreciated the paper Arnold wrote as a graduation thesis, and told him finally that he ought to be teaching air operations at the Command and General Staff School.[10]

Arnold knew now that attitudes about him at high levels were changing. Though he was still considered a maverick, Fechet had promoted him to lieutenant colonel in February, and this pleasant surprise, combined with the logistics assignment for the Air Corps' biggest-ever maneuver, indicated that his own chief, at least, had increasing confidence in him. In late October 1931, he learned that Fechet had given him another desirable assignment. He was to take command at March Field, near Riverside, California, where he would be in charge of some operational units as well as one of the Air Corps' larger installations.

On Halloween, the Arnolds were dressing for a costume party that was also to be a farewell party for them at the Fairfield Air Depot.[11] The family was to head east at 6:00 a.m. the next morning in their old Nash. After visiting Bee's parents and Hap's father for a few days at Ardmore, they were to board the Army transport *Republic* (formerly the German liner *Crown Prince Wilhelm*) in New York for the trip to California. The Army often moved personnel from coast to coast by ship rather than train in those days because it was cheaper.

Hap and Bee were in their costumes and ready to leave for the party when the telephone rang. It was Hap's father, announcing that the family bank, of which he had become the vice-president, had failed, and much of his money was lost. This bank, the Merion Title & Trust Company of Ardmore, was also Hap's bank; its failure meant that all the money he had in it was lost, so that the several checks he had made out that very day, to settle his bills before he left the post, were written on what was probably a defunct account. The only money the family now possessed was the children's education fund, which they had put in Bee's father's bank.

Bleak as this sounds, it is doubtful that the Arnolds could at first comprehend what was happening to them and the country. Though the national epidemic of bank failures had now begun, the whole phenomenon seemed so unreal that it took people some time to grasp it. The Arnolds' visit to Ardmore must have been a somber one; Dr. Arnold had been staggered by the failure of his bank, and Sidney Pool, Bee's father, was presiding over a bank which now teetered on the brink of failure. Yet Hap, Bee, and the children, still shielded by the Army from the harsh realities of civilian life during that period, boarded their transport in New York for what proved to be a peaceful and pleasant cruise down through the Panama Canal to San Francisco. It was only when they arrived in California in late November that the full impact of events bore down upon them. By that time, Bee's father's bank had crashed. He had suffered a stroke. His finance officer had absconded to Mexico. And the Arnold children's education fund was gone. Hap and Bee had several outstanding checks to cover, and no money with which to cover them.

They arrived at March Field in a drenching rainstorm at about 7:00 p.m. on Thanksgiving Day, feeling they had very little for which to be thankful. But there on the porch of the house to which they were directed stood Maggie, their cook (who had sailed with them from New York but had come down ahead of them from San Francisco) and Maj. Carl Spaatz (who commanded a combat wing at March) with his wife, Ruth.[12] A lavish Thanksgiving dinner was waiting for everyone at the Spaatz's quarters. Before they went to bed that night their spirits were somewhat improved.

In the morning, when they inspected their new Spanish-style home, they were delighted. The house had four bedrooms and two baths, a screened back porch, and a breakfast nook large enough for Hap to convert into a study.

The base itself was in the process of being refurbished when Arnold arrived. Built as a World War training camp, it was now mostly a flying school, and the old barracks were being replaced by attractive, permanent buildings. Arnold's first job was to phase out the flying school and convert the field into an operational base for fighters and bombers, some of which were already there. When his units came up to strength, he would be in command of two full groups—one of bombers and one of fighters. He appointed Maj. Joseph T. McNarney, the strict and sharp-tongued commandant of the flying school, to command the bombers; Maj. Frank O'D. "Monk" Hunter, a World War ace, to command the fighters; and Spaatz to handle the administrative chores as his executive officer.

Before he got very far with his military projects, Arnold found that he had a serious civilian problem. An Army uniform did not command great respect in America during the nineteen-twenties or -thirties. In Riverside, ten miles from the base, it commanded almost no respect at all. The people there, including the merchants, were not above posting signs that read: "Dogs and Soldiers—Keep Out." Relations between the Air Corps troops and the good citizens were so strained that Arnold arranged a meeting with the city fathers, hoping to relieve the situation. When he realized this meeting had done no good, he tried a new strategy. He declared Riverside off limits to all of his men and provided buses to take them to San Bernardino on their free days.

Riverside merchants soon felt the business loss so acutely that it was they who asked for the next meeting. At their request, Arnold agreed to cancel his off-limits order, but for the next several months he had his men paid in two-dollar bills so the Riverside shopkeepers would have a continuing reminder that March Field soldiers provided a sizable portion of their income.

Not content with this standoff, Arnold then set about trying to establish a positive relationship with the people of Riverside. He instructed each of his officers to join at least one of the town's service clubs, whether Kiwanis, Lions, Rotary, or any other. And he arranged special days for townspeople to visit the base, so he and his men could preach the Air Corps gospel to them. Henceforth, he had no more trouble with Riverside.[13]

In January 1932, the Arnolds received a series of sad letters from Hap's father, who, having lost all of his cash in the crash of his bank, was now on the verge of losing most, if not all, of the highly mortgaged houses and acreage he had bought through the years. "It would seem as though the nightmare of 1931 was being prolonged into 1932," he wrote them on January 16. He was willing to sell off some of his houses to raise cash in the hope of saving others, but "just now there is no market at any price." The second anniversary of his wife's death was two days ahead, on the eighteenth, and he confided that it further depressed him. "I shall never cease to miss the companionship of an undying love of more than fifty years."

By early 1933, it was evident that all of Dr. Arnold's property was lost, even though Hap had guaranteed a loan for him in a desperate effort to save at least some of it. One house after another was foreclosed because the doctor's tenants had no money to pay rent and he therefore had no money to make his mortgage installments. Out of compassion for him, Hap and Bee invited him to visit them, and in March he agreed. When he arrived they soon found that while he had lost his money, he had lost very little of his irascibility or his conviction that only his ways were the right ways.

During his visit, Prohibition came to an end, and Hap took delight in being able legally to mix drinks for his friends, though he still refrained from drinking himself, since he was convinced alcohol would aggravate his ulcers. His father, having quickly settled in as a member of the family, would walk into the living room just as the guests were beginning to feel mellow and say, "Where's my supper?" His custom was to eat at five, and he was not a man who believed in changing his customs. While Hap tried to pacify him, he would look around at the assembled company and say, "Why are you people drinking? You know you're not supposed to drink." Whereupon he would launch one of his well-practiced lectures on the evils of alcohol.

Inasmuch as Hap and Bee had no intention of disrupting their social life to comply with him, they finally arranged for him to eat in the kitchen at five o'clock with David, who also liked to eat early. David soon decided, however, that he didn't like to eat that early if he had to eat with his grandfather. Though the boy was only five years old, he was old enough to decide that Grandad was "a nasty old bastard."

More serious problems between Arnold and his father arose not from the old man's conduct at home but from his habit of instructing people he encountered on the base, soldiers and civilians alike. He found it almost impossible to watch men do anything without telling them how to do it better. This gave rise to some delicate situations because no one wanted to tell the commanding officer's father to go to hell.

A new base theater was under construction when he arrived and he especially enjoyed visiting the site because it seemed to him the men working on it needed a lot of guidance. One day the contractor visited Arnold at base headquarters and insisted that something had to be done. His men were civilians and they didn't have to take it any more.

Hap spoke sharply to his father that night, which proved of course that Hap, too, needed some instruction. When Hap persisted in his error, the old man took considerable umbrage, but he did, thereafter, stay away from the theater site. Fortunately for him, other activities on the base needed his attention. He began to spread his advice around, and there were no more complaints about him for quite a while because no group was getting a concentrated dose of him. One day, however, he discovered the repair hangars on the flight line. When he saw what the mechanics were doing with those aircraft engines, he couldn't resist pointing out their mistakes.

Here was an encroachment Hap had to view seriously. He didn't want a plane to crash because some mechanic had repaired its engine in compliance with his father's instructions. Unfortunately, the argument he had with his father about this issue caused a wound that never completely healed. Dr. Arnold, angry, depressed, and disappointed, got on a Greyhound bus and returned to Pennsylvania. A few months later, on October 27, 1933, he died in Ardmore.[14]

Arnold's unpopular sister Betty also dropped in occasionally while they were at March Field, and her visits were scarcely more successful than those of her father because Hap found it impossible to take seriously the subjects dearest to her—Arnold family history and the concerns of the D.A.R. (Daughters of the American Revolution), of which she was a devoted member. She was skillful at finding ways to insert Revolutionary War references into a conversation about something else. Let someone name a town in Pennsylvania and she would name a battle there "where our brave boys put the Red Coats to flight." At this point, Arnold would say something like "Yes, indeed. We had twelve thousand men and they had about four thousand."

He also took an irreverent view of family history, much to her discomfort. Whenever she began talking about distinguished ancestors, he would launch into stories about one great-uncle who barely escaped hanging as a horse thief, and another, a whisky taster for the Port of Philadelphia, who worked too diligently one day and killed himself when he fell off a ladder that was propped against a vat. What bothered Betty most was his insistence that these stories were true. Her visits to the Arnolds were not long, but Bee, whose dislike of Betty never subsided, would have been happier if she had made them even shorter.

The visitors Bee enjoyed most at March Field were the movie stars whose help her husband solicited while he was stationed there. Keenly aware of the value of public relations, Arnold had decided that it wouldn't hurt the Air Corps to be associated in the public mind with some famous film celebrities. Because he had already met such entertainers as Will Rogers and Mary Pickford, and because he was now the prestigious commander of a large California air base situated less than a hundred miles from Hollywood, he had easy access to almost anyone in the film industry. When the March Field base theater was finally completed, Jean Harlow, Wallace Beery, and several other stars came to

Riverside for the grand opening. Miss Harlow stayed at the Arnold home, which pleased Bee, except that she thought the beautiful blond actress's white dress was too tight. "And she's not wearing a brassiere," Bee whispered in an aside to Hap. Quite naturally, she was even more pleased when he brought home handsome male stars. "Mother loved the movie star bit," her son Bruce said later. "She always fell for a good-looking guy."[15]

Sometimes, however, such visits could lead to unexpected family complications. One day Hap brought home Ben Lyon, who had become an Air Corps reserve officer after starring in the famous air film *Hell's Angels*. All three of the Arnolds' sons plus several other boys, forewarned of the celebrated star's arrival, were waiting on the porch when Arnold and Lyon arrived. Arnold introduced Lyon to Hank and David but not to Bruce. Though it is likely that he simply didn't notice Bruce in the crowd of boys, Bruce felt deeply slighted and furious at his father, who had always aroused in him more awe than affection. "You son of a bitch," the boy said to himself, and running off to his room, burst into tears. So deep was his anger that he took a bitter vow against his father. "Some day I'll be big enough and old enough to get even with you," he resolved, "and until that time I'll take from you only what I have to take." Many teenage boys make such threats against their parents, but most of them quickly forget their grievance. It took about twenty years before Bruce finally forgave his father for this and other problems between them. "I never thought he was a good father," Bruce said in later years, "until I tried to be one myself."[16]

In retrospect, he could recall many happy images of his father during those years at March Field. It was true that Arnold seldom showed any physical warmth toward his sons. When they were small he might pick them up and give them piggyback rides, but after they were ten years old or so, he never hugged them, wrestled with them, or even touched them. He was a severe disciplinarian and he didn't engage them in idle chitchat—when he talked to them it was usually about a new airplane model, or some new gadget he had invented or discovered. He was an inveterate gadgeteer with an endless curiosity about how things worked and how they could be made to work better. Innovation was almost an obsession with him—he was as much attracted to new ideas and new methods as he was to new machines—and he made a serious effort to pass this restless curiosity on to his sons. But unlike his own father, he wasn't serious all the time. He loved to have fun with his family. He liked to get out and throw a football with Hank. He told the boys outrageous stories. He joined their checker, chess, or card games.

He helped them make paper gliders. He bestowed warmth and affection, but in his own controlled way. He was never a pal to his sons; he was always unmistakably a father, a figure of authority, and all three of them regarded him with a degree of awe. "Yet through it all," Bruce recalled, "the strictness, the too-busyness, the shyness, we all felt that he was something special. He was a man with a mission."

Movie stars were not the only people Arnold cultivated while he was at March Field. In 1924, Arnold had visited Donald Douglas at his Los Angeles plant, after Douglas had launched his own company and was building a special plane for a round-the-world flight. This was the first personal contact between the two men.[17] In 1926, just after Arnold was exiled to Fort Riley, he had already become familiar enough with Douglas to mention the possibility that he might like to leave the service and work for him. (Douglas told him in effect that he was needed in the service and should stay there.) By 1931, when Arnold came to March, they had become close friends. They saw each other often and went quail shooting together. But more important, Arnold, through Douglas, was able to keep himself well informed about the latest developments in aircraft technology. Douglas, more than any other manufacturer, gave him an opportunity to study the aircraft industry from inside, to learn about its needs, its limitations, and its potential output.

Arnold also cultivated, while at March, the friendship of the great California Institute of Technology scientist Dr. Robert Millikan, whom he had met in Washington during the World War. Millikan came to March one day and asked Arnold to help him with some cosmic-ray experiments.[18] Millikan wanted to conduct some tests in planes during flight, and Arnold provided the planes even though he didn't quite understand the research. While he had a good grasp of technology, he did not have a scientific mind, nor the patience for the scientist's slow methods, and he often referred to scientists as "longhairs." But Millikan made him realize how important they could be in the development of technology, and he never forgot it.

The Long Beach earthquake of March 10, 1933, which was to get Arnold into trouble again with higher authorities, also gave him an opportunity to know and cultivate a man who would be of pivotal importance to him five years later. When Col. Charles H. Hilton, the Fort MacArthur commandant, complained about Arnold sending a convoy of trucks loaded with government food and supplies to the quake victims without his authorization, the man who received his complaint was Gen. Malin Craig, commander of the Army's Ninth Corps Area, with headquarters in San Francisco. Craig was in command of both Hilton and Arnold. It was quite evident to him, after reading Hilton's report, that Arnold had indeed usurped Hilton's responsibility. Hilton, not Arnold, had been designated the disaster officer for Southern California. And Hilton was many years Arnold's senior in rank. Arnold would have some explaining to do if he was to avoid at least a stiff reprimand.[19]

It was July 20 before all the reports were in and Craig summoned Arnold to San Francisco for an explanation. Meanwhile, the general had found another reason to be annoyed at Arnold. In May, Craig had sent a telegram to March Field that said: "Can you take care of 1,500 CCC boys at your station effective next week?"

The Civilian Conservation Corps was one of many measures the new president, Franklin D. Roosevelt, was then instituting to stem the catastrophic nationwide economic panic. It was designed to employ hundreds of thousands of otherwise idle young men in such resource-conservation projects as reforestation and flood control. Arnold had nothing against it, but at the moment he was too busy to help out. He sent a return wire to Ninth Corps headquarters: "We are having maneuvers here now. All the combat type airplanes in the U.S. Air Corps are engaged. Cannot take care of CCC boys at present."

The following day, Craig's reply arrived: "You probably do not understand. This is an Executive Order of the President who says that CCC camps will be established and will be administered by the U.S. Army. Can you take care of 3,000 CCC boys effective immediately?"

This time Arnold's answer was affirmative and the boys began to arrive at March within a week. By July, the field was filling up with them and Arnold, whose attention had been caught, was already enthusiastic about this opportunity to preach the Air Corps doctrine to three thousand potential soldiers. But he didn't know how Craig felt about his initial impertinence in rejecting the project, nor did he know whether he could make Craig accept his reason for sending relief to the Long Beach quake victims without authorization. The reason had been simple enough. Those people needed help and old Colonel Hilton, whose job it was to help them, couldn't be found. Yet Craig, like Hilton, was getting along in age, and he was known to be a stern, strict soldier who liked to stick to the rules.

On the morning of July 20, Arnold took off for San Francisco in a

P-12 fighter plane that he had had assigned to him, with Lt. Eugene H. Beebe on his wing in another P-12.[20] He had explained to Beebe that he had some important business with General Craig at the Presidio. "I'm in trouble up there," he said. "Some of Craig's colonels are trying to court-martial me." But if Arnold was truly worried, he didn't show it. He was so cavalier about the matter that Beebe, unfamiliar with all the circumstances, didn't take the situation seriously. Though Arnold scarcely knew Craig, Beebe got the impression they must be old friends, especially when Arnold, with Beebe still on his wing, buzzed the tower at Crissy Field. As Beebe knew, Craig had strict rules against buzzing.

When they landed, two military policemen were waiting to put them under arrest and, in accordance with the commanding general's standing order, take them directly to his office.

As Arnold and Beebe settled into the back seat of the MPs' car, Beebe stared at Arnold in wonder. If he was already in trouble, why had he compounded it by buzzing the tower?

Arnold anticipated the lieutenant's question. "I wanted to give you a lesson," he said, "in how to get quick transportation."

When they were ushered into Craig's office, the general said, "Goddammit, Arnold! I might have known it would be you buzzing the tower."

Ignoring that little matter, Arnold saluted and got right down to business. In a tone of offended innocence, he said, "Sir, why am I in the doghouse?"

Craig recalled later that he was astounded by this cross young Air Corps colonel confronting him so abruptly. After a half hour of spirited conversation, during which members of Craig's staff enumerated the complaints against Arnold and he rebutted them, he was no longer in the doghouse. He had charmed the older man so completely that Craig promised to visit March Field at his earliest opportunity and see for himself what the Air Corps was doing down there.

Arnold was so elated when he and Beebe took off from Crissy for home that as they flew over the Tehachapi Pass (after stopping for gas at Bakersfield), he went right down on the deck and, with Beebe clinging to his wing, flew all the way to Cajon Pass about fifteen feet above the ground. Like Craig, he had forbidden buzzing in his command, but he didn't mind doing it himself when the situation was right.

Arnold's evident enthusiasm for flying during his years at March Field indicates that he had overcome his earlier fears. Yet the strain of flying, combined perhaps with his general intensity, his love of rich, sweet food, and his refusal ever to relax, brought on an episode which must have frightened him at the time, and to which, it can be said in retrospect, he should have paid closer attention.

On a flight later in 1933 back to California from the East, with two of his young fighter pilots flying on his wings, he stopped in Salt Lake City for refueling. The two young pilots, perhaps tired after the long formation flight west, wanted to lay over there until the next day. Arnold, always in a hurry, and possibly eager to show these youngsters that he wasn't so old himself, decided they would fly on to March Field, and since he was the boss, they did so. But at dinner on Arnold's first day at home, he seemed not to be hungry. His son Hank noticed that he just sat at the table, saying nothing and eating nothing.

Bee said to him, "Are you all right?"

"Yeah, I'm all right."

But by that time he was turning gray. All the color had left his usually florid face and his breathing was labored. Finally he laid down his knife and fork in apparent distress. Bee, possibly fearful that he was suffering a heart attack, sent Hank to get the base flight surgeon, who lived only two doors away. When the medical officer arrived, Arnold was stretched out in the living room, still in some distress but making little of his condition. Fliers, for fear of being grounded, don't like to advertise their illnesses—especially illnesses which resemble heart attacks. If the medical officer believed he had suffered a heart attack, he didn't say so. Not long after that, however, Arnold began flying bombers more frequently than fighters. In a bomber, there was usually a second pilot to take the controls if necessary.[21]

A few months after Arnold's meeting with Malin Craig in San Francisco, the general kept his promise to visit March Field. He flew south to watch a mass maneuver by the fighter and bomber groups under Arnold's command. He was so pleased, not only by the aerial display but also by the Southern California golf courses to which Arnold took him, that he made several more trips thereafter, the last one coming on a very auspicious occasion in 1935. Craig was then on his way to Washington to become the Army Chief of Staff, replacing Douglas MacArthur. By that time, Craig and Arnold were firm friends, all because Arnold, in sending relief supplies to Long Beach without authorization, had defied the Army regulations so dear to Craig.

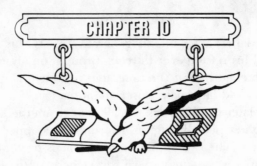

A rnold and his pilots undertook one other relief mission while he was at March Field, but for this one he received no criticism. During the winter of 1932–33, the blizzards were so heavy in New Mexico, Arizona, Utah, and Colorado that many remote Indian settlements in those states were stranded and threatened with starvation. When Arnold was asked if he could help these people, he had no idea how, but he said yes.

He assigned a bombardment squadron, under Capt. Charles Howard, to figure out a way to drop food from airplanes. It would be totally unfeasible to use parachutes, since in the windy mountains the packages might drift so far away from the target settlements that the Indians would be unable to get through the snowdrifts to recover them. Howard and his men finally devised a packet so well cushioned that, as one of them said, they could "drop a dozen eggs without breaking a damned one."[1] Arnold's pilots then located the settlements with the aid of Indian agents, and for several weeks, in Arnold's words, "bombed them with food." They had devised a dead-drop method that would still be useful many years later during the Berlin airlift.

Arnold's daily concerns at March Field were organization, training, and practice, and the development of new skills and techniques in military flying. His squadrons and wings staged one mission after another, many of them at night, trying to figure out what the flying conditions would be if there were another war, then simulating those conditions and inventing strategies or tactics to cope with them as best they could with the equipment they had. The bomb squadrons would conduct a mock bombardment raid and the fighter squadrons, taking off from other West Coast fields, would try to intercept them. All of this was done on the basis of calculated speculation. Everyone knew the aerial tactics in any future war would be unlike those in the Great War, but no one had formulated a tactical or strategic doctrine for future operations. Arnold, like everyone else in the Air Corps at this time, was groping toward such doctrines.

Dissatisfied with the mock bomb raids and fighter pursuits he was staging, he decided he needed a real bomb range and aerial gunnery range. In the Mojave Desert, northeast of Palmdale, he found the ideal location for such a range—the Muroc Dry Lake area. One trip to the fourteen-by-seven-mile dry lake convinced him that its bed would be "about the best and smoothest landing field imaginable." The soil was fine clay, its surface hard and "smooth as glass." Staking out a nineteen-by-nine-mile unpopulated tract, he began searching titles and found that the government owned part of it, the Southern Pacific Railroad owned part of it, and the state of California owned the rest. Since it was cheap desert land, he assumed it would be easy to arrange for the government to buy all of it. Actually, he didn't succeed in that project until 1939, but in the meantime, he didn't wait for legal niceties before using it. He set up his bomb and gunnery ranges there immediately, establishing an installation that is now the great test facility Edwards Air Force Base.

Arnold solidified a team of men at March Field who would be important to him for the rest of his career—men like Spaatz, Eaker, Hunter, McNarney, and Beebe. Spaatz was like a brother to him, in and out of his house all the time. On Sunday afternoons, they would sit in front of the fireplace playing chess and arguing about airplanes or air strategy.[2] One Sunday, during a game between Arnold, Spaatz, and Hunter, an argument arose as to whether it would be better to use 30- or 50-caliber machine guns in aerial combat. The heavier gun would be more effective, but its weight, and the weight of its ammunition, would diminish a plane's airspeed. Would the extra power of the 50-caliber gun compensate for this loss of speed? As the argument heightened, the decibel count in the room increased—not only because of passionate convictions but also because all three men, after fifteen or twenty years of flying loud propellor planes, had become partially deaf.

Finally the argument reached a point where it could no longer be settled by words. The three of them interrupted the chess game and went down to the ordnance department to weigh the two guns plus their ammunition. When they returned, the argument appeared to be settled. They quietly resumed their chess game and had played for several minutes when one of them said, "We forgot to weigh the linkage [the chain which feeds the machine gun bullets into the gun]." Without further ado they stood up and headed for ordnance again.

In late 1933 Spaatz was transferred to the Washington office of Gen. Benjamin Foulois, who was then Air Corps chief. On February 10, 1934, Arnold and Eaker were playing golf at a private course a few miles from March Field when a messenger arrived and said Spaatz, in Washington, wanted urgently to talk to them. They hurried back to Arnold's office and when they reached Spaatz, he told them a frightening story.

President Roosevelt, convinced that the Hoover administration had made fraudulent airmail contracts with the airlines, was canceling those contracts and asking the Air Corps to take over the job of flying the airmail. Furthermore, General Foulois had assured the president that the Air Corps was capable of handling the assignment. Arnold was to be responsible for carrying the mail in the western section of the country, which would include the routes connecting San Diego, Los Angeles, San Francisco, Portland, and Seattle, plus the routes between Salt Lake City and all of those cities. And he would be expected to start operations nine days later, on February 19.

Arnold told Spaatz he would get right to work on the job even though he knew he was flirting with disaster. As he later said, "My pilots [in the West] were mostly Reserve officers, none of whom, owing to the War Department policy of turning over Reserve officers in a squadron at the rate of 25 or 30 percent a year, had had two years' service. Very few of the 'regular' civilian air mail routes had been flown over by these officers. They had none of the special airline instruments; they must fly in whatever planes we had, including trainers. There was not —especially in the case of the open-cockpit fighter types that had to be flown—even enough space for the mail bags."

The plan was to have the Air Corps begin with fourteen of the twenty-six nationwide routes the airlines had flown. For this purpose, the Army would provide 122 planes and 200 pilots. But none of the planes was properly equipped. At that moment, the Air Corps owned only 274 directional gyros and 460 artificial horizons, very few of which were actually mounted on airplanes. As for radios, the corps had 172 transmitter-receivers, none usable at ranges beyond thirty miles.

On February 16, Foulois compounded his problem by telling the House Post Office Committee, "We have assigned to this work the most experienced pilots in the Army Air Corps. We have had a great deal of experience in flying at night, and in flying in fogs and bad weather, in blind flying and in flying under all conditions."

Actually, only 122 of the 262 pilots who were destined to fly the mail had more than two years' experience. Only thirty-one had more than fifty hours of night flying. Only two had as much as fifty hours of instrument time.[3] And only forty-eight had as much as twenty-five hours of bad-weather time. Such aviation authorities as Charles Lindbergh and Eddie Rickenbacker were predicting dire results if the Air Corps persisted in its intentions. On the sixteenth, the day Foulois testified and only three days before the regular runs were to begin, their predictions began to come true: three of Arnold's pilots were killed during route-familiarization flights through the Rockies.

Plans for the takeover continued nevertheless. Arnold established his command post at Salt Lake City. Eaker and his Pursuit Group, equipped with P-26 single-seat fighters, took the Los Angeles–Salt Lake City routes. Maj. Clarence Tinker, with his 2nd Bombardment Group, was to handle San Francisco–Salt Lake City. And one of his squadron commanders was given the Seattle–Portland–Salt Lake City routes.

Eaker could fit only fifty pounds of mail into each of his fighter planes (of which he had ten) if he wanted to leave room for the pilot, but on the day of his first run, the Post Office informed him he had 1,400 pounds of mail to carry. Thousands of philatelists, eager to have stamped envelopes from the first Air Corps airmail flights, had stuffed the letter boxes that day. Eaker called Arnold and asked him what to do with the 900 pounds of mail he couldn't carry. "Come on over here [to March]," Arnold said, "and I'll give you a bomber."[4]

Eaker picked up the bomber, but none of his pilots had ever flown one, so for the first week he had to fly as copilot on each of the aircraft's runs, teaching his fighter pilots how to fly it. Nevertheless, his was the only route that didn't lose a man.

The carnage began on February 22, the fourth day of the project. One plane crashed near Deshler, Ohio, another in Texas. A pilot on his way from Newark to Richmond crash-landed and fractured his skull. Another was lost in a snowstorm near Fremont, Ohio, and bailed out.

The next day, February 23, a pilot made a forced landing in the Atlantic and drowned. Already there had been a dozen or more crashes and six fatalities, counting the three men who died in practice flights. Roosevelt was so embarrassed he blamed Foulois for telling him that the Air Corps could do the job. And Foulois, having no one else to blame, said the bad weather was the villain. They agreed to cut the schedule and tighten the weather restrictions, but still the young, inexperienced, and ill-equipped pilots continued to crash. On March 8 and 9, four more were killed, bringing the total to ten. Roosevelt summoned Foulois and Chief of Staff MacArthur to the White House for another "shave and a haircut." He also put further restrictions on routes and flights, and more important, he hurried up his negotiations with the airlines toward new airmail agreements.

On June 1, the airlines finally resumed carrying the mail and the Air Corps was left to count its losses. It had suffered twelve deaths, sixty-six crashes, and untold humiliation. The public furor was so intense that Roosevelt felt compelled to appoint a special committee headed by former Secretary of War Newton D. Baker (soon referred to as the Baker Board) to investigate the airmail fiasco and the general condition of the Air Corps. Hap Arnold, however, emerged from this fiasco with his reputation intact because he had handled the most mountainous, most difficult section of the country with the fewest casualties.

As soon as Arnold returned to California after closing his Salt Lake City command post, he arranged a leave. He and Bee got in their car for a fishing trip to Jackson Hole, Wyoming, and had reached Salt Lake City when a telegram from Washington caught up to them.

At Air Corps headquarters, Foulois and his deputy, Gen. Oscar Westover, had been trying to think of projects that would earn the corps some good publicity to counteract the ridicule heaped upon it as a result of the airmail disaster. The first of the Martin B-10 bombers had just been delivered. A twin-engined, low-winged plane with a 900-mile range and an airspeed of 200 miles per hour, it was considered the marvel of its day. A flight of these planes to Alaska and back would serve the useful purpose of helping to map great stretches of uncharted northland, and it would also be a dramatic demonstration of Air Corps accomplishment. But no inexperienced young reserves would be sent on this mission. Maj. Hugh Knerr, an expert pilot and ingenious logistician, was named executive officer, and it was he who arranged for all the supplies and facilities that would be needed at all the fields where the planes would land, going and returning.

Much of the planning had already been done when Foulois decided that Arnold should lead the flight and began tracking him down with phone calls and telegrams. As soon as Arnold received Foulois's wire in Salt Lake City, he sent Bee home and proceeded to Wright Field in Dayton, where the flight was being organized. On June 29 he wrote to her from there: "Everyone in Washington thinks this is a wonderful assignment but to me it is only another job."[5]

His enthusiasm may have been dampened that day because he had just made final crew selections, which meant he had been forced to send home five pilots who had counted on going. He also had some reservations about the B-10s because they were brand-new and not thoroughly tested. "The new plane is an excellent one," he wrote to Bee, "but it must be properly prepared and the installation of equipment and instruments cannot be hurried. I believe that when we do start we will have the ships in such condition that we will have a reasonable chance of completing the flight."

A flight to Alaska is now such a simple, routine accomplishment that it may be difficult for a modern reader to understand why it should have been considered remarkable in 1934, seven years after Lindbergh flew across the Atlantic. But at that time, there were virtually no air routes north. No one had ever flown nonstop to or from the Alaska Territory. To go down in those north woods or mountains would be as disastrous as going down in the mid-Atlantic. And while Arnold's was not a nonstop flight, it was a ten-plane flight, which multiplied by ten the possibility of tragedy.

His ten bombers took off from Washington on July 19 and, averaging 820 miles per day, flew northwesterly with stops at Dayton, Minneapolis, Winnipeg, Regina, and Edmonton, then White Horse in the Yukon, before landing, intact and triumphant, at Fairbanks. Major Knerr, Arnold's executive officer, who took credit for the organization of the flight, nevertheless acknowledged Arnold's leadership as flight commander.

"That was one of the finest exhibitions of expert pilotage [a term which here denotes navigation through difficult terrain] that has ever been done," Knerr said later, "because we went up through rough country. And they literally cut strips out of the forest brush [for] our landings. . . . So with a strange airplane—and it was a difficult airplane to land—and arriving there at the proper time and getting the work done, [considering all the problems] Arnold was an excellent leader."

In Alaska they spent three days on a photo-mapping operation during which they photographed 20,800 miles of Alaskan wilderness, including the Mount McKinley massif, from the air. They also overcame a mishap that could have proved embarrassing.

One day while the crew was in Fairbanks, Arnold, Knerr, and the third flight leader, Maj. Ralph Royce, together flew three bombers down to Anchorage to inspect the airfield there. With them was a young pilot who was on the expedition as a photographic officer. Not yet having flown a B-10, he asked Arnold, while they were on the ground at Anchorage, if he could take one of the planes up for a short spin. Knerr advised against it because there were technical complications, especially in the fuel system, with which the man was not familiar. But Royce said to Arnold, "Oh, let him go. He's a good pilot."

The man was only a few hundred feet off the ground when

something went wrong and the bomber began to drop. But fortunately he was indeed a good pilot, and he managed to make a forced landing, with wheels up, on the beach of nearby Cook's Bay.

Watching the plane go down, Arnold looked sheepishly at Knerr, while Royce turned completely away from him. "You go bail it," Knerr said to Arnold, but, of course, all three of them hurried to the crash site. The pilot was unhurt. The plane was a mess. It had scooped up tons of greasy sand and debris. It looked as if it would never fly again. And with the tide rising to inundate it, there was a danger that it might soon disappear altogether.

The three men scurried around until they found some empty oil drums to fasten under the wings as floats, and when the tide came in, they got a fishing boat to tow it to the Anchorage dock, where it was lifted out of the water with a winch and put on a flatcar. The Anchorage Fire Department hosed it clean; then the expedition's mechanics, including Arnold's crew chief, Sgt. Henry Puzenski, went to work on it. The fuselage was suffering from dents in the nose and belly and these were hammered back into shape. The engines were hopelessly grimy, but Knerr had been wise enough to send ahead two spare engines and two sets of spare instruments, which were quickly installed. And when the other nine planes were ready for the return flight, so was this one.

On the way home they flew the 950 miles from Juneau to Seattle nonstop, thereby, in the words of the inscription on the Mackay Trophy, which Arnold won for the second time as a result of this feat, "linking the Territory of Alaska with the United States by air, without a stop on foreign territory, for the first time." From Seattle they flew by way of Salt Lake City, Omaha, and Dayton, landing at Washington on the morning of August 20, 1934.

It was a triumph for which Arnold received more credit than he deserved. For his leadership, he not only again won the Mackay Trophy, he also was awarded the Distinguished Flying Cross. The other men on the flight, for their participation, received no commendations at all, and they naturally resented this—especially Knerr, whose relations with Arnold were clouded by the incident for many years. Even after Arnold's death, Knerr expressed his resentment in an interview with Air Force historian Dr. Murray Green, who fortunately was able to put his mind at rest by quoting letters that proved that Arnold had gone to Deputy Chief of Staff Gen. Hugh Drum to plead for recognition of all the men connected with the flight. Arnold argued that every one of them should get the D.F.C. But General Drum, an infantryman, was not an aviation enthusiast—he had remarked at a hearing of the Baker

Board, of which he was vice-chairman, that he could see no reason why
the range of an Army airplane should exceed "three days' march by the
Infantry"—and he saw no merit in Arnold's plea on behalf of the other
men. Arnold therefore earned great public acclaim, but some private
enmity, for his part in the expedition.

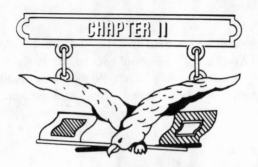

CHAPTER 11

There was one coveted recognition Arnold failed to win in 1934 and he was as resentful about it as Knerr was about the excessive recognition Arnold won for the Alaska flight. Arnold's D.F.C. and his second Mackay Trophy, plus the high marks he had earned for the organization and efficiency of his bomber and fighter groups at March Field, plus the praise he had won for his personal competence during the airmail disaster, continued to make him feel he deserved a promotion. In fact, General Foulois, during the ill-fated airmail effort, had told him that when the next vacancy for a star came up, it would be his.[1]

That would be a big jump—from lieutenant colonel to brigadier general—but there was no one who deserved it ahead of him, unless it might be Col. Frank Andrews. Andrews, who had graduated from West Point a year before Arnold, was an officer of such outstanding merit that everyone in the Air Corps, including Arnold, admired him. Andrews had graduated with Arnold from the Command and General Staff School in 1929, and the two had always been friendly. He had also graduated from the Army War College in 1933. He outranked Arnold as a lieutenant colonel by one year. But he had entered the Air Service in 1917, several years after Arnold, and in 1934 he was commanding a pursuit group at Selfridge Field, Michigan—a less impressive position than Arnold's, with a pursuit and a bomber group plus a large base under his control.

Arnold had told Bee about Foulois's promise of a star and it seemed to her that he was "feeling pretty good" about the possibility that he might soon be a general. But to his surprise and consternation he read the promotion list one day and learned that a colonel named James E. Chaney, a man who had never attracted much attention and was a year behind him at West Point, had been picked to get the star that Foulois had promised him.

As soon as he learned this, he called Bee and said, "I'm sorry you married such a bum."

"What are you talking about?" she asked.

"Didn't you hear the report that Chaney got the star?"

"Yes, I did," she said, "but that doesn't make you a bum."

He could not conceal his deep discouragement. "I don't know whether it's worth going on or not," he said. "I don't know what's ahead for me." But Arnold's discouragement never seemed to last long. This time he turned it into anger, went to Washington at the first opportunity, and marched right in to see General MacArthur, who was still chief of staff and whom he had known since 1912, when they both lived in Washington's Army and Navy Club. What, he demanded, did MacArthur have against him?

"I have to know," he said, "because my whole career depends on it."

MacArthur seemed bewildered until Arnold explained his visit. "I was told I was to have this air star," he said, "and Chaney got it."

MacArthur took some papers from his desk and glanced through them. "Your name wasn't even on the list," he said.

Arnold had been less than warm to Benny Foulois ever since the Mitchell trial, at which Foulois openly opposed Mitchell. After this episode, Arnold was never more than polite to him.[2] But despite his anger, he stopped even suggesting that he might quit the Air Corps. He would not give Foulois that satisfaction.

At about the time when Arnold was hinting he might quit the Air Corps, his daughter, Lois, ironically, was writing home that she might quit the University of Arizona in Tucson, where she had enrolled that fall after two years at a Riverside junior college.[3] She had done well at the junior college—earning straight A grades—and she had been welcomed into a sorority shortly after her arrival in Tucson, but she had also begun drinking as soon as she was old enough to date men who could buy drinks for her, and she was now beginning to find that drinking was more fun than studying. Besides that, her fellow students at Arizona were simply not up to her social standards. The girls weren't exactly sophisticated; the boys were too boyish, and she wasn't interested in boys—she was interested in men. She wanted to withdraw from Arizona and go to some other university where she could meet a better class of people.

Though her brothers already knew about her drinking by this point (years earlier she had told Bruce she could hardly wait till she was old enough to drink), her father was probably not yet aware that she took more than an occasional cocktail. But he was horrified by some other revelations in her letters, and when she wrote asking his permission to transfer to another school, he sent her a stinging reply, dated October 10, 1934, with some sharp words about her attitude:

I should hate to think that you really meant what you wrote. I hope that we did not get the meaning which you intended to convey. I don't believe that you are yellow—a quitter. I don't believe that you think that you are so much better than the average run of young America that you can not associate with them. I can't believe that you have made up your mind that you have developed so that you are far beyond others of your age.

If we are correct in our interpretation of your letter, you had better change your mind right away and get down to earth. Get this and get it straight—you are going to stay in the college where you are and finish this year. I am not a quitter and will not have any child of mine a quitter. Hence get busy and get the most you can out of the courses which you have selected.

Don't be a snob. The girls took you into their sorority and wanted you. Play the game. Otherwise you are going to have one hell of a time.

There is only one way to get educated for a position in the world and that is to stick to it and finish. You can't travel from one institution to another, change from one course to another. Some of these days you will be called upon to earn your own living, so while I am willing to foot the bills, you had better make the most of it.

Hoping that you will accept this in the spirit in which it is written, that of helping you out, I am, with love,

Your father

It was one occasion when he did not indulge Lois. But neither did he change her. In an undated letter apparently written about ten days later, she said: "I am about to die for want of a mature male. I am so tired of playing Dumb Dora for these college men, but it's the only way to secure dates—wide-eyed innocence." Later in the same letter, she asked, "Did you get any new West Pointers [at March Field]? . . . I do miss the Army so." These two tenuously connected thoughts might offer a clue to the workings of Lois's mind. She didn't care for civilian college boys. She was interested in Army men. West Pointers. And fliers. Men like her father.

It was not long before Lois alleviated her shortage of "mature" males. In letters to some of her father's young officers she let them know that her sorority house was full of girls eager to meet Air Corps fliers. Tucson suddenly became a popular stopover for cross-country flights by Arnold's bombers and fighters. But as a result, Lois had a problem to explain when she came home from school the following summer. She had flunked one of her science courses. She would have to go back for summer school to make up the credit.

This news astonished Arnold. If she could earn straight A's in junior college, why in hell should she flunk a course at the university? As he gradually learned, science class met at eight o'clock and Lois had a hard time getting up that early because she was staying out late at night. With whom? With one after another of Arnold's young pilots.

It was more than Arnold was willing to accept from her. Losing all patience, he informed her she was not going back to summer school. Indeed, she was not going back to college at all, and that was final.

"All I can think of," he said, "are the thousands of kids who can't get to college because of this goddamned Depression, and here you are flunking out because you can't make an eight-o'clock class. Your college days are over." He would enroll her in a secretarial school right there in Riverside.

Though this was a brutal blow to Lois, she soon found herself traveling the ten miles to Riverside every morning. But not necessarily to attend her classes at the secretarial school. She managed to find a congenial soda fountain where she could while away her time drinking Cokes. She just couldn't picture herself as a secretary.

The Baker Board hearings of April and May 1934, originated for the purpose of investigating the Air Corps' inability to carry the airmail, had become, in effect, another arena in the continuing battle between air men and doubters—ground and Navy men—over the potential uses of airplanes in national defense. With men like Hugh Drum of the Infantry declaring that no Army airplane's range should exceed three days' march by the Infantry, and the Navy's Rear Adm. Yates Stirling declaring that airplanes would be the "eyes" of the fleet but that "a shore-based air force" could function "only in narrow waters," the Air Corps' campaign for long-range heavy bombers was doomed. The Army ground forces, combined with the Navy, had so much political strength that all the long-range bombers in the world at that time would not have been able to budge them. But with Hitler gradually becoming a threat in Europe, and with the potential range of airplanes constantly increasing thanks to new technology, the Board felt obliged to make some recommendations that would appear to meet the Air Corps demands.

The result was the formation of the General Headquarters Air

Force on March 9, 1935, ostensibly to give the Air Corps a fast striking force, but actually to split the corps into two parts and lodge control of the striking force more firmly than ever in the hands of the Army General Staff.

Under this new setup, the chief of the Air Corps, General Foulois, would retain his position, but his main responsibility would be procurement and supply. The General Headquarters Air Force, commanded by Frank Andrews, who became a temporary major general for the purpose, would control a force of fighter and bomber groups but would have no procurement or supply authority. Andrews would take his orders directly from the Army General Staff, thus by-passing the chief of Air Corps, who would be in charge of an Air Corps with few planes. The only way Foulois would be able to exert any influence would be by failing to supply the needs of the G.H.Q. Air Force, thus keeping it on the ground. This separation of the two vital parts of the Air Corps so that neither had any control over the other was certain to cause lack of coordination, rivalry, envy, and friction between the two parts. Most Air Corps men considered the system insane at the time, but they were stuck with it and had to make the best of it.

Arnold was given command of the First (or Western) Wing of the G.H.Q. Air Force and promoted, behind Andrews, from lieutenant colonel to temporary brigadier general. His headquarters remained at March Field and his force consisted of three bomb groups plus three fighter units at March, Rockwell, and Hamilton Fields. But since an earlier reorganization had already put him in charge of all these units, there was no real change in his command.

There was a change, however, in operations. The thrust of the G.H.Q. operations was to prove the mobility of air power, the ability of the air arm to gather quickly with maximum force wherever in the country it was needed. By proving this ability to move and strike quickly, Andrews, Arnold, and other airmen hoped to demonstrate that the long-range bomber was the nation's primary defensive need.

Andrews, who some people thought had been selected to command the G.H.Q. Air Force because the General Staff considered him easily manageable, turned out to be a dynamic leader, as dedicated as everyone else in the Air Corps to the development of a long-range strike force. Though woefully limited by the B-10 and B-12 aircraft at his disposal, he quickened the pace of all of his units and devised every possible exercise to prove that wherever his planes might be needed, he could get them there on time. He also fought the ground generals and the admirals who were limiting acquisition of the new four-engine B-17 "Flying Fortress" bomber under construction by the Boeing Aircraft Company. And he encouraged the development at the Air Corps Tactical School, Maxwell Field, Alabama, of the strategic and tactical theories that were destined to become Air Corps doctrine by the time the United States entered World War II. These theories were based on the anticipated development of large, well-armed bombers, like the B-17, which would be able to hit vital enemy targets located hundreds of miles within enemy borders. In 1935 and 1936, the Air Corps almost had to bootleg such theories to its men because the Army ground forces, the Navy, and the majority of the political establishment were not ready to accept them, or even to have them taught. The prevailing political doctrine of the 1930s was that the nation could conceivably be forced into a defensive war but would never enter an offensive war. Hence there was no need for long-range bombers. The Navy would keep any enemy from American shores, and if an enemy did manage to land, the Army would deal with him. Though Hitler's threat to Europe was already becoming evident, no American politician, not even the very popular President Roosevelt, would dare suggest at that time the possibility that the United States might one day send a force across the Atlantic to oppose aggression.

Andrews, together with Arnold and his other subordinates, used the G.H.Q. Air Force, in their maneuvers, not only to demonstrate the mobility of air power, but to test, as best they could, the long-range theories being developed by the bright young instructors at Maxwell Field—men like Harold L. George, Muir Fairchild, Kenneth L. Walker, Claire L. Chennault, Robert Olds, Haywood S. Hansell, Jr., Donald Wilson, Laurence S. Kuter and others—who had been influenced themselves by such European air strategists as Guilio Douhet of France and Lord Hugh Trenchard of England.[4] But some of these men were misled, at that time, by the technology available to them. The fastest fighter plane they knew, the P-26, had an airspeed of only 220 miles per hour. The B-17, which was undergoing tests, was expected to fly at 250 miles per hour. This led many, though not all, Air Corps strategists to believe that the bombers of the future would be able to outrun the fighters and therefore would be able to fly their missions unescorted. It was a belief that persisted too long and was destined to cause grief during World War II.

Arnold wrote in his memoirs after World War II:

. . . we became convinced—at least I certainly did—that long-range,
heavy bombers must have not only increased fire power and mutual
support, but also a fast, maneuverable fighter escort which could go
with the bombers to their targets.

Part of this conviction came from a constant development, as
airplane types diversified and became more and more refined, of a
thought the Wright brothers had started to hammer into me in the
days when such terms as "fighters" and "bombers" were unknown
even to them: "Large airplanes built with the same shape and
relative dimensions as small ones, will not have the same relative
performance." . . . I should have preferred never to send any
unescorted bombers over Germany."[5]

Arnold seemed in these reminiscences to imply that it was the 1935
G.H.Q. Air Force exercises that convinced him long-range bombers
would need fighter escorts all the way to their targets. Future events
were to leave some doubt that he settled on this conviction as early as he
indicated.

Arnold enjoyed his association with the G.H.Q. Air Force because,
under Andrews's direction, it seemed to be doing something. It offered a
challenge. It invited experiment. It was attempting to develop, expand,
refine, and clarify the function the Air Corps should fulfill in national
defense. It was trying for the first time to decide in practical terms how
air power could and should be coordinated for the nation's maximum
benefit. Arnold found the work satisfying and so did his men. They were
now part of an increasingly tight-knit outfit that was getting something
accomplished, and around that fact they built an esprit de corps. But just
as some people had foreseen when the G.H.Q. Air Force was formed,
this esprit, this identification with one part of the Air Corps, tended to
separate the G.H.Q. men from the section under the command of the
chief of Air Corps. Arnold himself freely admitted that by the end of
1935, his loyalty was with the G.H.Q. rather than the chief of Air Corps.
"With the contention of General Andrews that his G.H.Q. Air Force
should not report to the Chief of the Air Corps at all, but should head
up directly under the Chief of Staff, we enthusiastically agreed." By "we"
he meant "I."

In early December 1935, the G.H.Q. Air Force held a maneuver in
Florida, the first aspect of which was to find out how quickly all of its
units could gather in one locality. Arnold's planes, coming from California, were allotted twenty-four hours to get to Vero Beach. His last one
was on the ground twenty-one hours and forty-five minutes after leaving
March Field, an excellent achievement for planes that cruised at no
more than two hundred miles per hour and had to stop several times to

refuel.[6] As for the rest of the Florida maneuver, Arnold didn't see much of it because he was summoned to Washington by General Craig, who was now the Army chief of staff.

Unimpressed by Florida on his first trip there and chilled by its unusual forty-degree weather, Arnold didn't mind the side trip to Washington until he found out why he had been summoned. Craig broke the news to him that as of December 28, he was to be assistant chief of the Air Corps under Gen. Oscar Westover, who had just been appointed chief to succeed Benny Foulois.

Once again Arnold astonished Craig. He protested that he didn't want the job. He would rather go back to March Field, he said, and even give back his general's star, than return to Washington as a desk soldier.

Craig listened patiently, perhaps with amusement since he knew Arnold well by this time, then told him to forget what he would rather do. Westover wanted him as his assistant and he, Craig, had already approved the appointment.

The matter may not have been decided quite so simply. Westover did admire Arnold, no doubt about that. Two years earlier after a visit to California (Westover was then assistant chief), he wrote a thank-you note to Bee Arnold in which he said, "March Field certainly made a wonderful showing in the Quarterly Test, and on each of my visits I have been impressed by the fact that March Field has not alone a wonderful Commanding Officer and wife of a Commanding Officer, but also has acquired a way of doing things, both in the military and social way, as to make it stand out comparatively among Air Corps stations."[7] A year later, Westover was instrumental in choosing Arnold to lead the 1934 Alaska flight. But Craig himself may have instigated Arnold's selection as assistant chief, and he had two obvious reasons for doing so. First of all, he clearly admired Arnold and was as entertained as he was sometimes shocked by Arnold's unorthodox methods. Since their original misunderstanding about the Long Beach earthquake relief, they had become fast friends. Secondly, Craig was sensitive enough to realize that the Air Corps was now almost bitterly divided into two camps. If the new chief was to come from the old chief's faction, then his assistant should be one of those fly boys from the G.H.Q. Air Force, and Arnold was the logical man. It would be unfair to ask Andrews to give up command of the G.H.Q., as a major general, and take over what should be a brigadier general's job as assistant chief. Andrews might not like to lose Arnold, with whom he got along very well, but he could hardly disapprove of Arnold's appointment. If he did, someone might suggest that he take the job himself.

Arnold's impulsive protest against becoming assistant chief was no doubt genuine. It meant the loss of his command and a return to Washington, a city he had never learned to like. But when he stopped to think of what else the job meant—a significant promotion, a seat next to the center of power, and the possibility that he might one day be chosen to assume that power—he decided to take it. When he returned to Florida to rejoin his units at the end of the maneuver there, Lt. Gene Beebe, who had become one of his aides, noticed that he had "come back happy" from his Washington side trip.[8] The two-day flight from Miami to March Field, December 15 to 17, was Arnold's farewell to his men and to the G.H.Q. Air Force. He was now in the camp of "the enemy."

In early January 1936, the Arnold family was again on the move, and again by car, but this time it was an abridged version of the family.[9] Hank was already in Washington, attending prep school and hoping to get into West Point the following autumn. Bruce, thanks to his father's influence, was able to fly east on a Douglas Aircraft Company test plane. Lois, who didn't look forward to the long car trip, got her father's permission to go by train. And Maggie, when informed that the Arnolds were moving to Washington, declined sadly to accompany them; as a black, she was concerned about conditions in the nation's capital.

"I just don't like the way my people live back there," she said. "I'm a country girl. Kansas and Ohio is one thing, but Washington is something different."

The Arnolds could only sympathize. With young David, a pet white rat named Minnie (the dog, Pooch, had also flown on ahead), and a carful of luggage, Hap and Bee set out across Texas, stopped over at Maxwell Field with Ira and Ruth Eaker, who were then stationed there, and arrived in Washington exhausted on a Saturday morning, only to learn that they did not have the Fairfax Hotel reservations they thought they had.

As they sat tired and dejected in their car outside the Fairfax, wondering where they would stay that night (they finally found rooms at the Brighton), Hap turned to Bee and said, "I don't want you to sign any leases. I want you to get a place to rent from month to month. I won't last three months in this city. Don't get tied up in anything. And further more, I will have no official social life. I will not go to parties where I have to wear a white tie. I don't like Washington. I don't like the life here."

Although he wore a perpetual smile on his face, Hap Arnold was prone to spells of gloom, and he was engulfed in one now at the prospect of life in Washington: "It had always seemed to me—and I knew the place pretty well—that the honking traffic jams, the waiting in anterooms, clerks colliding with their stacks of papers in the endless corridors, the sharp tongues at cocktail parties confiding what they seldom really knew, were not merely the Face of Washington, but much of its Inside Story. Friends or no friends, I thought, it was no place for me."[10]

He had an exceptional flair for description, but in this event at least, very little flair for prophecy. It would be ten years almost to the day before he finally escaped Washington for good.

For only a few hours did he manage to escape the Washington social life. On the telephone that night, General Westover informed him that one of his duties would be to represent the chief at official social functions.[11] Two days later, the Arnolds were invited to a white-tie affair at the home of General Craig.

"What are you going to do about that?" Bee asked Hap.

"I won't go," he said.

"You can't turn down Malin Craig."

"No, I guess I can't," he admitted. For the first time in his life he went out and bought white tie and tails. He was destined to give the outfit a lot of wear.

In his new job, Arnold found himself dealing with matters a good deal more complex than the operational procedures he had been helping to develop as a wing commander in the G.H.Q. Air Force. "The War Department, Congress, appropriations, public opinion, the definition of our program when nobody—not even the G.H.Q. Air Force —had any real program at all; the headaches of 'defending' our accident rate against the newspaper agitation begun at the time of the air mail disasters back in 1934, all became my problems as Assistant Chief of the Air Corps."

In addition, there was the problem of conflicting loyalties. He felt "a certain amount of embarrassment" because he was now "ranged with the Air Corps Headquarters, across the fence from the G.H.Q. Air Force." Despite his previous loyalty to G.H.Q., he soon learned that the Air Corps needed both sides, and that the two had better be brought back together as quickly as possible. Air Corps people had enough of a struggle against the appropriations inroads of the Army ground forces and the Navy without wasting their energies fighting each other. One of the first campaigns in which Arnold became embroiled was the effort to keep the War Department from using up a large portion of the Air Corps appropriations to buy short-range support planes, the kind Hugh Drum favored, for the Infantry. The stakes in this battle were high. It involved the very concept for which Air Corps men had been fighting since the days of Billy Mitchell, the concept which Douhet and Trenchard and the brilliant young strategists at Maxwell Field had been painstakingly refining for several years. If the Air Corps allowed itself to become primarily an Infantry support unit, the whole dream of building a long-range striking force would be shattered and the revolutionary new B-17 Flying Fortress on which airmen had based so many hopes might as well fly directly to the scrap heap.

In later life, Arnold felt that the development of the four-engine bomber represented "a turning point in the course of air power—of world power." And the B-17 seemed to him in recollection "the first real American Air Power . . . Air Power that you could put your hand on." But there is conflicting evidence about his attitude toward the B-17 during the early efforts to procure it in significant numbers for the Air Corps.

The B-17 was the first American airplane to help fulfill Billy Mitchell's dream of a long-range bombing fleet. The construction of the Barling bomber, which he inspired, was an earlier attempt to fulfill that dream. It failed because the air technology of the 1920s was not sufficiently advanced to create what Mitchell wanted. Ironically, it was Mitchell's most outspoken critic in the Air Corps, Benny Foulois, who finally got his cherished project off the ground.

In the spring of 1934, with aircraft technology becoming increasingly sophisticated, Foulois had cajoled the General Staff into approving the construction of a four-engine bomber that had an anticipated range of 5,000 miles, and could carry a ton of bombs at 200 miles per hour. He could never have sold the ground force generals on the notion that such a plane was needed to protect the United States itself, but he convinced them it would be useful in protecting two vital American territories —Alaska and Hawaii.

The Boeing Aircraft Company in Seattle submitted plans for such a plane, but there was some doubt that the Air Corps would be allowed to grant Boeing a contract because in 1932, when Franklin D. Roosevelt was running for president, the company would not allow him to enter its plant and address its employees, even though Republican candidates were allowed to do so. Many people in Washington believed that the

Roosevelt administration and the Democratic Congress would prevent the Air Corps from doing business with Boeing.[12] This belief proved unfounded and the Air Corps hired Boeing to build a four-engine bomber, which was eventually designated the XB-15 ("X" meaning experimental).

In August 1934, the Boeing, Martin, and Douglas aircraft companies all entered competition to create another plane, which, the Air Corps specified, should be able to carry a ton of bombs at 250 miles per hour, but with the much shorter range of 2200 miles. A year later, Boeing's Model 299, a four-engine, all-metal craft with five gun emplacements, which was a smaller but much improved variation of the XB-15, flew nonstop from Seattle to Wright Field in Dayton to compete against the Martin B-12 and the Douglas B-18, both twin-engine planes with limited capabilities. No Air Corps officials were on hand to see the Boeing entry land at Wright Field because it arrived two or three hours earlier than expected. It had cruised from Seattle at 233 miles per hour.

The competition was decided almost before it began. The Boeing 299 was a handsome machine, so big it made the other planes look puny. It could carry much larger loads farther and faster. It was also easy to fly. And it was so well armed that a newsman dubbed it the "Flying Fortress." As its modifications began, the 299 became the Y1B-17, and eventually, with several improvements, the celebrated B-17. But before that happened, there was a lot of travail.

On October 30, 1935, Maj. Ployer P. "Pete" Hill, chief of the Wright Field Flight Testing Section, decided he would fly the new Model 299, which his primary test pilot, Lt. Donald L. Putt, had successfully conducted through its competitive testing. Putt went along as copilot that morning, and Boeing test pilot Les Tower went along as an observer.[13]

When Hill took the plane off the ground, it had barely become airborne before it fell off on one wing and crashed. Hill was killed immediately. Tower later died of his injuries. Putt survived with a deep gash on his head. The cause of the accident was easy to determine. Boeing's Model 299 was the first plane built with internal locks on its aileron, rudder, and elevator controls. But in those days, as Putt later explained, "we didn't have any check lists. You got in, just as if it were an automobile, stepped on the starter and took off." Major Hill had taken off with the elevator control locked.

Though it would seem obvious that the plane should not be blamed for such an accident, people around Wright Field began to talk about it being "too big for a man to handle," and people in Washington, especially Navy people, who had always argued that the long-range bomber was a foolish waste of money, advertised the tragedy as sufficient proof that they were right. As a result of such uncertainty, the Boeing 299 was suddenly eliminated from the competition it had already won, and the Air Corps, on November 8, 1935, decided to buy eighty-two Douglas B-18s. The future Flying Fortress was now almost dead, but not quite. On January 17, 1936, Boeing was awarded a contract to build thirteen Y1B-17s, and the first one reached Langley Field near Washington on March 1, 1937.[14]

Between then and June 30, 1939, more than two years later, the Air Corps purchased only one additional B-17. Inasmuch as this airplane became the Corps' most powerful weapon during the entire war in Europe, such a delay in its procurement and development must seem difficult to fathom. But the reasons for the delay are traceable.

The closer the long-range bomber came to actuality, the stiffer became the opposition to it in the Army ground forces and in the War Department. Money for the military was scarce at the time, and the General Staff understandably didn't want to see a huge chunk of it spent on an idea that had never been tested in a real war. On May 28, 1936, for instance, Westover and Arnold presented to the War Department a request that fifty B-17s and eleven other "ultra-long-range" four-engine bombers be included in the budget for 1938. A week later, on July 6, Westover received a directive from the adjutant general that said: "The 11 Project 'A' [ultra-long-range] and the 50 Boeing 4-engine type aircraft now included in the Rearmament and Reequipment Program Fiscal Year 1938 will be eliminated and a standard 2-engine model substituted therefor in equal numbers. By order of the Secretary of War."

At that time, the secretary of war was Harry H. Woodring, who believed the nation's only military need was to defend its shores. But Woodring did not reach this decision without guidance from the chief of staff, who was Arnold's friend Gen. Malin Craig. A General Staff study, dated June 16, 1936, by Brig. Gen. George R. Spaulding, assistant chief of staff, and endorsed July 2 by Maj. Gen. Stanley B. Embick, deputy chief of staff, undoubtedly with Craig's approval, shows how Craig actually felt about long-range air power at that time and how little influence Arnold had managed to exert upon him. The concluding section of the study said:

a. Until the international situation indicates the need for [such] long-range types of bombardment aviation as the Project A and the 4-engine [Boeing] models, no more of that type should be procured except for experimental purposes.

b. That a medium range bombardment type such as the B-18 model will fulfill all reasonable military requirements and can be justified from the standpoint of initial cost, maintenance, expense and operating facilities.

On August 3, 1936, Secretary of War Woodring further instructed Westover that he shouldn't order the B-17s already included in the budget for fiscal 1937 until the thirteen planes due for delivery by the Boeing Company in 1937 had been received and tested. Arnold wrote a memorandum, dated September 11, 1936, recommending that at least twenty of the planes originally included in the 1937 procurement program be ordered without delay, but this recommendation was approved only with the same paralysing stipulations. The War Department had now begun a long series of delays and limitations that prevented the procurement of any more than the original fourteen Flying Fortresses until the latter half of 1939, when Hitler's invasion of Poland was imminent.

Did Arnold fight for the B-17 with his usual dynamism during this delaying action? Col. Hugh Knerr, who was then chief of staff of the G.H.Q. Air Force under Andrews, didn't think so.[15] Andrews himself had gone public in his campaign for the B-17, and Knerr, as his spokesman, was "carrying on the battle" before the budget committee of the War Department. Knerr later recalled that at several of the meetings, Arnold, as assistant chief of the Air Corps, sat at the table with the General Staff officers.

"Arnold would come in as an observer," Knerr said, "and the argument that I was carrying on got pretty hot and heavy. I looked toward Arnold for a little support but I got none. I personally believe it was because he had ambitions and he didn't want to get in the wrong."

Knerr's feelings in the matter could have been colored by his resentment of the fact that Arnold had been the only flier to win proper recognition for the 1934 Alaska flight. Knerr might also have felt that Arnold, when he left the G.H.Q. Air Force to become assistant chief of Air Corps, had defected to the enemy and had thereafter lost sight of the G.H.Q.'s needs. And Knerr definitely disagreed with testimony Arnold offered before a congressional committee in July 1936 that the Air Corps was not yet ready to become a separate air force. All of these factors may have contributed to Knerr's bitter belief that Arnold was not vigorous enough in his early support of the B-17 program. But Knerr was not alone in that belief. Gen. Orval Cook, then a major stationed at West Point, has recalled that Arnold, as assistant chief, entertained some fear that the B-17 program might eat up too much of the meager budget allotted to the Air Corps. Arnold wondered aloud to Cook, during one of his visits to West Point, whether the corps, in committing itself to the B-17, might be putting "too many eggs in one basket."

Arnold's close association with General Craig (they had become regular golf partners in Washington) must have conditioned him to some extent in the matter. He knew how to practice the art of the possible and he was developing some notion of how far he dared go in opposing his superiors. He may have argued privately with Craig about the B-17, but it is not surprising that he failed to dispute publicly Craig's decision to put the plane on ice, since it was Craig who had put him in the job he held. Arnold admitted in his memoirs that no one in the Army ground forces believed in long-range air power during the period between 1936 and 1938:

> . . . there were no responsible quarters, either, who still doubted that the airplane had become an indispensable weapon. But that meant as direct troop support, aerial reconnaissance for the ground forces, communications and transport. Bombardment on its own, to some extent—yes. But the twin-engined B-10s and B-12s seemed good enough for that. No powerful sympathy for the "independent air mission"—the kind of strategic air campaign which the B-17s and B-24s over Germany, and the B-29s over Japan were to carry out—existed in the War Department.[16]

He seemed to be admitting in that passage that his own arguments for the "independent air mission" had not budged his friend Craig, who was commanding the Army.

From the Navy, the Air Corps' "independent mission" was receiving even less sympathy. The Navy felt that any money being spent on long-range bombers might better be spent on battleships or even carriers, which were now getting some Navy attention. And the Navy had the ear of President Roosevelt, its onetime assistant secretary. Roosevelt was not yet at this time an air-power advocate.

There were two ways Navy people could have looked at the long-range heavy bomber. They could have seen it as a support weapon for their fleet, a land-based naval gun that could strike an enemy fleet hundreds of miles away. Or they could have looked upon it as an

altogether uncontrollable weapon that threatened their fleet and si-
phoned money from their annual budget. As it happened, Navy people
chose the latter view, because to choose the former view would have
been to admit that the long-range bomber, in *enemy* hands, could be an
effective weapon against the American fleet. Therefore they had to
pretend it wouldn't work.

This explains the Navy attitude about all the Air Corps tests,
beginning with those Billy Mitchell conducted in 1921, proving that
planes could sink battleships. Each time airplanes sank a battleship,
Navy publicists and supporters would raise its soul from the depths on a
tide of evasive words.

Until the B-17 actually appeared, the long-range heavy bomber had
been only a paper threat, but the Navy, having fared so badly against the
short-range bomber, was wary of it. On August 13, 1937, Lt. Col. Robert
Olds of the G.H.Q. Air Force, leading a flight of three B-17s (Capt.
Curtis LeMay was the navigator), located the battleship *Utah*—despite
foggy weather—in the Pacific during a controlled operation and soaked
her decks with water-filled "bombs." The Navy response to that performance was to classify the whole exercise "Secret," with the cooperation of the War Department, which shared the Navy's antipathy to the
long-range bomber.

Then on May 12, 1938, three B-17s in an Air Corps exercise in the
Atlantic, again led by Olds, took off from New York's Mitchel Field,
pinpointed the Italian liner *Rex* 625 miles at sea, and photographed it.
The Navy response to that performance soon reached the Air Corps
through General Craig. The very next day, May 13, 1938, Craig phoned
General Andrews to inform him that thereafter, the Air Corps would
limit its operations to an area within one hundred miles of the continental coast.

This was not actually a new rule. It had been promulgated by the
War Department on September 1, 1936,[17] at the apparent insistence of
the Navy, but no one in the Air Corps had paid it any attention until
Craig's verbal order was handed down in May 1938. Though that order
was never put on paper, it was rigidly enforced by the General Staff,
thus relieving the Navy, for some time at least, from further embarrassment by the Air Corps' long-range bombers.

The Air Corps' most outspoken advocates of long-range bombing
and an independent air force did not fare well at the hands of General
Craig. In February 1938, General Andrews was brought to Washington
and told that his G.H.Q. Air Force staff would thereafter be appointed
by the General Staff. Colonel Knerr was reduced in rank and eventually

"retired" from the Army. Lt. Col. George Kenney was sent to Fort Benning, Georgia, as an Infantry instructor. And Lt. Col. Joseph McNarney was transferred to an Air Corps post on the West Coast.[18]

In March 1939, Andrews was relieved of his G.H.Q. Air Force command, thus losing his rank as a temporary major general and reverting to the rank of colonel. He was sent to San Antonio as air officer of the Eighth Corps Area. Shortly thereafter, the G.H.Q. Air Force fell into virtual disuse.

Meanwhile, Westover and Arnold, working quietly within the establishment, were making no more progress than Andrews and Knerr in the cause of long-range bombers. In a May 13, 1938, letter to the assistant secretary of war, Arnold made a modest request for the development and procurement of an experimental pressurized-cabin bomber during fiscal 1939 and 1940. He got his answer on August 6 in a memorandum from the adjutant general:

> No military requirement exists for the procurement of an experimental Pressure Cabin Bomber in Fiscal Year 1939 or Fiscal Year 1940 of the size and type described. . . . Experimentation and development for F.Y.s 1939 and 1940 will be restricted to that class of aviation designed for the close support of ground troops and for the protection of that type of aircraft such as medium and light aircraft, pursuit and other light aircraft.

By that time, General Embick had already summarized for General Westover the General Staff's position on air power. National policy, he reminded Westover, focused on defense, not aggression. Defense of the seas beyond the coast was the Navy's function. The military superiority of large planes over small ones still had not been proved. Therefore, the Air Corps needed no plane larger than the B-17, and only a few of those, to reinforce Panama and Hawaii.[19]

When the Arnolds came to Washington in 1936, they had rented a house at 103 Bradley Lane in Chevy Chase. Hap's days at the Munitions Building were long, and when he came home, tired and often irritable from his frustrating attempts to "do business," as he called it, with the Navy, G.H.Q. Air Force, or General Staff, Bee would make him an Old Fashioned, which he liked as much for its sweetness as its whiskey. He drank only sparingly, but he still couldn't resist sweet desserts, and he had to fight a tendency to put on weight. Though Hap sometimes spoke of his ulcers, David, at least, thought of them as something out of the past, something from which he no longer suffered. He continued to fly enough to earn his flight pay, but he no longer had time to fly regularly. He seemed always to be on the go, and as soon as he did get home at night, the phone would begin to ring. The problems he was encountering in his work would sometimes provoke him into minor explosions, but Bee would caution him and his temper would quickly subside.

He would occasionally get out and play baseball on a Saturday or Sunday afternoon with David, who was in grammar school, and they would work together on model airplanes in the evenings. Prompted perhaps by a realization that he had never been close enough to his older children, Arnold made genuine attempts to get close to his youngest son; but at the same time he maintained strict discipline, and David was not completely comfortable with him. The fact was, the boy had seen so little of him through the years he felt he hardly knew him.[20]

Arnold's family problems with the older children seemed to be working out to his satisfaction by the summer of 1938. Hank was preparing for his third year at West Point. Bruce, after some difficulties adjusting to Washington schools, was set to enroll at the Naval Academy in Annapolis, which his father, despite the Air Corps-Navy contention, considered the next best thing to West Point. And the previous Thanksgiving Lois had married a handsome Navy flier, Ens. Ernest M. Snowden, and they were living in San Diego, where he was stationed.

Arnold had suffered through some stormy episodes with Lois. When the Arnold family had arrived in Washington at the beginning of 1936, she had enrolled in a secretarial school at her father's insistence. She wanted to return to California, where she had been promised a job at Consolidated Vultee Aircraft Company, but he said she could go only after she finished her course. With this incentive she worked hard and graduated from the school in six months. Then she left for San Diego in the summer of 1936, after a dramatic farewell to Washington from the door of the DC-3 airliner on which she was to travel. Standing at the top of the stairs, with the family looking up and waving goodbye, she launched into a long speech about the goddamned city of Washington and what a horrible place it was. "Thank God I'm out of it now," she concluded.

"Get the hell on that airplane!" her father shouted, and away she went.

At Consolidated in San Diego she became assistant editor of the plant newspaper, and it was there she met Ernie Snowden, who, like her father, was a dashing military aviator, but unlike her father, was a heavy drinker. Nothing could have suited her better. After their marriage they set up housekeeping in a spacious apartment, where Hank visited them in the summer of 1938. He soon found that any hope that Lois had settled down was at least premature. Ernie was at that time flying a catapult plane off the cruiser *Indianapolis,* which operated out of San Diego harbor, and he was able to spend most of his nights at home. The Snowdens, Hank discovered, held a party every night. The drinking was so heavy and the noise so loud that the police would sometimes drop in uninvited, but Ernie always seemed able to charm them. Or at least almost always. One night, his commanding officer, a party guest, was arrested, and the Snowdens, to avoid the same fate, had to flee up the coast to Laguna Beach. But they were back home the next night for another party.

One day while flying, Ernie ran out of gas and made a forced landing in the ocean. When the Navy informed Lois that his plane was down at sea, she sought immediate solace from a bottle. Ernie was rescued and returned home at 2:00 a.m., whereupon they drank together until dawn, when he went off to fly again. For Hank, it was a sobering summer.[21]

In the summer of 1938, a change occurred in the Army General Staff that was auspicious not only for Arnold and for air power, but for the entire nation in the years that followed: Brig. Gen. George C. Marshall became assistant chief of staff. Marshall was not at that time an air-power advocate, but he was a man with such remarkable insight and such an open, probing, all-encompassing mind that Arnold knew he now had a potential ally, or at least a man to whom he could "talk business." No one had to tell Arnold about the qualities of this unique soldier. Here was the same George Marshall of whom Arnold had said, in the Philippines in 1914, "That man will one day be the Army Chief of Staff."

Arnold said later that when Marshall arrived "he needed plenty of indoctrination about the facts of air life. The difference in George, who presently was to become one of the most potent forces behind the development of a real American air power, was his ability to digest what he saw and make it a part of as strong a body of military genius as I have ever known."[22]

Arnold's evaluation of Marshall's military genius is one that many military experts now share. Perhaps because he did most of his work during World War II behind a desk, Marshall has never received the public recognition he deserved. But when military men speak of him, they often lower their voices in respect.

It would, however, be interesting to know precisely what Arnold meant by the phrase, "the difference in George." The difference in George as opposed to whom? To Arnold's friend Malin Craig? It was perhaps admirable in Arnold that he did not publicly criticize his friends, and indeed, friendship aside, it is never easy for a brigadier general to criticize the chief of staff; but the result was that Arnold appeared sometimes to agree with a man whose views he didn't actually share. In the above passage he seemed to admit tacitly that his "indoctrination" of Craig hadn't taken hold. In his memoirs he wrote: "Looking at things as they were in 1936–38, how did our little Army Air Corps stand in relation to the air power of other countries as the war clouds took definite shape? . . . To be realistic, we were practically non-existent."

In early 1938 the Air Corps had no more than 1,650 officers and 16,000 enlisted men. Aside from thirteen B-17s, not all of which were yet delivered, its best bombers were the already obsolete B-10s and B-12s, plus a few B-18s, which were so inadequate they should never have been ordered. And its best fighter was the Boeing P-26, a slow, open-cockpit craft with fixed landing gear.

At about this time or shortly thereafter Arnold began to work seriously on the conversion of General Craig to the urgent cause of air power. Col. James H. Burns, an aide to Assistant Secretary of War Louis Johnson, and, like Arnold, a golfing partner of General Craig, remembered later one Sunday morning when the three men were forced to interrupt their game because of rain.[23] Arnold and Burns, who shared his feelings about the need to build up the Air Corps, jumped at this opportunity to talk to Craig while he was away from his earthbound staff. They took him down to "an obscure office in the Munitions Building" and talked airplanes to him for as long as they could get him to sit still. He seemed to weaken but they couldn't claim all the credit for that. With Hitler becoming ever more ominous in Europe, and waving his shiny new air force in the faces of everybody he wanted to intimidate, the American public was becoming so air-minded that even Craig and the General Staff were bound to feel the influence eventually. And when Hitler began to threaten Czechoslovakia in the summer of 1938, all of Washington suddenly noticed the imminent danger of a war in Europe.

Among those who were impressed by the German aggression was Harry Hopkins, President Roosevelt's closest adviser and one of the most important men in town. On September 12, Hopkins and Roosevelt were in an automobile in Rochester, Minnesota, where Roosevelt's son James was undergoing surgery, and were listening by car radio to a giant Nazi Party rally in Nuremberg. After hearing Hitler's harangue and his unveiled threats, Roosevelt snapped off the radio, turned to Hopkins, and told him to go looking immediately for new aircraft-factory sites on the West Coast. "The President was sure then," Hopkins later wrote, "that we were going to get into war, and he believed that air power would win it."[24]

Though Hopkins seemed to indicate that Roosevelt had simply changed his mind about air power after hearing Hitler's speech, the truth wasn't quite that simple. Hitler's rapid buildup of the German air force had made Roosevelt as air-minded as everyone else and Hopkins's own arguments had further influenced him. When Hopkins and Arnold got together after Hopkins's quick trip to the West Coast, Arnold had to do very little "indoctrinating." Hopkins was already with him, and perhaps a little ahead of him. He believed that the funds allotted to the Works Progress Administration, a Depression relief agency of which he was the director, could and should be diverted to the construction of new aircraft factories. Arnold, without disagreeing, pointed out also that the current painstaking, plane-by-plane mode of aircraft production would have to be changed, that the manufacturers would have to be persuaded to install production-line methods.

While Hopkins went back to Roosevelt with all the ideas they had exchanged, including some vague notions about the number of planes the nation might need, Arnold continued working on Craig during their golf games and whenever else he could talk freely to him.

Arnold was now functioning much of the time as acting chief of the Air Corps, because General Westover liked to get away from Washington to find out what was happening at his installations around the country and at the various aircraft factories with which the Air Corps was already doing some business. Though Westover enjoyed flying and insisted on piloting his own single-engine plane, accompanied only by a mechanic, many people in the Air Corps worried about him because he had started out as a balloon flier and had washed out several times before he earned his wings as an aircraft pilot. He was well liked and highly respected as an administrator but not considered a very good pilot.[25]

On September 21, 1938, while flying into Lockheed's Burbank, California, airfield, he made too low an approach and crashed at the end of the runway. The plane burst into flames, killing both Westover and his mechanic.

Capt. K. B. Wolfe, an Air Corps officer and engineering expert who was at the scene, called Arnold immediately with the tragic news.

It was a double shock to Arnold, first of all because Westover had become a valued friend, and second because he now found the entire weight of the Air Corps resting upon him until a new chief was named. And there was an excellent likelihood that he would be the new chief. But as the days passed with no announcement of his appointment, that likelihood seemed to fade.

There were, of course, other candidates, the most prominent of whom was Frank Andrews. Arnold had the highest respect for "Andy" and would gladly have served under him. At home one night, when his son Bruce mentioned that some people seemed to think Andrews should have the job, Arnold said, "Hell, I think Andrews should have the job."[26] But there was no announcement of Andrews's appointment, either. Then rumors began coming out of the White House to the effect that the president was holding up Arnold's appointment because someone had told him Arnold was an alcoholic. Supposedly he had gotten drunk and publicly disgraced himself while stationed in Hawaii. In fact, he had never been stationed in Hawaii, and since his apparent ulcer attack in 1920, he drank only occasionally, and then sparingly. Who could have told the president such a thing? The only person who was close to the president and also knew Arnold well was the president's military aide, Col. Edwin M. "Pa" Watson, a popular officer whom the President enjoyed because he was an excellent raconteur.

Watson and Arnold had been classmates at West Point until Watson was held back from the 1907 to the 1908 class. He had some academic difficulties that might have flunked him out were it not for his popularity with faculty and fellow students. For reasons that remain obscure, he did not like Hap Arnold and he didn't hesitate to say so. Many of their mutual acquaintances assumed, therefore, that he was the author of the slander against Arnold, but this has never been established positively, and it is possible that Watson was quite innocent. Some people believed the drinking rumor arose from a remark by *Army and Navy Journal* editor John Callan O'Laughlin in a letter to General Pershing. In any case, however the rumor may have arisen, it quite naturally damaged Arnold in the eyes of the president.

Arnold was still in limbo on September 28 when he was invited to a White House meeting called by the president.[27] On this date, British Prime Minister Neville Chamberlain was already in Munich, preparing to appease Hitler by bestowing Czechoslovakia upon him. With that in mind, Roosevelt urgently called to his office Secretary of War Woodring,

Secretary of the Navy Charles Edison, Secretary of the Treasury Henry Morgenthau, and their assistants; General Craig and his new deputy, George Marshall; Adm. Harold L. Stark, the Navy chief; Colonel Burns, acting as a War Department aide; Arnold as acting chief of the Air Corps; and perhaps most important of all, Harry Hopkins, who had met with Arnold several additional times since their first exchange of ideas.

Arnold was one of the few people in the room not surprised by what the president said that day. He and Hopkins had been saying much of it to each other during their meetings. And Hopkins had fully briefed him on the purpose of this meeting.

Roosevelt began by saying he had read the War Department's report on a proposed expansion of the ground and air forces, and he wasn't satisfied with it. A new Army post in Wyoming would not, in his opinion, scare Adolf Hitler one goddamned bit. What he wanted was airplanes. It was airplanes that would have an influence on Hitler.

Edison, Stark, Woodring, and Craig were taken aback by this outburst but quickly recovered and began to press for their own needs. If the country must have more airplanes, it must also have a bigger Army and Navy.

He hadn't called them in, the president said, to talk about the Army and Navy. They were there to talk about airplanes and how to get them. Aircraft factories would have to be enlarged and assembly-line methods inaugurated. The existing procurement bill would have to be changed and contracts arranged on a cost-plus basis so that manufacturers would be assured of fair profits as an incentive.

He then called on Arnold for an assessment of foreign aircraft strength, and Arnold estimated that France had only 600 serviceable military planes; England, between 1,500 and 2,200; Italy, 2,000 first-line planes and 1,000 second-line. But Germany, he said, had 6,000 combat planes plus 2,000 in reserve.

Arnold also pressed home the point that a large number of airplanes did not necessarily indicate air power. "The strength of an air force cannot be measured in terms of airplanes only," he said. "Other things are essential—productive capacity of airplanes, of pilots, of mechanics, and bases from which to operate. A sound training program is essential to provide replacements." And there would have to be a large, continuous flow of replacements, both machines and men.

It seemed to Arnold that the president understood all this, but what he kept talking about was airplanes, not pilots or schools or air bases. In addition to the mere 178 planes provided in the 1940 budget, he wanted another 10,000, which would cost, in his estimate, $300 million. And he wanted the factories enlarged to a capacity of 20,000 planes per year, because Hitler's potential enemies, especially France and England, would soon be desperately eager to buy planes from the United States.

Arnold, suddenly alarmed at the prospect of having 10,000 planes and not enough fields to keep them or pilots to fly them, suggested immediate expansion of the Air Corps to 7,500 combat planes plus 2,500 training planes. In this plan the president concurred.

Arnold was elated at the end of this meeting. He and Colonel Burns virtually hustled General Craig into a car and drove him to Arnold's office for what Arnold called "a get-rich-quick course in the elements necessary to make an air force." Though they had both been working on Craig for some time, he had not been fully converted until that day. But the president had shaken him mightily and forced him to see the light. "He [Craig] was a very apt pupil and from then on until his tour was completed," Arnold later recalled, "fought for our program."

On September 29, 1938, the day after that crucial White House meeting, Arnold was named chief of the Air Corps. Perhaps he had done himself some good with his performance before the president. But the steadfast support of General Craig, who had fought for his appointment despite their long-standing private disagreement about air power, and the relatively new but powerful support of Harry Hopkins, had not hurt his cause.

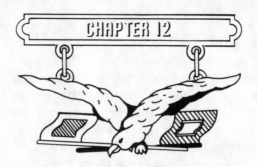

CHAPTER 12

A fter he took over as chief of the Air Corps, Hap Arnold could understand why his predecessor, Oscar Westover, had spent so much of his time away from Washington. The responsibility of running even the skeleton corps then in existence was enough to make any man want to get out of town. And the newly revealed possibility of building the corps into a real air force with the support of Roosevelt's urgent enthusiasm was bound to complicate the job rather than simplify it. The likelihood of large appropriations for the anticipated expansion soon attracted an endless number of government agencies—all of them, eager for a piece of what Arnold called "the Air Corps pie,"[1] telling him how much they loved the corps and how essential they were to its welfare.

But before there were any tangible signs of a feast, there was a surprising sign of continuing hunger. On October 5, 1938, the adjutant general sent Arnold a War Department budget memorandum which said "4-engine bombers will not be included in the estimates for FYs [Fiscal Years] 1940 and 1941."[2]

This meant either that Secretary Woodring, openly unsympathetic to Air Corps expansion, hadn't heard a word the president said at that historic September 28 meeting, or that he had decided to pay no attention to Roosevelt's orders, or that he assumed the money for Roosevelt's air force would come not from the Army budget but directly from the U.S. Treasury.

Oddly enough, the latter would not have been a farfetched assumption. President Roosevelt's perception of Hitler's intentions, and the dire consequences to America if Hitler were to conquer Europe, had brought him to the conviction that the United States must find ways to intervene against German aggression. But with American isolationist sentiment so strong, especially in the western part of the country, it would have been politically dangerous for him to declare openly for intervention. If he wanted to help Hitler's potential enemies he would have to do so by subtlety and subterfuge.

There was, it seems in retrospect, a certain degree of subterfuge in the initial aircraft production program he had proposed. It was not

186

altogether accidental that he had spoken mostly of aircraft, almost ignoring the need for bases, pilots, and technicians. He was expecting the British and French to provide many of the men and facilities these planes would require; in his mind, it was more urgent to produce planes for England and France than to build up American air power. He knew that if he wanted to expand American aircraft production, he would have to pretend he was doing it simply to strengthen American air defenses. He obviously did want to increase American air power, but as subsequent events proved, he wanted first to strengthen France and England in the hope that they could handle Hitler, thus relieving the United States of the necessity ever to do so.

Hap Arnold, new in his job and only recently acquainted with the president, could hardly be expected to perceive immediately the Byzantine workings of the Roosevelt mind. Arnold assumed that if Roosevelt said he wanted airplanes for the purpose of expanding the Army Air Corps, then that was why he wanted them. But Treasury Secretary Henry Morgenthau, a long-time observer of Roosevelt, realized that the truth was more complicated.

Roosevelt, unable to work with Woodring because of his isolationism but also reluctant to fire him for fear of arousing his isolationist friends in Congress, had turned for help to Morgenthau, who fully shared his alarm about Hitler, his new-found enthusiasm for aircraft production, and his eagerness to help Hitler's enemies. Morgenthau was delighted when Roosevelt called him to the White House on October 20 and told him he actually wanted to develop production not of 10,000, but of 15,000 planes per year.[3] He rushed back to the Treasury Building to tell his staff the good news. By this time, Morgenthau's own Byzantine mind was at work. If the increased American aircraft production was to help England and France in their coming hours of need, then the American Army Air Corps would have to be content to slow the pace of its own expansion. Was Arnold likely to understand that and accept it? Wasn't the whole matter too important to be left in the hands of an untried new major general? Morgenthau decided he himself had better learn something about the aircraft industry and the development of an air force.

He made a friendly call to the Air Corps chief, after which he said to one of his aides, "Next week I'm going to school with General Arnold."

In the meantime, Arnold, having caught Roosevelt's enthusiasm and accepted literally the aircraft figures he mentioned, had begun planning Air Corps expansion on the basis of those figures. But first he had to revolutionize the thinking of his own staff. "We had been fighting so hard and so long to get the few planes, the gasoline, the pilots, the mechanics, everything we had, that at first, even after Munich, it was difficult to get my staff to adjust their minds to a realistic plan."

Calling his staff together, he explained that because of events in Europe, it was time for them to work out an air program which would meet any eventuality. How many planes did they think would be needed?

He went around the table, asking each man. When he added up and averaged their replies, the estimate came to a mere 1,500.

The figure shocked him. He began breaking it down into various areas or possible war theaters. How many planes would be needed, he asked, to defend the Philippines? Hawaii? Alaska? Panama? The figure began to expand, but even then, the highest estimate he could get from his staff members was 7,500 planes. Already thinking in much larger terms himself, he left in his office the easel on which he had written the figure. In the years that followed, he would point to it whenever one of his men seemed to be "thinking in small terms."

One man who knew how to think in large terms without Arnold's prodding was George Marshall, assistant chief of staff until October 15, 1938, and thereafter deputy chief of staff. Marshall's influence within the General Staff had increased quickly since his assignment to it the previous summer because the quiet force of his personality and the sharpness of his reasoning were difficult to resist. Impressed by Arnold's arguments about air power, he was already telling his economy-minded General Staff colleagues that the B-12s and B-18s they had bought to save money would not be good enough to put up against planes then being built in Europe, that they would have to start buying B-17s despite their higher cost. How many B-17s? He didn't know, and when he tried to find the data needed to make an estimate, he discovered that the General Staff had no such information.[4] So he called Arnold and together they worked out what Arnold described as "an entire air plan for the War Department," a plan that, with refinements and modifications, became the basis for setting World War II requirements.

The details of this plan were reflected in a report by Arnold to Assistant Secretary of War Louis Johnson on October 27, 1938, and a memorandum from Arnold to Tooey Spaatz (then executive officer of the G.H.Q. Air Force's 2nd Wing but soon to become Arnold's planning chief), on November 17, 1938. The report to Johnson, which detailed the plans for expansion of the aircraft industry (Arnold had already gathered the company heads and told them what he expected), showed how completely the Air Corps chief had caught Roosevelt's fever. These plans envisioned "an ultimate production capacity of 40,000 airplanes per year. . . . 20,000 a year as the first objective." The maximum output of American factories at that time, Arnold said, was about 2,500 planes per year, working one shift per day. To increase that number he suggested not only enlargement of present plants and construction of new ones, but also the use of three shifts per day. The companies, most of which were on the West Coast, where labor was limited, would have to build subsidiary plants in the East, where labor was plentiful. And the government itself might have to build some plants. But remembering his procurement experience in the World War, Arnold cautioned against bringing the auto industry into aircraft production. He was still convinced that car-makers didn't understand the peculiar problems of plane-making.

In his memo to Spaatz, Arnold foresaw "10,000 airplanes . . . to be provided to the Air Corps by the end of a two-year period." Of those 10,000 planes, 2,320 (the legal limit imposed by Congress at that time) were already under order. Of the 7,680 to be procured, he expected that 2,000 would be built in government-owned plants, and the aircraft industry would provide the rest. In the fully assembled force there would be 5,620 combat planes, 3,750 trainers, and 630 miscellaneous planes.

The balance of the memo concerned itself with budget, procurement procedures, personnel, training, operations, and so forth. But nowhere in the document, or in Arnold's report to Johnson, is there mention of the possibility that the plan might fall short, or that some of the planes on which the Air Corps was counting might be sent instead to England or France. Arnold seemed at the time to be still blissfully uninformed of Roosevelt's and Morgenthau's real intentions.

Unbeknown to Arnold, Morgenthau was already negotiating with French banker and diplomat Jean Monnet, who was representing France in that country's effort to buy American military aircraft. The French, despite their somnolent Premier Edouard Daladier, were finally awakening to the fact that they might need some airplanes if they wanted to protect themselves against Hitler. And the British, despite Prime Minister Chamberlain, were beginning to realize they would need many more planes than they had.

One possible factor in awakening the French, who were now producing for themselves about forty-five military planes per month, was a series of conversations[5] on October 1 and 3 between Monnet and Charles Lindbergh, who had visited Hitler's Germany several times, and was an avowed admirer of the Germans. Having already seen the extent of Hitler's military buildup, he impressed upon Monnet the need for

France to become serious about the matter and to hasten its rearmament. A few days later, Lindbergh again went to Germany, toured several more aircraft plants, and on October 18 foolishly accepted a medal from Hitler's deputy, Hermann Goering. While Lindbergh was not very astute about politics, he understood aircraft; when he again passed through France with the story of what he had seen, M. Monnet, a man who was astute about almost everything, took his message very seriously.

Lindbergh was so overwhelmed by what he had seen in Germany that on November 2, 1938, he wrote Hap Arnold a letter from France, not exactly warning him of Germany's progress in aviation, but informing him of it:

> This is the third consecutive year during which I have had the opportunity of watching the German aviation development, and I am more impressed on each visit with the rate of their progress and the magnitude of their program. Germany is undoubtedly the most powerful nation in the world in military aviation and her margin of leadership is increasing with each month that passes. She is developing her research facilities as rapidly as she is increasing the rate of production. The design and performance of German aircraft are excellent and improving greatly each year. In a number of fields the Germans are already ahead of us and they are rapidly cutting down whatever lead we now hold in many others.
>
> My object in writing to you at this time is to tell you how essential I believe it is for us to keep in closer touch with Germany, especially in regard to military aviation. . . . I wish that you yourself could make a trip to Germany in the near future to see what is being done in that country.

As it happened, Arnold had planned a trip to Germany the previous summer for the very purpose Lindbergh mentioned, but his superiors had dissuaded him from it "for diplomatic reasons." After receiving Lindbergh's letter, he was sufficiently aroused to reopen the possibility, but, as he explained in his November 17 answer to Lindbergh, Woodring and Craig had again vetoed his plan. If Arnold had gone to Germany and the Nazis had been as boastfully open with him as they had been with Lindbergh, he might have brought back some useful information. But he would have needed forty-eight-hour days to do everything he did in the latter months of 1938 and still have time for a trip to Germany.

He was now so consumed by his job, and stayed so late at the office, that Bee and David felt like a widow and an orphan. In a letter to Lois and Ernie Hap wrote:[6] "We are quite busy, not keeping the water running but trying to keep it from running too fast. It seems that one thing is barely started [when] another comes into being."

For Christmas, Lois and Ernie came east from San Diego, Hank came home from West Point, and Bruce from Annapolis. But none of them had more than fleeting moments with their father as he hurried in and out of the house.

Finally, Bee protested. "This may be the last time we'll have the whole family together," she pointed out. She insisted that he spend the days before Christmas at home.

He agreed, and he kept his promise, but he also had a special telephone installed in his den, and there he spent his days and his evenings, so his family still saw very little of him.

Bruce was especially eager to talk to him because he had a story to tell.[7] Just before their release for Christmas leave, his whole class at Annapolis had been marched into an auditorium to hear and see a presentation by two officers.

"When you leave here," one of them said, "you'll be wearing Navy blue for the first time in public. People will ask you, 'Can an airplane sink a battleship?' We're here to tell you an airplane cannot sink a battleship."

Thereupon they unveiled a large cardboard battleship model with overlays. They ripped off one overlay of "armor" after another and each time there would be another overlay beneath it, until they finally reached the case-hardened steel hull. Perhaps airplanes had sunk some old, obsolete battleships, but no airplane could sink a modern ship like this one.

Bruce, having grown up in the Air Corps, didn't believe their story, was in fact appalled by it, but being acutely aware of his father's arguments with the Navy, couldn't wait to tell him about it. After several days at home, however, he still hadn't had a chance to mention it.

Finally he arranged to tell Hank a short version of the story, in a loud voice, right outside the door of his father's study. It was the kind of ploy Arnold couldn't resist. He came bursting out of the room bellowing, "Who the hell told you all that nonsense?"

After listening to the whole story, he rushed to his telephone and called Adm. John Towers, once a fellow student at the Wright brothers' flying school, now the chief of naval aviation. But what could Towers do other than laugh? Though he might even agree with Arnold, as a naval aviator he had no more influence over sea officers than Arnold had over ground officers.

In January 1939, Arnold's expansion plans met new complications.

With Roosevelt and his associates leaking rumors that the president would soon ask Congress for enough money to build an eight- to ten-thousand-plane Air Corps, it seemed logical to expect that the aircraft manufacturers would be happy and eager to get going. But were they? Not quite. They had become disturbed by the concurrent rumors that the government itself might build some aircraft plants. If the aircraft companies increased their capacity during the crisis and then found the government producing its own airplanes after the crisis, they might face bankruptcy. In addition, they weren't quite sure how the government defined the crisis. Already the French and English were shopping for planes. Were the companies expected simply to supply their needs, plus the eight or ten thousand planes the expanded Air Corps would want in the next two years? And what were the needs of the French and British? They were still at peace, but the danger of war was increasing. Should the American aircraft industry prepare itself only for the present and foreseeable future? For the day when the French and British might mobilize totally? For the day when the entire world, especially the United States, might mobilize totally?

The industry was not ready to move until some of those questions were answered, and Arnold didn't have the answers. When he tried to get the companies into action on his Air Corps expansion plans, he could assure them of the urgency that they start now and promise that the government would pay later. But urgency was only one of their considerations.

While Arnold was wrestling with this problem, he was hit by another shocking development. After all of Roosevelt's talk about 10,000 planes a year, he had tested the political atmosphere, then sent a special defense message to Congress on January 12, 1939, asking for only 3,000 planes. At about the same time, Arnold was informed by the General Staff that when he testified at the House hearings on War Department appropriations for 1940, he would be ordered to ask for even less money than he had requested the previous year. Only 219 new aircraft could be procured in 1940 despite the crisis in Europe, he was told, because that would bring the Air Corps to the congressionally established legal limit of 2,320 planes. Instead of expanding, his force seemed suddenly to be shrinking. The situation was now so absurd it could only be obscured by something equally absurd. And it was.

In mid-January, Arnold learned that the president, in his efforts to circumvent the deliberate sloth of Secretary of War Woodring, had signed an executive order, drafted by Treasury Secretary Morgenthau, that gave the procurement division of the Treasury Department jurisdiction over all purchasing for the Army and Navy. Morgenthau had argued that he needed such authority because Woodring and Arnold were resisting his efforts to send airplanes to France and England.

Arnold had first tasted Morgenthau's power in late December 1938, when Morgenthau, after negotiating with Monnet, had arranged for a five-man aircraft-purchasing team from France to visit the United States. Permission was necessary because of the security policy of the Joint Army-Navy Aircraft Board, which stipulated that no secret parts or devices on U.S. planes could be released to a foreign country. Morgenthau asked the Army and Navy to waive this policy for the benefit of the beleaguered French.

The Army balked. Woodring wrote to Morgenthau on December 29, 1938, that he would reveal no secrets to the French until Morgenthau could say for certain that their orders were genuine, and that allowing them to buy planes from American companies would not impede the expansion of the Army Air Corps.

Morgenthau, unable to guarantee French orders for planes they hadn't even been permitted to examine, contacted Woodring to complain that this letter had "put me on the spot."

The secretary of war in turn said he had written it because of pressure "from my own shop."

The heaviest pressure had come from Arnold, whose sympathy for the French and British did not obscure the fact that his job was to expand the U.S. Army Air Corps. Arnold's stated objection to giving the French such open access was that it violated the security policy of the aircraft board. His more serious objection arose from the fact that the French had indicated their intention of ordering 600 planes, many more than Arnold felt his Air Corps could spare. He also, though not openly, disapproved of Morgenthau's interference in a matter which only the White House and the War and Navy departments should have the power to decide.

He soon found out how the White House felt about that. On January 16, 1939, President Roosevelt summoned several Army, Navy and Treasury officials to his office. It was his desire, he said, that they give immediate assistance to the French purchasing team, which was now in California awaiting permission to examine the new, experimental Douglas 7-B light bomber at the company's Santa Monica plant.[8]

Woodring pointed out that this plane, developed partially with government funds, featured several secret components.

Assistant Secretary of War Johnson, who seldom got along with Woodring but agreed with him on this issue, asked the president if he was specifically ordering them to release the plane to the French.

Roosevelt said that was exactly what he wanted.

Morgenthau had prevailed. Arnold realized now that his Air Corps enjoyed only a secondary place in Roosevelt's plans to build aircraft. But he did not lose sight of the fact that Roosevelt was the boss. As soon as he learned of the president's direct order, he sent a telegram to a subordinate in Santa Monica, instructing him to show the plane to the French —after its secret parts had been removed.

None of this was as yet public knowledge, but a tragic mishap on January 23 launched an embarrassing exposure of the whole affair.[9] Having received Arnold's approval, Douglas officials that day arranged a flight in the experimental bomber for a member of the French mission, Air Ministry engineer Paul Chemidlin. Douglas test pilot John W. Cable was at the controls when the plane went into an inexplicable spin, four hundred feet above the Douglas plant, and crashed into the company parking lot. Ten people on the ground were injured and nine automobiles demolished. The pilot emerged from the plane before it crashed but hit the ground and was killed before his parachute had time to open.

M. Chemidlin was found in the wreckage of the plane with a broken leg and several lacerations but no serious injuries. Of much greater concern than his condition was the question of how he should be identified in news stories about the crash. Because of the vocal isolationist sentiment in the country, the visit of the French aircraft-buying mission had not been publicized. And under existing regulations, it would be difficult to explain how a representative of a foreign government had been authorized to fly in a new and secret American bomber. It was decided, either by officials on the spot, or after consultation with Washington, that the injured man in the plane should be identified as a Douglas mechanic named "Smithins." This subterfuge was effective just long enough for newsmen to get around to the Santa Monica hospital at which Chemidlin was recovering from his injuries. There was something strange about a Douglas mechanic who spoke French so fluently and English with such a pronounced accent. On the twenty-sixth, when it was no longer possible to conceal M. Chemidlin's identity, the Douglas Company issued a statement confirming it.

General Arnold, much to his regret, happened to be testifying about Air Corps needs before the Senate Military Affairs Committee when its isolationist members learned of the newspaper accounts transforming Smithins into Chemidlin. Senator Bennett Clark of Missouri, an ardent isolationist, asked Arnold if he could explain the peculiar circumstances of the crash.[10]

The War Department was aware of the French mission's presence in the country, Arnold said, and was also aware that these representatives of the French government were going to inspect the new Douglas bomber.

And whose decision was it to allow representatives of a foreign power to inspect a new, secret, experimental bomber?

That decision, Arnold indicated quite truthfully, had originated with the secretary of the treasury, but he could assure the senators that all secret equipment had been removed from the plane before the flight.

The questions now descended on him thick and fast. "Does the Secretary of the Treasury run the Air Corps?" "Does he give orders about Air Corps procurement?" There was no graceful way for Arnold to explain why Morgenthau was exercising powers that should have belonged to the War and Navy departments. He ended by raising more questions than he answered, and by explaining almost nothing. He soon wished he had explained even less.

The very next day, when Morgenthau was called to testify before the same committee, he pointed out that Arnold had signed the telegram authorizing the flight. He did not disclose that it was at his insistence, and even then only after a direct order from President Roosevelt, that Arnold had sent the telegram.

The president, in a press conference that same day, showed his annoyance at being embarrassed by the isolationists and the way his own people had handled the entire matter. Two days later he voiced his dissatisfaction to his old friend Morgenthau in a stern private session. To Arnold he said nothing at the time, but as Arnold was becoming aware, Franklin Roosevelt had a way of remembering everything.

On April 26, 1939, the president signed an appropriations bill that directed the War Department to order 571 bombers and fighters—a measure that slightly alleviated the Air Corps' scarcity of planes. But the embarrassment of the Chemidlin crash did not alter Roosevelt's and Morgenthau's intention of sending as many planes as possible to France and England. The desperate need for those planes in preparation for almost certain war against Hitler was as evident to Arnold as it was to the president, and it put both of them in a difficult situation because they shared the responsibility of building up American air power. But while that was only one of Roosevelt's responsibilities, it was Arnold's sole responsibility and therefore his first priority. He decided in this instance that the best way to serve his commander-in-chief was to resist him as much as he dared without disobeying him. He realized now that he had a lot of fighting to do before the Air Corps got enough planes with which to fight. Meanwhile he went to work getting the corps ready for the day when there would be enough planes.

It seemed to him that despite the current bottleneck, the day would eventually come when the corps would need as many as 100,000 pilots. At the moment, it was turning out only 750 per year. Even if all these graduates were to become instructors, there wouldn't be enough of them to guide 100,000 cadets through preflight, primary, basic, and advanced schools for several years to come. If he was to get the pilots trained, he would have to find instructors elsewhere. He decided that at least for primary training, he would enlist civilian flying schools throughout the country, furnish them with planes, send their instructors to Randolph Field in San Antonio for indoctrination in Air Corps methods, and then give them so much per head for each cadet they trained.

When he tried out this idea on his staff, most of them were incredulous. Lt. Col. Ira Eaker, for one, argued that such a policy would be "just plain murder,"[11] and Col. Carl Spaatz agreed with him. It was inconceivable to them that civilian instructors could teach the rudiments of military flying, which required more demanding, more daring performance and therefore much greater risk than civilian flying. They argued and pleaded with Arnold not to make such a dangerous mistake. He listened to them, then calmly announced that he intended to do it anyway.

He invited the owners of several civilian schools to Washington and when he presented his proposal to them, they were, in his words, "flabbergasted."[12] After a long conference among themselves, they sent a representative to him who said, "We might be able to do the job, but it would entail an initial expenditure of a couple of hundred thousand dollars for each school."

They would have to build barracks and mess halls and expand all their facilities. Arnold knew that. He also knew he had no authorization to provide the money for it. But within a year or so, he would have to have a steady stream of pilots, and there was no time to waste.

The suggestion he made was as risky as it was unorthodox. "You can borrow the money, can't you, until I get a congressional appropriation?"

Before the afternoon was over, he had talked them into this chancy proposition. And before World War II was over, 190,000 young Air Corps pilots (including the author of this book) had undergone their primary flight training at civilian flying schools.

Still without sufficient funds or authorization, Arnold also began ordering primary trainer planes from companies like Ryan, Fairchild, Steerman, and Stinson. From Vultee he ordered the basic trainer, BT-13, which was so noisy it was soon dubbed the "Vultee Vibrator." And from North American he ordered the advanced trainer, the AT-6. These were to become standard Air Corps training planes until the end of World War II.

In 1939, he also encouraged plans for the development of the Consolidated Vultee B-24 "Liberator," a four-engine long-range bomber that was expected to out-perform the B-17; and the Lockheed P-38 "Lightning," a beautiful, twin-engine, double-fuselage fighter that looked like two planes embracing each other.

While Arnold in Washington was scrambling for the best men and equipment he could find, some of the Air Corps' brightest strategists, notably the members of the Air Corps Board and the faculty of the Air Corps Tactical School at Maxwell Field, were wrestling with the question of how to approach an anticipated air war whose exact nature would not be known until it happened. Arnold's principal role in their deliberations was to state the problems, ask the questions. Thereafter, he encouraged these strategists—men like Harold George, Kenneth Walker, Orvil Anderson, Edgar Sorenson, and Mack Snyder—to express their most critical views on "any question that was asked, any problem that was posed." Anderson recalled that "even while Arnold was Assistant Chief, he sent down directives to the Air Corps Board, established what we were to pursue."

One key problem that had been argued informally for several years within the Air Corps was the fighter-versus-bomber controversy. In any future war, would the corps have greater need for fighters or bombers?[13] Would bombers be able to defend themselves on long missions, or would they need fighter protection? When the national policy was defensive, how was it possible to justify investment in bombers, which were patently offensive weapons? On the other hand, how could a fighter, which was primarily a defensive weapon, damage the enemy enough to help win a war? These arguments were destined to continue until the grim realities of the air war over Europe imposed a somewhat tardy and therefore expensive solution. It was a solution which did not fit the prevailing theories of 1939.

Because almost all airmen believed in the airplane as an offensive weapon, the Air Corps strategy had always been based on offense, even when the nation's psychology was defensive. The bomber, therefore, was the darling of the corps. No airmen argued that fighters were superfluous, but many thought their future was limited, especially since it was becoming apparent that the foreseeable four-engine bomber would have a much longer range than the foreseeable fighter planes. Air Corps Board members like Anderson, Sorenson, and Snyder argued, however, that these developments would not eliminate the need for fighters, but that the range of fighters would have to be increased, because unless bombers were escorted by fighters on long missions into enemy territory, the bomber losses would be prohibitive.

This proved to be a minority opinion. The bomber advocates tended to disagree with it because they were imbued with the doctrine that the bomber would always get through. And fighter advocates, of whom Arnold's old friend "Miff" Harmon was a leader, took exception because they didn't believe the range of fighter planes could be significantly lengthened without sacrificing combat performance. Increased gas loads and decreased ammunition loads, for instance, would lengthen the range of fighters, but a shortage of ammunition would make them vulnerable to enemy fighters, and the extra gas would make them more flammable when hit. The fighter advocates at Maxwell Field argued, therefore, that it would be useless to send fighters all the way with the bombers because they wouldn't be able to protect the bombers when they got there. The bombers, they argued, should be armed to protect themselves.

This argument prevailed in 1939, and for more than three years thereafter, because the technological limitations of the time made it difficult to refute. The result was the development of bombers that bristled with guns but because of this excess weight were limited in their bomb loads; and the development of fighters with ranges so short they could escort the bombers only for pathetically inadequate distances. Arnold would one day be plagued by the fact that he accepted the majority view of his strategists on this question.

With Hitler preparing to occupy Czechoslovakia (which he did on March 16, 1939), while France and England finally scrambled for weapons to resist him, the danger of war in Europe was increasing daily. And in Washington, confusion reigned as the American armed forces struggled to expand despite the resistance of the strong isolationist faction in Congress. The clouded future made everyone in America uneasy and prone to believe rumors, especially the young men who would have to fight any war that might come.

Arnold's son Hank was now in his third year at the Military Academy, which, being part of the Army, was almost as much a rumor factory as it was a school. The rumors were piling up so fast there in the

spring of 1939 that Hank, on March 8, wrote an amusing letter to his
father in the hope of finding out, from a man in authority, what to
believe:

> We've got about 20 good "sinkoid" rumors floating around, and also
> we've heard bits about all kinds of bills up before Congress which
> may or may not directly affect us. How about this probation bill
> putting all new officers on three years probation after they
> graduate? . . . Also, how about the three year marriage rule? The
> first class [seniors] and a lot of my classmates are plenty concerned
> about that. The first class also can't quite figure out where they are
> going to get their primary flight training. We've heard about all
> primary being given at twelve civilian flying schools and only basic
> being given at Randolph. How about it, and also how will it affect the
> number that will be washed out? Next is the rumor that no men
> graduating from here after 1940 will be allowed to take Air Corps.
> Verdad, or no es verdad? [True or not true?] We got thousands of
> rumors, any kind you want.

His father was able to reassure him about only one of his rumors. In
a letter to Hank three days later, he said nothing about the civilian
primary schools. As for the three-year marriage rule: "I think it would
be a good thing. A young officer just entering the Army has a heavy
financial load to carry just to keep himself." And as for post-1940
graduates not being allowed to choose the Air Corps: "This is not even a
good rumor—you will have to do better than that. How about graduates
after 1940 not being allowed to eat lunch?"

A month later, on April 14, Hap and Bee were about to get in their
car and drive up to West Point to see Hank when they got a radiogram
from Charles Lindbergh, who was on the liner *Aquitania* approaching
New York from Europe. He would be landing that evening. Arnold,
anxious to get more details from him about the tense situation in
Europe, replied by radio that he would be spending that night at the
Fountain Inn, Doylestown, Pennsylvania. About midnight he got a call
there from Lindbergh, who had been besieged and jostled by an
unprecedented mob of newsmen and photographers when he disem-
barked. It was Lindbergh's first trip to his native land since 1935, when
he moved his family to Europe in the wake of the kidnapping and
murder of his infant son. To America and to the world he was one of the
great folk heroes of all time, but he was also an exceptionally private
man who didn't appreciate the attention and adulation that followed
him wherever he went. He wanted to see Arnold, he said, but where
could they meet without attracting a crowd?

Where better, Arnold asked, than a place as well guarded as the

Military Academy? "How about meeting my wife and me at West Point for lunch at the Thayer Hotel?"[14]

When Lindbergh arrived at noon, he found the Arnolds alone in the main dining room of the Thayer. To help preserve Lindbergh's privacy, the manager had closed the room to everyone else. For three hours Arnold listened while Lindbergh talked about the strength of Hitler's air force and what American airmen would have to face if the country were to go to war against Germany.

"Lindbergh gave me," Arnold later recalled, "the most accurate picture of the Luftwaffe, its equipment, leaders, apparent plans, training methods, and present defects that I had so far received. . . . Lindbergh felt that Hitler held the destruction of any major city on the continent, or in Britain, in his hands."

When they left the hotel, they walked over to the Plain, where the Army baseball team was playing Syracuse, and sat down in the grandstand. "For the rest of the afternoon," Arnold recalled, "while he continued to tell us about Hitler's air force, we sat unnoticed in the grandstand, surrounded by rooting cadets, and right behind a row of reporters from the New York papers, which were trying desperately to locate Lindbergh all over the East."

Later in the afternoon, the Arnolds introduced Lindbergh to their son Hank, but aside from Hank, only two cadets even noticed that the lanky, curly-haired man with the visiting general was the famous trans-Atlantic flier. Before Lindbergh's departure, Arnold asked him to serve on a board that would determine what kinds of planes the Air Corps should try to procure during the next five years. Lindbergh agreed to do so, and for the next two years, he worked with Arnold, supplying the Air Corps with valuable information about European, and especially German, aircraft. Arnold's use of Lindbergh's knowledge, at a time when the Air Corps had no intelligence-gathering agency, proved enormously advantageous in the effort to improve American planes. But it did not help Arnold in his relations with President Roosevelt, who distrusted Lindbergh, first of all, because the man had accepted a medal from Goering, and second, because he soon became a leader of the America First Committee, one of the nation's most notorious isolationist groups.

The spring and summer of 1939 gave Arnold a foretaste of the life he would live until the end of World War II. He was now embarked on a seemingly endless campaign to get more money from Congress, develop better airplanes, hasten the aircraft companies into producing them at an ever-increasing rate, build bases from which they could operate, recruit men to fly and maintain them, create schools to train these men, and choose the right officers to lead them. In 1939, he had also to prevent Morgenthau from taking away planes he desperately needed and sending them to France or England; he had to figure out, in a constantly shifting situation, just how many planes and men he did need, or would need in case of various eventualities; and he had to convince a lot of doubting people—in Congress, in the ground forces, and in the Navy—that the Air Corps actually needed long-range bombers.

All of this, unfortunately, kept him on the verge of financial distress, because while he was marvelously adept at cultivating people whose help he needed, this entailed a lot of expensive entertaining. Besides maintaining a sizable house and keeping three boys in school, he was now paying for a succession of lunches, dinners, and parties, and in those days there was no special fund to help high-ranking officers pay for social expenses connected with their work. "We had a pretty bad four years in that house [on Bradley Lane]," Bee later remarked. "Many times . . . I had no help at all and was doing all the housework. . . . A great many people came into Washington, and Hap was hospitable. 'Come out to the house. We've got a couple of guest rooms.' It was nice, but it was difficult and it was expensive."[15] It was especially difficult for Bee each summer to be in the eastern part of the country, as she still suffered dreadfully from hay fever.

In June, both Hap and Bee were distressed to learn that Bruce was leaving the Naval Academy owing to a combination of academic difficulties and general unhappiness.[16] His academic problems arose from the fact that during his boyhood years in California he had attended a school with such low standards that he could get by easily without studying. Consequently, he had never learned to study, and when he enrolled at Washington's Western High School, one of the nation's top-rated secondary schools, he was far behind his classmates and didn't know how to catch up. His general unhappiness stemmed partly from his problems in school and partly from his relationship with his father; but Arnold probably didn't realize this, as sensitivity was not one of his more prominent virtues. Bruce had always felt that his father treated him differently from the other children. He hadn't yet forgiven his father for not introducing him to Ben Lyon on the porch that day at March Field seven or eight years earlier. When, almost finished with high school, he had mentioned that he wanted to go to West Point, his father had refused to take him seriously. "You want to go there," he said, "just because your brother's there." When he enrolled in the Naval Academy, he was reenforcing within himself a feeling that he was being sent to a branch of the service his father loathed. If he was not welcome in his father's branch, it must mean that, for some reason, his father was rejecting him.

As he prepared to leave the Naval Academy, depressed and miserable, he wasn't sure what to think of himself. It seemed that whenever he had failed at something in the past, his father had said not "I'm sorry," but "What the hell are you going to do now?" Less than eager to hear that again, Bruce decided not to return to Washington.

His father, anticipating this possibility, sent an aide to see him. The aide, a captain, was sympathetic to the young man because he too had once left the Naval Academy under similar circumstances. "I'll bet you're getting ready to sign onto a ship," he said to Bruce. "That's what I almost did."

Bruce admitted it was exactly what he intended.

"You can do that if you wish," the captain said, "but you've got to face the old man sometime. It's easier to get it over with right away."

Sufficiently persuaded, Bruce returned home. His mother cried. His father bellowed, "What the hell are you going to do now?"

Nothing had changed. "I'd like to try for West Point," Bruce said.

"You can't go to West Point," his father insisted.

Having just been dismissed from the Naval Academy, Bruce could hardly argue that. He decided to go to New York, see the World's Fair, and figure out what to do with his life. The decision came quickly after he left Washington. He knew that each year some soldiers were selected through competition to attend West Point. He would enlist in the Army and, with luck, win one of the soldier appointments, then enter the academy whether his father liked it or not.

When he called home to announce proudly that he had enlisted, his father, still angry and disappointed, said, "It better not be the Air Corps."

Suddenly Bruce became just as angry. "I wouldn't be in your goddamned lousy outfit," he yelled, and slammed down the receiver.

A week later, his father, apparently feeling some remorse but not quite able to unbend enough to admit it openly, sent another officer to talk to Bruce. "He wants to know what he can do for you," the officer said.

"You can tell him," Bruce said, "that what I want him to do for me is to leave me to hell alone."

Arnold seemed to sense now that he had better back off and let the young man find his own way in the world. He may also have begun to sense that he was paying a penalty for his career, which had kept him away from his children so much of the time while they were growing up; but even if he did sense this there was very little he could do about it. His career was now taking so much of his time it separated him more than ever from his family.

In the summer of 1939, he saw Lindbergh frequently. He appointed him to the board on which Lindbergh had agreed to serve.[17] He took him to congressional hearings and introduced him to influential congressmen who needed to be told about the rising strength of Germany. He also introduced him to scientists like Dr. Vannevar Bush, and to George Marshall, who was to become Army chief of staff on September 1, when General Craig retired.

Once, after a luncheon with Dr. Bush, a distinguished electrical engineer and president of the Carnegie Institution, Arnold and Lindbergh had a few minutes to chat in Arnold's office.

Arnold said to Lindbergh, "Do you mind if I ask you a personal question?"[18]

Lindbergh said, "Go ahead."

"What are you shooting at?" Arnold wanted to know. "Have you set a goal for yourself, or do you just take life as it comes?"

Life was sufficiently complex, Lindbergh observed, without trying to foresee the future. So he seldom worked for a very distant objective. He liked to feel his way along and let life have a hand in guiding its own direction.

Arnold, after listening to this, said he felt the same way. He had never set any definite objective as his life's work.

Before that summer ended, however, he was destined to see before him a definite objective that would constitute his life's work. On the evening of August 31, Lindbergh came to his home for dinner. Arnold was alone. Bee and David were at Nag's Head, North Carolina, where the climate gave Bee at least some relief from her hay fever. Lindbergh brought with him Col. Truman Smith, who had been for four years the American military attaché at the embassy in Berlin. The three men, like most Americans that same evening, talked about the appalling situation in Europe. Hitler had now signed an alliance with Italy and a ten-year nonagression pact with Russia. And of more immediate concern, he had issued an ultimatum to Poland that was actually a demand that the Poles completely surrender. Though Arnold and Lindbergh didn't yet know it as they sat down to dinner, the Polish government, that evening, had rejected Hitler's demand. The next morning at dawn, the German army invaded Poland.

Hap Arnold's father,
Dr. H. A. Arnold.

Hap Arnold's mother,
Louise Harley Arnold.

The Arnold home
in Gladwyne, Pa.

Mrs. Hap Arnold
as a young woman,
with twin brothers
Jack and Henry
and sister Lois in
foreground,
outside the
family home in
Ardmore, Pa.

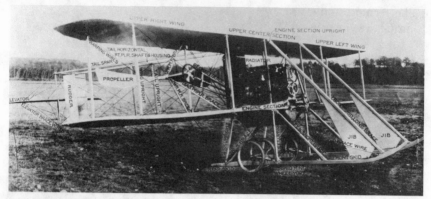

Wright B-model, with nomenclature.

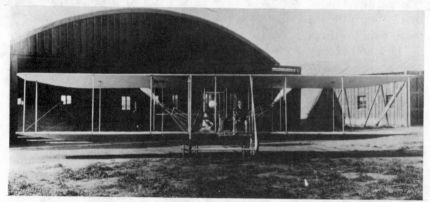

Hap Arnold in a Wright C, College Park, Md., 1912.

Hap Arnold, 1912, in
the Wright C.

Air Force bomber
drops phosphorus
bomb on the
battleship
Alabama,
1912.

Bruce, Lois, and Hank at the Presidio in
San Francisco, about 1922.

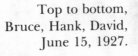

Top to bottom,
Bruce, Hank, David,
June 15, 1927.

Barling bomber that Arnold contrived to destroy in 1929.

Bruce, Hank, Hap, and Lois at air show in Los Angeles, 1932.

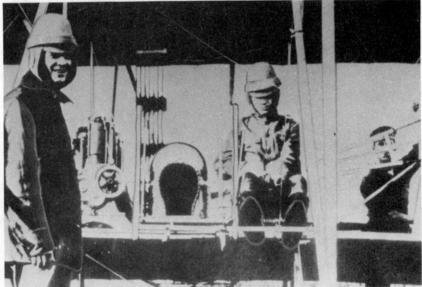

Hap Arnold and Tommy Milling, 1932 (*top*) and 1911 (*bottom*).

Hap Arnold, 1934. Taken in
Fairbanks, Alaska, at the time of
the Alaska flight.

B-10s led by Hap Arnold returning from pioneer Alaska flight, flying
over Washington, D.C., before landing at Bolling Field.

General of the Army Henry H. Arnold and Mrs. Arnold,
Washington, D.C.

Harry S. Truman presenting Distinguished Service Medal to
Hap Arnold.

CHAPTER 13

T he beginning of the war in Europe created immediate repercus-
sions in America. Among other things, it threatened to end the
shipment of all aircraft and other weapons to France and England at a
time when these Allies against Hitler needed them most. The terms of
the isolationist-sponsored U.S. Neutrality Act of 1935, and subsequent
revisions of it, prevented the sale of American weapons to any belligerent nation, whether it was an aggressor or a victim. Though President
Roosevelt had opposed the bill, he had signed it reluctantly because he
feared it reflected the will of the electorate. He was such a political
animal that the one thing to which he always paid attention was the
mood of the voters.

In 1937, when Japan invaded China, he had dodged the provisions
of the Neutrality Act and sent aid to the Chinese by calling the invasion
an "incident" rather than a war. But he could hardly pretend that the
conflict now engulfing Europe was simply an incident. As soon as France
and England declared war on Germany, he had to acknowledge that no
more planes and weapons could legally be delivered to them.

To Hap Arnold this might look like an immediate blessing, because
all the planes the French and British had ordered might now go to the
American Air Corps by default. But it was a blessing he didn't welcome.
Contrary to the impression he had created in his contention with
Morgenthau, he was in favor of sending to France and England all the
planes that could be spared. He sympathized with their cause against
Hitler, and he recognized as well that their orders had provided much of
the money that allowed the U.S. aircraft industry to expand. His quarrel
with Morgenthau concerned only the ratio of planes for the Allies and
planes for his skeletal Air Corps; he didn't want Morgenthau to send all
available planes abroad and leave him with virtually none. But neither
did he want to take for the Air Corps all the planes now being produced
for the Allies; he had neither the money to buy them nor the men to fly
them. And the Allies desperately needed them.

Fortunately, the aircraft companies and the British, with Roosevelt
pretending not to notice, worked out a subterfuge that at least alleviated

204

the problem until it could be solved. The companies began shipping their planes north to the Canadian border and leaving them precisely on the international line. British workers would then come forward and pull them across, thus technically avoiding delivery in the United States. It was a clumsy arrangement and far from satisfactory but it did permit the continuing delivery of planes during the two months it took Roosevelt to convince Congress that Hitler's victims should be allowed to buy weapons, on a cash-and-carry basis at least. When the problem of selling planes to the belligerent Allies was eliminated in early November —with the French and British needing more planes than ever—Arnold's problem of keeping a few for his Air Corps was exacerbated. If he was to succeed in his task of expanding the Air Corps, he might have to go to the mat against Morgenthau, and perhaps against the president himself.

He did, however, have an important new ally in George Marshall, who, by coincidence, had become chief of staff on the very day Hitler invaded Poland. Marshall, as deputy chief of staff under Craig, had been astonished by the attitude of his General Staff colleagues about air power. He had discovered something most airmen had known for years—that the Air Corps had almost no representation on the General Staff and that the officers on the staff had little interest in the air. "I found everyone on the Staff hostile to Air, and the young air officers were going to Congress and stirring up everything—and the [situation] was in a general muddle. They had something to complain about because they were not getting recognition."[1]

Marshall, while he was acting chief of staff, had already made one important move to correct this situation. On August 4, 1939, he had brought former G.H.Q. Air Force chief Frank Andrews to Washington from his "exile" in San Antonio, promoted him to brigadier general —thus restoring to him one of the two stars he had lost when he was sent to Texas—and appointed him assistant chief of staff for operations and training. But the recall of Andrews had not been an easy move to make because the men who had relieved him of his G.H.Q. Air Force command, presumably because of his public campaign in favor of long-range bombers, were still in control of the Army. "For the first time I can remember," Marshall later told his biographer, Forrest C. Pogue, "Woodring, [Louis] Johnson and General Craig all acted as a unit in opposing [the] action." Marshall insisted Andrews was the man he had to have, and, "after a stormy session," they finally agreed. Woodring, Johnson, and Craig were then learning something that many other people, including even President Roosevelt, would eventually discover —that while George Marshall seldom raised his voice, the force of his personality was difficult to resist. Marshall soon put Andrews to work on an Air Corps expansion plan and assigned a brilliant young major, Laurence S. Kuter, to help him with it.

After becoming chief of staff, Marshall took another step toward making ground officers air-conscious by adding the study of air power to the Command and General Staff School curriculum. And when the Air Corps study group of which Lindbergh was a member (called the Kilner Board after its chairman, Brig. Gen. Walter G. Kilner) recommended on September 1, 1939, the development of a huge bomber, which was to become the B-29 "Superfortress," Marshall enthusiastically joined Hap Arnold in endorsing it. "This establishes for the first time a special mission for the Air Corps," Marshall said.[2] His statement had pivotal significance because it was the first acknowledgment by a commanding general of the Army that the Air Corps had a distinct offensive function of its own, in addition to its responsibility for support of ground forces.

Once this concept had been accepted, the development of the B-29 was a logical and necessary step. The expanding Air Corps, in its "special mission," would eventually need a successor to the B-17; given the months and years it would take to develop such an immense and complex machine, there was no time to lose. Yet if Arnold had known in 1939 what headaches the B-29 would eventually give him, if he had known that it would one day put his entire career and reputation in jeopardy, he might have been more cautious in endorsing it.

Lindbergh's participation in recommending development of the B-29 produced an ironic twist two weeks later, when Arnold felt the need to ease him out of his Air Corps work. By this time, Lindbergh had become an avowed isolationist, and he planned to make a nationwide radio speech the evening of September 15, pleading with Americans to stay out of the European war. On the previous day he showed the speech to Arnold who tactfully suggested, after reading it, that he discontinue his Air Corps activities while he was taking part in politics.[3]

After Lindbergh left his office, Arnold may have informed Secretary of War Woodring about the speech because the next day, Lindbergh's friend Col. Truman Smith went to Lindbergh with a White House "feeler," which had descended from Woodring to Arnold to Smith.

If Lindbergh would cancel his radio speech opposing American entry into the war, Smith said, the administration would create for him a new cabinet post, "a secretaryship of air." General Arnold had felt he must pass the offer on, Smith added, because it had come from the secretary of war's office. But when Smith asked Arnold if he thought Lindbergh would accept it, Arnold had said, "Of course not."

He was quite right. Lindbergh, who already despised President Roosevelt with passion, rejected the feeler scornfully, but he retained his friendship with Arnold, whom he had come to regard as "a grand fellow."

Arnold's preoccupation with the need to create a large Air Corps soon put him in contention with Maj. Gen. Delos C. Emmons, the commander of what was left of the G.H.Q. Air Force. Emmons, who outranked Arnold, felt the G.H.Q. should be strengthened immediately so it would be ready in case the country came under attack. Arnold, who didn't anticipate an imminent attack, wanted to use the best men in the G.H.Q. to train the new men coming into the corps in ever-increasing numbers. Col. Carl Spaatz, an observer of the friction between Arnold and Emmons, remarked later that "there were only a certain number of officers in the Air Corps then, and in building up Hap's program, he had to tear down Emmons's program. In building up the training he had to tear down the tactical."[4]

Spaatz considered Emmons "a very fine man," but more conservative than Arnold. "He couldn't have done Hap's job in building up the Air Force. . . . He wouldn't have moved fast enough." It seemed to Spaatz that Emmons was expecting the Germans to come swooping down on the United States, whereas Arnold "saw that the war was going to be fought eventually in Europe, and the thing to do was to get personnel into training commands, training centers, and get the production of airplanes going and build up the Air Force."

Emmons, despite his rank, was not strong enough to stand up to Arnold, who was now attacking his job with whirlwind force, building air fields and schools, developing and ordering planes, worrying about the "bugs" in new models, pleading with Congress for more money, fighting off Morgenthau for delivery of planes, weeding out officers who didn't seem inclined to move fast enough, and trying to find out exactly what was happening in Europe, what kind of equipment and tactics the new Air Corps would have to develop if it was to match and surpass the European air forces.

To this end he increased his contacts with scientists like Vannevar Bush, Robert Millikan, C. F. Kettering, James B. Conant, Arthur Compton, Frank Lilly, and Theodor von Kármán.

One day he invited George Marshall to come to lunch with several of these distinguished men. Marshall was astonished to find himself in such company. "What on earth are you doing with people like that?"[5] he asked.

"Using them," Arnold said. "Using their brains to help us develop gadgets and devices for our airplanes—gadgets and devices that are far too difficult for the Air Corps engineers to develop themselves."

One day Arnold made a phone call to von Kármán, a California Institute of Technology physicist and aeronautical engineer, and asked him to come to Washington for a visit.[6]

"I had first met him in 1936," von Kármán recalled, "when he was commanding officer at March Field. . . . He was a stocky, broad-shouldered West Pointer with inquisitive eyes and a blunt but acute way of asking questions. . . .

"I met him again in 1938, shortly after he became Chief of the Army Air Corps, a famous meeting at which we discussed rockets as a means of assisting bomber takeoff. There was never any doubt in my mind that he was the greatest example of the U.S. military man—a combination of complete logic, mingled with a far-sightedness and superb dedication."

In 1939, Arnold's meeting with von Kármán was more urgent. The U.S. Army Air Corps would never become preeminent, he said, unless it did some experimental work to advance the art of flight. Did von Kármán have any ideas in that direction?

"In my opinion," von Kármán said, "the first step is to build the right wind tunnel. It should be large enough to contain a full-scale airplane engine installation and should be capable of generating winds of at least four hundred miles per hour."

Seeing the quizzical expression on Arnold's face, von Kármán added, "Of course, a tunnel of this size will require forty thousand horsepower. Maybe you don't wish to invest in such a large and revolutionary piece of equipment?"

"On the contrary," Arnold said, "that's exactly what we do want, the highest combination of speed and size. It's about time the Air Corps stopped begging to be allowed to catch up to other agencies and started taking the lead."

Von Kármán returned to California and with Arnold's authorization went right to work designing a twenty-foot, 40,000-horsepower wind tunnel, which was soon built at Wright Field and was the first of its kind. When it was built, its first problem was already waiting: there was an acute need, as Lindbergh had already observed,[7] for the development of better and more powerful aircraft engines.

Early in 1940, General Marshall called General Arnold and several senior Air Corps staff officers into his office to hear a presentation of the

Air Corps expansion plan on which General Andrews (as assistant chief for operations and training) and several members of his staff had been working. Arnold and most of his men were familiar with the provisions of the plan because there had been a lot of give and take between them and the Andrews staff during its development. It was basically an Air Corps dream of its own expansion. Andrews was an Air Corps man and so was Major Kuter, the project officer. But while the plan contained few if any surprises for the Air men, Marshall himself had not yet seen it, and without his approval it would never become anything more than a dream.

Kuter made the presentation, which called for a huge expansion of the corps into a fifty-four-group organization, with all the procurement of planes and equipment, construction of air fields and facilities, and recruitment of men that such an undertaking entailed. Though everyone knew by now that Marshall was more sympathetic to Air than any of his predecessors, no one was sure how he would feel about such an enormous bite out of the Army budget for a corps that had always been treated like the Army's orphan.

Marshall listened carefully without comment, and when Kuter was finished, astonished everyone by asking, "Why is this a fifty-four-group program? Why not fifty-six, or sixty-four, or more?"

After Kuter caught his breath, he said, "Sir, while presenting this program to the many agencies involved we have had to answer countless questions. Yours is the only one that has never before been asked. All others have been suggestive of less ambitious efforts." Fifty-four groups was as many as the Air Corps could accommodate within the immediate future, he explained, but it would be possible to enlarge that number later.

That was all Marshall wanted to know. "The program is approved," he said. "Let's get on with it."

If Arnold had had any doubts about Marshall's cooperation, they were eliminated that day. Kuter, recalling later the relationship between Marshall and Arnold, described it this way:

> It defied description by usual categories. There was no back-slapping, no banter or chit-chat that you'd expect between old pals. I saw them together many times and was occasionally alone with them in Marshall's car en route to meetings. They were simply two senior officers who had known each other for thirty years with mutual friendship. I never heard them call each other by nickname or first name.
>
> Without question, Arnold had great respect for Marshall. I suspect that Marshall had a lot of affection for Arnold. I never heard

them argue though they may have done so in private. Marshall was always senior but I never heard of his pulling rank over Arnold. Arnold was free to announce his intentions and plans. I never heard of him asking Marshall's permission. Theirs was a unique top-side relationship.[8]

But while Arnold now had Marshall squarely on his side, the same could not be said of Morgenthau. The embarrassing Chemidlin affair of January 1939 and the conflicting testimony by the two men over who had authorized the French representative's flight in a classified American plane had caused a breach between them, which widened as the aircraft companies concentrated increasingly on foreign orders. In February 1939, the British purchasing mission had ordered 650 planes from North American and Lockheed for $25 million. A few days later, the French ordered 615 planes from Douglas, Curtiss, Martin, and North American for $60 million. This business was enormously important in helping the companies begin an expansion that would eventually be vital to the United States. And in light of the fact that the budget for fiscal 1939 allowed the Air Corps to buy only $32 million worth of planes, the foreign orders had not at first damaged the Air Corps. But when Congress authorized an expansion to 5,500 planes, the corps found itself in serious competition with France and England for delivery of those planes. By the beginning of 1940, American aircraft companies had a backlog of $630 million in unfulfilled contracts, $400 million of which was from foreign countries.

The foreign countries, now at war, were so desperate for quick delivery they were willing to pay a bonus for it. But since the companies were producing at maximum capacity, a speedup in foreign deliveries could only come at the expense of Air Corps deliveries. In the Air Corps contracts with the companies, there was a provision for a penalty of up to fifteen percent for late deliveries. Therefore, if the French or British were willing to pay a bonus, they had to begin by reimbursing the companies for the penalties that late delivery to the Air Corps would entail. But for countries which desperately needed aircraft, an extra fifteen percent or more was an insignificant expense.

Both Arnold and Morgenthau understood all of this, though Morgenthau knew much more about the extent of foreign "bonus" payments since his Treasury coordinating committee had arranged the foreign business, and he allowed no Air Corps representatives on that committee. But Morgenthau was still not satisfied with the proportion of planes going to the Allies. On January 8, 1940, he secured Roosevelt's approval for allotment to France of twenty-five of the first eighty-one

Curtiss P-40 fighter planes the Air Corps had ordered. "I did a magician's trick for you," he told one of the French representatives. "Pulled twenty-five planes out of the hat."[9]

Four days later, after learning about the loss of those planes, Arnold carried by hand a memorandum to Secretary Woodring protesting the situation. "Certain foreign governments," his memo said, "have express-ed a desire to obtain delivery of airplanes contracted for by the Army Air Corps prior to deliveries being made to the Army Air Corps. Further, expressions have been made which indicate that in the future requests may be made to set aside work now being done on Army airplanes to expedite foreign deliveries. . . . More requests by foreign governments for the diversion of aeronautical equipment will undoubtedly be made."[10]

Arnold had two main objections to this diversion: it would delay Air Corps expansion; and if foreign countries were given top priority, his Air Corps, for some time at least, would end up with inferior planes.

But even in this protest, Arnold was careful to make two points clear: "It is very desirable to have as many foreign orders as possible placed in the United States," he wrote, "as it increases the productive capacity for airplanes, engines, and their accessories, thus making us better prepared for any emergency." And in conclusion, he reaffirmed his loyalty to the commander in chief. "Should a decision be made by those in authority that such diversion should be made, the Chief of the Air Corps will carry out his instructions to the letter."

When Arnold testified secretly before the House Military Affairs Committee on March 5 that the Air Corps would have to pay an extra $20 million for 2,100 new planes, partly because of foreign orders, he was acutely aware of the delicacy of his situation, as the above statement indicates. But he seems to have overestimated the discretion of congress-men and underestimated the intensity of President Roosevelt's feelings in the matter.

The White House meeting March 12 at which the president castigated Woodring and Arnold, and threatened to send Arnold to Guam if he didn't cooperate, was not the only meeting on the subject in the Oval Office that day. The president met privately with Morgenthau, his military aide, Gen. "Pa" Watson, and his confidential secretary, Stephen Early. At that meeting, Arnold had no friends. Morgenthau was annoyed not only at Arnold's testimony, which exposed the division within the administration, but also at the refusal of Woodring, Johnson, "and particularly" Arnold to release to the Allies "certain engines and designs still classified as secret." Morgenthau's effectiveness was "just being ruined" by Johnson and Arnold, he told the president. He couldn't function that way, and if the president wanted him "to do this thing," he would have to do something about the situation.[11]

It was then that Roosevelt called in Early and Watson. Early reminded him that he, Early, was in the War Department when Arnold was there "running a mimeograph machine on government time and government stationery sending out propaganda against the coordinated air force." (Though the reference is slightly confused, Early was obviously referring to the 1926 incident that resulted in Arnold's exile to Fort Riley for continuing the Billy Mitchell air-power crusade.)

The president, after listening to Early, said, "Well, if Arnold won't conform, maybe we will have to move him out of town."

As Morgenthau described it, this private meeting between the president, Early, Watson, and himself ended with the president saying in very forceful language "that Johnson has to announce that he likes this [Treasury Department procurement] board; he likes to have Secretary Morgenthau in charge of it; . . . and that it is functioning well and that he and Arnold are going to conform."

Furthermore, he instructed Early to tell Johnson that "from now on [there is to be] no publicity from the War Department except from the central bureau, and that Arnold has to keep his mouth shut."

By four o'clock, after this meeting and the larger meeting at which Arnold received his threatening lecture, Morgenthau was so elated that when he returned to his office he said to members of his staff, "Oh, boy, did General Arnold get it!"

Arnold himself, in a memorandum of record the next day, said, "It was a party at which the Secretary of War and the Chief of Air Corps were to be spanked, and were spanked."[12]

Once again Arnold had miscalculated how far he could go in resisting a superior, and once again, though it was not announced to him, he was in a kind of exile. As the weeks passed, he noticed that he was no longer invited to the White House, even for meetings which concerned the Air Corps.

When Arnold went home after his dressing-down by the president, he was so pessimistic he told Bee she had better get ready to pack their belongings.[13] And he had reason to talk that way. Any time a president of the United States threatens to send one of his generals to Guam, it is no joke. Arnold's job was undoubtedly in jeopardy. His authority had been seriously impaired, yet his responsibility—to expand the Air Corps and prepare it for a possible war—remained the same. And he could get little help or comfort from Secretary of War Woodring or his assistant, Louis Johnson, because they themselves had been "sent to Coventry," and in addition were constantly feuding with each other.

It is not surprising that Arnold's temper shortened and his impatience developed an even finer edge during those trying days in 1940. When he would come home fuming about Morgenthau's latest maneuver, Bee would try to calm him. But her efforts to maintain equilibrium in the house were made, as it later developed, at great expense to herself.

There was one thing, however, about which both of them could be proud and happy in the spring of 1940. Their son Bruce, having enlisted in the Cavalry after his difficulties at Annapolis, had taken the soldier's examination for West Point and had won an appointment on his own merit, without any help from his father.[14] It seemed to Bruce that for the first time in his life his father showed real pride in him. But when Bruce came home on leave that spring, it was also evident to him that his father was distracted by other matters and his temper was short. On the morning Bruce returned to camp, for instance, his father drove him to Union Station and on the way they came up behind a car that was standing still at a stop sign. Arnold slowed down as if he had seen the car, but instead of stopping, he absently slammed into the rear of it.

His anger rising, he jumped out of his car, ran up to the car he had just hit, and shouted at the two men in it, "What the hell were you stopped for? There wasn't anyone coming! You should have moved on!"

Though he was obviously in the wrong, having hit them from behind, the men were apparently intimidated by the force of his wrath. "Yes, sir," the driver said, and drove away.

Fortunately, Arnold no longer had to do much driving—as chief of Air Corps he was entitled to a car and a chauffeur. But the first chauffeur assigned to him had turned out to be a secret tippler, and after several occasions when Arnold got the uncomfortable feeling that he was sitting behind a drunk driver, he contacted the motor pool and asked for a new one.

On call there at the time was a young private from Norfolk, Virginia, a country boy who had been in the Army since 1936. This was Bruce Simmons.[15] When he reported to Air Corps headquarters in the Munitions Building, he was subjected to an hour-long interview with Arnold's secretary, Miss Suzy Adkins, who tried to give him some inkling of how demanding her boss could be and in particular how quickly he liked to move. Finally she ushered him into Arnold's private office.

The general's first question was, "Do you drink?"

"No, sir," Simmons said nervously. He had never before seen a general.

"You know," Arnold said, "I'm supposed to have a sergeant as my driver, not a private."

Simmons studied him a moment and said, "Well, sir, you can make me a sergeant."

Thus began a relationship which would last until the day Arnold died. He gradually developed a nagging affection for Simmons comparable to the feeling he already entertained for that secretary in his outer office, Miss Adkins, whom he had inherited from General Westover. Adkins was a plump brunette about thirty years old, not beautiful but with a pleasant face that fooled some people into thinking she might be easy to get around. As they soon learned, her smile concealed a strong will. She was the one person in Arnold's office who showed no fear of the general. When she got angry at him, she would refuse to speak to him, and he would send Simmons for a box of candy to pacify her. She was apparently quick to sense the difficulty he had dealing with women. She didn't hesitate to differ with him. Yet she would not allow anyone else to say a word against him. Simmons believed that "she loved that man," and that Arnold, in his way, loved her, though nothing improper ever passed between them. Arnold once remarked to Simmons that she was "as smart as some of the damned generals."

By this time Arnold was virtually losing his ability to function as a pilot, not only because he was so busy, but also because, when he became Air Corps chief, General Craig had decreed that as long as he held that job he would not again fly alone or in a single-engine plane. Having just lost General Westover in the crash of a single-engine plane he was flying himself, Craig had decided he didn't want to lose another Air Corps chief. He had told Arnold to choose a personal pilot and keep him on hand. Arnold chose Capt. Eugene Beebe, with whom he had often flown at March Field, but who had then gone to Wright Field to become a bombardment project officer.[16] As soon as Beebe reported for duty in Washington, Arnold had introduced him to Craig, who told him, "Son, your main job is to keep Hap alive. You'd better do it." When they weren't flying, Beebe occupied a desk in Arnold's office and helped with administrative matters.

Though Arnold acknowledged the benefits of foreign orders in hastening the expansion of U.S. aircraft plants, he was quite unaware in 1940 of another benefit, which was destined to become tangible in late 1943, just when he desperately needed it. In April 1940, the British

Purchasing Commission, headed by Air Marshall Arthur T. Harris, approached North American Aviation president J. H. "Dutch" Kindelberger and asked him to manufacture for them under license as many Curtiss P-40s as possible. Kindelberger, convinced that the P-40, with its small Allison engine, could not face up to Germany's fighters, suggested instead that he design a fighter for the British.[17] When Harris and his colleagues agreed, Kindelberger and his staff went to work, and using as the basic model a plane the Air Corps had rejected after a crash, they designed within a 120-day time limit the plane that would one day become famous as the P-51 Mustang. But, when the time came to select an engine for this plane, it suffered the same fate as the P-40. The best liquid-cooled engine available in America was the Allison V-1710, and it generated only 1,200 horsepower. The first batch of P-51s delivered to England in November 1941 were so underpowered that the British didn't know what to do with them. Neither did the U.S. Army Air Corps. Officials at the corps' Wright Field test facility didn't welcome the sight of the Allison engines because they had become convinced that liquid-cooled engines were too vulnerable to enemy bullets. When they learned that the P-51 was also too underpowered to face an enemy, they gladly put it aside. The British had inspired the development of the P-51, and it would remain for them to save it from oblivion. Arnold would one day have reason to thank them for that.

In 1940, however, Arnold, despite his sympathy for the British, had a limited view of their helpfulness. On May 15, about a week after becoming British prime minister, Winston Churchill sent an urgent plea to Washington not only for thousands of planes and engines, but for ships, artillery, rifles, ammunition, and machine tools. With the German army rolling toward Paris and the British retreating toward Dunkirk, he was sufficiently desperate to take anything the United States could spare. Morgenthau was eager to accommodate him, and once again Arnold felt he had to resist despite the presidential strictures that had been placed upon him. But this time, Marshall was on hand to intervene in his favor. He, too, was willing to give the British everything that could be spared, but he pointed out that there wasn't much left to give.

During a May 22 conference at the Treasury Department, Morgenthau asked that 100 planes, already in use by the Air Corps, be turned over to the British. Marshall looked to Arnold and asked him how much training time his units would lose if those planes were surrendered.[18]

After making an unexplained calculation, Arnold said that those 100 planes, which the R.A.F. would use up in three days at its current loss rate, would cost the Army Air Corps six months of training time.

The Air Corps then had only 160 pursuit planes for 260 qualified pilots, and it had only 52 of the 136 heavy bombers it would have had were it not for the diversion to foreign countries. Marshall, after listening to this, sided with Arnold and turned down Morgenthau's demand. Arnold heard no more of the matter but he could be sure the president was informed of it.

Meanwhile, President Roosevelt, on May 16, had made a plea before Congress that might give hope to the still puny Air Corps, and to the British if they could hold out long enough against Hitler. Arnold had prompted Marshall to encourage this plea, since he himself no longer had access to the president, and when he learned that Roosevelt's address was to be broadcast, he called in Tooey Spaatz and Ira Eaker, both now on his staff, and told them to listen to it.[19] He himself would listen to it elsewhere.

When the president's address to Congress came over the radio, Spaatz and Eaker were both astonished at his concluding statement. "I should like," he said, "to see this nation geared up to the ability to turn out at least fifty thousand planes a year."

Arnold returned to his office to find both Spaatz and Eaker staring at him in consternation. How could he have let the president make such a preposterous statement, they asked him. The whole aircraft industry that year was turning out less than ten thousand planes.

Arnold looked at them and smiled. "If I had asked for twenty-five thousand," he said, "I would have gotten fifteen thousand. Now I've asked for fifty thousand, and if I don't get twenty-five thousand, you boys won't be here a year from now."

He was coming to his office now at seven each morning and staying until at least seven in the evening. It seemed, at least to Eaker, who knew him well, that the strain of too much work was beginning to show in his face. If he was particularly irritated about something, or hadn't had enough sleep, he would "come to the office pretty ragged." He was also suffering from occasional spells during which his heartbeat would increase rapidly. If he didn't take the medicine prescribed for this problem his face would flush and the veins in his neck would enlarge. But most of the people around him considered these nothing more than symptoms of his recurring impatience with men who couldn't think and move as fast as he did.

With the advent of summer, Arnold had to take some time off for the graduation of his oldest son, Henry, from West Point; and after that, for Hank's marriage to a beautiful New York model named Kaye Hickey. Arnold's pride was mixed with disappointment. Hank's eyesight barred him from pilot training.

France had fallen shortly after Roosevelt's call for 50,000 planes a year, and Congress reacted by giving the president all the money he wanted for his rearmament program. Suddenly the 50,000 planes per year looked like a dream about to come true. Within two weeks after Congress supplied the funds, the Air Corps had closed contracts for 11,000 planes. Legal officers at Wright Field were signing as many as a thousand contracts a day for everything from aircraft to potatoes. Arnold observed that the funds now available were enough "to stagger any mere officer," and "seemingly sufficient to buy anything for anybody at any time."

All this money and all these contracts amounted to just so much paper, however, and did nothing to solve his immediate problem. It would take planes and guns to fight the Germans if the need arose —which it might at any time, since they now controlled the whole European continent—but he still didn't have much more than paper to throw up against them. And Morgenthau continued to chip away at him. On June 5, Arnold protested to Marshall against Morgenthau's plan to send a shipment of P-36 fighters to Sweden. On July 9, Morgenthau arranged delivery of 3,350 aircraft engines to England. On August 9, he asked for the release to the British of 50 more Allison engines that the Air Corps desperately needed.

On August 14, Arnold finally arranged a conference with the new secretary of war, Henry L. Stimson, whom Roosevelt had appointed to replace Woodring after the fall of France.[20] Stimson, as Arnold soon realized, did not intend to be a figurehead like Woodring. A Republican who had been secretary of war in William Howard Taft's cabinet and secretary of state under Herbert Hoover, he was the only man in public life who advocated stopping the Japanese in 1931 when they first invaded China. He was a tough, crusty, intelligent, and prestigious old man whose health was poor but whose tongue was sharp. He shared Morgenthau's concern about Hitler but he also understood the pressing need to develop an American air force.

With Stimson that day was Robert P. Patterson, a former circuit court of appeals judge in New York who was replacing Louis Johnson as assistant secretary of war. A veteran of the First World War, Patterson was so convinced of the nation's need to rearm that he had enlisted in the Army reserve and was serving a two-week stint as a private in a training camp when he was named assistant secretary of war. It was surely the most rapid promotion in the history of the U.S. Army.

Arnold pointed out to Stimson and Patterson that if "the policy of giving the British priority over all deliveries" was continued, he couldn't promise to meet his 1941 and 1942 schedules for Air Corps expansion. The English now had so many engines on order, for instance, that within a short time they would be getting 1,500 American engines a month while the U.S. Army and Navy combined would be getting only 500. Already, thanks to a decree the previous day by Secretary Morgenthau, "every other Allison engine from now on" would go to the British, and it was the Allison engine that powered the P-40. While the P-40 was beginning to look inadequate compared to some of the new European fighter planes, it was still the best plane the United States had.

Patterson at first defended the Morgenthau policy. By giving this equipment to the British, he said, the United States was helping them overcome the Germans, so that we might avoid the necessity of having to make use of the materiel later ourselves.

That brought Arnold to an overriding concern that had been occupying his mind since the fall of France. He no longer had much confidence that the British could hold out against the Germans. As a military man, he was perhaps less impressed than most civilians by Winston Churchill's famous fight rhetoric. A nation couldn't fight with words alone, and the British had very little else. He apparently shared a growing belief that a German invasion of England could come at any moment. It was his opinion, he said, that any planes being built for delivery to England six months into the future would get there too late; that the whole crisis in Europe would "probably be over in a period of a month"; and that the U.S. Army should now concentrate on building its Air Corps because if too many planes were given to the British, those planes would "be used against us if the Germans lick the British."

The possibility of Hitler's conquering England was not pleasant to contemplate, but in the summer of 1940 it was a possibility that military planners had to take seriously. Stimson made Arnold no promises that day, but he did have a better picture of the cold military realities he faced. And he seemed to realize immediately that a system in which the secretary of the treasury dictated to the War Department was intolerable.

Soon thereafter Morgenthau learned he was dealing with someone quite different from Woodring, and Arnold's problems with Morgenthau, as well as his procurement problems in general, began gradually to diminish.

At a September 27 White House conference, to which Arnold was, of course, not invited, even President Roosevelt seemed to become aware of the Air Corps' lack of preparedness. He began the meeting by urging, probably at Morgenthau's instigation, that B-17s be made available to the British. Stimson, noticing that Marshall looked eager to speak, invited him to do so. Though Stimson didn't know it, Arnold had asked Marshall to "object strenuously to turning over any of our heavy bombardment." Marshall had promised he would do the best he could, and as usual, he got right to the point. Aside from a few squadrons in Hawaii and the Philippines, he revealed, the Army had only 49 bombers fit for combat.

Stimson noticed that when Marshall made this observation, "the President's head went back as if someone had hit him in the chest." At the end of the meeting, Stimson felt that both Morgenthau and Roosevelt "finally saw the situation we were in."[21]

Since March 12, the day of his magisterial castigation, Arnold had not been in the White House, but Roosevelt's attitude toward him seemed to be softening now. Harry Hopkins had defended him from the start, as had George Marshall, which might explain why he wasn't dismissed in July with Woodring and Johnson. And on September 19 he had perhaps enhanced his reputation at the White House, though not elsewhere, when the Air Corps commissioned the president's second son, Elliott, a captain.[22] (To the cynical public outcry that followed this appointment, Arnold answered that he was looking for good officers and young Roosevelt was qualified.) But what seemed to bring Arnold back into Roosevelt's favor more than anything else was the growing evidence, now that Hitler had conquered the European continent, that Arnold had been right to insist that the Army Air Corps needed planes as urgently as did France and England. Despite all the planes Morgenthau had sent to those countries, France was now totally defeated and England was almost helplessly awaiting invasion, while the United States, after the talk about 50,000 planes a year, had on hand only 49 heavy bombers and perhaps 250 fighters ready to defend her shores.

In October, when Marshall wanted to appoint Arnold deputy chief of staff (for air), making him the first air man ever to sit so high on the General Staff, Roosevelt raised no objection. Arnold received the promotion on October 30. (Though he then appointed Maj. Gen.

George Brett acting chief of Air Corps, he relinquished none of his control over the corps.)

A few weeks before Christmas, and approximately nine months after his banishment from the White House, Arnold was invited to a small dinner party there.[23] Arriving early, perhaps because the president had invited him early to allow time for a private chat, he found Roosevelt sitting beside a table loaded with cocktail fixings.

In his usual blithe and hearty manner, as if there had never been the slightest misunderstanding between them, the president said to him, "Good evening, Hap. How about my fixing you an Old Fashioned?"

He didn't explain how he happened to know that it was Arnold's favorite drink. The general still drank only sparingly, but when he did, it was usually an Old Fashioned or some other sweet cocktail. The president, a good host, had apparently gone to the trouble of finding out Arnold's preference, but his courtesy was lost on Arnold, whose immediate reaction was to recall that this same man had almost refused to appoint him Air Corps chief in 1938 because of the rumor that he was a drunk.

Still eager to erase that impression, Arnold engaged in a bit of ludicrous hyperbole. "Thanks, Mr. President," he said, "I haven't had one for about twenty years, but I assure you I'll enjoy this one with you, tremendously."

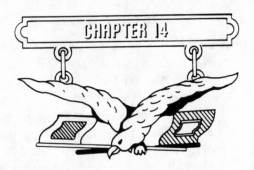

CHAPTER 14

Arnold's reconciliation with President Roosevelt and Stimon's success in easing Morgenthau toward the background brightened the prospects for Air Corps growth but did not produce immediate results. During one week in November 1940, for example, the aircraft industry delivered only two tactical planes to the Air Corps, the bulk of the output going to the British, whose desperate need in those dark days and nights of the Battle of Britain could not be doubted. Arnold now had at least some confidence in the British ability to resist Hitler. While the American ambassador in London, Joseph P. Kennedy, was sending back gloomy predictions of the early demise of Great Britain, Arnold's own "ambassador to London," Col. Carl Spaatz, who had gone over there to study developments from an airman's viewpoint, was sending back optimistic reports.[1] The Germans could not invade England, Spaatz insisted, until they defeated the Royal Air Force, and in the Battle of Britain so far, they did not appear able to do so.

On January 17, 1941, Arnold received a letter from Maj. Gen. Frank Andrews, whom Marshall had sent to Panama the previous November (with his second star restored) to command the Canal air defense. Andrews was appalled when he got there to learn that there wasn't any air defense worthy of the name. "I am not happy about our air situation here in Panama," he wrote to Arnold. "If there were an air raid, we would not be able to put up much of a show."

What Andrews desperately needed was airplanes, but Arnold had none to offer. "Frankly I am worried about aircraft production," he wrote in a January 22 reply. "We are leaning over backward to give everything to the British . . . there will be no relief for several months."

In a wistful, handwritten postscript he added, "All I can say is that we hope to get planes for everyone but at this writing it is only a hope."

Fortunately for Arnold and for the Air Corps, he was now getting important help from a new associate who had been unknown to him only a few months earlier. On November 7, 1940, at the instigation of Robert Patterson, Stimson had appointed Robert A. Lovett to a post of his own creation—assistant secretary of war for air. Lovett, a wealthy

New York stockbroker and director of the Union Pacific Railroad, had been a naval aviator, in command of U.S. Naval Air Squadron Number One, during the First World War. He had come to Patterson's attention because, during a Union Pacific inspection trip in the summer of 1939, he had taken it upon himself to visit the West Coast aircraft companies. With war looming in Europe, he wanted to know how the U.S. aircraft industry was progressing. He might also have been interested in its investment potential. A skillful and well-trained business observer, he looked at several companies and was distressed to find them far behind their British and German counterparts. For the benefit of his partners, he wrote a report of this trip. James Forrestal, one of his neighbors on Long Island and a man destined to become secretary of the navy, asked for a copy of this report, which he then showed to Patterson. As a result, Patterson called Lovett to Washington and Stimson hired him.[2]

Lovett and Arnold got along well from the beginning. Arnold said later he found in Lovett "a man who possessed the qualities in which I was weakest, a partner and teammate of tremendous sympathy, and of calm and hidden force. When I became impatient, intolerant, and would rant around, fully intending to tear the War and Navy Departments to pieces, Bob Lovett would know exactly how to handle me. He would say with a quiet smile, 'Hap, you're wonderful! How I wish I had your pep and vitality! Now . . . let's get down and be practical.' And I would come back to earth with a bang."[3]

Lovett, recalling their association, has said, "I'd see that Hap would be very bouncy, then he'd have fits of depression. He'd think things weren't going well. He needed help. He was a young boy in many ways. Not sophisticated. . . . His great gifts were not adequately appreciated because there was quite a little jealousy among the other services. The Air [Corps] had grown rapidly. Hap showed a great deal of self restraint in some ways, but he was flamboyant and aggressive. [He had] enthusiasm. [To him there] wasn't anything that couldn't be done."[4]

There were things, however, that Arnold didn't like to do, and one of them was to handle the tedious duties of administration. His vision of administration was to think of something that ought to be done and tell somebody to go do it right away. He could not comprehend or tolerate delay. Concepts like definition of duties, coordination of projects, standardization of procedures, and communication through chains of command might be desirable but they took too much time. Whatever he wanted done, he wanted done immediately, and if that necessitated a violation of orderly process, so be it. Through no fault of his, the Air Corps administrative setup was so unwieldy that he almost had to ignore it in order to get things done. Though it was a fast-growing organization that operated almost separately from the Army, it was still ultimately subordinate to the Army and dependent on it for most of its needs, including quartermaster supplies, engineering, ordnance, medicine, and other special services. And thanks to the 1935 reorganization, it was divided within itself in a way which worked against cohesion. The G.H.Q. Air Force still existed, under the command of Lt. Gen. Delos Emmons, and its job was to do the fighting, but without much regard for any of the important support functions essential to a fighting unit. The rest of the Air Corps, which handled planning, logistics, transportation, procurement, training, and construction of facilities, was separate from it and now under the command of Maj. Gen. George Brett, whom Arnold had made acting chief of Air Corps. Arnold himself, as deputy chief of staff for air, was nominally in control of both parts, but the G.H.Q. habit of independence, plus the fact that Emmons was senior to him and outranked him, made his control over the operational units tenuous. While he actually did run the whole Air Corps by the sheer force of his personality, he hadn't really managed to consolidate its parts.[5]

When Lovett discovered this organizational situation, he declared it "appallingly bad." He had spent two years in England studying the structure of the R.A.F., and though he agreed with Marshall and Arnold that this was no time to strive for a completely independent air force, he favored a reorganization that would give the corps more autonomy and much more cohesion. He went to Stimson and asked for authority to develop a plan. Stimson gave his blessing and Lovett went right to work.

Arnold, released by Lovett from some of his Washington responsibilities, intensified his pressure on the training command to hasten the output of crews, and turned up the heat on the aircraft companies to speed up the production of planes.

His pilot, Gene Beebe, later said of him, "His idea of a good time was to work all day, then go to Bolling Field [in south Washington], fly all night to Los Angeles [in a DC-3], arrive in the morning, visit about five aircraft plants, then go to someone's house for dinner that night."[6]

F. W. Conant of Douglas Aircraft recalled that Arnold would come into the plant, gather together the engineers and designers, take note of the fact that some plane they were making could fly perhaps three hundred miles an hour, and then say, "I want four hundred miles an hour. Why in the hell can't somebody give it to me?"[7]

"You'd begin to wonder," Conant said, "why the hell you couldn't do it—how you would do it. He was always a step ahead of everybody. . . .

You never thought the things he asked you for were possible, but then you did them."

Col. K. B. Wolfe, one of Arnold's top production engineers, was often amazed at the way he played the manufacturers against the training commanders. "He would say to a manufacturer, 'Damn it, you told me you were going to have [so many] fighters this month. Now I've got the [pilots] trained and where the hell are the fighters?'

"Then he would get hold of a training commander and say, 'Look, you've got to have [so many] crews by [such a time] because we're going to have that many airplanes." [8] He soon had people racing against each other to get the work done.

Because Boeing couldn't make enough B-17s to satisfy him, he forced Boeing to license Douglas and Lockheed to build them. Then he made Douglas and Lockheed construct new plants in which to do the building. Because the labor supply on the Pacific Coast wasn't big enough at that time, he made all the large companies build additional plants in Texas or the Middle West, where labor was plentiful.

Dutch Kindelberger of North American built a plant between Dallas and Fort Worth in March 1941 because Arnold had called him in and told him to do so.

"We had to finance it on our own money," Kindelberger recalled. "They [the Air Corps] didn't have any money for this. I was scared to death for a long while there because I didn't even have a piece of paper. I was building six hundred trainers for Hap, and building a factory [near] Dallas, and the net worth of North American was obligated several times over. And I hadn't any contracts yet." [9]

Within three years, that plant near Dallas would be employing 43,000 workers and turning out thousands of P-51s and B-24s.

Donald Douglas has told a similar story. One day in late 1940, Arnold called him from Washington and said, "Don, you're going to Tulsa to run a plant." [10]

"The hell I am," Douglas said.

"The hell you aren't," Arnold insisted. "You're there now."

Before he knew it, Douglas had a $36-million plant in Tulsa employing 16,000 people. By 1943, Douglas would also have a $45-million plant in Oklahoma City employing 20,000; a $33-million plant in Chicago employing 11,000; a $30-million plant in Long Beach employing 40,000; a $20-million plant in El Segundo employing 21,000; and his original $30-million home factory in Santa Monica employing 44,000.

By 1941, the demand for aircraft was so great that the big automobile companies had gone into the business of building planes. Arnold was still convinced, from his World War I experience, that they would never develop the knack for it, but William S. Knudsen, an auto industry expert in mass production, was by that time coordinating the nation's rearmament production program, and he thought otherwise. To keep an eye on the plane-making efforts of the auto makers, Arnold sent to Detroit one of the great aeronautical geniuses of all time, Maj. Jimmy Doolittle.

For several years, Doolittle had been a civilian working for the Shell Oil Company, but he had never dropped his Air Corps connections. In August 1939, after a trip to Europe, he had come to Arnold with a report that predicted the imminent outbreak of war, confirmed everything Lindbergh had said about Hitler's air force, and described its strength in terms that the war later proved uncannily accurate.[11] With this report, Doolittle had also offered his services to the Air Corps.

"I want you back on active duty," Arnold had said, "but it will take an act of Congress to get you back."

Doolittle was then a reserve major and the Army was forbidden by law to call field-grade officers back to extended active duty. By July 1940 Congress had revised the law, thanks largely to Arnold's lobbying, and Doolittle was the first field-grade reserve officer to return to uniform. Arnold had immediately sent him to the Allison Engine Corporation in Indianapolis, a rather self-satisfied subsidiary of General Motors, which was not very rapidly turning out engines that were not very good. Since theirs was the only large, liquid-cooled engine available in the United States, and since they weren't likely to have any competition in the near future, the people at Allison had to be coddled, wheedled, threatened, and inspired to do better work and do it faster. Doolittle was the ideal man for it and he did the best he could. While he was at Allison, he also conducted instrument-flying experiments with the P-40, which resulted in a whole new set of training procedures for bad-weather flying. There were few things connected with airplanes that Doolittle couldn't do, but teaching the auto-makers to build planes was one of them, and some problems were never solved. Arnold's warning that auto-builders didn't make good plane-builders would eventually prove to be quite accurate.

Despite Arnold's endless prodding of the plane-makers, he still had, in the spring of 1941, an Air Corps of only nine operational groups —fewer than five hundred planes in total. And he was still accusing President Roosevelt of sending too many planes to England. On March 10 he found out that the president had "objected very strenuously" to a

March 6 memorandum he had written for Marshall, a memo which decried his continued lack of combat aircraft and suggested that England was getting more planes than the United States could spare.[12] Arnold didn't seem able to make the president understand "the necessity for an air force in being" as opposed to an air force in prospect. Perhaps the time had come to approach the problem from another angle. He decided to go to England himself and find out firsthand what the British really needed, what they were doing with what they had already received, and what they could tell him about America's needs in the event that the United States entered the war.

Bee, Lois, and her husband, Ernie Snowden, drove him to New York on April 9 so he could catch the Pan American Clipper to Bermuda on the first leg of his flight. Lois and Ernie were then living in Pensacola, Florida, where he was stationed, but had come north on leave for a visit. In New York, Arnold made connections with Maj. Elwood P. "Pete" Quesada, his aide and companion on the trip. Quesada, who was well known in the Air Corps for his flying skill, had been one of the pilots on the famous "Question Mark" flight, which set an air endurance record of 150 hours, 40 minutes, in 1929. (Others on that flight were Carl Spaatz, Ira Eaker, Harry A. Halverson, and Roy Hooe.)

Flying to Europe was a roundabout experience in 1941, before the days of nonstop airliners and before the Air Corps' North Atlantic route via Newfoundland and Greenland had been opened. Arnold and Quesada, plus sixteen other venturesome passengers, took off on the clipper bound for Portugal at 1:15 a.m. on April 11 and stopped at Bermuda and the Azores before reaching Lisbon, which was then a center of international intrigue.[13] Because Portugal was a neutral country and one of the few gateways to and from conquered Europe, people from all the warring nations moved in and out of it, exchanging information or whatever else they might have to sell.

Arnold, not yet accustomed to being considered an important man, "hardly knew what to expect" from the English. He was sure he would get to meet Air Chief Marshal Charles Portal and his subordinates and perhaps even Lord Beaverbrook, the British newspaper publisher Churchill had named production coordinator. But Arnold did not anticipate any fuss over him. "In the United States, I was definitely in the 'minor league,'" he later observed. "I had not reached the 'major league' status in the military setup." He was astonished, therefore, to find that a British welcoming party of three, headed by Air Marshal John C. Slessor, had flown all the way to Portugal to greet him.

After checking in at the Hotel Abbis, Arnold and Quesada took time for a bath; then, at breakfast with Slessor and his companions, they learned that the British were eager to get right down to business. First of all, what could the Americans do about the German submarine campaign in the Atlantic, which was so effective that it threatened England with blockade and starvation? Second, what could they do about the B-17 Flying Fortress, several of which had been sent to England, but had so far proven useless in combat? Gun turrets were freezing up and guns were failing to fire at the high altitudes for which the plane was designed. These were but two items on a long list of the plane's operational flaws. And third, did the Americans actually believe in the daylight precision-bombing method for which the B-17 had been created? The British were there to tell Arnold right away that daylight bombing wouldn't work. It would be too costly. Even before he reached England, Arnold had reason to wonder whether he shouldn't have stayed at home.

A suite had been arranged for Arnold and Quesada at the Dorchester, where Portal lived, and the first evening, when they dined with him, he annoyed Arnold immediately by asking for a copy of his proposed agenda. What subjects did Arnold want to discuss during his stay? Arnold didn't have an agenda. But he soon found the British unprepared to talk about some of the subjects he considered important, and vice versa. It seemed to Quesada that Portal's formality, combined with his repetitious urgency in asking for things from America, was irksome to Arnold.

One of Arnold's questions to Portal concerned British bauxite supplies for aluminum production. He was talking about the manufacture of 75,000 military planes, which might require more aluminum than the United States could spare. It suddenly became apparent that Portal was staggered by the concept of 75,000 planes. This was Arnold's first introduction to a British attitude that he encountered repeatedly during his visit. When he talked about opening a North Atlantic route so American planes could be flown rather than shipped to England, the British seemed skeptical that American fliers could navigate such a route. When he talked about storing two million gallons of gasoline at a Newfoundland transit base, they found it "somewhat staggering."

To Quesada, Arnold soon confided a feeling that the British had set their sights too low, that if they were going to win the war they would have to do "a hell of a lot more" than they were then planning to do. "It was discouraging," Quesada recalled, "that they would talk about squadrons whereas we would talk about groups."

The talks nevertheless turned out to be much more cordial and productive than early indications had led Arnold to expect, and the fuss the British made over him pleased him as much as it mystified him. On his third day, after meeting high British air officers and American diplomats, he visited Beaverbrook, who proved to be one man in London with ideas as large as his own. Beaverbrook listened to Arnold talk about the planes and materiel and men he considered necessary to win the war, then called Churchill and suggested the prime minister interview this American airman. Beaverbrook also immediately granted Arnold's request for two Spitfires, two Hurricanes (both fighters), two Wellingtons (medium bombers), and two night fighters for American experts to study. And he cordially invited Arnold to see "everything the British had." But most important from an air strategist's viewpoint, he told Arnold that the Germans had reduced British aircraft production by as much as one-third in some months by bombing their factories. And the Germans never used more than five hundred planes. Arnold, who envisioned the use of eight hundred or one thousand planes per raid, became increasingly confident that American air power, when fully realized, would have the capability of winning this war for the Allies.

On his third night, April 14, he was invited to a dinner given by Australian Prime Minister Robert G. Menzies, which made him feel that as far as the British were concerned he was in the "big league." At this dinner, in addition to Menzies, were Field Marshal Sir John Dill, chief of the Imperial Staff; Admiral Sir Dudley Pound, First Sea Lord; Portal; several members of the cabinet and of Parliament; and the new American ambassador, John G. Winant. Arnold was bombarded with questions about America, especially about its labor and production situation and the prospects of the United States' entering the war.

He was on his way back to the Dorchester after this dinner when he was enveloped in the sound of wailing sirens. The guns barked, the bombs began to burst, and the fires began to erupt. He was experiencing his first German air raid.

Hurrying to the hotel, he went up onto the roof with Quesada to watch the attack and the defense. "The sound of the bursts came closer and closer," as he described it, "and the sky grew red beyond the city—flats and warehouses were burning. The German airplanes seemed to be concentrating on the center of London. The antiaircraft guns in Regent's Park opened fire with ear-splitting cracks. The German planes were soon directly overhead. The noise was deafening with the firing of guns and the bombs dropping—and then, almost as quickly as the raid had started, the noise rapidly receded and all was silent again. leaving the sky bright from the fires." At midnight, a new batch of

German planes arrived, sending Arnold and Quesada back up to the roof to watch once more.

"I can say rather frankly," Quesada recalled, "the horrible effect of these night attacks had a profound impact on both of us. Very profound, including Arnold. And the ability to see thirty or forty raging fires at one time in a large city had an impact on us, and to see the calm of the next day, and to see business and commerce progressing as usual, had another unusual effect on us. We came to a sort of opinion, an intuitive opinion, that the British didn't know what they were in for. We sold them short, in other words. We thought they didn't realize the magnitude of all the real effect of this night bombing. Well, it turned out that they were right and we were wrong."[14]

On the seventeenth, Air Vice Marshal Sir Richard Peirse, commander in chief of Bomber Command, flew Arnold and Quesada over Cambridge to look at German bomb damage and repeated to him substantially what Slessor had said—that daylight bombing was impossible. This was an astonishing statement coming from Peirse because he was considered one of Britain's foremost advocates of precision bombing, a modus operandi that American air strategists were now accepting as sacred doctrine. Since Peirse's appointment the previous October, his planes had been concentrating their attacks on two specific targets that had to be hit precisely if they were to be damaged at all—oil installations and invasion barges. But after a few daylight attempts they were now flying only at night, when precision was impossible. With their American planes they had received an American invention, the Sperry bombsight, and had tried it, but Peirse and his aides insisted it was useless because it required a more-than-twenty-second straight course on the target approach, with no evasion to escape antiaircraft fire.

Arnold was not convinced of the uselessness of the bombsight but decided he had better have the problem studied. "I think the British have much to learn about bombing," he noted in his diary, "but who am I to question two years of bombing in a real war? Hence, the study as soon as I get back."

On the eighteenth he had to borrow a dinner jacket from Air Corps Col. Martin "Mike" Scanlon, the air attaché at the American embassy, because he had received, to his unexpected delight, an invitation for a weekend with Churchill and his official family at Ditchley Park castle in Oxfordshire. Because all British road signs had been removed to confuse the Germans in the event of invasion, the chauffeur who drove Arnold and Averell Harriman (who was in London on a special mission for President Roosevelt) lost his way and reached the well-kept seventeenth-century castle an hour late; but that didn't matter, since Churchill's conversation seldom reached high gear until after midnight. On this occasion he talked until three in the morning.

"Russia," he said, "is like an amoral crocodile, lurking in the depths, waiting for whatever prey may come its way." He didn't explain the distinction between an "amoral" and a "moral" crocodile. At that time Russia had not yet been drawn into the war by Hitler's invasion.

In a series of more important remarks, Churchill confided to Arnold that the British would be able to do very little against the Germans in 1941 or 1942; that the Battle of the North Atlantic could and "must" be won by American aid; and that the United States should send long-range bombers as quickly as possible. "England may not always win battles," he said in the best British schoolboy tradition, "but always wins wars."

After dinner Churchill engaged in a series of quips against the Royal Air Force, which hadn't been damaging the Germans enough to satisfy him, but Portal answered him so sharply that Arnold soon came to consider him (as did many other people) "one of the most brilliant of the British Chiefs of Staff."

On April 21, Beaverbrook invited Arnold to dinner and posed for him a sobering question: "What would you do if Churchill were hung and the rest of us were in hiding in Scotland or being run down by the Germans? What would the people in America do? We are up against the mightiest army the world has ever seen."

The consensus of the people at Beaverbrook's dinner was that "Germany could establish a bridgehead in England any time she was willing to make the sacrifice. . . . It was not a question of whether [the Germans] could make the attack but whether the British could keep them from extending the bridgeheads."

By this time, Arnold was again less than sanguine about England's chances of survival. Though the men he met seemed determined to fight to the end, a certain pessimism pervaded most conversations. Were the British simply painting the bleakest picture in the hope of getting the most help? That possibility occurred to Arnold but he discounted it. The country seemed to him in desperate straits. On the debris-strewn streets of bomb-battered London people moved to and fro with solemn faces. The one thing that gave Arnold some encouragement was the British Air Defense, commanded by Air Marshal Sir Sholto Douglas. It seemed to Arnold that the Fighter Command was really fighting, but that the Bomber Command under Peirse was pathetic. And he didn't know what to think about British research and development. He was taken aback when Sir Henry Tizard, Britain's science coordinator, told him that many of the airplanes and some of the engines the United States was developing "might be thrown into the scrap heap." Was that just sour grapes? Not necessarily. In contrast to what America was building, Sir Henry offered Arnold the engineering plans for a plane currently being developed by the British—a fighter plane that didn't even have a propellor. It was powered by something called jet propulsion. Arnold decided he had better look into that.

While Arnold was in London trying to deal with British problems as they came up, he was forcibly reminded that he still had some difficulties with the U.S. Navy. He met Rear Adm. Robert L. Ghormley, then the special U.S. naval observer in London, who was working on the formation of an Anglo-American military commission. Arnold suggested to Ghormley that there should be an American air officer on the commission. He pointed out to Ghormley that "war today is an air war," and that "the Air alone can bring Germany to its knees if anything can." As Arnold should have realized, that was no way to talk to a Navy man. Ghormley "would have none of it." Arnold wrote in his diary, "He is all wet because the British have a strong combination Air-Army-Navy against which we have Army-Navy." But at least he had found one man in London who seemed unimpressed by the power of the German bombers.

On his next-to-last day Arnold was again surprised when he learned that King George VI wanted to see him at Buckingham Palace. After "a long walk down seemingly endless corridors," which were cold because most of the palace windows had been shattered by bombs, he entered a room and there was His Majesty. They shook hands and talked for more than a half hour about "everything from Hitler to Washington, from war to peace." Gradually it occurred to Arnold that he was taking up too much of the king's time. But how did one end a conversation with a king? "People always tell you how to enter and greet a king," he said to himself, "but why is it that no one ever tells a fellow how to leave a king? What do you say?"

What Arnold said was, "Sir, I know you are a very busy man and have a lot to do, so I will leave." The king shook hands again and smiled affably. But when Arnold made his way alone back down the long chilly corridors to the room where he had left his hat, the king's aides there were astonished to learn how he had ended the interview. One of them said, "My God! You don't leave the King! Not ever! The King always leaves you!"

On his return to Washington, Arnold decided to assemble all the senior Air Corps officers at the Bolling Field Officers' Club and tell them his impressions of the situation in England. But before doing so he had two meetings at the White House with President Roosevelt and Harry Hopkins. After the second meeting, he called Quesada into his office and said, "Pete, you've got a job. You've got to make my talk tonight. I can't make it."

He gave Quesada the distinct impression that President Roosevelt had noticed his negative impression of the English situation and had forbidden him to make his speech for fear he might spread his pessimism about England.

While the president may not have appreciated Arnold's opinions about the plight of England, he had apparently begun to appreciate the way Arnold was handling his job, because in June 1941 he approved the plan Robert Lovett had been working on, a plan to reorganize the Air Corps and give it more autonomy. On June 20, a revision of Army Regulation 95-5 established the Army Air Forces (to replace the Army Air Corps) with an air staff of its own and a chief of the Army Air Forces who would also be Army deputy chief of staff for air. Arnold, who was to fill those two roles, would continue his current duties, but henceforth he would have official control over the entire organization. For this solidification of his authority he could thank not only Lovett but General Marshall, who later said, "I tried to give Arnold all the power I could. I tried to make him as nearly as I could Chief of Staff of the Air without any restraint."

The first piece of work produced by the fledgling air staff was a remarkable document which became known as AWPD-1. Named after the air staff's recently formed Air War Plans Division, it was a projection, and as it happened a remarkably accurate one, of the Air Forces' role in any war that might arise against Germany and/or Japan. Largely the work of four exceptional thinkers—Col. Harold George, Lt. Col. Kenneth Walker, Maj. Haywood Hansell, and Maj. Laurence Kuter—the plan assigned four basic war tasks to the Air Forces. It would defend the air over the Western Hemisphere. It would support the defensive strategy in the Pacific during the initial phases of the war if both Japan

and Germany became adversaries. It would wage an unlimit-
ed strategic air offensive against Germany as soon as possible, including
support for an invasion of the European continent. And finally it would
soften Japan for invasion by waging an unlimited strategic air offensive
against its homeland. The document added hopefully that with regard
to both Germany and Japan, "If the air offensive is successful, a land
offensive may not be necessary."[15]

The inclusion of Japan as well as Germany in this theoretical war
plan was a result of aggressive Japanese expansion policies in the Far
East. From the day they invaded China in 1931, the Japanese had been
regarded by the United States as a potential enemy. The China campaign (still in progress ten years later); the notorious Axis Pact between
Japan, Germany, and Italy; the massive enlargement of Japan's army
and navy; and the growing possibility that the Japanese might try to
capture the oil fields of the Dutch East Indies made it imperative that the
United States prepare contingency plans to stop them. If Japan were to
conquer all or even most of East Asia, American interests there would be
seriously threatened.

In August 1941, Stimson, Marshall, Lovett, and Arnold all approved the plan, and in September, President Roosevelt accepted it,
incorporating its key features into his own calculations of what would be
needed to defeat the Axis powers. The special strategic mission of the
Army's air arm was at last formally recognized. Arnold now had
concrete authorization to build openly, without hindrance from Army
ground generals, the kind of air force he had been trying to build for the
last three years.

Still smarting at the British remarks about the B-17 in combat, he
sent Gen. George Brett to London to find out if the plane was actually as
inept and hopeless as they claimed. And to make sure the British didn't
outstrip the United States in the new field of jet propulsion, he put the
Bell Aircraft Corporation to work on the prototype of a jet fighter plane,
using as a basic model the specifications he had brought back from
England.

In August, at Marshall's invitation, he attended the Argentia
(Newfoundland) Conference between Roosevelt and Churchill, at which
the Atlantic Charter was promulgated. The purpose of the conference
was to serve notice on Hitler that America sympathized entirely with his
enemies. The Atlantic Charter was a declaration in favor of all the
freedoms, national and personal, that Hitler was trying, with fearsome
success, to suppress. It declared that neither the United States nor Great

Britain sought territorial aggrandizement, and that both nations, after the war, would foster the basic freedoms of all people, vanquished as well as victors.

While the president and the prime minister worked on the wording of the charter, their top generals and admirals conferred about more concrete military possibilities. Once again Arnold was disappointed by the narrowness of British thinking and appalled by the number of aircraft and amount of materiel they were seeking from America. They wanted four thousand heavy bombers at a time when the United States was producing only five hundred a month. Yet they didn't seem to have any long-range plan that anticipated the defeat of Germany or even the invasion of the European continent.

"British long-range plan," Arnold wrote in his diary, "is to keep giving as little as possible in remote areas where they can meet Germans on even terms, always hoping for a break—a miracle—an internal breakdown of [German] morale." To Arnold, who operated on that typically American assumption that nothing is impossible, the realistic outlook of the British, which simply took into account the virtual helplessness of their situation, was almost insupportable. He was incapable of thinking in terms of a standoff. It seemed to him inexcusable to plan for anything less than total victory.

A few days after his return to Washington on August 14, Bee and David (who was now "getting to be quite a large boy, growing by leaps and bounds") departed for their annual anti-hay-fever sojourn at Nag's Head, leaving him alone in their big, empty house. Bruce was still at West Point, where summer vacations had been eliminated and the four-year course cut to three years because of the critical world situation. Hank, married and the father of a baby boy, H. H. Arnold III, was a second lieutenant stationed in Panama and impatient to become a first lieutenant. He was also disappointed because he hadn't been assigned to the troop command he expected to get.

"Don't take it too hard," his father advised in a letter. "I don't believe I ever got the command I thought I was going to get and I never could tell what I was going to do next, but taking it all in all, my life in the Army has been a very pleasant one. I have yet to get an unpleasant station in spite of the fact that I have been banished, exiled and all the other things that have happened to me."

Though he felt a growing need for good officers, Arnold seemed less than eager to hire one particular outstanding man who became available in the early summer of 1941.[16] Col. Hugh Knerr, who had been retired from the Army for medical reasons but whose health was now apparently sound, had been trying since May to return to active duty. His possible reemergence brought back echoes of the mid-1930s struggle for the B-17, air power, and an independent air force. Knerr had not yet forgiven Arnold's self-restraint in that struggle, which he and Frank Andrews had led, and which he himself had never abandoned even though, like Andrews, he had been "exiled" by the War Department for his part in it.

In February 1938, after being relieved as chief of staff, G.H.Q. Air Force, Knerr had been demoted to lieutenant colonel and sent to Fort Sam Houston in San Antonio as air officer for the Eighth Army Corps Area. He was assigned to the same "remote" office there that Billy Mitchell had occupied during his "exile," and as soon as he settled into it he was "mortified to see an open-top latrine in the opposite corner." He was soon further mortified to find the outer office clerks walking in and out to use this latrine. The Army was teaching him a lesson.

Strange things began happening to Knerr in San Antonio. "The frustration of my routine and strain of the G.H.Q. experience brought on a recurrence of sciatica traceable to a crash . . . in 1923." When the flight surgeon discovered this, he "put me in the hospital where I remained unwillingly for several months." In January 1939, Knerr "agreed to retire" and was sent before a retirement board. During the board's deliberations, a psychiatrist made the claim that "I had a psychosomatic indication resulting from my persistent battles for the B-17." Knerr noted that "subsequent examination at Walter Reed [Hospital] cleared me."

In April 1939, as a civilian, Knerr continued his crusade for a separate air force by sending a paper to President Roosevelt, deploring the fact that Air Corps operational units had been subjected to the chief of Air Corps (Arnold). As a result, he charged, "convenience of administration always took precedence over efficiency in operation." What was needed, he wrote, was "a United States Air Corps within the War Department, with a Chief of Staff for Air reporting direct to the Secretary of War."

Four weeks later, in a letter to Andrews, Knerr stated that Arnold was "furious" about this paper, as he may very well have been. Though the president apparently gave it some attention, nothing was done about it. It could hardly have been forgotten, however, when, in May 1941, Andrews wrote to George Brett, then acting Air Corps chief under Arnold, asking him to reactivate Knerr as a brigadier general and send him to Panama to run Andrews's maintenance command there.

Knerr at that time was working in the Sperry Corporation Research Laboratories. On June 5, he ran into Arnold at lunch in Washington. Arnold mentioned the letter from Andrews and asked Knerr if he did indeed want to return to duty. Knerr said he did. Then for some inexplicable reason he added, "as soon as war is declared." Shortly thereafter, in a letter to Andrews, Brett, presumably under Arnold's orders, said he couldn't make Knerr a brigadier general.

While Andrews was trying "to find a way to get around" Brett, Knerr and Andrews exchanged letters that revealed some important currents of feeling within the Air Corps during the years of its struggle for expansion.

On June 18, 1941, Knerr wrote to Andrews about his continuing campaign, waged in letters and magazine articles, for an independent air force. He felt he was making some progress, but "the biggest problem left is to devise a means that will ensure having as its first air marshal FMA [Frank M. Andrews] instead of HHA [Henry H. Arnold]. Frankly, I am stumped. Looks like the only way to do it would be to discredit the leadership of HHA while FMA was fighting for the things that the present war has proven to be essential to victory. Although he lifted no finger to help me when I needed it I can't quite come around to smearing him. Besides it might discredit the whole movement if someone picked up the idea. I could be accused of personal motive. So [it] looks like the old slicker is sitting pretty again."

Andrews, in a June 23 reply to this letter, took a carefully measured view. "I have not been doing much thinking lately on the question of higher organization of air power . . . except to retain the conviction . . . that it cannot be developed under an organization which considers it as an adjunct of surface forces; even with a man as broad minded and as far seeing as Marshall at the head of the Army. No matter how progressive Marshall may be himself the rank and file of the Army has not changed materially. . . .

"With reference to your dilemma about HHA, don't let that influence you in any degree. Arnold is capable all right. The main objective now is to get started. He is probably the best man available to head it up. He is a much better politician than you or I, as he very clearly demonstrated when he sat back and let us butt our heads against a stone wall and kept himself in the background. Whoever handles this thing initially has got to be a good politician."

The June 20 reorganization of the Air Corps, giving it a large measure of autonomy, foreclosed the possibility of creating an independent air force at that time, and virtually stilled the debate on the subject. Knerr, referring to the organizational change in a note to Andrews, said, "Arnold beat us to it." He might better have said Arnold, Marshall, Lovett, and Stimson had beaten them to it. All four agreed that 1941, with war approaching, was not the time to separate the Air Corps from the Army. The Air Corps was simply unable to take responsibility at that point for all the peripheral services the Army was providing for it. But Arnold's vigorous campaign for an independent air force in the closing days of World War II and Marshall's active support of that campaign after the war indicate that the two men had agreed, perhaps as early as 1939, that this would be a desirable goal when the right time arrived.

During July of 1941 Andrews continued his efforts to bring Knerr to Panama as a brigadier general, but Brett remained "obdurate in his opposition." In a phone conversation between Andrews and Arnold on July 27, Andrews again asked for Knerr. Arnold said he had talked to Knerr about the move (presumably at the June 5 lunch) and felt convinced that Knerr didn't want to go. Arnold's remark may not have been as disingenuous as it must have sounded, since he could easily have interpreted Knerr's words "as soon as war is declared" to mean "not now."

An assessment of all the available evidence indicates that Arnold, while admiring Knerr's ability, had reason to feel less than warm toward him. He may very well have been dragging his feet about returning Knerr to active duty. But he had too much respect for Andrews to refuse the request when Andrews put it to him directly. In August, Knerr's recall to duty was approved, at which point a new snag developed: the Surgeon General rejected him on medical grounds. The reason: "It is not the policy of the War Department to place returned officers on active duty who have had mental or nervous conditions of such significance as to lead to retirement."

Under the circumstances, the Surgeon General's judgment seemed unfair. Hugh Knerr's subsequent service during World War II proved that it was an uninformed judgment. But meanwhile, throughout 1941, the decision kept Knerr off active duty.

On September 24, 1941, Arnold wrote another memorandum, this time to Secretary Stimson, complaining once more that too many heavy bombers were going to England, especially in light of the fact that the British didn't like America's best heavy bomber, the B-17. He asked that medium and light bombers plus pursuit planes be sent to England because they would be more useful there, and that heavy bombers be kept at home to build an American strike force.

The memo seemed to suggest that he could more easily spare the lighter planes, but a conversation between Arnold in Washington and General Marshall in Memphis the next day, September 25, illustrates sharply that, even in late 1941, the Air Forces was still woefully short of more than heavy bombers.

Marshall was in Memphis observing the Army's extensive summer war maneuvers. Arnold called him about a problem that had arisen in delivering dive bombers for the climax of the exercises, scheduled for November.[17]

Arnold began by reminding Marshall that there were only two dive bomber groups in the current maneuvers, one of which was supposed to go to the Philippines in early December, making it unavailable in November.

"How many will you have in November?" Marshall asked.

"We have just the two groups."

Marshall didn't seem to grasp the problem. "With one short, how many will be left?" he asked.

"We'll just have that one group in the maneuvers."

"And at the present time you have how many?"

"Two."

"You have two of yours?"

"Two of ours, and they're not both equipped with dive bombers. One's equipped with light bombers but they're both dive bomber groups."

Later in the conversation, Marshall said, "Now let me see if I have got this straight. What you want to know is whether we should go ahead and send that dive bomber group to the Philippines."

"That's right. And be short one in November."

"How's that?"

"And be short one in November."

"When does it sail?"

"The first of December."

"It doesn't sail until the first of December?"

"Yes sir."

Marshall laughed. "Why'd you have to call me this afternoon?"

"Because I have to make the decision now," Arnold explained. "They'll have to be called away from maneuvers on September thirtieth if they go to the Philippines. They'll have to pack up their equipment and pack up their planes."

Marshall could hardly gainsay that but he still didn't quite understand Arnold's dilemma. "We will have one group, anyway, won't we?"

"Not dive bombers," Arnold said. "They'll be light bombers."

"We won't have any dive bombers?"

"We have only one group of dive bombers." What he was trying to convey was that the group he intended to send to the Philippines was the only dive bomber group actually equipped with dive bombers.

"That's the only one in prospect?" Marshall asked.

"That's the only one we have right now."

"Well, I know it's the only one we have right now, but . . ."

"There won't be any more deliveries," Arnold announced.

"No more deliveries?"

"For some time."

But his lack of dive bombers did not concern Arnold as much as his lack of heavy bombers. And his concern about heavy bombers was intensified by the British reports that the B-17 performed badly in combat. The Air Corps was so deeply committed to the B-17 that Arnold would be in trouble if it fell short of expectations. He was somewhat relieved when George Brett reported from England that the British disliked the plane only because they had misused it. Their training and maintenance were poor, and so was their flight planning. They had made "no attempt to institute check lists for takeoff and landing." There was "no inspection system in effect." One pilot was sent on a mission without ever before having flown with his crew. Neither he nor the crew had flown a B-17 above 2,000 feet before this mission, in which they had to fly above 25,000 feet. The pilot had never before used Boeing oxygen equipment, nor had he ever feathered an engine or operated the automatic pilot. The crew had never used the interphones or fired fifty-caliber machine guns.[18]

Brett also sent word of another B-17, which on August 15 had attacked the German battleships *Scharnhorst* and *Gneisenau* at Brest. After dropping its bombs, this plane had been attacked for a total of twenty-three minutes by two Heinkel 113s and five Messerschmitt 109s. "Approximately 20 cannon shells" hit the plane and six of them burst inside the fuselage. Several crew members were killed or wounded. The bomb-bay doors were jammed open. The left aileron was "practically shot away." The trim tabs were shot away and the rudder was damaged. Yet the plane returned to England. People would tell many similar stories about Flying Fortresses during the next four years, but this one was especially reassuring because it was the first such story.

Despite Brett's encouraging report, Arnold was aware that his reputation was riding on the uncertain prospects of the B-17. He was in fact so keenly aware of it that in the late fall of 1941 he considered deemphasizing the use of heavy bombers and placing his reliance instead on an unmanned projectile plane that was an improved version of the "bug" he had tried to promote during World War I. Charles F. Kettering of General Motors, the creator of the original "bug," was also the creator of the modernized missile. He had successfully tested a model with a two-hundred-mile range (which could be lengthened) and had proven it was now possible to control it by radio. Arnold, disturbed by the casualties he would have if he sent huge armadas of heavy bombers over Germany, gave the bug serious consideration. But ultimately he had to abandon the project. "We finally came to the conclusion unanimously," he explained, "that even with the most improved type of 'bug,' the best we could do from England would be to hit Paris or some of the other large cities in France, Belgium or Holland. We could not get at the real heart of our enemy—interior Germany itself."[19]

Instead of developing the bug, he asked for authority, and received it December 2, to go ahead with the plans for the superbomber, which eventually turned out to be the B-29.

One weekend late in 1941, Hap, Bee, and Dave went to West Point to see Bruce, who was now in his second year there. Hap himself flew up Friday afternoon because he couldn't spare the time to drive, but he had Simmons bring Bee and Dave in the grey-and-black family Pontiac.

"Leave at three," he said to Simmons, "and be there at nine."

Simmons was incredulous. "General, that only gives me six hours."

"I don't give a goddamn," Arnold said. "You be there at nine."[20]

With fourteen-year-old David in the front seat and Bee in the back, "scared to death," Simmons drove the country roads at seventy-five and eighty miles an hour. Nevertheless Arnold "cussed me out when I got there" twenty minutes after nine. Simmons knew him too well by this time to take the cussing seriously, but when Arnold added, "I can drive it back in six hours," Simmons had the uneasy feeling he meant it.

At the academy, Arnold found his son Bruce in the quad, walked up to him, and without so much as a hello, said, "You will not get married until you've been out of West Point a year and you've saved a thousand dollars. Do you understand that?"[21]

Bruce had matured sufficiently by this time to remain unflustered. He had caught on to the fact that whenever his father had to say something unpleasant to someone, he would cover his embarrassment by blurting it out abruptly. He wasn't capable of taking a person aside when a delicate matter arose and quietly discussing it.

Bruce looked at him and said, "My God! I'm not even in love."

"I can't support two boys and their wives," his father said. "Just remember that."

Bruce understood now what was bothering him. Hank's wife, Kaye, had a tendency to overspend Hank's salary.

When Bruce told his father he wasn't even in love, he was being slightly less than candid. The previous summer, plane manufacturer Donald Douglas's daughter, Barbara, a student at the University of Southern California, had decided to transfer to an eastern college. On an exploratory tour of several eastern schools, she and her mother had dinner with the Arnolds in Washington. When Hap learned that Barbara was going up the Hudson to visit Vassar, he suggested she stop at West Point and visit his son Bruce. She liked the idea, and after reaching Vassar in nearby Poughkeepsie, let Bruce know she was coming to the academy.

He had never met her. But as he stood in the lobby of the Thayer Hotel with a friend, waiting to be paged, a girl walked across the lobby who was so beautiful that he turned to his friend and said, "I don't know who that is, but that's the girl I'm going to marry." It was, of course, Barbara Douglas, and in the late fall of 1941, he still had her more than casually in mind.

That Sunday afternoon, Arnold did drive his Pontiac back to Washington, but fortunately for Simmons, Bee's mother, Annie Pool, had also shown up at West Point and decided to ride back with them. Since there was no room for Simmons, Arnold arranged for him to fly back. Mrs. Pool, then in her late seventies, enjoyed speed so much that whenever she rode with her son-in-law, whose company she obviously enjoyed, she would cry out, "Throw it to her, Hap! Throw it to her!" while her daughter in the back seat would plead, "Mother! Keep your mouth shut!"

Hap Arnold didn't need any encouragement. He was determined to beat Simmons's record. In his hurry, he went speeding through one town the wrong way on a one-way street, until he encountered a car going the right way. It extracted the front fender of his Pontiac; fortunately, no one was hurt. He explained to Simmons later that the other driver had cut in front of him. But the other driver had not prevented him from making it to Washington in six hours.

On November 5, Arnold wrote a note to Donald Douglas in Santa Monica: "Confidentially, I may be able to get away for a trip to Los

Angeles, arriving there late in the evening of Dec. 6th and remaining around there until the 7th, 8th, 9th and 10th. If my memory doesn't fail me, quail season is still on during that period and I wonder if you have any idea as to how a fellow might be able to get out somewhere and see two or three of them flying."

One purpose of this trip west, besides quail-hunting, was to take part in the sendoff for the crews of thirteen B-17s, which were on their way to the Philippine Islands.[22] The Japanese were making such ominous moves in the Far East that it was not unreasonable to think they might declare war on the United States. Arnold believed, as did most American military men, that if the Japanese did launch a war, they would begin by attacking the Philippines. And he was still as woefully short of planes on the islands as he was every place else—he had a total of only twenty-six B-17s in the Philippines. An extra thirteen hardly represented adequate reinforcements, but he had no more to spare.

By late November, Japan had two diplomats in Washington, Admiral Kichisaburo Nomura and Saburo Kurusu, conducting negotiations with the State Department. These negotiations, which were generally assumed to represent the last chance for continuing peace in the Pacific, were obviously going badly. Nevertheless, American military men seemed unable to grasp the probability that guns would soon be firing and bombs exploding. Arnold, for instance, would hardly have planned to go quail-hunting if he had been at all suspicious that the country was at the very brink of war.

In Arnold's case, however, there was some excuse for a lack of urgency. Even on December 4, his last day in Washington before leaving for the coast, he had no current information about what was happening in the Pacific.

"I had no reason," he later recalled, "to believe the Japanese fleet had left the east coast of Asia days before, had headed eastward through the mandated islands, and was now a short distance from the Hawaiian Islands. That bit of information—about the Japanese fleet being loose, known to many War and Navy Department officials—had never been given to me. Like most officers in the War Department, I was under the impression that, if a Japanese attack occurred, it would be made first against the Philippines and then would be carried down the east coast of Asia to Singapore, to the Islands of Borneo, Java and Sumatra." The Air Corps at that time had no intelligence organization of its own, and was not always privy to Army Intelligence information.

As it happened, Arnold picked a good time to get out of Washington. On December 4, the Chicago *Tribune* and Washington *Times-Herald*, both isolationist papers, exposed the existence of a document called "Rainbow Five," a joint Army-Navy paper that outlined military strategy to be pursued in the event of war against Germany and Japan. It was the kind of contingency plan that the defense establishment of every nation should have ready at all times as a guide to follow if suddenly attacked. But to the *Tribune* and the *Times Herald,* it was a "Roosevelt administration project to expand the Army and Navy to ten million men and send American expeditionary forces of five million men overseas to fight Germany, Italy and Japan." And they denounced it so vehemently that the noise was heard throughout Washington.

In the midst of the furor, a rumor began to circulate that the *Tribune* and *Times-Herald* had obtained their copy of "Rainbow Five" through an Air Forces captain, who had given it to isolationist Sen. Burton K. Wheeler of Montana. This supposition, never verified, led to another supposition, never verified, that Arnold must have given the document to the unidentified captain. The matter was delicate at the time, not only because national security was at stake, but because Congress was then debating an $8-billion supplementary defense bill. Arnold, according to the rumor, had divulged "Rainbow Five" in the hope of reducing aircraft exports to England. It was a rumor that made no sense. The disclosure of "Rainbow Five" to the isolationists was more likely to bring about a reduction of Army and therefore Air Forces appropriations, which the isolationists were always trying to do, than a reduction of aircraft exports, which brought money into the country and created jobs. It was a rumor typical of many that circulated in Washington during the uneasy days and weeks of late 1941. There is no evidence that President Roosevelt or General Marshall gave it a moment's credence. And it was destined to be forgotten after the events of December 7.

After taking off from Washington, Arnold, with Gene Beebe as his pilot, flew first to Knoxville, where he inspected an aluminum plant. Shortages of aluminum still seriously hindered the expansion of the aircraft industry. On the sixth, they arrived at Hamilton Field, north of San Francisco, where Arnold assembled the officers scheduled to fly the B-17s to the Philippines that night. The first leg of the journey would be to Hawaii; the early birds would arrive in the morning, the later ones about noon. Arnold wasn't worried about that leg of their trip, but it seemed to him at least possible that by the time these men reached the South Pacific, Japan might have declared war. So he gave the crews a short talk, warning them that they might run into trouble, might have to use their guns "somewhere along the line" before they reached their destination. What he had in mind was the danger of passing Japanese-mandated islands like Truk. He didn't even dream of the bloody chaos they would find when they tried to land, the very next day, at Wheeler Field on Oahu.

At midnight, after waving goodbye to the last of these thirteen B-17s, Arnold and Beebe retired for a short night's sleep; the next morning they flew to Bakersfield, where they met Donald Douglas and his father. After a drive of several miles, they came to the ranch property of a friend of Douglas's who had given him permission to hunt there. Before noon, Beebe had shot his legal limit of quail but the others had not, so they returned to a house on the property in which the caretaker and his wife lived. The owner retained one section of this house, including a kitchen stocked with food and beer, for himself and his guests. While the hunting party ate lunch, they could hear voices on the caretaker's radio through the wall but they thought nothing of it.

Douglas, realizing his elderly father wasn't much of a walker, suggested that he stay at the house and wait for their return. "Why don't you play the radio to amuse yourself," he said.

When the hunters returned, about three p.m., Douglas's father came running out to tell them Pearl Harbor had been attacked.

The caretaker, behind him, said, "I heard something about that while you-all were having lunch, but I didn't think you'd be interested."

Beebe recalls that the immediate reaction to the news was stunned silence. Douglas recalls that Arnold finally broke the silence when he looked off into the distance and said, "I've been trying to tell . . . Roosevelt something like this was going to happen."

They hurriedly threw their gear and their quail into the car and headed for the Bakersfield Airport. When they flew from there to March Field, they found their "old stamping ground" in total commotion and confusion. Arnold first called General Marshall, who suggested he fly to San Francisco and help prepare the Army commander there, Gen. John L. DeWitt, for the possibility of a sneak attack. After several more phone calls, and after putting March Field on a "war status," he and Beebe again took off, just before dark, this time for San Francisco, then Washington. Because the weather was bad, it took almost forty hours to fly across the country. Fortunately, Arnold was able to get some sleep on the way. It would be several days before he got any more.

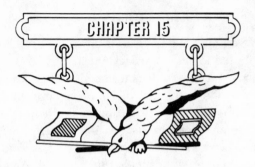

CHAPTER 15

At about four o'clock in the afternoon of December 9, 1941, Beebe brought the general's DC-3 down out of the thick overcast and landed at Bolling Field. Arnold said to him, "I'll see you at the office," then leaped out of the plane and into his waiting car.[1] During the weather delays on the flight east, he had spent most of his time on the phone to Washington, so when he arrived at his Munitions Building office, he already had considerable information about the Japanese attack and the extent of damage it had done. He was quite prepared to blame the Navy for what had happened. How could the Japanese have launched an attack from two hundred miles north of Hawaii when, if his information was correct, a U.S. naval task force was on maneuvers north of Oahu, directly in the path of the raiding planes?[2] As soon as he reached his office he was confronted by other questions, which indicated the Navy might not deserve all the blame. Why, for instance did it take three or four hours after the first Japanese attack in Hawaii before most of the Air Forces' P-40 fighters could get off the ground? And how could twelve Air Forces B-17s have been caught on the ground and destroyed in the Philippines? Fortunately for Arnold, these questions would never embarrass him personally because he had no control over the use of Air Forces units in Hawaii or the Philippines. Operationally, the Air Forces were still part of the Army and the air commander. But while the dismal lack of air performance on December 7 and 8 may not have embarrassed Arnold, it did infuriate him. "I had always believed that our airmen would fight it out in the air," he said. "They should never have been caught flat-footed on the ground. It was a very sad blow to me."

More important, it demonstrated a problem he would have to cope with throughout the war. It was his job to put those hard-earned planes and crews together. But what was the point of sending air units overseas to fight if ground force generals like Walter Short in Hawaii and Douglas MacArthur in the Philippines allowed them to sit idle and be destroyed on the ground? MacArthur on December 10 sent him an effusive radiogram about the gallantry of the air crews in the Philippines. "Their losses were due entirely to the overwhelming superiority of enemy force," he said. "No unit could have done better. . . . No item of loss can properly be attributed to neglect or lack of care. . . . You may take pride in their conduct." But he did not explain why, despite adequate knowledge of what had happened in Hawaii several hours earlier, he had allowed so many planes to be sitting in tidy rows on the airfields when the Japanese attackers arrived. Arnold called the Philippine air commander, Gen. Lewis H. Brereton. He couldn't explain it either. He said they didn't have enough airfields for dispersal. Arnold called the Hawaiian air commander, Gen. F. L. Martin. He said General Short had ordered the planes to be grouped tightly together on the ground so it would be easier to guard them against possible sabotage. The Japanese bombers had found this tight grouping delightfully convenient. Martin also said many of the air crewmen were being used for other purposes. Trained mechanics, for example, were assigned to military police and patrol duties.

None of this made any sense to Arnold. At home that night he found it difficult to explain the debacle to Bee because he still didn't understand it himself.

Why weren't the planes dispersed, she wanted to know. Why weren't there more airfields in the Philippines?

"Because MacArthur wouldn't have them," he said to her. "He insisted that if we got an increase of squadrons and wings, the Army had to have the same increase, and Congress wouldn't go for it."[3]

The more hideous aspects of the situation were now bearing down upon Arnold. For three years he had been warning President Roosevelt that if too many planes were sent to England, the United States might end up without air power at a moment when it would be most sorely needed. That dire prediction had now come true. The Army Air Forces were facing a long, hazardous war with only 159 four-engine bombers on hand and a total of only 1100 planes that could even claim to be combatworthy. These included P-40 fighters that, as Arnold knew, were obsolescent and might soon be made obsolete by the Japanese Zero. In Hawaii and the Philippines, the two cornerstones of American Pacific defense, the Zero already had the better of the P-40. Of course, the Zeros had been airborne during the battles while most of the P-40s were on the ground—presumably the P-40 would do better when flown into battle. But after the Japanese attacks, were there enough of them left in the Pacific to make a showing? And even if he managed to scrounge replacements for those that had been destroyed, would the ground force commanders out there know how to use them?

Arnold's first reaction to this desperate situation was to increase his work load and the work of everyone around him. In his office the day began at 8:00 a.m. now—except for Arnold, who usually arrived at seven—and ended about 8:00 p.m. Everyone on the staff had a red emergency telephone at home so he could be reached at night, and there were no more free Saturdays or Sundays; Arnold decreed a seven-day week for the duration.[4] He wanted to make sure everyone around him knew there was a war in progress, and everyone soon did. Whenever a member of his staff asked to be sent out for combat duty, someone was likely to accuse him of wanting a rest.

Arnold also took immediate steps to strengthen his staff, which General Marshall sometimes criticized as too old and lacking in initiative. On December 12, Arnold called Jimmy Doolittle, who at that time was still in Detroit, trying to hasten the auto industry into aircraft production.

"How quickly can you be here?" Arnold asked. "I want you on my immediate staff."

"Will tomorrow be all right?" Doolittle asked.[5]

When Doolittle arrived in Washington he learned that he was to be the staff troubleshooter, and his first problems needed immediate solutions. In the opening days of combat, according to the reports, the bombs in some of the planes refused to drop, machine guns refused to fire, and a lot of other things simply didn't work. Doolittle's assignment was to make those things work, and quickly. Though he didn't solve all the problems, he did so well that Arnold soon sent him to the Martin plant in Baltimore to decide whether the Air Forces should cancel production of the B-26, twin-engine, medium bomber—a plane the Martin Company called "the Marauder" but a lot of pilots were beginning to call "the Murderer." Too many fliers were crashing in it. Doolittle recommended a change in training methods "because we were training people to fly a normal airplane and the B-26 was not normal." He admitted it was an "unforgiving" airplane, one that didn't allow a pilot to make repeated mistakes, but he liked it.

When Arnold read his report, he called him in and said, "I want you to take a B-26, fly it under any and all conditions, then go down . . . and show those boys that flying this ship is no different from flying any other."

When Doolittle flew to the B-26 transition school, all the student pilots, by prearrangement, had been lined up along the ramp. Suddenly they were amazed to see a B-26 coming in to land on only one engine, a feat believed to be impossible. Doolittle touched down smoothly, taxied over to the assembled men, got out, and said to them, "Now what is it you don't like about this airplane?"

Before he left several days later, all of them had learned to land on one engine.

On the afternoon of Sunday, December 21, President Roosevelt had a meeting in his White House study with his top military men —Secretary Knox, Adm. Harold Stark and Adm. Ernest King of the Navy; Secretary Stimson, General Marshall and General Arnold of the Army. Arnold was surprised and delighted to be included in such august company. "From that time forward," he observed, "there was no doubt about the Commanding General of the Army Air Forces being a member of the President's Staff."[6] In his own eyes, Arnold was still a Pennsylvania farm boy who had never imagined himself a member of such a high council. His wide-eyed and evident pleasure at finding himself there seemed to amuse and charm men like Roosevelt, Stimson, and Marshall.

British Prime Minister Churchill was arriving in Washington the next day, Roosevelt announced, with a staff of eighty-two cabinet ministers, admirals, generals, and aides. They would be well prepared to discuss war aims, joint strategies, and materiel needs. The president wanted his men to be equally well prepared. They now had a whole day to think about it.

Arnold's first significant meeting, with British Chief of Air Staff Sir Charles Portal and Air Marshal Arthur Harris (who had been in the United States for seven months purchasing aircraft), brought out one potential disagreement of major proportions. Portal was eager for the arrival of American bombers in England (he didn't mention his dissatisfaction with those he already had) but he was obviously not so eager for the arrival of American crews. He said he now had more bomber pilots than he had planes and he implied that instead of sending Air Forces units, the Americans should simply send bombers, which could be immediately incorporated into the R.A.F. Though Arnold could see this as another move to siphon off American aircraft, thus further delaying the development of a real American air force, and though he had no intention of letting it happen, he refrained from arguing the issue at this meeting. Portal also said he thought it was the Navy's job to attack Japan. This was a clear implication that whatever strength the Air Forces had to offer should be spent in the effort against Germany. Arnold didn't argue this issue either. He agreed with it in part, but he also recognized it as a potential matter of contention between his Air Forces and the Navy. He was already familiar with the attitudes of the Navy's gruff, argumentative, and intransigent Ernie King, who insisted that America's major war effort must be in the Pacific against Japan. Arnold could see in the making a tug-of-war for his airplanes between the British on one side and the U.S. Navy on the other. Though the admirals had consistently and stubbornly resisted the allocation of raw materials and factory space to heavy bombers rather than to warships, they could be expected to demand their share of these heavy bombers as soon as they realized how useful a big, long-range plane could be in attacking Japan.

This first meeting between the British and Americans as wartime allies produced some generalized agreements on aims and strategies. Most important from Arnold's viewpoint was the decision to concentrate first on Europe rather than the Pacific, and Churchill's concession that the Americans should start heavy bombardment operations against Germany as soon as possible, from British bases and with their own units. The latter was a clear victory for Arnold, who promised, much too optimistically, to have his first bomb group in England within three months. But even after winning this preliminary skirmish, Arnold realized there were many underlying issues that had not yet been joined. He was to feel some heavy and conflicting pressure soon from the British and from the U.S. Navy.

The pressure was quick in coming. After the Washington meetings, Arnold took Portal on a short trip to Florida, where they fished, sat in the sun, and got to know each other. They had what Arnold called "a wonderful time," but if he thought he was softening Portal, he was misjudging the man. As soon as Portal returned to England, he sent back the kind of request Arnold was most eager to forestall. The R.A.F. wanted 250 B-17s to use as submarine chasers in the British coastal command.[7]

This request infuriated Arnold. It insulted America's premier airplane by suggesting it would be suitable only for patrol duty, not for its original purpose as a deep-penetration bomber. And it pursued the apparent British intention of trying to absorb American planes into the R.A.F. rather than giving the United States a chance to build its own air force.

At the same time, the Navy's pressure on the Air Forces was increasing. Already the admirals were beginning to see the virtues of the B-17s they had so strenuously belittled.[8] Squeezed by the demands from both sides, Arnold decided to play one against the other. In late January he invited to his office Air Marshal Harris, who was still in Washington, and treated him to a convincing display of emotional heat. The result was a cipher telegram from Harris to Portal, dated January 29, 1942, and marked "Most Secret":

> Arnold asks me to tell you that so far as he can judge at present he aims to get up to 20 heavy bomber groups into U.K. this year. . . . But this is likely to be adversely affected by certain tendencies now growing in force e.g. in spite of lip service to the agreed grand strategy the Far East looms ever larger and more insistently in the thoughts of the highest ones in the land. Added to this the Navy has now realized the limitations of the flying boat and covets the heavy bomber in quantity. Recent successes against Jap. ships lend weight to their case and in any event they have always opposed the bomber plan by fair means or foul. . . . Our proposal to sidetrack 250 B-17s to Coastal Command has made the airmen here very hot under the collar. "We are thereby playing straight into the Navy's hands." As to what he wants you to do about it Arnold was not clear, but in general he expressed an urgent desire that you should fight every proposed diversion of H.B.s [Heavy Bombers] from the bomber force and from direct action against German territory. . . . He implores your backing in the fight against diversion.

"Diversion" was a cry which would often arise from the U.S. Army Air Forces during the next two years. The British could always be depended upon to help Arnold fight the Navy's efforts to divert heavy bombers to the Pacific. But in some of Arnold's other struggles against diversion they were not so helpful. On February 19, Portal wrote Arnold a soothing letter that neither settled nor promised anything. Despite its friendly tone, this letter pointed out to Arnold that the B-17's bomb load "is less than that of the B-24 and our own heavy bombers, and consequently its diversion to a Coastal Command role involves the least loss of hitting power."

Harris, in his conversation with Arnold, had mentioned another criticism of the plane in combat. The machine guns in the B-17C, the latest model the British had received, were not set in power turrets, and the plane had no tail guns. The gunners would hit nothing, Harris warned, unless those guns were set in proper emplacements.[9]

These British disparagements of the B-17 must have shaken Arnold. The basic American air-war plan depended upon that plane. If it failed, there was only the B-24 to fall back on (at least until the unproven B-29 was developed), but very few people in the Air Forces considered the B-24 as good a plane as the B-17. Perhaps the British were misusing their B-17s, as General Brett had reported, but even so it was difficult to explain the plane's poor record in combat to date. On twenty-two missions (mostly two or three planes per mission) Fortresses had aborted eighteen times before reaching primary or secondary targets. That was a statistic difficult to answer. The only thing Arnold could do was to report each of the plane's newfound flaws to Wright Field and to the Boeing Company in the hope that they would be corrected. He was too deeply committed to the plane to abandon it.

He was just as deeply committed to the basic American air doctrine, which the British were seriously questioning. His whole plan for a massive bombing offensive against Germany, envisioned as the main United States contribution to the war in Europe until an invasion of the continent became feasible, was based on the belief, almost universally held in the Air Forces, that with the well-armed B-17 and the newly developed Norden bombsight (which during tests had reportedly placed a bomb in a barrel from 25,000 feet), it would be possible for huge armadas to conduct pinpoint raids against precisely selected German targets in broad daylight. The British, who had tried daylight bombing, were reiterating that such tactics would not work against German defenses. And they were also pointing out that the Germans had failed in their attempts to use daylight bombing against British defenses. If he wanted to bomb Germany, they said, he would have to be content to do as they did—drop great loads on large cities at night.

Arnold did not intend to relinquish a plan that he and his fellow airmen had cherished ever since the appearance of the B-17. But he did have some serious discussions about the plan with the man he had selected to fulfill it—his old friend Carl Spaatz.[10] When Spaatz came back from England the year before after observing the Battle of Britain, Arnold had got him his first star and then assigned him to Wright Field. Spaatz, who was never intensely absorbed in technical details, pleaded for some other post, but Arnold had said, "That's where you're going."[11] After Spaatz had been in Dayton a week or so, he came back to Washington and went into his act again until Arnold relented and made him chief of the air staff. He was one man on whom Arnold felt he could always rely. The two of them decided that, whatever the British might think, daylight bombing was possible, and that it would be much more conducive to winning the war than dropping bombs blindly and indiscriminately on civilians at night.

With Spaatz now the overall commander of the newly formed Eighth Air Force, an organization that existed on paper only at that time, Arnold called in another dependable old friend, Ira Eaker, who had taken over the fighter defenses on the West Coast the day after the Pearl Harbor attack. When Eaker arrived in Washington on January 8, Arnold said to him, "You're going to England. I want you to fly over there and negotiate with the British for headquarters, airdromes, communications, all the stuff we'll need. Understudy the British and work out the plans. Then I'll get you some bombers and some crews. You'll be in charge of the Eighth Air Force Bomber Command."

"Bombers!" Eaker exclaimed. "But I've been in fighters all my life!"

"That's why I'm giving you this job," Arnold said. "I want you to put some fight into the bombers."[12]

"What do I do for a staff?"

"I can spare two or three good men," Arnold said. "Beyond that I suggest you find yourself some civilians. You take a smart civilian, you can make him a smart officer in six weeks or so. But if you take a dumb officer, you'll never make him a smart officer."

After following this advice, Eaker left for England six weeks later with a staff of six (three career officers and three converted civilians) but with no airplanes, to create the Eighth Bomber Command. Spaatz stayed behind at Bolling Field to organize the Eighth Fighter Command, and to hasten the shipment of supplies, planes, and crews. The American air offensive against Germany had begun—with seven men in civilian clothes on a civilian airliner.

During the hectic days after the American entry into the war, Arnold found out what it was like to run an organization that suddenly had to assume life-and-death responsibilities all over the world. While he was fencing with the British and with the U.S. Navy, he was also involved in the much more immediate and desperate problem of getting emergency planes and supplies to the Philippines, where MacArthur and his men were trying, without much success, to beat back the invading Japanese. Shortly before Christmas, Arnold and Marshall dispatched 125 pursuit planes on two ships by way of Australia. They also diverted 15 B-24s to Manila by air. They weren't confident that any of these planes would reach their destination but they had to make every possible effort to save the Philippines. At the same time, Hawaii, Panama, Alaska, and all the continental American commands were pleading for more planes. Arnold could only tell them to get in line and wait.

The problem of putting the right men in the right jobs was another increasing headache because, as Arnold had indicated to Eaker, there weren't enough outstanding men in the small officer cadre of the peacetime Air Corps to fill all the vital posts created by the war. As time would tell, he had, in fact, an amazing number of remarkable men at his disposal. But he also had some deadwood. He was aware that some of the men he had appointed to important positions before the war, especially some of the men his own age, long-time friends and associates, lacked the drive and the dynamism to handle big jobs under wartime conditions. He knew he would have to relieve some of them, and just in case he might forget to do so, Marshall kept reminding him.[13]

After the war, Marshall said, "My main difficulties [with Arnold] came from the fact that he had a very immature staff. They were not immature in years, because they were pretty old but . . . they were not trained at that kind of staff work and they were busy taking stands . . . about promotions. They were already getting more rapid promotions than anybody else. . . . But his staff was always agitating about that. And the less [rank they had] the more they were busy talking about a separate air corps."[14]

Marshall kept urging Arnold to reach below his "antique staff officers and passé fliers" for promising, aggressive young men who knew how to get things done. And Arnold was doing so as fast as he could. He already had his eye on Lauris Norstad, Emmett O'Donnell, Harold George, Orvil Anderson, Charles P. Cabell, and Laurence Kuter, but he didn't feel he could raise them peremptorily over the heads of the older men on his staff. In the case of Kuter, who was still a major when the United States entered the war, Marshall disagreed. Marshall had gotten to know and admire Kuter when Arnold assigned the young officer to work on the General Staff.

"Why don't you make that fellow a general?" Marshall suggested one day.

"I can't," Arnold said. "I'd lose my whole staff."

Marshall waited until the January 1942 list was being prepared and added Kuter's name for promotion to lieutenant colonel. Then he waited for the February list and added Kuter's name for promotion to brigadier general. Thus Kuter, still a major until the fifth of January, was a general on the second of February. Arnold was delighted because he shared Marshall's admiration of Kuter, who was as diligent as he was resourceful. Arnold once told his son David that Kuter and Norstad were "the brains of the Air Force." And since it was Marshall who had promoted Kuter, none of Arnold's staff men could complain to him about it.

Marshall, however, wasn't yet satisfied with the work of the air staff. One day two of its members went to Arnold with a plan to ease the submarine menace in the Atlantic by securing the Azores. Arnold was sufficiently interested to ask Marshall to listen to it, and Marshall in turn asked Kuter to attend.

The two officers made their presentation, which called for the use of one amphibious division and the support of a small Navy escort force. Marshall listened carefully and asked two questions. "Where will the amphibious division come from?" And, "Does the Navy have available a small escort force?" They didn't know. He thanked them and ended the meeting but asked Kuter to stay.

When he and Kuter were alone, he described the presentation heatedly as "magazine type writing." It passed the buck upward. It was in no sense a staff study. It presented a problem and told the chief to go solve it.

"As the upcoming deputy chief of air staff," Marshall concluded, "one of your duties will be to make sure that half-baked, exciting material of that sort never gets as high as General Arnold again."[15]

Arnold, in his own efforts to make the best use of his brightest young officers, formed a new advisory council, which began in mid-February with just two members, Norstad and Cabell. One morning they found themselves together in Arnold's anteroom. They had been told to report to him but they hadn't been told why. Cabell had reason to be nervous about the meeting. He had met Arnold only once and had quite thoroughly disliked him. In April 1941, after returning from England, where he had taken part in a study of the R.A.F.'s system of aerial reconnaissance photography, he had stopped in Washington en route to Wright Field to brief Arnold. This was the first time Cabell had ever talked to his chief and he didn't consider the talk satisfactory. As he later recalled, "He listened to part of my report, then he would interrupt, sort of back me against the wall, shake his finger at me and tell me all the things that were wrong about the Air Force in general and reconnaissance in particular. He was not critical of my report so much as he was critical of the things I was reporting on, and why we were not doing a better job in our own Air Forces on reconnaissance and photography. But the thing that impressed me most was, he seemed to be holding me responsible for this lack of progress—holding me responsible for all the ills of the Air Force."[16]

It was soon evident that Arnold had come away from that first meeting liking Cabell better than Cabell liked him. When Cabell and Norstad were called into Arnold's office, he began by showing them a new Air Forces organizational chart with a little box leading out from the commanding general's box. In this box were the words "advisory council."

"You two boys," Arnold said, "will be my advisory council. I need a small office that reports directly to me and can help me with my problems. What I want you two boys to do is to do my thinking for me—my long-range, blue-sky thinking. I don't want you to get into daily operations. As a matter of fact, if I ever catch you mixing in with daily operations, I'm going to fire you both. You two sit down and decide what help you need in your office and all those details. I leave that up to you. But remember that you don't report through anybody else. You report to me directly. . . . Now drop whatever else you've been doing and go to work on this."

When Cabell and Norstad went to work they were still bewildered by their directive, but they made one important determination between themselves. "We were going to work with the staff and not against the staff. We would be helpless otherwise."

Every morning they made their rounds of the various departments within Arnold's office: they were so often together that Arnold's secretary, Suzy Adkins, began calling them "the twins." There was suspicion among staff members at first. Some people called the two men "the Gestapo." Others called them "the kibitzers." Orvil Anderson in the plans section, who never thought very highly of the advisory council, called them "the kids."[17] But Arnold, who was now almost swamped with work, found them useful.

"What I want you to do is sit down and think," he told them. "Think of the problems confronting us. Bring in new ideas. If you bring in one new idea every two or three days, I'll be satisfied." He apparently was satisfied. Though he kept rotating the personnel, sometimes enlarging the group to five members, sometimes contracting it to two or three, he maintained the advisory council for the next four years, and out of it came a succession of bright young officers, most of whom achieved three or four stars before they ended their careers.

All these men had one thing in common—they were quick and adaptable. They had to be in order to accustom themselves to Arnold's helter-skelter administrative methods. After the war began, he more than ever lacked the patience to restrict himself to the normal chain-of-command method of doing things. If he wanted something done, he wanted it done immediately. But his office was now a large organization with hundreds of officers and civil servants in a bewildering maze of branches and sections. As Kuter recalled, "Directives launched into this elaborate new machine might spend days and weeks gathering coordinations and approvals."

Arnold never did get accustomed to that.[18] "I toss a new idea to you staff fellows and what happens?" he would say. "A long time later I get a list of the staff's projects that will have to be deferred if mine is to be implemented, and sometimes the implication that my idea isn't as good as yours anyway. All I get back are reasons why it can't be done."

The one thing it was dangerous to tell Arnold was that something couldn't be done. He was quite capable of saying, "Maybe you can't do it but I can and you're fired." On several occasions he stopped officers in the corridor, sometimes officers he didn't even know, and sent them off on projects that had suddenly come to mind.

One day, he stopped an officer in the hall and said, "I want you to go to Los Angeles for me and find out some things from the aircraft companies."

The man said, "Yes, sir, I'll go right away and get the orders cut for myself."

"I didn't tell you to get any orders cut," Arnold said. "I want you to get in my airplane and go."

His insistence on doing things immediately kept his staff somewhat jittery, but it also hastened the war effort by making them move at double time. In February he realized he needed a training center for nonflying officers, but when he brought it up, his staff told him it would take three months to secure a site, three months to build the school, and another three months to find the instructors. "Hitler won't wait that long," Arnold said, "and neither can I."

He picked up the phone and pretended to call Gen. "Miff" Harmon, his chief of staff, who happened at the moment to be in Shreveport, Louisiana. After faking a few preliminary pleasantries, he said, "How long will it take you to get me Louisiana State University? You think you can get it for me in three or four days? Well that's great. I'll tell you what I want. I want a place to establish an Officer Candidate School. . . . We may have as many as two or three thousand candidates, maybe more than that before we get through. But you think you can get it for me in three or four days. Well, that's wonderful, Miff. Thank you very much."

Though Suzy Adkins in the outer office was the only person on the line, Arnold had succeeded in fooling the staff members with whom he was conferring. Maj. Gen. Walter Weaver, who had been a classmate of Arnold's at West Point and was now acting chief of Air Forces, stood up and said, "May I be excused?"

Arnold said, "By all means."

A few days later he received a call from Weaver in Miami Beach. Because of the war, the tourist business there was bad. The Air Forces could take over three hundred hotels at once.[19]

Arnold figured that the cost of leasing these hotels would be $119 per man, whereas school construction costs at the time would be about $1,000 per man. Though he had difficulty convincing the War Department of this saving, he eventually succeeded, and before he was through the Air Forces had taken over about five hundred hotels for its training program, which was now bursting its seams.

When Weaver secured the Miami Beach hotels, Arnold was already on the verge of relieving him as acting chief of Air Forces. His adroit Florida transaction came too late to save him. In March, Arnold sent him to Knollwood, North Carolina, to take over the Eastern Technical Training Command. At the same time, Arnold's old friend Maj. Gen. Jake Fickel was relieved as commander of the Fourth Air Force in California and put in charge of the Western Technical Training Command. Under the pressure of wartime needs, Arnold was finally developing the ruthlessness that Marshall demanded of him, and for which some of his old friends would never forgive him.

The immediate cause of Fickel's replacement (by George Kenney) was an inordinately high accident rate among the P-38 fighters in his command. The twin-fuselage plane was beautiful and graceful in the sky, but it had a tendency to nose in if not flown properly, and many pilots were being killed. Under Kenney, Gen. Barney Giles took command of operations. He called Arnold and asked him about putting dual controls in three or four P-38s and starting a school at Muroc Dry Lake to give the young pilots some extra instruction.

Arnold wasn't sure it was possible to put dual controls or an extra seat in a P-38. "You'd better take it up with Wright Field," he told Giles.

"I have taken it up with Wright Field," Giles said, "and they told me it couldn't be done. But I'm telling you now, I've already done it."[20]

That was the way Arnold liked to hear people talk. With his blessing, Giles started the school at Muroc, where he made his pilots learn to fly the P-38 on one engine. The accident rate was cut by about two hundred percent, and Arnold filed the name of Barney Giles in the back of his mind.

Arnold had a different kind of trouble with another fighter plane he was counting on—the cigar-shaped P-47 Thunderbolt, manufactured by Republic Aviation Corporation. It was a plane developed by Alexander de Seversky, a distinguished aircraft designer and Republic's principal owner. De Seversky, a long-time air-power advocate, had written a popular book, *Victory Through Air Power,* which became the basis for a Disney movie and made him a prominent public figure. He seemed to enjoy flying around the country in his company's planes, setting speed records and making speeches about air power. Arnold was increasingly annoyed at this because he thought de Seversky was making speeches when, as Republic's chief operating officer, he should be making airplanes. While he was busy setting his speed records in flight, Republic's output of P-47s was lagging behind Arnold's expectations.

Arnold did not keep his dissatisfaction to himself. As he explained to his son Bruce, de Seversky had made a beautiful airplane; but the Air Forces didn't need *an* airplane, it needed five thousand of them, and de Seversky didn't seem able to turn them out in that kind of quantity.[21] Before long, Arnold's feelings became known in the aircraft industry. De Seversky, who happened to be in California when someone told him what Arnold was saying, went to see Donald Douglas in Santa Monica. He wanted to know why Arnold was cutting him out of the war program.[22]

"Well, Sasha, I guess you know why," Douglas said. "He's peeved at you because he hasn't thought you were paying attention to your business."

De Seversky did not deny that there might be something to that.

"Do you want me to call him up," Douglas suggested, "and ask him what about it?"

"Yes, call him," de Seversky said.

Douglas made the call and Arnold said, "Tell the guy to come in. If he's ready to go to work, we want him."

De Seversky did go to see Arnold but they did not have a meeting of minds. Arnold continued to believe de Seversky was too much of a perfectionist to adapt himself to the sort of mass production the war required. He ended their conversation by demanding that de Seversky divorce himself from the operation of the company and replace himself with a man whom Arnold nominated. In effect, Arnold was demanding that de Seversky fire himself from his own company if he wanted the company to do business with the Air Forces. De Seversky ultimately capitulated and the output of P-47s began to climb.

Arnold and the Army Air Forces gained a measure of new prestige on February 9, 1942, when he took his place as a member at the first formal meeting of the Joint Chiefs of Staff, a body of four men —Admirals William D. Leahy and Ernest King, Generals Marshall and Arnold—which thereafter constituted the American High Command. The concept of the Joint Chiefs was born at the Argentia Conference in August 1941, when the Americans felt the need for an agency to parallel the British command structure. President Roosevelt had invited Arnold

to the Argentia Conference at the request of Marshall and the insistence
of Harry Hopkins, who continued to support, within the White House,
both Arnold and air power. Thereafter, Arnold remained a member of
what was to become the Joint Chiefs because Marshall needed him and
Roosevelt accepted him.

The naval members, on the other hand, or at least Admiral King
and his aides, never did wholeheartedly accept him. Since the naval air
chief, Adm. John Towers, was not a member of the Joint Chiefs, they
could see no reason why the Army air chief should be so honored. But
Marshall was eager to have Arnold included for two obvious reasons.
First, he was genuinely convinced that the Army air arm was now so
important a part of the nation's military system that it deserved
representation; and second, without another general at his side, he
could be out-voted consistently by the Navy. Though he believed Leahy
to be a fair and honorable man, he was also aware of the pressure Leahy
would feel from King and other Navy men on issues of contention
between the Army and Navy.

Leahy assumed chairmanship of the Joint Chiefs at Marshall's
behest. Already retired after a term as chief of naval operations, he had
become governor of Puerto Rico in 1939, and after the fall of France,
American ambassador to the Vichy French government. Marshall suggested that Roosevelt bring him home to head the Joint Chiefs because
"I thought the Navy couldn't resist this, and from what I had learned, I
was willing to trust Leahy to be a neutral chairman."

Marshall knew he was destined to have trouble with Ernie King,
who was replacing Adm. Harold Stark as chief of naval operations.
Everybody had trouble with King. One morning at about this time, when
King came to Marshall's office for a talk, Marshall couldn't see him
immediately because he was engaged in a delicate conversation with
someone else. After waiting a few minutes, King left in high dudgeon.
When Marshall heard about it, he hurried to King's office to explain and
apologize.

"I think this is important," Marshall said to King, "because if you or
I begin fighting at the very start of the war, what in the world will the
public have to say about us. . . . We can't afford to fight. So we ought to
find a way to get along together."

The best reply he could get from King was: "We'll see if we can get
along, and I think we can."[23]

But King was an unbending man. Gen. Dwight Eisenhower, at that
time chief of the Army operations division, is reported to have referred
to him in a confidential part of his diary as "a mental bully." On

February 23, 1942, two weeks after the first formal meeting of the Joint Chiefs, Eisenhower wrote: "Admiral King is an arbitrary, stubborn type with too much brain and a tendency toward bullying his juniors. But I think he wants to fight, which is vastly encouraging."[24]

King did indeed want to fight. The great fighting record of the Navy in World War II is partly a reflection of his insistent personality. But unfortunately for Marshall and Arnold, who had to cope with him, he sometimes seemed as willing to fight the Army as he was to fight the Japanese. And he was so eager to fight the Japanese that he sometimes seemed unable to understand or accept the Allied grand strategy, agreed upon by Roosevelt and Churchill, to hold off the Japanese while concentrating on the defeat of Germany.

King's most formidable aide on the staff of the Joint Chiefs, Rear Adm. Charles M. "Savvy" Cooke, who was also chief of naval war plans, often acted as if he had been made in King's image and likeness. Orvil Anderson, the Air Forces chief of plans, could not get Cooke to recognize him as an equal on the staff.

Cooke, referring to Arnold, said to Anderson one day, "Where do you get the queer idea that your man is a chief of staff?"

"By edict," Anderson answered. "By some new terms the president made up."

"He's not a chief of staff," Cooke insisted. "He is definitely—and you might as well face up to the fact—he is subordinate to the War Department."[25]

Admiral King, at Joint Chiefs meetings, would often indicate, not in words but by his behavior, that he shared Cooke's point of view. When Arnold addressed himself to King, the admiral was not above aiming his reply to Marshall, as if it were Marshall who had spoken, or as if it should be assumed that Marshall had put the words in Arnold's mouth. There was a tradition in military councils that equals addressed equals, but King, when he refused to address a full member of this body as an equal, was going far beyond tradition. He was telling an upstart he didn't belong where he was. King was a battleship admiral who had only lately come to acknowledge the importance of air. Though he had earned his wings at the age of forty-nine, he was hardly an aviator. Sometimes he seemed to blame Arnold personally for the fact that airplanes were now threatening to make his battleships obsolete.

Cooke was quite literally correct in his remarks to Anderson. Arnold was not a chief of staff. But neither was Leahy, although he was now called the president's chief of staff, whatever that might mean. And Arnold was unquestionably subordinate to the War Department. But so was King subordinate to the Navy Department. If the president decided the War Department should have two generals on the Joint Chiefs of Staff to balance the Navy's two admirals, that settled the matter. It didn't mean, however, that Arnold would have an easy time with the Navy.

The first of his serious Navy troubles in wartime began on February 14 when King formally asked him to allocate to the Navy four hundred B-24s and nine hundred B-25s (twin-engine, twin-tailed North American "Mitchell" bombers) for submarine patrol. To Arnold it appeared that the admirals, after years of belittling and resisting the very idea of an air force, had suddenly decided they wanted one, now that they were beginning to see what such a force would look like and how useful it could be.[26] He saw this innocent request as the Navy's first move toward the formation of a second American air force, which would duplicate the functions of the Army Air Forces. But these were beliefs he couldn't state flatly because he couldn't prove them. Nor could he deny that there was an acute need for long-range bombers to find and attack submarines; he had been preaching that doctrine for years. How then was he to foil this attempted Navy raid on his still-small bomber force?

On February 25 he drafted a letter to King saying: (1) that land-based planes had long been recognized as the Army's responsibility; (2) that the Army already had the personnel, facilities, bases, maintenance, and supply organizations to operate such planes; (3) that the Army also had pursuit planes designed to protect these bombers in flight and on the ground; and (4) that the Army, recognizing the submarine menace, was willing to perform the antisub function itself, under Navy supervision if necessary. The principle had been established, he reminded King, that the mass of the nation's air striking power should be under one command. King's request violated that principle since it would establish two separate air forces with all the attendant difficulties of coordination.

On March 5, King wrote a surprisingly mild answer. Perhaps Arnold misunderstood the intended mission of these heavy bombers. They were needed in northern climes because seaplanes didn't work in icy seas. As to whether the Navy had a right to heavy bombers, he said quite reasonably that "no arbitrary limitations as to the type of aircraft or weapon should restrict the effectiveness of either the Army Air Forces or Naval aviation." And the submarine menace was so serious the Navy urgently needed the planes. In light of this, he hoped Arnold would reconsider.

On March 16, after what he deemed sufficient reconsideration, Arnold came up with a compromise that neither he nor the Navy welcomed. "I propose to recommend the establishment of a Coastal Command, within the Army Air Corps [sic], which will have for its purpose operations similar to the Coastal Command, Royal Air Force. This organization, operating when necessary under the control of proper Naval authorities, can readily meet the requirements of convoy escort, patrolling, and protection of shipping."

Though he didn't like it, Arnold's Air Forces were now in the antisubmarine business, which meant that several hundred heavy bombers would have to be diverted from their primary task of attacking Germany. But at the same time, the Navy's threat to get into the air force business was at least temporarily subdued.

On March 26, the Navy took operational control of the Air Forces antisubmarine units. Within the next two years, the Air Forces patrol sighted 241 German U-boats and was able to attack 147 of them. This operation was so successful that Arnold never did manage to get out of the antisubmarine business.

A more serious problem with the Navy arose over the question of where to send aircraft as they became available. But this problem was not limited to the Navy. The demand for more air strength was now so universal in all theaters of war that it gave rise to a malady Arnold called "theater-itis." "During those early war days when we did not have combat units, personnel, or equipment," he later recalled, "we were all in a quandary as to what dispositions to make of our meager forces. Everyone wanted them."

In the Philippines, where most of MacArthur's planes had been destroyed on the ground during the first Japanese attack, the lack of air power and materiel forced his troops to retreat to the Bataan Peninsula and the island fortress of Corregidor, which guarded Manila harbor. But because of the shortage of food and the inability to resupply these troops, it was obvious that malnutrition would soon necessitate their surrender. On February 22, 1942, President Roosevelt ordered Mac-Arthur to escape the Philippines by submarine and proceed to Australia, where he would become supreme commander of Allied forces in the Southwest Pacific.

As soon as MacArthur reached Australia on March 17, he, too, began pleading for more planes. The Hawaiian command, meanwhile, was already pleading for planes and men to guard against a repetition of the December 7 attacks. And commanders on the Pacific Coast were frantically asking for help against the possibility that the Japanese might soon arrive unannounced in Seattle, San Francisco, or Los Angeles.

It was this panic which gave strength to the Navy arguments that Europe could wait. The Japanese had to be handled immediately. Arnold didn't agree. He had said during the Arcadia conference with the British, "The way to win the war is to hit Germany where it hurts the most, where she is strongest—right across the Channel from England, using the shortest and most direct road to Berlin." He still believed that.

On January 27, the Combined Chiefs of Staff (British and American) had decided that the first U.S. heavy bomb group should be assigned to England. And on February 16, the Combined Chiefs' planners, shortly before Ira Eaker and his staff took off for England, began preparation for the first two heavy groups to follow them.

By this time, King and his aides were already expressing deep concern as to whether they could continue to hold the Japanese in the Pacific without more men and airplanes. And when someone showed him a copy of the Air Forces War Plan (AWPD-1), which the Navy should have been shown as a courtesy the previous summer, he was so furious he tried, though without success, to have it repudiated by the Joint Chiefs of Staff.

During March, the Army General Staff, with the help of the air staff, drew up a plan for an operation code-named "Bolero," which envisioned the invasion of the European continent in the late summer of 1942, after an intensive campaign of aerial bombardment against German targets. How two men like Marshall and Arnold, usually so astute and practical, could have deluded themselves about such an impossibility, is difficult to fathom. It has been suggested that Marshall decided to plan for a 1942 invasion fully aware that it was impossible —especially in light of expected British resistance—but convinced that such preparations would bestir the British, thus insuring that the invasion could be launched at least by 1943. But Arnold tacitly admitted later that he had taken the project seriously at the time, which would seem to indicate that Marshall did likewise, since they were so close. Arnold in his memoirs said that he thought in the early months of 1942 he would have enough planes by autumn to support the invasion.[27] The whole matter illustrates how little the Americans knew when they entered the war about the effort it would take to defeat Germany and Japan.

On April 1, the president held a secret meeting at the White House (with all the participants coming in the back door to avoid attention) for the purpose of discussing the Bolero plan. Stimson, Knox, Stark, King, "Pa" Watson, Marshall, Hopkins, and Arnold attended. Roosevelt read the plan aloud and discussed it paragraph by paragraph. Then Hopkins said pointedly, aware as he was of Navy recalcitrance, "I want to be sure that everybody is in accord with this program. Admiral King, do you see any reason this cannot be carried out?"

King said, "No, I do not."

It appeared that, whatever the merits or demerits of the Bolero scheme, the Army and Air Forces had at least reaffirmed the doctrine of concentration of power against Germany, and had thus prevented diversion of strength to the Pacific. But King was not an easy man to overcome. In time they would hear more from him on the subject of diversion to his Pacific theater. They would also hear more from Douglas MacArthur about diversion to his Pacific theater. MacArthur and King didn't agree about many things—they assuredly did not agree about whose theater the Pacific was—but they were both certain that the Pacific was the primary theater in which to fight the war. And they were a hard pair to resist.

In the midst of the planning for Bolero and the efforts to satisfy the demands for air strength in so many theaters, Arnold held a 10:00 a.m. staff meeting one Sunday in early March to find out why he was receiving conflicting reports about plane deliveries from factories to Air Forces units.[28]

One reason, as it turned out, was his own helter-skelter method of gathering information. He was constantly on the phone with manufacturers or Air Forces people in the field, trying to find out for himself what was happening. It was perhaps a good way of keeping informed about certain things, but it was a poor method of compiling statistics. His hit-and-miss figures seldom agreed with those of his materiel division. And to complicate matters further, the two sets of figures weren't likely to agree even if they were both accurate because there were two ways to calculate aircraft deliveries.

Ordinarily a plane was not put on the "accepted" list until it had been delivered in flying condition. But quite often a manufacturer would collect on his parking lot a backlog of planes, complete except for some part, possibly even as important as the engine, which was to be made and supplied by a second company. In many instances, it was not only fair but necessary to consider these planes "accepted" so the manufacturer who had completed his job could be paid, and thus finance his future output.

Though Arnold knew all this, he found it hard to accept the notion that at any given time he didn't know exactly how many airplanes he had in operation, nor could he receive calmly reports that airplanes "accepted" a month or so earlier had not yet reached the units to which they were consigned.

The purpose of this Sunday morning meeting was to straighten out the confusion in the system of acceptances. Among those present were Miff Harmon, Larry Kuter, and an officer named Col. Oliver S. "Steve" Ferson of the materiel division. A quiet, soft-spoken man, with "every external appearance of being steady, outwardly calm and even placid," Ferson was the air staff's chief authority on the numbers and status of aircraft in operation. That, of course, made him the chief target of Arnold's impatience.

After Arnold's data on aircraft "acceptances" had been presented, Ferson "slowly and methodically" itemized the aircraft which had been "accepted" despite the lack of engines or other components. When his list varied from Arnold's list, Arnold quickly took the attack, with his customary insistence and impatience. As Ferson listened to Arnold's criticism of the materiel command data, he "began to flush under the strain." His face reddened and the veins in his neck expanded.

Finally, when Arnold paused, Ferson opened his mouth as if to defend himself, but no words came forth. Pitching forward, he fell dead of a massive heart attack on the carpet in front of Arnold's desk.

Arnold ended the conference and told everyone in the office to go home and take off the rest of that Sunday, but he himself stayed at his desk for another hour or so. Though he mentioned it to no one, he must have noticed the similarity between Ferson's symptoms and his own flushed face and bulging veins during the short spells that occasionally overcame him.

Despite the fears he may have harbored about his own health, he refused to slow his pace. Since the country went to war he had been leaving home at 6:30 a.m., seven days a week, and returning about 9:00 p.m., except when he traveled. He had time to say little more than hello and goodbye to Bee and David, the only two members of the family still at home. Even when he did try to relax, late in the evening, the phone would ring. Bee and David set up a series of codes to let him know who was calling so he could decide whether to take the phone, but despite their efforts to screen calls, he took most of them.[29] He was so absorbed in his work, so worried about the problems of the war, that he had room in his mind for nothing else.

It was a brutally difficult time for Bee. Though proud of Hap, she was losing touch with him. Though close to the world-shaking excitement in which he was involved, she was not a part of it. She had lost her husband to the war. The magic that had made them celebrate their wedding date every month in the early years of their marriage was long since gone. There was no time now even for the comradeship they had enjoyed in more recent years. These losses were much more difficult for her to absorb than anyone near her realized. While she seemed unchanged on the surface, her loneliness was beginning to bear down upon her. But even Hap didn't seem to notice.

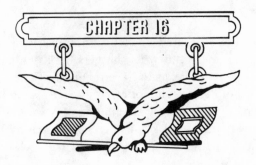

CHAPTER 16

I n March 1942, at Marshall's behest, the Arnolds moved from Bethesda to a commodious house, Quarters #8, at Fort Myer, across the Potomac in Virginia, near the Pentagon Building, which was then under construction. For wartime security reasons, Marshall wanted the top Army commanders to live within the protection of a military reservation.[1] He himself lived just down the street from Arnold's new home. They often went to work together.

Shortly after the Arnolds moved to Fort Myer, Lois came to visit them. Unpredictably playful as ever, she answered the phone one evening with the words, "Sadie's house. Girls of your choice." It was Marshall. "I seem to have the wrong number," he said. Later, with a smile, he asked Arnold, "Are we running a house of prostitution on this base?" Because Marshall looked stern and didn't do a lot of smiling, some people thought he didn't know how. But David Arnold, who got to know him well during the Fort Myer years, found him a very warm and thoughtful man. Bee considered him one of Hap's closest friends. It has been noted that even President Roosevelt addressed him as "General Marshall." When Marshall and Arnold were at work together, they addressed each other formally, as General Kuter has observed. But when they were alone together, or in social situations, they called each other Hap and George.

In addition to his strictly military duties, Arnold somehow found time for a lot of peripheral matters, even during the early months of the war. He corresponded with Irving Berlin about the possibility of Berlin's composing a new Air Forces anthem.[2] With Ira Eaker, he completed editing a book entitled *Army Flyer*, which they had written together to stimulate enlistments. (It was published in May 1942.)

From President Roosevelt on March 7 he received a private, handwritten "Dear Hap" letter that he could hardly ignore: "I am a bit concerned because Elliott has a rather bad chronic case of haemoroids [*sic*] that need to be operated on. He rightly insists on going through with his new assignment but when he gets back, I hope you can give him enough time off in Texas to have them taken out."

One day Arnold got a call from Clark Gable asking for an appointment. He had met Gable during the filming of *Mutiny on the Bounty* and they had become good friends. But when Gable arrived for his appointment, he was accompanied by an MGM press agent who did most of the talking.

"We'd like to have Mr. Gable serve in the Air Forces," the press agent said.

Arnold said, "Great. He can do a job for us."

The press agent, perhaps remembering the enlistment of Elliott Roosevelt as a captain, said, "We'd like him to go in as a captain."

Arnold said politely, "I don't think that's the route to go."

The press agent tried to persuade him. Arnold became angry. Finally he turned to the silent Gable and, perhaps forgetting the enlistment of Captain Roosevelt, said, "You just don't come into a service as a captain when you've had no military experience."

Gable and the press agent departed, but that night, Gable called Arnold and said, "I've been thinking of what you told me and I agree. I should start as a private."[3]

He did so, and served with such distinction in the Eighth Air Force that he had risen to the rank of major by war's end.

The need for technological and mechanical advances was so apparent as the early combat reports began arriving in Washington that Arnold decided to launch a new Air Forces proving ground under his direct control at Eglin Field, Florida. Though it might duplicate some of the work being done at Wright Field, he didn't care because he was perpetually annoyed at the Wright Field engineers. They were always telling him why his ideas wouldn't work. He wanted an agency that would find out whether his ideas worked by trying them. He chose Gen. Grandison Gardner, a veteran of the materiel division, to command the installation, and a few days after it opened he flew down from Washington with Gene Beebe to try out one of his ideas—skip-bombing against enemy ships. It seemed to him that if a plane came in low and dropped its bomb into the water before reaching the ship, the bomb would skip or ricochet into the side of the ship, where it was most vulnerable.

Gardner, after experimenting with the idea, decided it wasn't quite practical as Arnold had conceived it because the skipping dissipated the impact of the bomb. But from Arnold's idea, the men at Eglin developed a similar technique that did increase the effectiveness of bombs against ships.[4]

With the inauguration of the Newfoundland–Greenland–Iceland air route to England and the construction of bases in those frigid locations, Arnold felt the need to prepare the men who would be stationed there. As a result, Eglin Field established the "Arctic, Desert and Tropic information Center," which became a permanent Air Forces school.

Another Arnold idea, which he developed with Gen. Gene Reybold, chief of the Army Engineers, soon proved useful at new Air Forces fields throughout the world. Whenever the Army took a new piece of territory, there was an immediate need for an air base on it. But most warplanes were now too heavy to land and take off safely on fields that, after a rain, could suddenly become quagmires, and the installation of paved runways was a lengthy process. Arnold and Reybold conceived the idea of pierced steel planks, about ten feet long and two feet wide, which locked into each other to form a long steel carpet over a flat field.[5] This steel carpet made an awesome racket when a plane landed on it or took off from it. But it could be installed in two days and it was an effective substitute for a paved runway.

In early March, responding to President Roosevelt's insistence "that we find ways and means of carrying home to Japan proper, in the form of a bombing raid, the real meaning of war,"[6] Arnold called in Jimmy Doolittle and told him to select a plane that "would go 2000 miles carrying 2000 pounds of bombs and take off short." The plan, Arnold said, was to bomb Tokyo with planes that would take off from a Navy carrier and then fly across Japan to land at an American base in China.

After Doolittle had spent some time and thought on the project and had selected the B-25 as the best plane for it, he went into Arnold's office one day and said, "I know more about this mission, I know more about the aircraft, I know more about the crews than anyone else. I would like to lead it."

Arnold said, "I need you badly here, Jimmy. I'd rather see you stay on my staff."

Doolittle did not conceal his disappointment. Finally Arnold said, "Well, I'll tell you what. If it's all right with Miff [Harmon], it's all right with me."

Doolittle saluted, ran as fast as he could to the chief of air staff's office, and said, "If you have no objections, General Arnold has no objections to me leading the operation."

Harmon said, "I have no objections."

The jubilant Doolittle was on his way out when the phone rang. As he left he heard Harmon say, "But, Hap, I just told him he could go."[7]

On April 18, Doolittle led sixteen B-25s from the carrier *Hornet* to targets mostly in Tokyo. Eight of his men were captured after crashing off the coast of China and three of them were eventually executed by the Japanese. Altogether nine of his eighty men died as a result of the raid, and all the B-25s were lost. Though the damage to Japan was minimal, the mission did have three salutary effects. It was the first American offensive move against Japan, and therefore boosted the morale of the American people. It showed the Japanese that their homeland was vulnerable. And it forced the Japanese to divert much of their fighter-aircraft strength from active war fronts to home defense.

On May 6, Arnold heard from another country—China. He received from the president that day a secret memorandum that said: "I gather that the air ferry route to China is seriously in danger. The only way we can get certain supplies into China is by air. I wish you and Mr. Lovett would confer immediately with Dr. Soong . . . on alternative air routes." Just in case Arnold might miss the urgency of this message, Harry Hopkins affixed to it a note of his own: "The President is very anxious that you see Soong today sometime, if you can."

The general military situation in China at the moment was in even greater disarray than usual. Chiang Kai-shek, in a message to Roosevelt, said he was at a "critical stage such as I have never experienced before." The Japanese were still pushing back his armies, and to make matters worse, they were threatening to cut the airline route from China to India. With his message, Chiang sent his brother-in-law, banker T. V. Soong, to Washington, to ask for more money and help. The most immediate need was an air-cargo operation that could fly essential materials into China.

In 1942, some American military men had already come to the conclusion that sending supplies to Chiang Kai-shek was only slightly more useful than sending them to the Japanese. There is no indication that Arnold had yet embraced that belief, but he positively did not want to use planes in China that he could otherwise use in the planned air offensive against Germany. He would have been quite content not to hear from China at this time, but since the president had spoken, he saw

Soong on May 6 and assured him everything possible was being done to keep supplies moving to China.

Arnold may have hoped that would take care of the matter for the moment, but it didn't. Roosevelt, recognizing the desperate need to keep Chiang Kai-shek operating, however ineptly, against Japan, strongly suggested to Arnold that he assign fifty heavy bombers (B-24s) to the China–Burma–India hump route. Arnold indicated both his reluctance and his concurrence in an amusing May 9 memorandum to Col. Hoyt S. Vandenberg of his staff:

> Note the attached memorandum to the President relative to aerial operations for carrying supplies into China. The proposition for utilizing 50 B-24s for this purpose is one that will require some study. On the other hand, someone must make a decision as to whether these bombers will be of more importance in the long run utilized in this manner than if they were utilized to bomb Germany.
>
> I am of the opinion that we, for the time being, should take the affirmative and assume that they could be used to better advantage for carrying supplies into China because the President of the United States has directed me to put this line in, regardless of any difficulties that may be encountered.

As if the overseas demands for airplanes were not enough, Arnold was now getting requests from fellow Army generals who hadn't yet gone abroad to send them planes for their personal transportation. He fulfilled some of these requests. On May 7 he sent a C-45 transport plane to Maj. Gen. George S. Patton of the Armored Corps, who was then commanding the Desert Training Center in California. But he was not so generous with some of the ground force generals who had spent the peacetime years resisting Air Corps growth. To one lieutenant general who said to him, "Say, Hap, where is that transport plane that you're supposed to get for me?" he replied, "Still on the drafting board, just exactly the same place it was three years ago when I asked you to buy it for us."[8]

Among the matters that had been decided at the secret April 1 Bolero meeting in the White House was the question of sending American bombers to the R.A.F. The British had asked for thousands of them, to be incorporated into their own bombardment fleet.

Arnold argued in front of the president that since America was now in the war, American young men should fly whatever bombers the United States could send to England. And Arnold's argument prevailed. But it wouldn't be easy to make the British happy about this.

Arnold decided in May to go to England himself and explain it to Portal. Marshall and Hopkins had flown to England in April to sell the

British on the Bolero plan, but they had not told Churchill and Portal they were to get no U.S. bombers. They had enough trouble winning British approval for Bolero without spreading such bad news. In fact, they weren't yet certain the British had actually approved invasion of the continent.

Churchill had tentatively agreed it might be practical, but not until the spring or summer of 1943, and he had suggested that a North African landing should precede it. To clarify some of these matters, Marshall sent Major General Eisenhower along with Arnold. Also on the trip were Maj. Gen. Mark Clark of the Army, Rear Adm. Jack Towers, Arnold's naval counterpart, Col. Hoyt Vandenberg, Col. Gene Beebe, and several British officers stationed in Washington.

Their "stratoliner" left Bolling Field at 7:15 a.m. the morning of May 23 for Montreal and Goose Bay, Newfoundland, before heading out into ice and fog over the Atlantic. After 540 miles of blind, treacherous flying, they had to return to Gander and try again the next day.[9] On the second attempt they made it to Prestwick, Scotland, the morning of the twenty-fifth, though the weather was still bad. Since it was impossible to fly to London, they boarded a train that evening and arrived there early in the morning of the twenty-sixth. Portal did not meet them for a reason he explained charmingly in a note Arnold received later that day: "Going to the station at 6 a.m. would mean that I should fall sound asleep at 3 p.m. just when I should be listening to what you were saying."

After checking in at Claridge's, Arnold had breakfast with U.S. Ambassador John G. Winant and U.S. Army Commander in England, Maj. Gen. James E. Chaney of the Air Forces. Chaney was the man who won the brigadier general's star Arnold thought he should have received in 1934. Since Arnold, with three stars, had now surpassed him, that incident was long forgotten. The two men had always been cordial to each other, but Arnold was poorly disposed toward Chaney at the moment because he wasn't cooperating fully with Ira Eaker in the formation of the Eighth Air Force Bomber Command.[10] Chaney wanted Eaker in his headquarters and under his direct command. And since he was theater commander, his argument had force, but that was not the way Arnold wanted it and it wasn't the way he intended to have it. Chaney was too conservative for him. He had decided that Spaatz and Eaker, not Chaney, would command the air offensive against Germany.

None of this came up during their breakfast, but Chaney did cast some doubts upon the efficiency of two American pursuit planes, the P-38 and P-39. Arnold didn't like to hear that, either. He would have more to say to Chaney later. His thoughts at the moment concerned the problem of breaking the bad news to the British about the bombers they would not be getting.

At 10:00 a.m. he reached Portal's air ministry office and, in his words, had a "long talk about everything but why I came over. Then a short talk on the main issue. That was the first indication that the task was not going to be an impossible one."[11]

Arnold didn't yet know the British very well. He seemed to think that if they didn't explode when you hit them, it meant they didn't intend to hit back. Portal, without exploding, took Arnold immediately to Churchill, who also seemed to be sweetly reasonable.

Present at 10 Downing Street were Jack Towers, lend-lease coordinator Averell Harriman, and several British airmen. Arnold quickly explained the American decision to send the R.A.F. no bombers. He said America had plenty of exceptional young men who could fly American planes better than the young men of any other nation. One purpose of lend-lease, and of producing planes for foreign countries, had been to build productive capacity for the United States when it was needed. It was now needed. The American people wanted the United States to have an air force, and they wanted action quickly in Europe. The American decision did not mean there would be fewer American planes operating out of England. It meant only that Americans of the Eighth Air Force rather than Englishmen would be flying those planes.

The prime minister said he understood the desire to have American pilots fly American planes, and he favored it. But he pointed out the necessity for maximum impact against the enemy in the shortest possible time. The Allies must, he said, have the maximum number of planes in action dropping the greatest possible number of bombs. And it was a question of maintaining strength now, for the next few months, not a year from now. He couldn't understand, he said, why the Americans were raising an issue about five thousand planes for the British from an anticipated production of sixty thousand planes per year.

Arnold listed for him the demands for those planes from war theaters throughout the world, including British theaters such as the Near East. Churchill then called on Towers, who said the U.S. Navy problem was simple. From the sixty thousand planes produced, the Navy would need only torpedo bombers, dive bombers, patrol bombers, and fighters. That was all.

Arnold, painfully aware of Admiral King's increasing demands for B-24s, asked Towers if the Navy didn't also need some heavy bombers, which were, after all, the central items under discussion.

Thus confronted, Towers, with aplomb, said "Why, certainly."

At the close of this meeting, Churchill and Arnold walked together for a half hour in the garden, after which Arnold noted in his diary: "I may be mistaken but I believe that we can sell our point." Because Arnold had that ingenuous American habit of exposing his entire argument openly from the start, he seemed to feel the British were equally direct. In time he would come to know them better.

He noticed a great change in London. "People are not the diffident, harried, listless ones I saw last year. They have pep and show an interest in life. The city is cleaned up. Bomb marks are rapidly disappearing." He went to visit Eaker's command at High Wycombe and found it "a fine place." Eaker seemed ready to fly as soon as he got some airplanes, and his first airdromes were nearing completion.

At an air ministry conference on the twenty-eighth, Arnold had more trouble with the U.S. Navy than with the British. His friend Towers, whom he had genuinely liked ever since they were fellow students at the Wright brothers' flying school, annoyed him during this meeting when he said the Navy could send no help for the British coastal command. The Navy had "too many other activities at home," he said. And when the question of providing more transport planes arose, he suggested that Arnold stop B-17 production at the Douglas Long Beach plant and build cargo planes instead. When one of Portal's aides asked him what the Navy was willing to give up to help the British, he said, "Nothing the Navy could give up would help." Arnold was furious at this. It seemed to him that the Army Air Forces "was expected to give everything to everybody." From then on, he decided, he would "take a much more hard-boiled attitude."

While he was having his troubles with Towers, the British were preparing to do a little more work on him. Because he was the giver and they were very conscious of being the receivers, they could hardly be ungracious. But Portal did point out that it would be a few months at best before the Eighth Air Force could operate against Germany, whereas he had trained pilots who could fly all available American bombers immediately. If Arnold would send the heavy bombers to the R.A.F., he would be willing, he said, to give them back as soon as American units were ready for them. It sounded like a reasonable proposal, but Arnold resisted it when he realized his units could never get ready if they had no airplanes.

He was also invited to visit the headquarters of the British bomber command, which was now under the direction of Air Marshal Harris,

whom Arnold had known in Washington. Harris had already constructed what he called his "conversion room," in which there were three-
dimensional photographic displays of the horrendous damage the
R.A.F. had already inflicted upon German cities during their night
bombing raids.[12] Harris and Eaker, though they were personally the best
of friends (Harris, in a letter to Arnold, had said of Eaker: "He's a great
man"),[13] were engaged in a lively dialogue about that other important
difference of opinion between the Americans and the British: night
versus day bombing. Harris took Arnold into his conversion room to
show him what the R.A.F. night bombers had done to Rostock on the
Baltic, and to the Heinkel aircraft factory at Marienehe. Arnold was
impressed. "I could see that R.A.F. Bomber Command was doing a
magnificent job. Their operations gave us something to shoot at." But he
was not sufficiently impressed to send heavy bombers to the R.A.F., or to
abandon the American daylight precision-bombing plan.

On May 30, in one last attempt to work on Arnold, Churchill invited
him, together with Harris and Eaker, to the prime minister's official
country estate, "Chequers." It was perhaps more than coincidental that
Harris was planning for that same night the biggest bombing raid ever
staged by the R.A.F. or by any other air force—1047 planes, against
Cologne. Arnold had already spent some time at dinner trying to sell his
British hosts on daylight bombing when Harris received the anticipated
news and announced that the R.A.F. had just completed its unprecedented mission. Arnold later noted with a touch of chagrin, "Of all the
moments in history when I might have tried to sell Mr. Churchill and his
R.A.F. advisers on the future of American precision bombardment by
daylight, I had picked the night when they were selling their own kind of
bombardment to the world."[14]

Churchill said to Arnold that night, "Your program apparently will
provide an aerial striking force equal to, or in some cases larger than,
that provided and planned by us. Perhaps your program is too ambitious. You are trying to do within a few months what we have been
unable to accomplish in two or more years."

The next day he agreed that the Americans should keep the heavy
bombers for themselves. But he didn't explain to Arnold why he was so
sure the American plan was too ambitious. In fact, he was quite sure
there would be no major American air offensive against Germany in
1942 for the same reason there would be no invasion of the continent
that year—because he intended to insist that North Africa be invaded
first, and many of the American bombers assigned to the Eighth Air

Force would have to be diverted to that operation. Though Arnold had apparently won his point and persuaded the British to concede, the actual results were yet to be seen.

While in England, Arnold decided definitely that Chaney would have to go. But only Marshall had the power to relieve an Army theater commander. Arnold discussed this problem with Eisenhower and Clark, two of Marshall's aides. Then in a separate conversation with Clark, he decided Eisenhower would be the ideal replacement for Chaney.

On the morning of June 2, when Arnold left London for home, Chaney rode with him to Northolt Airport. In the front seat with the driver was Capt. Beirne Lay, Jr., of Eaker's staff, who had acted as Arnold's secretary during his stay in England. As they drove toward the outskirts of London, Chaney said to Arnold, "General, I know how busy you've been, at meetings with the British. I haven't had a chance to talk to you about my plans. I welcome this opportunity while we're alone to give you my thinking."

Arnold, blunt as usual when he had to say something unpleasant, turned to Chaney. "I would suggest you concentrate your immediate plans," he said, "on a change of station."[15] Glum silence prevailed the rest of the way to the airport.

It was 3:30 a.m. British time (12:30 a.m. local time), June 3, before Arnold and his party landed at Goose Bay, after flying against head winds that cut their airspeed to 135 miles per hour. They rode in jeeps to the mess hall where they were served a greasy breakfast of roast beef, fried potatoes, and string beans, all cold.

Arnold said to the commanding officer, "What the hell kind of food is this for an American Air Forces base?"[16]

The officer said, "We're sorry, General, but we can't make much fuss about it because we have a contract with the Canadians and they run the mess."

"I'll be damned if they're going to run a mess like this," Arnold declared. "If our boys have to sit up here in this God-awful hole with no recreation, and in such a terrible climate, at least they're going to have good food."

He took out his pen and wrote a telegram to one of his aides in Washington. A plane was to leave Bolling Field the next morning, it said, loaded with pancakes, fresh eggs, sausages, bacon, oranges, beef —everything. The Goose Bay mess was to be improved until it was the best in the Air Forces. "And if it's not," the telegram warned his aide, "you're in trouble."

☆ ☆ ☆

A few days after his return to Washington, Arnold was subjected to a major embarrassment, which raised new questions about the Air Forces and the B-17, the weapon upon which Arnold was building his major hopes. On June 3 and 4, the Navy scored its great air victory at Midway, sinking Japan's four best carriers and reversing the trend of the war in the Pacific. Also in that battle were fourteen B-17s from the Seventh Air Force's 11th Bombardment Group, which had been sent to Midway in anticipation of the battle. The day after the battle, as soon as the scope of the victory was apparent, the Seventh Air Force claimed that the Fortresses had scored twenty-two direct hits from about 20,000 feet, many of them on carriers, battleships, and cruisers. When the facts were determined, these claims had to be scaled down to one probable hit on a transport.

As Arnold said later, he and other advocates of high-altitude precision bombing "were criticized from all around the compass," not only for the sorry performance but for the outrageous claims. "[We] were called upon, time and time again, to make a restudy to be sure we were on the right track. Should we continue our high-altitude precision bombing, when we might have been making dive bombing or low altitude attacks?"[17] He and his B-17s were now under pressure both in the Pacific and in Europe. Ironically, Adm. Chester Nimitz, the Navy's Pacific commander, began asking King to procure more B-17s and B-24s, but not as bombers. Like the British, he wanted to use them simply for patrol.

The concept of daylight bombing came under further critical scrutiny after thirteen B-24s led by Col. Harry A. Halverson bombed the Ploesti oil fields in Rumania on June 12, from a base in North Africa. The plan for this mission, brilliantly conceived by Col. Orvil Anderson and approved by both Arnold and Marshall, was to cut oil supplies to the German armies in Russia by knocking out the huge Rumanian refineries that fed them. Since there couldn't possibly be enough bombers available for large-scale, high-altitude pattern bombing, Anderson's design called for ninety-nine B-24s to stage a surprise, low-altitude skip-bombing raid from nearby Syria.

Because it gradually became obvious that nowhere near ninety-nine planes could be made available, Anderson scaled his plan down to thirty-three planes departing from North Africa. Even that many bombers could place more than three tons of bombs on each of the eleven prime targets—but only if those targets were easy to see. Anderson stipulated that the mission should not be staged unless the day was absolutely clear.

Despite this, Halverson took off with only thirteen planes on a cloudy day and bombed through an overcast. The mission did more damage to the prospects of daylight bombing than it did to the Ploesti refineries.[18]

In June, an argument developed between MacArthur and the Navy, one that would eventually affect Arnold and the Air Forces. Shortly after Midway, MacArthur, as supreme commander in the Southwest Pacific, proposed that he capture Rabaul with the use of one amphibious division (presumably Marines), a Navy task force including two carriers, and a large force of land-based bombers. On June 11, King told Marshall the Navy was already planning such an operation, using MacArthur's troops as a backup force; and on the twenty-fifth, he told Marshall that the Navy's broad strategy was a northwesterly advance through the Solomons. Marshall liked this idea but proposed MacArthur rather than Nimitz as its commander.[19] The Navy was not enthusiastic about letting MacArthur command anything. Three days later MacArthur warned Marshall that the Navy intended to assume complete control in the Pacific, and that he should beware of King. Finally Marshall settled this unseemly squabbling by deciding that the Navy would invade Guadalcanal and Tulagi.

MacArthur was not an easy man with whom to argue. One of Arnold's old colleagues, George Brett, had been finding that out since March, when Arnold made him Southwest Pacific air commander. The MacArthur-Brett bickering became so serious that Marshall sent an Air Forces colonel on his staff, Samuel E. Anderson, to find out what was happening between them. When Anderson returned, he was summoned to a meeting with Marshall and Arnold.

"Shall I relieve Brett?" Marshall asked.

Glancing at Arnold, whom he understood to be a close friend of Brett, Anderson swallowed hard, then said, "Yes, sir."

Marshall asked, "Why?"

"Because, sir, as long as Brett is there, you won't have any cooperation between ground and air. And I don't think you plan to relieve General MacArthur."[20]

Anderson didn't know that, while Arnold admired Brett's administrative skills, they had not been close friends since 1938, when Brett tried hard for the chief of Air Corps job, which went to Arnold. To replace Brett, Arnold sent George Kenney from the Fourth Air Force in California. It proved to be one of the best choices he ever made. Without losing his own strong individuality, Kenney pleased MacArthur from the start by his enterprising and imaginative use of the few airplanes he had.

In June, Tooey Spaatz, after organizing the flow of Eighth Air Force planes, men, and supplies from the United States to England, took off himself for London to assume command of the Eighth. To team with his bomber commander, Ira Eaker, who was already in England, he took along Gen. Frank "Monk" Hunter, another friend of Arnold's from the March Field days.

The night of Spaatz's departure, his wife, Ruth, bade him a tearful farewell. He did his best to comfort her, but with his usual economy of words. "Relax," he said. "I'll be back within six months. By that time, Hap will fire me."[21]

Throughout the war, Arnold kept sending his closest friends and best staff members overseas, not to punish but to reward them. In July, after Marshall established a United States Army Forces headquarters in the South Pacific, perhaps as a buffer between MacArthur and the Navy, Arnold relinquished his chief of air staff, Maj. Gen. Millard F. "Miff" Harmon, to command it. (He replaced Harmon with the obscure but efficient Maj. Gen. George E. Stratemeyer.) Time after time, Arnold had told his personal pilot, Col. Eugene Beebe, about his disappointment at having to spend the entire First World War in Washington. He was determined that in this war the outstanding men around him would see action, even if it meant recurrent disruption of his own staff. Eaker, Spaatz, Hunter, Harmon, Kenney, and others already overseas were the vanguard of a long parade of Arnold associates he would send to combat theaters.

One day in June, he said to Beebe, who had been hinting subtly that he would like overseas duty, "You can go now, but find me somebody who can take over the flying part of your job."[22]

After choosing an ideal replacement—Capt. Clair A. Peterson, who had also served under Arnold at March Field—Beebe went to Davis Monthan Field in Tucson, Arizona, to put together a B-24 group that he would lead to China. A letter Arnold wrote to him in Tucson on July 13

indicates how difficult it was for Arnold to release men on whom he had
learned to depend:

> I do want to tell you that it was with honest-to-God real regret that I
> let you go. I thought about it for some time and finally decided that I
> would be selfish to stand between you and your first chance to put to
> test in the field your professional knowledge and training. . . . I
> appreciate, Gene, more than I can ever tell you, the very able
> assistance you have rendered me during the last four years. . . . At
> this moment I feel as if I have lost my right arm.

As the summer progressed, Arnold was confronted by more aircraft
worries. In late June he received a report from the Pacific that indicated
the Japanese Zeros were beginning to outlast the American P-39s and
P-40s in battle.[23] During the early weeks of the war, the American
fighters enjoyed a one-to-four loss advantage in engagements with the
Zeros. But during June, twenty-two P-39s were lost while bringing
down seventeen Zeros; and ten P-40s fell while destroying eleven
Zeros. The 39s and 40s would have to be replaced soon by P-38s and
the new Republic P-47s.

By late July, the Ford Motor Company had fallen so far behind in
deliveries of B-24s that Arnold asked Charles Lindbergh to go to Detroit
and find out if anything could be done. Lindbergh returned on August
11 with very little encouraging news. Arnold, who had visited the Ford
plant himself on July 31, was not surprised. He was more than ever
convinced that auto companies didn't know how to make aircraft. And
he had also become ambivalent about the B-24. He told Lindbergh the
combat squadrons greatly preferred the B-17. "When we send 17s out
on a mission, most of them return. But when we send the 24s out, a
good many of them don't."[24] The B-24, with its small-surface but aero-
dynamically efficient Davis wing, could fly faster and carry a heavier
load than the B-17, but when something went wrong, it also dropped
faster because it lacked the advantage of the B-17's larger, kitelike wing
surface.

In the spring and summer of 1942, Arnold realized that an
enormous need had arisen for quick transportation of men and supplies
to war theaters throughout the world and that he had to do something
about it. His response was to create what soon became the largest airline
the world had ever seen—the Air Transport Command.

At that time, the Ferry Command was already "in business," flying
combat planes and some personnel, first to England, then to all theaters

outside the Western Hemisphere. And the Air Service Command was "in business," flying mostly supplies and equipment to such places as Iceland, Greenland, and the Caribbean. But there was so much duplication of work and the two agencies got along so poorly with each other that Arnold decided to consolidate them, by stages, into one large military airline.

To command the operation he appointed a man of proven ability, Col. Harold George, and at the end of April he made him a brigadier general. But George's experience was largely as a pilot and a military planner. He had flown one of Billy Mitchell's bombers that sank the German battleship *Ostfriesland* in 1921; and both at Maxwell Field and in Washington he had been a leader in the development of the Air Forces' basic war strategy. He had never run an airline and he needed help from someone who had.

By chance, President Roosevelt received a phone call one day that provided a solution to George's need. The call was from a long-time Roosevelt friend, C. R. Smith, a big, gruff Texan who was president of American Airlines and already a legend in the airline business for his quick but intuitive decisions and his rapport with people.

As was his custom, Smith got right to the point in his conversation with the president. "You can tell Hap Arnold," he said, "if he needs someone to run his goddamned air transportation, I'm available."[25]

As soon as the president relayed this information, Arnold called Smith, who shortly thereafter became Col. C. R. Smith, deputy commander of the A.T.C. under George. Standing side by side, the two men looked like Mutt and Jeff—Smith, about six feet four and slightly rumpled, as if he had just been working on an aircraft engine (which he sometimes did); George, almost a foot shorter and splendidly attired in his well-cut uniform. But they worked together as if they had been born to be partners, with George concentrating on the military aspects of the operation while Smith organized the airline aspects. They got on so well they became lifelong friends.

Smith joined the Air Forces, at considerable financial sacrifice, not only because he could see the value of becoming involved in such a major enterprise as A.T.C., but for another reason Arnold could appreciate. Smith had been excluded from the experience of World War I because, as he said, "My mother had seven children and no father for them." At that time, he was already supporting the family. After the war, he attended the University of Texas for four years, then, in 1928, learned to fly for a small Texas airline. Six years later he was president of American Airlines. He had met Arnold through their mutual friend

Donald Douglas in the early thirties and was impressed by the cheerful brightness and vigor of this smiling Air Corps colonel, but the two never became close friends.

When the United States entered World War II, Smith, as an airline executive, realized perhaps even more than Arnold how essential air transport would be. "Wars in the past had been fought with steamboats," he later observed. "It was obvious that this war was going to cover the world and you can't fight wars with steamboats all over the world, so we had to build up an airline."

He and George began the job with a twelve-room office in the Munitions Building, several people inherited from the Ferry Command, and no airplanes except those in transit to operational units around the world. With Arnold's help, they chiseled a few planes for their first air routes (until he was able to start a steady flow coming to them from the factories); then, after developing a priority system for passengers and cargo, they began scheduled flights. Whenever they needed a directive to get something done, Arnold would give it to them. But Arnold's cooperation arose not only from his realization of the need for military transport but from his long-time vision of aviation as a means of mass transport. He had often spoken to his sons about the days to come when air travel would be as common as a bus ride. By developing the A.T.C. into a worldwide airline, he was pointing in that direction, creating a model for today's great worldwide airlines systems. And he was soon pleased with the two men he had chosen to run it. He later said of the A.T.C., "Once it had established its bases around the world and General George and General C. R. Smith were operating it, I was able to forget about it."[26]

There were problems in the beginning, however, and one of them arose in the person of Juan Trippe, president of Pan American Airways, who felt no need for an A.T.C. Arnold had only to provide the planes and Pan American would do the whole job for him. Or at least the whole overseas job. "We're the only airline," he said, "that has the experience and capability of flying overseas."[27]

Arnold, who did not consider it his job to build Pan American into a monopoly, said to Trippe, "I'll give you your share, but before this war is over, I'm going to have every major airline in the United States flying overseas, hauling military cargo." Though there had been talk of confiscating or militarizing all the airlines, Arnold decided he didn't favor that. It seemed to him that the individual lines could operate more effectively on their own, under the direction of the A.T.C. and in compliance with its priority system.

Trippe, however, was angered by Arnold's decision and though he had to abide by the arrangement, never did reconcile himself to it. When C. R. Smith began recruiting airline executives to help run the A.T.C., he was not able to get cooperation from Pan American.

Again that summer Bee Arnold went to Nag's Head for relief from her severe hay fever, taking David with her and leaving Hap alone in Washington. Becoming aware, perhaps, of the way she had been cut out of his life by the war, and of the growing gulf between them, he stopped to see her at Nag's Head on one of his trips south and involved her in a project that would not only give her something to do but would also fill a serious need. The Air Forces, he said, should have some kind of unofficial organization to help men with special problems, and to help the families of men who were killed or wounded. Would she fly to Washington and talk to Bob Lovett about the idea?[28]

She was in Washington the next day, and a few days later Arnold held a meeting of his entire staff with their wives. He talked to them about the need for an Air Forces relief society, asked the wives if they would volunteer to work for it, then turned to Bee and said, "You'll take charge of it."

She did so with such enthusiasm that she soon had forty thousand Air Forces wives all over the country contributing their time, and hundreds of industrialists contributing money. "But without solicitation," she claimed later with a smile. "We weren't allowed to solicit for funds."

The Air Forces Relief Society under Bee Arnold helped thousands of distressed or wounded airmen and thousands of bereaved families throughout the war, but it did not help bridge the gulf between Bee and her husband. She became as involved in her work as he was in his, and they saw even less of each other.

On July 6, the first B-17 reached the Eighth Air Force in England, flying the Atlantic via the Greenland–Iceland route, but it was an occasion for only qualified satisfaction. By this time, Arnold realized how cleverly Marshall and he had been slickered out of Bolero. The apparent British concurrence in the Bolero plan to launch a massive air offensive against Germany and then invade the continent at least by the spring of 1943 was fading away as President Roosevelt listened to Winston Churchill's insistence on a prior operation under the code name

"Torch"—an invasion of North Africa in the autumn of 1942. On July 22, Bolero was officially abandoned in favor of Torch. Then, on August 7, against Arnold's advice, the Navy invaded Guadalcanal. Suddenly, the entire strategy of the war seemed to have changed.

The decision to abandon Bolero was so frustrating to Marshall that it diverted his focus, at least temporarily, from Europe toward a Pacific strategy. Arnold, despite his great respect for Marshall, disagreed with him about the Guadalcanal invasion because he didn't think the Navy was yet strong enough to manage it. He predicted the Navy would start it, then come crying to the Army and Air Forces for help. And his prediction was proved true even before the August 7 landings on Guadalcanal. In late July, Admiral King had begun to demand air help, and with Bolero abandoned, it was almost impossible to ignore his demands. In an August 11 memorandum of record, Arnold wrote:

> At noon, in a talk between Admiral King and General Marshall, the general trend seemed to be that added emphasis must be put on the Pacific: that that was where we would, in all probability, fight the main battle rather than in the European theater.
> In spite of every protestation that [I] could make, it seems as if the weight is moving in that direction. Admiral Leahy, at the Joint Chiefs of Staff meeting this afternoon, came out quite positively for operations in the Pacific as against operations in Europe.
> None seemed to think in terms of winning the war. All seemed to think in terms of meeting the easiest enemy first.

In a memorandum to Marshall entitled "Air Force Voice Crying in Strategic Wilderness," Arnold complained: "The air plan to win the war is completely abandoned in turning to Torch and the South Pacific."

But once the Torch decision had been settled, Marshall could do no more about it than Arnold. The abandonment of Bolero was as hard a blow to him as it was to Arnold. When Marshall's new man in Europe, Dwight Eisenhower, learned on July 22 that it would be Torch rather than Bolero, he said this was, in his opinion, "the blackest day in history." And he was the man assigned to command the North African invasion. Marshall, under the influence of his disappointment at the cancellation of Bolero, had then agreed to send to the Pacific several hundred planes that were originally intended for the Eighth Air Force in England.

Arnold had once promised to have 3,640 combat planes in England by April 1943. He knew now that the Pacific would get about a third of those planes and that North Africa would get another third of them, meaning that the air offensive against Germany, which was the basic foundation of Air Forces war strategy, would have to be delayed or maybe even abandoned. Since all of this was carefully guarded information, how would he explain to congressmen and other influential people in Washington, people who might even have the power to cut Air Forces appropriations, why he wasn't launching the heavy blows he had been promising against Hitler?[29]

Spurred by this pressure, Arnold began passing it on to Eaker, urging him to get started, even though he had only one group of B-17s, which had just reached England.

On August 14, Eaker noted in his diary this pressure from Arnold. On August 17, Eaker himself led the first American offensive thrust against Hitler—a twelve-plane bombing of the railroad yards at Rouen. It was not an impressive start. The Germans hardly bothered to oppose it. As the summer of 1942 turned into autumn, Eaker got a few more groups, but Arnold's dream of a massive air offensive against Germany couldn't possibly materialize, at least until 1943.

When Admiral King announced in June that the Navy, not MacArthur, would stage and command the island-hopping offensive through the Solomons toward Japan, he had reminded Marshall that the Navy was accepting the Army's control of the European theater inasmuch as the European war was primarily a land war. Therefore the Army should accept the Navy's control of the Pacific theater inasmuch as the Pacific war would be primarily a sea war.[30] If the Army didn't like that, he said, the Navy would launch its offensive without the Army's help. In effect, King then prepared to do just that. But as the Guadalcanal invasion day approached, he realized he didn't have enough aircraft, especially in light of the danger to his carriers if they were exposed to Japanese land-based planes. Carriers could operate against other carriers in the open sea but they were woefully vulnerable to land-based planes, most of which had greater range than carrier planes.

King, realizing his needs by late July, had begun to demand planes from the Air Forces to strengthen the Guadalcanal operation. When the Marines invaded Guadalcanal on August 7, the Japanese, aware of its importance as an air base, counterattacked quickly, sank four U.S. cruisers, and forced the American naval task force to retire, leaving the 1st Marine Division stranded on the beaches. After three days of going it alone, the Navy's operation, commanded by Adm. Robert Ghormley, was in deep trouble. The fighting was to drag on for months. But when Arnold was asked to send more planes to the South Pacific, he pointed out that 900 American planes were already in that area, plus another

280 en route, while the Japanese, according to best intelligence estimates, had only 535 planes there. Furthermore, Arnold insisted, there weren't enough air fields to accommodate any more planes.

He considered the Navy's adventure on Guadalcanal a local action that got in the way of the overall war plan—a plan to which he still clung even if Marshall, King, Churchill, and Roosevelt had abandoned it. "Though everyone agrees that success in the Pacific theater will not win the war," he said in an August 21 memo to Marshall, "we are planning to concentrate more airplanes there." The war could be won, he declared, only by attacking German industry "relentlessly from now on."

King was not impressed by any of these arguments. On September 2, Arnold said to Stimson, wearily, "King never lets up. He has not receded one inch from any of his demands upon us, and I prophesy that he will eventually get them all."[31]

At a Joint Chiefs of Staff meeting on September 15, King and Arnold argued bitterly. King wanted, for the Pacific, fifteen air groups originally intended for England but now reserved for North Africa. Marshall indicated that without those planes, Torch might have to be postponed. (Though he didn't like the Torch operation, it was his responsibility to make it work.) Arnold repeated that what the Navy needed was not more planes but improved airfields and a better supply system. The only thing they could do with the planes, he insisted, was to park them on fields, while their crews would miss training and go stale. "In England," he said, "they could be used against the Germans every day."

King said, "We must keep the theater saturated."

"What is the saturation point?" Arnold demanded. "Certainly not several hundred [planes] sitting on airdromes where they can't be used."

At this point, Marshall announced that Arnold was planning to go to the Pacific to look into the situation for himself. Admiral Leahy quickly interrupted the hopeless argument to suggest that the decision be postponed until Arnold's return.[32]

Arnold was so exasperated by the entire matter that he wrote in his diary the next day: "The Navy is hard pressed at Guadalcanal. It does need a shot in the arm. It needs it badly. But in my opinion the shot can best come by getting new leaders who know and understand modern warfare."[33]

The next day, before Arnold's flight to the Pacific, Marshall called him in and gave him some fatherly advice. When he got out there into that unfriendly naval atmosphere, he should first of all listen. He should not get mad. And he should "let the other fellow tell his story."

Arnold flew to Hawaii on September 21, to talk with Nimitz at Pearl Harbor. The cool, shrewd Navy commander of the entire Pacific was surprisingly optimistic and quite convinced that Guadalcanal could be held. He said the Japanese had only half as many men there as the Americans, and their shipping losses had been prohibitive. Within the past two or three months, including the Battle of Midway, they had also lost 650 planes. The bombardment of Germany, he said, was "of no use."[34] The war could be won in the Pacific.

On the twenty-third, Arnold and his party, which included Col. Charles Cabell, landed at New Caledonia (south of the Solomons and east of Australia), where Admiral Ghormley had established his head-quarters on his flagship. Ghormley and his air strategist, Adm. John S. McCain, were awaiting Arnold with what seemed to him "blood in their eyes."

This was his theater, Ghormley informed Arnold, and nobody was going to tell him how to run it.

Arnold, perhaps recalling Marshall's advice, held his temper. All he wanted, he said, was some information. The personal tension seemed to him to ease after that, but he still felt Ghormley showed the strain of the military situation. He had been so busy, the admiral said, he hadn't been able to leave his headquarters for about a month.

Marshall or no Marshall, Arnold wasn't going to let such an opportunity pass. Maybe that was the cause of some of Ghormley's troubles, he suggested. No man could sit continuously in a small office, fighting a war, "without suffering mentally, physically and nervously."

Ghormley's immediate concern was logistics. He had eighty ships in the harbor at New Caledonia that couldn't be unloaded. And Guadalcanal was short of gasoline, but it was difficult to get his ships into the harbor there past the Japanese sea and air pickets.

The image of eighty ships loaded with supplies standing idle in the harbor when "the planners of Torch were going nearly crazy in their search for ships" staggered Arnold. Why couldn't the ships be unloaded? One of Ghormley's aides said it was because they didn't know what was on them, so they'd have to be sent to New Zealand, unloaded, then reloaded with new manifests.

Before Arnold had quite digested this, McCain informed him that the Navy had to have B-17s, and a lot of them, for long-range patrol. The Navy's PBY flying boats simply wouldn't do. The Navy also needed Army fighters to stop the Japanese bombers that were sinking American supply ships. And the only fighters he really wanted were P-38s, of which very few were available. Both Ghormley and McCain repeated Nimitz's refrain that the B-17s and the Air Forces fighters were being wasted in Europe. (Actually very few bombers or fighters had yet reached Europe.) McCain told him, "Here is where they can be of use. Here is the only place where they can get results. MacArthur may need them, but we need them more than he does."

Arnold could remember the days, in the not-far-distant past, when neither MacArthur nor the Navy could see much need for big bombers, but on that score he held his tongue.

Gen. Alexander M. Patch, the Army's ground forces commander in the area, who had accompanied Arnold to the meeting, said when they left that as far as he could see, the Navy had no logistic plan. He told Arnold he had already given the Navy and Marines twenty thousand pairs of shoes and tons of other items out of his own reserves because they had undersupplied themselves; and they were short of both airfields and gasoline simply because they had miscalculated their needs.

(From his visit to Ghormley's headquarters, Arnold emerged with only one piece of good news, and that was personal rather than military. Ernie Snowden, Lois's husband, had been on the carrier *Wasp* when it was sunk earlier in September, but he had survived and was thought to be en route to San Diego.)

From New Caledonia, Arnold flew on to Australia, 750 miles west, and landed at an airport 50 miles beyond Brisbane because it was the only one with runways long enough for the B-24 in which he was traveling. George Kenney met him and flew him, in a much smaller Lockheed Hudson, back to Brisbane, where MacArthur was waiting. There was nothing fancy about Kenney's plane. It had no passenger seats: Arnold sat on a coil of rope, Cabell sat on a box of ammunition, and Kenney squatted between them. But for Arnold, this flight was one of the few reassuring legs of the entire trip. Though Kenney had been in Australia only a month, after replacing Brett, he assured Arnold he was having no trouble with MacArthur now, and didn't intend to have any. (As Arnold later learned, Kenney had already amazed MacArthur by airlifting a whole brigade of troops to Port Moresby, on his own initiative, when the Japanese threatened the airfields there.) "We're going to win it out here," he said, "and I'm going to get along with General MacArthur."

Arnold's half hour alone with Kenney pleased him more than the two hours he spent with the histrionic supreme commander of the

Southwest Pacific. What MacArthur said that day, as reported in Arnold's diary, does not make him seem, in retrospect, as astute as he was reputed to be. The Japanese, he declared, were better fighting men than the Germans. He didn't have enough troops to hold them. The Australians were not even good militiamen. The Japanese could take New Guinea and the Fijis any time they pleased, after which they would control the Pacific for a hundred years. And their move into the Aleutians was part of an eventual move into Siberia. As for the European war, no second front could be established from England because it would be impossible to build enough bases to provide air cover. And any move into North Africa was a waste of effort.

With this last assessment, at least, Arnold could agree. He wasn't completely surprised at the other extraordinary attitudes because Delos Emmons, now the Hawaiian air commander, had recently visited Mac-Arthur and had reported some views of his that were even more outlandish. The Japanese, MacArthur had told Emmons, would take the Solomons, Fiji, New Guinea, Hawaii, then South America. And the United States was in greater danger of invasion by them than by the Germans because the U.S. Navy couldn't stop the Japanese.

Arnold in his diary did not comment on MacArthur's predictions, most of which must have seemed insupportable even in those difficult days, but he did note that their talk "gives me the impression of a brilliant mind—obsessed by a plan he can't carry out—dramatic to the extreme—much more nervous than when I formerly knew him. Hands twitch and tremble—shell shocked."

From Brisbane, Arnold flew to Espiritu Santo, the westernmost island in the New Hebrides, where the Air Forces and the Navy had established a primitive air base for the Solomons campaign. The 11th Bombardment Group, commanded by Col. Laverne G. Saunders, a onetime football star at West Point, was stationed there in the company of mud, mosquitoes, malaria, and a Navy fighter squadron. At this fighting-men's level, the Air Forces and the Navy were getting along nicely together despite their shared misery. Since they had almost no maintenance men, the B-17 crews were repairing their own planes and sleeping under the wings, but they were flying daily missions against the Japanese on Guadalcanal, and they had only one complaint. Their lifeboats, they said, were built to hold four men, and as there were eight men in each crew, four of them had to cling to the sides, uncomfortably exposed, when they went down in these shark-infested waters. Arnold promised he would do something about that.

Saunders gave him a tour of the base in a jeep but didn't suggest he stay overnight because there was no mess hall.[35] Of the thirty-six planes with which the group had left Hawaii in late July, twelve had been lost but the other twenty-four were still flying missions. Six were out on patrol this afternoon. Before Arnold left, they returned with the news that they had sunk two Japanese transports. Arnold was so impressed he decided to recommend Saunders for his first star. "Saunders deserves much credit," he wrote in his diary, "for looking after his men and at the same time carrying on such successful operations." There was one other heartening thing about Saunders. Unlike some of the generals and admirals to whom Arnold had spoken, this flying colonel had no doubt that the Japanese would eventually be driven back.

The next day, September 28, at 4:30 p.m., Arnold arrived on Ghormley's flagship again, for a conference with him and Nimitz (who had flown in from Hawaii), Kenney, and Gen. Richard Sutherland (representing MacArthur), and Miff Harmon, representing his own South Pacific command. The meeting was devoted largely to generalities, and Arnold emerged from it with several depressing conclusions. The Navy's big drive in the Solomons was now considered "a limited offensive" to stop the Japanese from further advance. The Navy did not intend to help MacArthur any more than necessary, but the Navy and MacArthur agreed on one thing—the Pacific was the only important war theater.

After listening to both sides, Arnold was more than ever convinced that there had to be unity of command in the Pacific. The Japanese, with fewer troops, were pushing the Americans around because the man in command of the Japanese could concentrate his forces at any point of attack without having to talk some other commander into helping him. But the prospects for a unified American command were dim because neither Nimitz nor MacArthur would accept it unless he were named supreme commander.

When Arnold returned to Washington, he was greeted by two items of good news for a change. On October 1, the first U.S. jet plane, a fighter built by Bell Aircraft from the English plans he brought back in 1941, had successfully completed its maiden flight. Also, of more immediate interest, the first B-29 Superfortress had taken to the air September 21. Arnold was counting on the B-29 to be the weapon that would force Japan to surrender. But without a unified command in the Pacific, who would be in charge of the B-29 fleet when it was ready? And what assurance was there that it wouldn't be fractured like the B-17 fleet, instead of being concentrated, as he was certain it should be, against the Japanese homeland?

At the October 6 meeting of the Joint Chiefs of Staff, King and his aides listened politely while Arnold outlined his impressions of the Pacific situation, after which King simply reiterated his contention that the number of aircraft in the Pacific should be maintained "at the point of saturation of available facilities." Additional airfields were now being built, he said, to accommodate more planes. Leahy then said if additional planes were needed in the South Pacific, they should be sent there rather than to England. Despite his trip, Arnold's argument with the Navy was right back where it had started.

After private briefings with Marshall, Stimson, and President Roosevelt, Arnold received a request to visit Navy Secretary Knox and tell him about it. This meeting went smoothly until Arnold began outlining his differences with the Navy.

Knox stopped him with the announcement that he didn't care to hear him criticize the Navy.

Arnold said he was simply presenting the facts as he had found them. He had not asked for this interview, and if the Secretary didn't care to hear what he had to say, it was all right with him. That ended the interview.[36]

Shortly after his return, Arnold summoned to Washington from Wright Field the men who designed and procured lifeboats and other emergency equipment for heavy bombers. After assembling this team in his office, he had them inflate one of their four-man boats in front of his desk. Then he chose eight of them and said, "Climb in."

"But it's only a four-man boat," one of them said.

"I don't care if it's a four-man boat or what it is. Climb in."

Needless to say, they didn't fit. But that was not enough. He instructed them to get bathing suits and try it in the Potomac, climbing into the raft from the water, the way downed airmen would have to do it at sea. "When you get through," he said, "I want to talk to you some more."

By the following day, they fully understood the problem of an eight-man crew trying to get into a four-man lifeboat. As a result, the B-17s and B-24s were soon carrying two five-man boats plus a four-man boat, so that even if one boat was bullet-riddled, there would be two left.[37]

On November 8, 1942, the North African invasion began, but Arnold still had mixed feelings about it. The Eighth Air Force, after a few skeleton missions, was now reduced to virtual impotence, and whatever strength it had was devoted to keeping submarines away from the African landing forces. The United States had now been at war for one year, and so far nothing had happened in accordance with the original plan of exerting the major effort against the German homeland. Arnold still believed in that plan, but all he could do was wait.

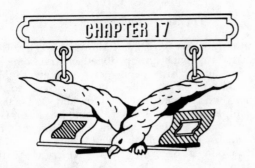

As the year 1943 began, Hap Arnold was coming to the realization that his problems with the British were more complicated than he had imagined, partly because the British themselves were more compli- cated than he imagined. He had watched in astonishment as Prime Minister Churchill, by diplomatic sleight of hand, turned the Bolero invasion of the continent into the Torch invasion of North Africa. And now the North African campaign was progressing so steadily that Roosevelt and Churchill had scheduled a two-power conference, to begin officially January 14, at the sunny French Moroccan port of Casablanca.

When Arnold left Washington for this conference on January 9, with the rest of the American contingent, he didn't know what surprises Churchill might be planning. Had he been privy to some of the communications between Churchill and his top military men in recent months, he might have been better prepared for what was to take place at Casablanca.

In an October 22, 1942, "Note on Air Policy," Churchill had written:

> The utmost pressure must be put upon the United States authorities here and in America to utilize their Fortresses and Liberators in support of our sea communications during Torch. . . . At present the United States are perservering with the idea of the daylight bombing of Germany . . . without escort. So far they had not gone beyond the limits of strong British fighter escort. They will probably experience a heavy disaster as soon as they do. We must try to persuade them to divert these energies (a) to sea work, beginning with helping Torch, . . . and (b) to night work. . . . We should urge them to build Lancasters [the best of the British four-engine bombers] for us. . . . We should urge the development of the Mustang with the right engines. It would be much better if they could be induced to build 70,000 aircraft of the right kind in 1943 than a hundred thousand of those they are now projecting.

In a "Most Secret" November 2 memorandum to Portal, Churchill had written:

The first American heavy bomber group arrived in this country accompanied by its fighter group, together with some eighteen thousand American Air Force personnel as long ago as the end of July. By the end of September the number of American Air Force personnel has risen to about fifty-five thousand. So far the results have been pitifully small. Far from dropping bombs on Germany, the American daylight bombers have not ventured beyond Lille. . . . Meanwhile, the American public has been led to believe that a really serious contribution has been made by the American Air Force.

Addressing himself in this memo to the American daylight bombing methods, Churchill Wrote:

Considering the American professional interests and high reputations which are engaged in this scheme, and the shock it would be to the American people and to the Administration if the policy proved a glaring failure, we must expect most obstinate perserverance in this method.

And in a January 10, 1943, memorandum to Sir Archibald Sinclair, the secretary of state for air, who also had reservations about the American air effort but was now trying to soften the prime minister's criticisms, Churchill wrote:

I have never suggested that they [the Americans] should be "discouraged" by us, that is to say, that we should argue against their policy, but only that they should not be encouraged to persist obstinately and also that they should be actively urged to become capable of night bombing.

Arnold did not know about these harsh assessments Churchill had been making privately of the American air effort in England. He did know, of course, that the British still disliked the B-17 and wanted America to produce Lancasters; and that they still wanted the Eighth Air Force to begin nighttime rather than daytime bombing. But he was convinced they would change their minds about both the B-17 and day bombing once the African campaign was over and the Fortress fleet in England could be built to its intended strength. Arnold had never envisioned the Eighth Air Force attacking targets in Germany with a force as small as it now had in England. He had hoped by now to have several hundred B-17s over Europe, but the diversion of planes to the Pacific, and to Churchill's own Torch operation, had kept the size of the Eighth Air Force down to less than one hundred heavy bombers.[1] The whole concept of daylight precision bombing depended upon fleets so large and with so much fire power and bomb power that enemy defenses would be unable to cope with them. In his view, the daylight bombing theory hadn't yet been tested because he hadn't yet been able to send over enough planes to try it properly.

On the way to Casablanca in a new four-engine Douglas C-54 transport, Arnold, Marshall, and their aides landed at Bathurst in West Africa, where Gen. C. R. Smith and Gen. Tom Hardin of the A.T.C. were waiting to greet them. Smith was in Africa because Arnold had learned, in early December 1942, that the Navy planned to develop an air transport service, which, in effect, would duplicate the A.T.C.[2] A day or so later, Arnold met Smith in the Munitions Building corridor and said, "I want to see you."

They went into Arnold's office where he said, "We've got to do something about Dakar." With North Africa under Allied control, the West African port of Dakar assumed great importance as a landing place for transatlantic cargo and passenger planes. "I understand there's four hundred thousand tons of shipping in the harbor and they've got a railroad and an airport. You'd better go over there and take them over."

"Suits me," Smith said. "Give me a letter."

"I won't give you a letter," Arnold said. "Go over there, see what's wrong, and take care of it." [3]

Knowing Arnold, Smith went immediately to Dakar and made arrangements with the French governor general to assume control of the harbor, the railroad, and the airport, which he then undertook to enlarge. He hadn't been there long when he became aware of the real reason Arnold had sent him. An American admiral arrived one day with a representative of the State Department, apparently intent on doing for the Navy what Smith had already done for the Air Forces.

Smith had gone to bed early that night and was asleep when the State Department man came and told him that the admiral wanted to see him. The first thing the admiral said was, "I understand you've made quite a lot of engagements over here. Can I see the letter that authorizes you?"

Smith said, "No, you can't because there isn't any letter. I have my verbal instructions from General Arnold and I did just exactly what he asked me to do."

"That's extraordinary behavior," the admiral exclaimed.

Smith became impatient. "Well, look," he said, "we came over here and took over this goddamned place and we're building an airfield here now. As long as I satisfy General Arnold, I think I'll get along pretty good in the military service, and when I don't satisfy him I won't. If you've got any complaints about what I've done, take it up with him. I'm going back to bed."

Arnold was both pleased and amused to learn all this from Smith. In Dakar, at least, he had moved fast enough to beat the Navy. He was slightly alarmed, though, at some of the information Smith had managed to pick up. For instance, Smith knew that President Roosevelt was arriving in Africa on the cruiser *Memphis* for a Casablanca conference with Churchill, and that Marshall and Arnold were on their way to the same conference, as was Admiral King. And from Casablanca, Arnold was off to China for a conference with Chiang Kai-shek. How had Smith learned all this? From Air Forces headquarters in Washington? Not at all. He had picked it up from gossipers on African A.T.C. lines. It made Arnold wonder about the American security system.

After arriving in Casablanca, Arnold himself heard some gossip that sounded like considerably more than gossip, and that alarmed him so much he immediately sent a cablegram to General Eaker in England, directing him to come as quickly as possible to Casablanca.[4] Eaker, who had become the Eighth Air Force commander when Spaatz went to North Africa as Eisenhower's air commander, was surprised to hear from Arnold in Africa. He knew nothing of the Churchill-Roosevelt conference (which said something for British security) but he knew Arnold well enough to waste no time getting to Casablanca. On the fifteenth, he arrived at the villa Arnold was occupying within the Anfa Hotel compound at the edge of the city. Arnold, who was in the bathroom shaving, emerged to greet his old friend with lather on his face but without his usual smile.

He had learned, he said, that the prime minister had asked the president to discontinue daylight bombing. And the president had agreed that the Eighth Air Force should join the R.A.F. in night bombing. "What do you think of that?" he asked Eaker.

He knew very well what Eaker thought of it. Having been engaged in day bombing for more than four months of Eighth Air Force operations, Eaker was in a better position than anyone else to defend the strategy. And unlike Arnold, he was a man of tact and diplomacy. Arnold was intelligent enough to know that he himself was not the best man to argue the case for daylight bombing. He had neither the detailed knowledge nor the patience to prevail over Churchill.

"In my judgment," he said to Eaker, "the American Chiefs of Staff will join the British Chiefs in acceding to Churchill's request. And that will settle it because if Roosevelt accedes, it'll finish daylight bombing for the Eighth Air Force in England. It occurred to me that the only chance we had to get the Prime Minister to change his view was to have you come down and see him. I've heard him mention you favorably. If you can't convince him that we should continue daylight bombing, I think we're finished with it. I'm going to try to arrange a meeting for you tomorrow."

It was three days before Churchill had time to talk to Eaker. Meanwhile, Eaker and his aide, Capt. James Parton, settled into a room in Arnold's villa and went to work. First Eaker wrote a two-page paper, "Why Have U.S. Bombers Not Bombed Germany?," which explained that most of his planes had been taken from him (six hundred of them went to Torch), the weather had been unfavorable, the submarines in the Atlantic had demanded attention, and he didn't yet have long-range fighters to escort and protect the bombers over Germany. But he concluded that if his force was rebuilt as planned, the B-17s would be bombing Germany before February.

He and Parton then wrote another paper, "The Case for Day Bombing," which was almost seven single-spaced typewritten pages when they finished it. Aware of Churchill's fetish for brevity, the two of them spent a whole day boiling this paper down to a memorandum of less than one page which made eight points:

1. Day bombing was more accurate than night bombing.
2. Therefore it took fewer planes to destroy a target.
3. U.S. day bombing and British night bombing (around the clock) would give the Germans no rest.
4. Air congestion in England would be relieved if Americans flew in the daytime, the British at night.
5. U.S. crews were trained for day bombing and would have to be retrained for night bombing.
6. U.S. planes and equipment were designed for day operations.
7. Day bombing would destroy Germany's fighters by exposing them to the B-17's twelve 50-caliber guns.
8. Americans could ignite obscure targets by day, which the R.A.F. could find at night by the light of the fires.

Eaker met Churchill at his villa, submitted his short brief, and talked to him for a half hour, after which Churchill indicated he would drop his case against day bombing. But just to make sure Churchill had been sufficiently bombarded by the American argument, Arnold also sent Spaatz and Frank Andrews to see him. (Andrews had succeeded

Eisenhower as theater commander in England.) And on the nineteenth, Arnold himself had lunch with Churchill, impressing upon him the contention that the big American bombers, with long-range fighter escort, could protect themselves against the Germans. After all this, Churchill must have been exhausted by the argument. Finally he promised he would "say nothing more about it." Churchill's surrender was incorporated into a policy paper called the "Combined [day and night] Bomber Offensive." The American airmen had survived their most serious challenge from the British. They had only to prove they could survive the coming challenge from the Germans.

The Casablanca conference ended on January 23 and Arnold, with Clair Peterson at the controls, flew to Algiers the next day, en route to China. He had in his pocket a letter of introduction from President Roosevelt to Chiang Kai-shek explaining the purpose of the trip. Roosevelt wanted Arnold and Chiang to work out ways of transporting more supplies into China, and more planes for Gen. Claire Chennault's air force, "in order that you may carry the offensive to the Japanese at once." He also wanted Chiang's assurance that the Chinese army would take part in a campaign to drive the Japanese out of Burma—a campaign agreed upon in principle at Casablanca.

All of this sounded simple enough, but Arnold knew it was not. Chiang was a harder man to pin down than Churchill, and even when he was pinned, no one could be sure what he was pinned to. In addition, only one of the American military men in China, General Chennault, was able to get along with him. Chennault was an operational genius but not very interested in logistics. The American Army commander in China, Gen. Joseph "Vinegar Joe" Stilwell, Chiang's chief military adviser, held the generalissimo in such contempt he referred to him openly as "Peanut Head." And neither Stilwell nor his air commander, Gen. Clayton Bissell, an excellent logistician, could get along with Chennault, their subordinate, who generally sided with Chiang against them.

Already tired from the Casablanca conference, and subject to occasional spells of unexplained stomach distress, Arnold might well have done without the China trip. But someone had to go and mollify Chiang, who was angry at having been omitted from the Casablanca meeting, and Arnold had been elected because air help was about the only thing the United States could offer China for the coming year.

At New Delhi, Arnold and his two fellow travelers, Army Gen.

Brehon Somervell and British representative Sir John Dill, met Stilwell and the British commander in India, Gen. Sir Archibald Wavell, who seemed to Arnold "brilliant but worn out." When Wavell showed him his plan for driving the Japanese out of western Burma, Arnold observed with his usual lack of tact that it was not a plan at all "but merely several pages of well written paragraphs telling why the mission could not be accomplished."[5]

He reached Dinjan on February 4, planning to spend the night and get some rest at an A.T.C. base there, but when he heard that Stilwell and Dill had taken off for K'un-ming, he said, "If Stilwell can go over the Hump at night, so can we." He promptly ordered Peterson, his pilot, to go to the operations building for briefing.[6]

There had been very few flights over the Hump at night, but General Bissell and his pilot were traveling with them, and Bissell's pilot indicated he was familiar with the 525-mile two-and-a-half-hour route, which was important because they would be flying over some very high mountains and, at intervals, ground held by the Japanese.

Peterson took off and climbed through rough air to eighteen thousand feet. The first indication he might have trouble was when the navigator, who had never before flown above ten thousand feet, turned giddy from lack of oxygen and couldn't function. About the same time, Peterson realized that Bissell's pilot didn't know much more about the Hump than he did. At the midway point, there was supposed to be a beacon; they couldn't find it. The radio operator tried to get the K'un-ming station but couldn't raise it. He could get other Chinese stations, and Japanese stations, but not K'un-ming. As he later learned, there was a fifty-mile-per-hour tail wind that night. After two and a half hours, by which time they should have been near their destination, they still couldn't see it. In fact, they were beyond it.

Peterson went to the rear and told Arnold they were lost. Though Arnold showed no emotion at this news, he later confided his fears to his diary: "There is always the possibility of Jap planes being abroad. They probably have radar. . . . If we turn back into the wind do we run out of gas in the mountains? Do we jump? If so, when? . . . What should we take with us if we have to jump? What will the people back home think if they hear that the Commanding General, U.S. Army Air Forces, and the Commanding General, Tenth Air Force [Bissell] and the others with us have been taken prisoners? What are the best shoes to wear in hiking through the jungle?"

Meanwhile, Peterson had gone into a square search pattern. Bissell's pilot was not very confident of this expedient. Glancing at the altimeter, he said, "If you fly too far north, you're not high enough." In other words, they were approaching mountains higher than eighteen thousand feet. Peterson checked his gas supply. If they turned back to Dinjan now, they wouldn't make it; they would run out of gas in the mountains through which they had come. He was trying dismally to think of other options when the radio operator announced he had found K'un-ming on his dial. Peterson turned on his radio compass and began homing in on the K'un-ming station. A few minutes later, the navigator, who had been given oxygen, took a bearing and fixed their position. They had overshot K'un-ming but were now on course back toward it. Finally, at 1:45 a.m., more than six hours after takeoff, they landed safely with only a few gallons of gas in the tanks.

Arnold said nothing to Peterson that night, and even the next morning, all he said was, "Pete, I think we ought to plan our trips better." It was apparently as close as he could come to admitting that he shared the blame.

In K'un-ming, Arnold talked to Stilwell, Bissell, and Chennault. From Chennault he got a clear picture of the air situation in China "but to my astonishment, in spite of his Air Corps and Tactical School training, he was not realistic about the logistics of his operation."

The next day, after a flight to Chungking and a chair ride up a steep stairway to a mansion which Stilwell called "the Peanut's Berchtesgaden," Arnold met Chiang Kai-shek for the first time.[7] During their almost three-hour luncheon talk, Chiang kept hammering on the same theme. He didn't like the present setup. He wanted Chennault to command all air forces in China, independent of Stilwell and Bissell. Chennault was the one outstanding air tactician in the Far East. Someone else could handle his administrative work for him if he took command.

Chiang also wanted a firm commitment for five hundred more U.S. planes. And he didn't care to talk about logistics. It seemed to Arnold he "wanted to build up the Chinese Air Force in numbers, regardless of whether or not there was gasoline for the planes to use."

Later that afternoon, at a larger conference, Sir John Dill presented the Combined Chiefs' plan for the reconquest of Burma. Chiang didn't seem interested.

The next morning, Sunday, February 7, Chiang wanted to see Arnold alone. After breakfast in his frigid room, Arnold trudged up the long flight of stairs, through four inches of snow, to the mansion, where Chiang and T.V. Soong were waiting.

"I am going to be very frank with you—more so than I usually am,"

Chiang said. "The conference so far has been a failure and I want you to tell the President so for me."

He reminded Arnold that his army had been fighting for six years, without trucks, often without food, and without getting supplies from anyone. If, as the Combined Chiefs said, they considered China important, why didn't they send supplies? Russia got convoys. China should get at least ten percent of what Russia was getting. But when he asked Bissell for things, he got nothing but explanations as to why there weren't more planes and more tonnage.

"Tell your President," he concluded, "that unless I can get these three things, I cannot fight this war and he cannot count on me to have our Army participate in the [Burma] campaigns."

The three things he insisted on were an independent air force under Chennault, 10,000 tons of supplies per month over the Hump, and 500 more U.S. airplanes by the following November.

Arnold's reply was, for him, a model of patience, perhaps because Chiang's demands "threw me back on my haunches for a few minutes." But as he said to Stilwell later, he'd be damned if he would carry such a message back to the president. After the usual courtesies, he, too, talked tough.

"I am sincerely disappointed in your message to the President," he said, "for it is not in any way in accordance with my understanding of what has occurred."

He had already issued orders to increase the number of planes on the Hump run from 62 to 137. He planned to bring the tonnage up from 1,700 to 4,000 monthly by April and keep raising it as quickly as possible thereafter. Chennault had asked for medium bombers because he said heavy bombers couldn't operate in China. But heavy bombers could most certainly operate there, and he was sending 35 of them.

"I have outlined plans for creating one Chinese fighter squadron, then another. . . . I also outlined plans for creating four bomber squadrons in the same manner. . . . These plans may bring 500 planes to China, but not by November. As yet I have not received your O.K. . . ."

"As to the independent air force for Chennault, I am not in a position to approve such an organization, but I assure you I will repeat the remarks, as given to me, to the President."

Eventually the other conference members were brought in and the talks continued until early afternoon, with both sides repeating their stands. In the end, Chiang seemed to agree that he would help the Burma campaign, and he insisted that the Chinese would fight on under any circumstances; yet at the same time he left a veiled impression that they wouldn't do too much fighting unless he got his way. When Arnold departed, he was no more certain of Chiang's intentions than when he arrived, but he had a better understanding of why so many people had trouble dealing with him.

"The generalissimo does not impress me as being a big man," he wrote in his diary. "He casts aside logic and factual matters as so much trash. . . . Apparently he has had the power of life and death so long that he expects, and his subjects give him, the answer that he wants. Accordingly, he does not have to think through. It makes no difference as long as he has his way. . . . In any event, he did not impress me as being in the same class as the President or the Prime Minister."

Returning from China by way of the Middle East and Europe (Japan controlled the Pacific almost as far south as Australia), Arnold recalled that the Air Forces had set up an emergency refueling station at a place called Salala on the Indian Ocean in Saudi Arabia. He decided to detour and land there, just to see how the boys were doing, to make sure they didn't feel forgotten at this remote outpost. When Peterson set down their B-17, the desert wind was blowing clouds of fine sand, but the commanding officer, a nonflying lieutenant named Pike, was right there to greet them.[8] He had about twenty men living in tents and eating at an improvised mess hall. They hauled their gasoline up five miles from the water by camel, in five-gallon cans. The heat of the desert pressed down on them and there was no relief, no entertainment, nothing to alleviate the monotony. When Arnold asked Pike how things were going, he said, "Fine."

He showed Arnold and Peterson around, which didn't take long, then brought them to the mess hall, where they and their crew had an excellent meal, all from cans.

"Is there anything you need?" Arnold asked Pike.

"No, sir," said the lieutenant. He either thought it improper to bother the commanding general with small details or he knew instinctively that by impressing Arnold he'd get what he needed.

Arnold looked around, saw a phonograph, and tried to play it, but it didn't work. "What's the matter with this?"

"We broke the mainspring, sir."

"Then you need a new phonograph, don't you?"

"Well, we could use one, yes, sir."

Before Arnold was through nosing around, he decided there were a lot of things these men could use, and when he landed at the next American base, he gave the commander there a list of items to be sent immediately to Salala. Shortly after their return to Washington, he called Peterson into his office and said, "Remember that Lieutenant Pike in Salala? I've looked into him. I found out he wants to go to flight school and become a pilot. You see to it that he does."

Arnold arrived back in Washington the afternoon of February 17 and had been home only one day when he received some chilling news from Seattle. On September 21, 1942, the first B-29 had undergone its maiden test flight with Boeing's best test pilot, Edmund T. "Eddie" Allen at the controls, and afterward he had pronounced the plane a winner. That had been a great relief to Arnold because, on his authority, the U.S. government was spending more money on the development of the Superfortress than on any other war project except the atomic bomb. But the public knew nothing about the bomb. Everyone had read about Arnold's huge bomber. He had bet his reputation that the plane would deliver.

Since the day of its maiden flight, however, the B-29 had exhibited so many shortcomings that it couldn't possibly be ready for combat before 1944, and some experts doubted it would ever be ready. The giant plane was designed to fly so high its cabin had to be pressurized, but in altitude tests the pressure had caused rivets to burst. When that had been corrected, the complicated new navigational system developed bugs. Then questions arose about the engine's cooling system.

On February 18, 1943, the day after Arnold returned from China, Eddie Allen took off from the Seattle airport in the second B-29 test plane. After twenty minutes in the air, he reported calmly to the tower that he needed a landing clearance because his number-one engine was on fire. Several minutes later he reported to the tower, "I'm coming in with a wing on fire." He didn't quite make it. With flames trailing from the stricken wing, he hit some high-tension lines and crashed into the side of a packing plant, killing himself, his crew, and several plant employees.[9]

When Arnold learned of the tragedy, he called Gen. Oliver Echols, the Wright Field commander, and said, "Look, we're in trouble about this thing. What're we going to do?"

Echols said, "I'll send you some of our best people."

Gen. K. B. Wolfe of the materiel command went immediately to Washington and Arnold put him in charge of a committee to study the entire B-29 project. But that didn't silence the criticism. Reactions reached Washington within hours, especially from executives of other aircraft companies, men who had already told him the B-29 was too sophisticated an airplane to be developed in time to help win the war. Even some of the Boeing executives were so shaken by the crash that they seemed about to lose faith in the plane. Arnold would soon have to decide whether all those millions had been wasted on the B-29. If so, he would have a lot of explaining to do to the president, the Congress, and the American people.

Of more immediate concern was the declining strength of the Eighth Air Force in England.[10] On February 9, while Arnold was in India en route home from China, he had received through Marshall a radiogram from Andrews asking him to stop in England and discuss a buildup of Eaker's B-17 force. The message said: "Bomber strength deteriorating rapidly to point where raids cannot be made in sufficient strength to disperse anti-aircraft."

None of this was news to Arnold. Thanks to all the diversions, he simply didn't have the planes to rebuild the Eighth immediately. But there was no need to go to England to tell that to Andrews and Eaker. He was too tired, after Casablanca and China, for a side trip.

A few days after his return to Washington, he came down with what he called "the darnedest spell of the grippe I have had in years." He had barely gotten back on his feet when it was time to go up to New York to welcome Mme. Chiang Kai-shek, who had come to the United States to argue her husband's case with the president—and while she was there, to do some shopping. (By the time she was through shopping, the A.T.C., at the prodding of the State Department, had to provide a four-engine C-54 cargo plane to carry all of her luxuries back to China for her.)[11] When Arnold returned home from New York, he was exhausted, but he wasn't ready to admit it. He had already slipped back into his seven-day-week routine. Early in the afternoon of Sunday, February 28, he went to the White House for a discussion of his China trip with the president. Marshall was also there, as were Sir John Dill and General Somervell. After the meeting, in midafternoon, Arnold went home to Fort Myer for a rest. Bee was there, with David, which should have been comforting to him but was not; the fact that he and Bee now saw so little of each other had raised barriers between them which made it more difficult for them to get along when they did see each other.

Arnold had been home only a short time when he complained of chest pains.[12] Bee became concerned, but when she tried to talk to him about it, he was uncommunicative. As his condition apparently worsened, she became alarmed and, without his consent, called the post medical officer of the day, Dr. Lee B. Martin, a young captain, who came immediately.

When the doctor arrived, Arnold did not welcome him. He was not sick, he said.

Mrs. Arnold insisted he was sick. "He's very stubborn," she said to the doctor. "I can't do anything with him."

Martin perceived quickly that the two were not getting along well. Arnold seemed reluctant even to speak to his wife. He obviously hadn't wanted her to call the doctor. Perhaps he realized that a serious illness on his medical record might force his retirement. He was reluctant also to speak to the doctor, but Martin examined him anyway.

Had there been any incident that preceded the onset of the chest pains, Martin asked.

He had been at the White House that afternoon, Arnold said, and yes, he had been involved in a rather heated argument. But he refused to attach any importance to that. It was silly to suggest that he was sick.

To Dr. Martin, however, he exhibited "the cardinal signs and symptoms of a coronary," and the young doctor said so.

"You don't know what you're talking about," Arnold insisted.

"I'm going to give you an injection," Martin said.

He would do nothing of the kind, Arnold insisted. He wasn't sick and he wasn't having any injections.

Martin, trained to believe that when someone is sick, the doctor is the boss, said to him, "General, roll up your sleeve."

Arnold, no doubt amazed to hear a captain talk that way to him, rolled up his sleeve.

After administering the shot, Martin said, "I think you should go into Walter Reed."

Arnold said, "I won't go. There's no need."

Mrs. Arnold suggested the doctor call Walter Reed. Instead, he called the Air Forces' chief flight surgeon, Gen. David N. W. Grant, and explained the situation. Grant said he would arrange for an ambulance.

Martin, turning back to Arnold, said, "Now, we'll put you on a stretcher and carry you upstairs to bed."

Arnold said, "No damned captain is going to tell me what to do. I'll walk."

"You'll go on a stretcher," Martin said, and he did.

The ambulance came that evening and at Walter Reed, the young doctor's diagnosis was confirmed by an electrocardiogram. Arnold had suffered a severe coronary. The long hours of work, the efforts to supply and control the nation's air power all over the world, the contention with the Navy and the British, the hectic trips, the enormous responsibilities —in short, the war, and perhaps, too, his growing difficulties with Bee, had finally caught up with him. In a few days he was released from Walter Reed, only to be transferred to the Biltmore Hotel in Coral Gables, Florida, which—at his behest, as it happened—had been converted into an Air Forces wartime convalescent hospital.

Back home for a day or so before the flight to Florida, he called Dr. Martin, the strong-willed captain, and invited him to his quarters. He had developed so much respect for this young man who had dared speak up to him that he wanted to take him to Florida.

Martin tried to back off. He had never flown, he explained, and he suffered from a fear of flying.

Though Arnold didn't say so, he could understand such feelings. "Think nothing of it," he said. "I'm going to transfer you to the Air Forces."

That afternoon, Martin was an Air Forces captain on his way to Florida in a B-25, with Arnold, Arnold's son David, and Bruce Simmons aboard. Simmons had been in the infirmary about to have his tonsils removed when Arnold called and told him to get up and get out of there. He was going to Florida. "They can take your tonsils out down there," Arnold said. Bee Arnold chose not to go.

At the Coral Gables Biltmore, Arnold was installed in a tower suite from which he could look down on a private golf course, Biscayne Bay, and much of Miami. He could also see a pool in which bass were jumping, but despite his continuing pretense that he wasn't really sick, he took little interest in such things during the first few days after his arrival.

For the purpose of assessing Arnold's condition as well as treating him, Secretary of War Stimson sent down his own physician, Col. Russell V. Lee, who had been a nationally known Palo Alto, California, heart specialist before his wartime enlistment in the Medical Corps. Lee put Arnold on a strict regimen and remained in Coral Gables to make sure he stuck to it. As he began to feel better he did some fishing, and he and Simmons took short walks and rode the Air Forces crash boat in the bay. He played golf, a few holes at a time. At Lee's behest, his staff tried to leave him alone, and he was surprisingly good about leaving them alone. After two weeks he was playing eighteen holes of golf a day with scores in the eighties. "Pretty good for an old man," he said in a letter to his son Bruce.[13] Actually it was amazing, especially in light of his golfing style. He never took a full swing. He simply brought the club back halfway, then leaned into it. He sacrificed distance for accuracy, and while his technique amused his fellow players, it actually worked for him.

His recovery was remarkably rapid, and as he recovered, he continued to maintain the pretense that he had never been sick. "I was sort of worn out," he wrote to Lois, "so I came down here for a rest and am having a delightful time."[14] To Bruce, now a first-classman at West Point, he indicated it was because of his case of "the grippe" that the doctors "shipped me off . . . for 2 weeks' recuperation." To Hank he later wrote: "I had a couple of weeks of rest and recreation down in Florida recently and managed to get in quite a lot of golfing and fishing."[15]

To Lois he also maintained the pretense that all was well between Bee and himself. "I have been trying to get your mother down here and maybe will be able to get her here for a couple of days." But Bee did not visit him while he was in Florida.

Arnold was back in Washington in time for the Joint Chiefs of Staff meeting on March 21, which he attended silently. His staff did everything possible to help him slacken his pace, and for a few days he appeared to do so. Then without warning he pushed his throttle forward and brought himself back to speed, hurrying up the people around him rather than allowing them to slow him down. On March 24 he wrote an enthusiastic letter to Andrews in England (and another the next day to Harry Hopkins) about the report of his committee of operations analysts, which indicated that German industry might be paralyzed by the destruction of "not more than sixty" strategic targets.

"On the basis of our preliminary studies," Arnold told Andrews, "the destruction of the ball-bearing industry would apparently have the most far-reaching effects upon German industry of any of the targets studied." Thus did he point the fateful way Eaker's B-17s would eventually take to the German ball-bearing center at Schweinfurt.

It was becoming apparent, however, that despite the old Air Corps theory of the heavily armed, self-defending bomber, Eaker's B-17s might need fighter protection on their forays into Germany. Since the late autumn of 1942, Eaker had been pleading for auxiliary gas tanks for the P-47s in his fighter command, but there was resistance, even by his fighter commander, Monk Hunter, and by many of the fighter pilots, to the addition of tanks.[16] They argued that extra gasoline would make flying torches of the P-47s, as well as making them slower and less maneuverable. Hunter, worried about his pilots, argued for safety.

Eaker, worried also about the bombers, insisted there was little point in having fighters if they couldn't accompany and protect the bombers. But their argument hung in the balance, first of all because Eaker's demand for extra fuel tanks was unfulfilled so far, and secondly because, even with extra tanks, it was doubtful that the P-47 could reach the heart of Germany.

By this time, however, the North American P-51 Mustang, a hopelessly sluggish airplane when it was powered by a 1,300-horsepower Allison Engine, had been reborn, at the suggestion of the British, by the substitution of a 1,600-horsepower Rolls-Royce Merlin engine. Suddenly it was beginning to act like a potentially great fighter plane. But like all other fighter planes of the period, it lacked range.

Arnold had put Maj. Gen. Barney Giles, now his director of military requirements, to work on the problem.[17] It was Giles who had earlier solved the P-38 training problem by adding a piggyback seat for instructors. He called North American president Dutch Kindelberger and told him the Air Forces wanted to put three hundred more gallons of gasoline in the P-51.

Kindelberger said, "Impossible!" The wings would not be strong enough and neither would the landing gear.

"Have a P-51 on the line tomorrow morning at ten o'clock," Giles said. "I'll fly out there tonight. And have some of your design engineers there, too."

The next morning, after examining the plane, Giles said, "Take out the radio set behind the pilot and put in a hundred-gallon tank. Then open up the wings and put in bulletproof tanks the entire length."

Though Kindelberger and his engineers didn't believe the plane could take such a load, Giles, who had been an aircraft engineering officer for most of his career, was convinced it could. "Put the tanks in as soon as possible," he said. "Then fill them with water and give the plane a thorough test."

They did, and within a few weeks, the water-laden P-51 underwent and passed a series of tests that would eventually have a profound effect on the course of the war in Europe.

In early April, Arnold had to face a question he had been dreading since the moment of his heart attack. In light of that episode, would he be allowed to continue on active duty? Army regulations said no. And only the president, as commander in chief, had the power to override those regulations. Dr. Lee, who had taken up Arnold's case, was able to convince Stimson and Marshall that Arnold was strong enough to continue. But Stimson and Marshall, in addition to feeling a need for Arnold, both had further reasons to side with him. Stimson's health had been delicate for some time, and Marshall had been walking around with a pronounced heart murmur for several years. (Dr. Lee Martin had once examined him and concluded he didn't have long to live.)[18]

Even with the blessing of Stimson and Marshall, Arnold needed Roosevelt's approval if he was to remain commanding general of the Air Forces. Dr. Lee made an appointment at the White House to argue for him, after Arnold gave him some advice about what to say.[19]

The president listened to Lee's description of Arnold's heart attack, his recovery, and his current condition, then said, "Hap works hard and he has to fly a lot. If he continues as commanding general, is it likely to endanger his life?"

Lee said, "Yes, Mr. President, it might. But he has asked me to point out that whenever his combat crews go on missions, they endanger their lives. He sees no reason why he shouldn't do so."

Roosevelt said, "Fair enough," and Arnold's job was saved. But Marshall called Dr. Lee every month thereafter for a report on Arnold's health.

One Friday Arnold impatiently banged the button on his buzzer, as he was wont to do, and got Maj. William F. "Bozo" McKee, one of eight young Army officers Marshall had transferred to the Air Forces to help improve Arnold's staff. "Get down here immediately," Arnold shouted into the box.

McKee already knew him well enough to hurry. "I'm very much concerned about the defense of North Africa," Arnold said. "I want an air defense plan, coordinated with the General Staff, and I want it by Sunday."[20]

Though McKee thought the job was too big to finish in two days, he knew better than to say so. He had found that he could tell Arnold something shouldn't be done, and Arnold would listen, even though he might disagree. He encouraged argument. He didn't want yes-men. But only a fool would tell him something couldn't be done. Returning to his desk, McKee worked night and day through the weekend. Sunday noon he reported to Arnold.

"Sir, I have the plan but I couldn't get the War Department coordination." Perhaps because it was a weekend, he hadn't been able to find the General Staff officers he needed.

Arnold said, "To hell with 'em. We'll go ahead with our own."

After reading the plan, Arnold buzzed his chief of staff, Stratemeyer, and said, "I want Major McKee to go to Africa immediately."

Stratemeyer reminded Arnold that McKee was on the staff of Gen. Gordon Saville, director of air defense. Stratemeyer may also have had in mind McKee's youth and inexperience in Air Forces methods, and the fact that he was a nonflying officer. That was an important liability in the minds of many veteran airmen, but it apparently made no difference to Arnold. "I don't give a goddamn who he works for," he said. "You can send him in my plane." By the end of the day, McKee, who had never flown a plane, was on his way to Africa to tell Tooey Spaatz what kind of an air defense he needed. (Before the end of his career, McKee became the first nonflying officer to win four-star rank.)

Arnold's celebrated impatience, possibly exacerbated by his heart condition, directed itself now against Spaatz in North Africa, and eventually against Eaker in England. He followed one hurry-up memo to Spaatz with another, which asked Spaatz not to be impatient with him for his impatience. "I have been impatient all my life," Arnold wrote (as if Spaatz didn't know it), "and probably will be until the end of my days, but that's my makeup and that's that."[21]

He began soon to unload a lot of his impatience on the Eighth Air Force, which weather and lack of planes had limited to two raids over Germany in February. By the end of March, gradual attrition had so reduced its meager fleet that Eaker had to suspend all attacks against the German homeland lest his bomber force dwindle away. His B-17s hit such safe targets as Rouen, on March 28; Rotterdam, on March 31; Paris, on April 4; and Antwerp, on April 5. Meanwhile, Eaker's repeated pleas to Arnold for more bombers may have exasperated Arnold even though, or perhaps because, he thoroughly sympathized with them. In a March 24 letter to Eaker, he said:

> I sincerely appreciate your problems. . . . I am also aware of the
> embarrassment which undoubtedly results in your conferences with
> Air Chief Marshal Portal on the buildup of your Air Force. However,
> as you can well realize, I am unable to definitely and finally commit
> myself to any set of figures or dates at this time.

He hoped, he said, that Eaker would have nineteen heavy bomb groups by June 30 and thirty-seven groups by December 31. But he could make no promises.

Eaker, taking a forlorn view of Arnold's letter, sent him a bitter essay at the end of the first week of April, entitled "The Position of the Eighth Air Force." It began by proclaiming that "the current position of the Eighth Air Force is not a credit to the American Army. After sixteen months in the war we are not yet able to dispatch more than 123 bombers toward an enemy target."

In mid-April, Arnold was able to send four new B-17 groups to England, but these would hardly give Eaker enough bombers to launch the long-anticipated air offensive against Germany. On April 23, Eaker came to Washington for ten days at Arnold's behest to present the Combined Bomber Offensive plan, also known as the Eaker Plan, to the Joint Chiefs of Staff. While Eaker was in Washington, Arnold, curiously, wrote a letter to Andrews, who, as the Army's European theater commander, was now Eaker's boss. It was a restless, frustrated letter, criticizing the Eighth Air Force and its fighter and bomber commanders, but not Eaker, its overall commander.[22] Since the letter attacked one man, Col. Newton Longfellow, the bomber commander, whom Eaker later defended, it could hardly have been inspired by Eaker, who in any case was not likely to inspire a letter criticizing his own command. The most likely explanation of the letter is that it arose out of Arnold's impatience, suddenly ignited by remarks he heard from staff members. It was also a plea for advice from Andrews, whose judgment Arnold had always trusted almost as much as his own:

> I am rapidly coming to the conclusion that our bombing outfit in the Eighth Air Force is assuming a state of routine repetition of performance and perhaps finding many excuses and alibis for not going on missions, which with more aggressive leaders might be accomplished. . . . Information I receive from England is . . . that our fighter pilots are looking for excuses to go to the Savoy. . . . May this not be the result of having a leader who is not sufficiently aggressive? Has Monk Hunter lost his spirit—his dash? I know he isn't the Monk Hunter I used to know. He seems to be playing safe on most of his missions. . . .
> Is not the same thing true of the Bomber Command? Does it not lack an aggressive leader? Is the staff what it should be? . . . Let me have your frank reactions to the above.

On May 1, Andrews answered Arnold, agreeing with him that both Bomber and Fighter Command should be more aggressive, but reserving judgment on what should be done about it. Unfortunately, this was the last letter Arnold would ever receive from his old friend and long-time rival for American air leadership. On May 10, Andrews was killed during a flight from England to Iceland when his plane crashed against an Icelandic mountain. Later, Arnold was to say of Andrews, "All Air Corps officers saw in him the leader among the Air Force generals who might become one of the outstanding combat commanders in the war."

On the day Andrews died, however, Arnold had problems of his own. While preparing for the Trident conference between Roosevelt and Churchill, scheduled to begin the next day in Washington, he suffered another heart attack and was rushed to Walter Reed. Once again the doctors had difficulty keeping him inactive. He wrote a note to George Marshall that very night. But at least he was willing to admit now that something was wrong with him. "This is one hell of a time for this to happen. My engine started turning over at 160 when it should have been doing 74 to 76. For this I am sorry."

Marshall —who was busy that day with the Senate Foreign Relations Committee, the next day with the Andrews memorial service and the welcoming ceremonies for Churchill and his entourage, and the ten days after that with the Trident talks—didn't get to see Arnold in the hospital, but in a note on the eleventh he took cognizance of Arnold's restless nature: "I want you to be very careful not to worry about our affairs here because if you do that will mean an indefinite stay in the hospital. We will manage and you devote yourself to yourself."

Three days later, on the fourteenth, Marshall felt compelled to issue a further warning:

> A note came in yesterday that you planned to leave Sunday [May 20] for Oregon. I think this is fine, but I was concerned to learn that you plan to leave there at the end of the month *in order* to make an address at West Point. Please don't do the latter. Your Army future is at stake and I don't think you should hazard it with a matter of such trivial importance. Get solidly on your feet and absolutely refrain from any inspections, interviews, speeches, or anything in the way of business. It is vastly important to you, and it certainly is to me, and to the Air Forces, that you make a full recovery, and you cannot do it if you overrun your own internal machinery.

Arnold recovered from this attack even more quickly than he had in March. Within a day or so, he had begun to appreciate the nurses at Walter Reed, a fact he later jocosely admitted in a letter to Gene Beebe about what he called, rather forgetfully, "the second time I was ever in a hospital in my life."[23]

"Had I realized what a pleasant experience it would be," he wrote to Beebe, "[I] would have spent more time [in hospitals] in the past. It's no punishment to have a bunch of good-looking gals feeding you, taking your TPR [temperature, pulse, and respiration] and giving you a bath. By the time I'd been there three or four days my blood pressure hardly raised more than 100 points per bath."

After ten days at Walter Reed, Arnold was ready for fishing, resting, and recuperation in Oregon—a recuperation that was hastened by the fact that he and Bee were now getting along better. She and her brother, Hank Pool, went along for what Arnold later described as "a swell trip." The fishing was good. "The red sides were plentiful and we got our share of them."

The fishing wasn't good enough, though, to make him heed Marshall's advice about skipping the West Point graduation. Marshall may not have realized that Arnold's middle son, Bruce, was one of the graduates. Arnold was now so proud of what Bruce had accomplished after a shaky start that he refused to miss the ceremony. He and Bee were at West Point the first day of June and he delivered the commencement address. As was the case with Hank, however, Bruce had been unable to fulfill one of his father's most cherished dreams. His eyesight disqualified him from flight training. He was assigned to the Anti-Aircraft Artillery and posted to Camp Davis, North Carolina.

The Eighth Air Force situation had become so worrisome to Arnold that three days after his heart attack, on May 13, Robert Lovett flew to London to find out how Washington might better be able to help Eaker. The problem of supplying bombers had been relieved to such an extent that on the day he arrived, Eaker had written in a letter to Arnold, "this is a great day for the 8th Air Force. Our Combat crew availability went up in a straight line today from 100 to 215. That is because the five new groups have finished their two weeks' training and are off this afternoon on their first mission." But their first mission was a short, easy one to St. Omer, and this illustrated a problem that was becoming daily more acute as the Germans shifted fighter strength west to meet the American daylight bombing threat. Eaker had realized for some time the need for long-range fighters to escort his bombers. It was one thing to accept prewar American Air Corps doctrine in theory; quite another to persist in it after combat experience proved it didn't work. The B-17s, despite their unprecedented armor and fire power, couldn't fully protect themselves against concerted attack by German fighters. Eaker had faced up to that in the autumn of 1942 when he began asking for auxiliary gas tanks for his P-47 fighters. In an April 5 letter to Arnold he emphasized the still unfulfilled request. He had by that time received some wing tanks, but they were less than satisfactory. Lovett's visit gave Eaker a chance to make it clear that he would lose fewer B-17s over Germany if he had fighters that could escort them all the way to their targets.[24]

When Lovett returned to Washington, he wrote two memoranda to Arnold (June 18 and 19) assessing the needs of the Eighth. The latest Messerschmitt 109, he said, had a definite edge on the P-47, but there were ways to improve the P-47. And one of those ways was to add auxiliary tanks. "It is increasingly apparent," Lovett informed Arnold, "that fighter escort will have to be provided for B-17s on as many missions as possible."

He suggested that the twin-fuselage P-38 might be suitable. (Actually, as it was learned later, the P-38 could not maneuver well enough to cope with the German fighters.) More important than his P-38 suggestion was a remark he made at the end of his first memo, which seemed almost like an afterthought but was soon to assume great significance. "High hopes are felt," he said, "for the P-51 with wing tanks." Day by day, more and more people were beginning to think seriously about the potential of the improved P-51.

Lovett's assessment wasn't Arnold's first warning that long-range fighters were going to be an absolute necessity. In late May, Col. Emmett "Rosie" O'Donnell, a one-time West Point football hero (and teammate of Blondie Saunders), who had distinguished himself as a B-17 commander in the Pacific and was now a member of Arnold's council, went to England to find out what could be done for the Eighth Air Force. On his return, he wrote a report, dated June 12 and entitled "Ineffective Fighter Support to Bombardment in the U.K." It seemed to him the fighters were doing almost nothing to protect the bombers:

> If the P-47 airplane does not actually have the ability to escort on fairly deep penetrations, we have been badly fooled and our planning is extremely faulty. . . . The large number of fighters we have allocated to the U.K. are not paying their way if their participation in the bomber offensive comprises escort across the Channel only. This in effect simply insures the bombers' safe delivery into the hands of the wolves.

Arnold did not dispute either O'Donnell's or Lovett's conclusions, but neither did he turn his full energy to the solution of the fighter problem. The fighter was essentially a defensive weapon, and Arnold's mind was always on the offensive. He wanted to strike damaging blows to

Germany and only the bombers could do that. It was not surprising, therefore, that when he returned to work after his heart attack, his mind was on the bombers. It seemed to him he had sent a lot of them to England. What were they doing? Why weren't they flying more missions? Why weren't the bomber and fighter commanders more aggressive? As for the fighters, in a June 22 directive, he turned that problem over to Barney Giles:

> Attached are Mr. Lovett's comments on the P-47 situation in England. This brings to my mind very clearly the absolute necessity for building a fighter airplane that can go in and come out with the bombers. Moreover, this fighter has got to go into Germany. . . . About six months remain before deep daylight penetration of Germany begins. Within this next six months, you have got to get a fighter that can protect our bombers. Whether you use an existing type or have to start from scratch is your problem. Get to work on this right away.

In this directive, Arnold also pointed out that the P-38, though useful in Africa, accelerated poorly and was too slow to bother the big-league German fighters on the western front. As for the P-51, he didn't even mention it.

It is notable that while he told Giles it would be six months before the Eighth was ready for deep penetration of Germany, he was already demanding of Eaker that he get going immediately. He had heard about all the difficulties—weather, maintenance, combat attrition—but in spite of difficulties, he wanted results. How could he justify the dispatch of so many planes to England, how could he tell the Navy they couldn't have those planes, if they weren't now being used effectively against Germany?

On June 12 he had cabled Eaker about "the low percentage of airplanes your organization has been able to keep in commission." To solve the maintenance problem, he said, Eaker needed "a clearcut supply and maintenance plan" and "an Air Service Commander with sufficient initiative, force and executive ability to carry out this plan."

He had already suggested as air service commander Hugh Knerr, who had finally been allowed back into the Air Forces with the rank of colonel. Though Arnold and Knerr could hardly be called friends, Arnold's high regard for Knerr's ability is indicated by his description of the job for which he was recommending him.

Three days after his cable, on June 15, Arnold sent a letter to Eaker criticizing him because he hadn't yet fired his maintenance officer, his bomber commander, or his fighter commander:

I am willing to do anything possible to build up your forces but you must play your part. My wire was sent to you to get you to toughen up—to can these fellows who cannot produce—to put in youngsters who can carry the ball. . . . You have to be tough to handle the situation.

On June 28 Arnold sent Eaker another cable blaming him for being so slow to fire his fighter commander. The next day, Eaker exploded in a five-page letter to his old friend. He hadn't relieved his bomber and fighter commanders earlier, he said, because he didn't have proper replacements. Now he had found the men he wanted. Brig Gen. Fred L. Anderson would be the new bomber commander and Maj. Gen. William Kepner would be the fighter commander. For air service commander, he would be glad to have Hugh Knerr. (It proved to be an excellent choice. Knerr did the job so well he was a major general by the end of the war. But unfortunately, his estrangement from Arnold, who had recommended him, was never resolved.)

Having got the business end of his letter out of the way, Eaker turned to his personal relations with Arnold:

I have always felt the closest bond of friendship between us as two individuals. I have never thought that you placed quite the confidence in me officially as an officer, as you did as a friend. I sometimes thought that you were tough on me officially in order to make certain that nobody had a feeling that I got the positions I held through our personal friendship, and to make doubly sure that you did not allow that friendship to influence you unduly toward me officially. . . . I shall always accept gladly and in the proper spirit, any advice, council or criticism from you. I do not feel, however, that my past service which has come under your observation indicates that I am a horse which needs to be ridden with spurs.

A week later, on July 7, Arnold wrote Eaker a letter that he must have hoped would clear the air between them:

I want you to get this firmly in your mind that had I not had confidence in you—confidence in your ability, I would never have built you up for the job that you now have. I give you full credit for having the inherent ability—the knowledge and judgement that goes with the command that you now hold. That being the case, I see no reason in the world for any fears or suspicion as to our relationship entering your mind. But you must know me well enough by this time to know that I am very outspoken. I say what I think and do what I think best, so when you hear these rumors, comments, criticisms or what-have-you, always remember that if there is anything serious you will be the first one to hear of it and it will come from me direct.

It was a letter Eaker must have found just slightly less than reassuring. While it reaffirmed their friendship, it also restated one of Arnold's creeds—that his warm feelings for you wouldn't save your job if he thought you weren't doing it right.

By mid-July, Giles had determined that if any fighter plane in prospect could fill the need for a bomber escort into Germany, it was the P-51. Tests at North American had proven that the plane could carry its extra gas load easily. At Giles's suggestion (he was now chief of the Air staff), Arnold ordered 181 Merlin-powered Mustangs for delivery to England. But they couldn't possibly get there until late autumn. Meanwhile, the war wouldn't wait. The Eighth Air Force would have to fight the Germans with what it had.

On July 25, the Eighth began its first significant offensive against targets within Germany. The gradual increase in Eaker's bomber fleet and a sudden change in the weather were as responsible for this initiative as the change in command leadership. On this date, a divided force of Fortresses hit Kiel, Hamburg, and Warnemünde. The next day Hanover was the target. On the twenty-eighth, 302 B-17s bombed aircraft factories in Kassel and Oschersleben. On the twenty-ninth, they returned to Warnemünde and Kiel. And on the thirtieth it was Kassel again. They had dropped more than a thousand tons of bombs on Germany in a week. But they had also lost one hundred bombers, and one thousand crewmen had been killed or captured. It would be impossible to sustain such losses indefinitely. The Eighth had to pause for rest and reinforcement.

During this time, plans had been in progress for the mission Arnold suggested in March against the German ball-bearing center in Schweinfurt, deep in Bavaria. It was scheduled for August 10, but weather forced its postponement. For a week the bad weather continued, forcing postponement also of a mission scheduled August 13 against the Messerschmitt aircraft factory in Regensburg. On August 17, these missions were combined, with 146 Fortresses led by Col. Curtis LeMay going to Regensburg in the hope of luring away the German fighters while 230 Fortresses led by Brig. Gen. Robert Williams struck the Schweinfurt ball-bearing plants. The weather was again uncooperative. The Regensburg force took off on time, but the Schweinfurt force was so long delayed by ground fog that the German fighters were able to attack both formations in turn. The Flying Fortresses and the German fighters that day fought the biggest and most ferocious battle in the history of aerial warfare up to that time. An undetermined number of German fighters went down. The Messerschmitt plant in Regensburg and several ball-bearing plants in Schweinfurt were badly damaged. But the B-17 losses were almost catastrophic. The German fighters, perhaps 500 in number, had shot down 60 American bombers, damaged another 50 so badly they would never fly again, and damaged another 100 so badly they would need extensive repairs. There was no doubt now that the Fortresses were going to need fighter escort on missions into Germany.

CHAPTER 18

In mid-July 1943, Arnold flew to California for five days for the purpose of "putting the fear of God in the West Coast members of the aircraft industry."[1] Production had dropped off slightly and he wanted everyone to know he wouldn't tolerate it. "I hope I needled some of [their] complacency and self-satisfaction out of them," he said in a letter to Gene Beebe, who was now commanding a bomb group in China. To this he added a wholly superfluous afterthought. "I guess I don't have to explain to you that I'm personally never satisfied."

His doctors were trying now with limited success to keep him from working full days. Col. Fred M. Dean, a fighter pilot with such a distinguished record in Africa that he became a member of Arnold's council in July, noticed that he was still coming into the office at 7:30 a.m., but he would try to leave at 3:00 p.m. He also tried to nap for twenty minutes after lunch each day. Nevertheless, he found time to read twenty to fifty cables from the various theaters of action each morning. He digested and answered several memoranda daily, attended meetings of the Joint Chiefs, consulted with Marshall, talked to an endless stream of visitors, wrote a dozen or more letters (usually with staff help), and discussed a bewildering variety of projects with members of his council and his staff.[2] The one thing he didn't do was conduct formal staff meetings. He had sat through so many such meetings during his career he knew very well they were a waste of time. He preferred to work directly on each problem with the man he had assigned to solve it.

When one of his staff members brought him a proposal it had better be short and to the point. "He would read it while [you] were standing there talking to him," Dean later recalled. He would be talking about some other subject as he read, but if the staff officer thought he was wandering from the subject and tried to bring him back to it by mentioning something in the brief, he would say, "You said that here." Though it might not seem so, he had been reading while he was talking. He had, Dean soon learned, "a tremendous faculty for being able to do more than one thing at a time."

In a briefing one day to prepare him for a Joint Chiefs meeting, he read what his staff thought he should know about the subjects on the agenda, then began asking questions so penetrating and so difficult nobody in the room could answer them. Finally he threw everybody out of the room. "Do your lesson," he said. "You haven't done your lesson."

"He never tried to win a popularity contest," Dean recalled. "I have seen four-star generals time and again backing out of his office saying 'Yes, sir, yes, sir, yes, sir.'" But Dean also concluded, "He wasn't a mean person. He [simply] could not tolerate incompetence, laziness, [or] poor judgment."

Among the visitors to his office one day was a group of five men led by Gen. Dave Grant, the Air Forces chief flight surgeon, and Col. Howard Rusk, who had developed the Air Forces program for rehabilitation of wounded men. With them were three young pilots, limping noticeably. All five had angry expressions on their faces.

At Grant's suggestion, each of the young pilots rolled up a pants leg to exhibit artificial legs made of papier-mâché. Returning from combat as amputees, they had been sent first to an Army general hospital. When they were returned to the Air Forces for Rusk's rehabilitation training, they were wearing these pathetically inadequate paper limbs.

"Is this what you get when you give your leg to your country?" one of them had asked.

"I fell down getting on a bus," the second one said, "and almost got run over because the rivets fell out."

Arnold, after hearing their stories, became so visibly angry Rusk thought he was about to suffer a stroke. He reached out and banged down every button on his squawk box. Moments later, the room was full of two- and three-star generals. Even Robert Lovett, whose office was next door, came in to investigate the commotion.

By this time Arnold was pacing back and forth behind his desk. "This is the goddamnedest outrage I ever saw!" he cried. "I'm too old to fly these airplanes and so are all of you. These boys are doing it for us. They're fighting for our lives. I spend all my time trying to get them the best airplanes, the best gasoline, the best clothes, the best food, the best of everything. By God, they're going to have the best legs!"

Grabbing his telephone, he got the Army surgeon general on the line and began chewing him out unceremoniously. "Not only are we going to get these boys the best legs available," he said. "We're also going to do some research to develop some better legs. And if you don't get started on it in thirty days, I'll go directly to the president."

Before he was finished, Arnold had lobbied through Congress a new law that established a prosthetic research program and provided veteran amputees with the best artificial limbs science could devise.[3]

Two days after the costly Schweinfurt-Regensburg mission on August 17, Churchill and Roosevelt with their staffs got together in Quebec for the Quadrant conference. The main argument at Quebec concerned the question of when or whether the British planned to commit themselves to an invasion of the continent. The Americans were eager but Churchill had been dragging his feet for some time. Arnold, in a May 1 memorandum of record, had written: "It is becoming more and more apparent that the British have no intention of invading France or Continental Europe." At Quebec, one way in which they tried to divert attention from the subject was by criticizing Arnold for his persistence in daylight bombing. The losses at Schweinfurt and Regensburg gave them such a persuasive argument that even Marshall was swayed by it. Arnold's chauffeur, Sgt. Bruce Simmons, who overheard some of the private discussions on the subject, felt that Marshall was turning against the strategy but that Harry Hopkins still favored and supported it. Marshall pointed out that Arnold was losing a prohibitive number of planes. Arnold kept insisting to Marshall and to the British that daylight bombing was going to work, that it hadn't yet had a fair chance.[4] But he was beginning to have his doubts, which he confided privately to Lovett. "Hap was having a hell of a time hanging on," Lovett recalls. Was he actually losing faith in daylight bombing? "I think so. I can't document it but I think he was beginning to worry about it because the attrition rate was too high."

Having defended it so staunchly, however, Arnold had to do everything possible to make it work. On August 31, he flew to England to help and encourage his beleaguered friend, Ira Eaker. The Schweinfurt-Regensburg raid had so shattered the Eighth Air Force that it had been unable to launch another mission for ten days, and then, on August 27, only as far as Calais. The day Arnold arrived, the B-17s went to Paris on another "milk run." But while he was there, on September 6, Eaker was able to piece together a fleet of 338, which he sent to Stuttgart. Again the big bombers were savagely attacked and 45 of them went down.

Eaker had been pleading steadily for long-range fighter support, and in late August, before leaving for London, Arnold had promised him some P-38s and P-51s, but he couldn't say when they would arrive. When Arnold got to England and saw the condition of the planes returning from missions to Germany, he quickly developed an even sharper understanding of Eaker's plea. On September 3, Arnold himself took up the chorus in a cable to Marshall: "Operations over Germany conducted here during the past several weeks indicate definitely that we must provide long-range fighters to accompany daylight bombardment missions."

He followed this with another cable, apparently designed to cancel a previous commitment to divert more fighters from England to North Africa for use in Italy:

> Believe it would be a great mistake to divert P-38s from U.K. to North Africa at this time. The battle for complete destruction of German Air Force is approaching most critical stage. 8th Air Force must be built up rapidly—more rapidly than planned—to administer a knockout blow while they are groping for any respite they can get. . . . I realize the desire of Eisenhower to get as many airplanes as possible but strongly recommend that the answer to his request for P-38s be "No," repeat, "no."

On this trip to England Arnold saw for the first time with his own eyes what a beating the B-17s were taking. But he also saw, from aerial photographs taken not by the Eighth Air Force but by the British, what a beating these Fortresses were administering to German industry. Despite their losses, he decided they were indeed hurting Germany. And until such time as an invasion could be launched, they would continue to be the only American weapons hurting Germany. His faith in daylight bombing, though it may have been shaky when he arrived, was strengthened now. Even the Schweinfurt raid, costly as it had been, seemed worthwhile to him when he studied the photographs of damage to the ball-bearing factories. And when Portal spoke to him about the importance of knocking out those factories completely, he decided the Fortresses should go back to Schweinfurt without delay to finish the job they had begun.

"I know you'll get to it," Arnold said to Eaker, "as soon as the weather permits."[5]

He did not say, "as soon as I send you long-range fighters." Arnold and Eaker agreed that the war wouldn't wait to be fought. They had to keep fighting it with whatever weapons were available. They didn't dare give the Germans time to rebuild and repair the damage already done to their industries. But Arnold did concede now, more positively than ever before, that long-range fighters were desperately needed. He had been somewhat late in coming fully to this realization. Writing about the P-51 in his memoirs, he took upon himself some of the blame for its slow development. "That we did not have it sooner was the Air Forces' own fault."[6] But once he realized the need, he rushed the production of P-51s with his customary urgency.

The P-51s did not arrive in England quickly enough, however, to alleviate the pain of the second Schweinfurt mission. Within two weeks after Arnold returned to Washington, he was again becoming impatient for more action against Germany. On September 7, 9, 15, 16, 23, and 26, Eaker's Fortress fleet, not yet recovered from the battering at Stuttgart and hampered by more bad weather over Germany, hit targets in France, but never with more than 300 planes. Arnold couldn't understand this. He had sent almost a thousand B-17s to England. Why was Eaker dispatching only 300 at a time? "To us here in the United States," he wrote to Eaker September 20, 1943, "it looks as if the employment of large numbers of heavy bombers has not been followed through by your headquarters and staff. . . . Since my visit to England the impression in my mind is that you still figure on employing small numbers of 300 or maybe 400 at a time." Despite Eaker's explanations, Arnold seemed unable to accept the fact that so many of the bombers he had sent to Europe were lost or damaged beyond repair.

Eaker on September 27 sent his Fortresses back to Germany in the hope of bombing Emden by radar through an overcast, but only 305 bombers could make the trip and the results were indifferent. In Washington on the twenty-eighth, Gen. Laurence Kuter, now assistant chief of air staff for plans, prepared at Arnold's direction three radiograms to "put more heat on the Eighth Air Force" and "build a fire under Gen. Eaker."

"Your bombing through the overcast," one of these messages said, "indicates an additional type operation which should result in more bombs on the German fighter factories. . . .What are your views as to the possibility of using your entire force during the bad weather now approaching for bombing within as well as on top of the overcast?"

Another message said: "When North African fighter groups escort bombers it is a matter of honor that hostile fighters shall not be permitted to attack the escorted bombers. Do your fighters have that spirit?"

With all this impatient encouragement bombarding him from Washington, and with new B-17 groups arriving now at an increased rate, Eaker decided in early October that he was ready once again to tackle the Germans. On October 4, 326 B-17s hit Frankfurt and only twelve were lost. On the eighth, ninth, and tenth, they hit military targets in Bremen, Gdynia, Marienburg, Anklam, and Münster. But in those three days, 88 of them were shot down by the Germans.

Eaker received a congratulatory cable from Arnold on the eleventh:

> The employment of larger bombing forces on successive days is encouraging proof that you are putting an increasing proportion of your bombers where they will hurt the enemy. Good work. As you turn your effort away from ship-building cities and toward crippling the sources of the still-growing German fighter forces the air war is clearly moving toward our supremacy in the air. Carry on.

Eaker did exactly that. On the fourteenth, he sent 291 Fortresses back to Schweinfurt. Those bombers soon found themselves up against several hundred German fighters in what still ranks as the most horrendous air battle of all time. Despite constant attacks from every angle, the B-17s flew across Germany and inflicted even more damage on the Schweinfurt ball-bearing plants than they had done in August. But again 60 Fortresses failed to return home. These 60, added to the 100 lost since October 4, represented a depletion of Eaker's force that he could not afford.

Arnold, expecting an adverse reaction in Washington, sent Eaker an extraordinary cable the next morning. Apparently forgetting the cable he had sent four days earlier, which described the German fighter forces as "still-growing," he now wrote:

> It appears from my viewpoint that the German Air Force is on the verge of collapse. . . .We must not (repeat) must not miss any symptoms of impending German collapse. . . .Can you add any substantial evidence of collapse?

In view of what the German air force had done to the B-17s at Schweinfurt the previous day, Eaker was hard put to supply any such optimistic evidence. He sent a cablegram describing the battle and assuring Arnold that despite the losses, "this does not represent disaster." He was ready to continue the fight. "We must show the enemy we can replace our losses," he said. "He knows he can't replace his."

At a Washington press conference on the fifteenth, President Roosevelt hedged in response to questions about the loss of 60 bombers in one day. Arnold, apparently unsatisfied by Roosevelt's reaction, rushed into print in support of the Eighth Air Force:

This attack on Schweinfurt was not merely a spectacular air raid. It was an engagement between large armies—a major campaign. In a period of a few hours we invaded German-held Europe to a depth of 500 miles, sacked and crippled one of her most vital enterprises.

We did it in daylight and we did it with precision, aiming our explosives with the care and accuracy of a marksman firing a rifle at a bull's-eye.

We moved in on a city of 50,000 people and destroyed the part of it that contributes to the enemy's ability to wage war against us. When that part of it was a heap of twisted girders, smoking ruin and pulverized machinery, we handed it back, completely useless, to the Germans. Ball-bearings cannot now pour from this ruin, and no moving machinery will operate without ball bearings.

It was a much more glowing description of the second Schweinfurt raid than the facts warranted. Though the ball-bearing plants had been badly damaged, they had not been rendered "completely useless." And the Eighth Air Force was now in critical condition. On the fifteenth, Eaker again asked for long-range fighters—P-38s and Mustangs. On the twenty-ninth, Arnold informed him that all the P-38s and P-51s intended for Africa and the Pacific were being diverted to England. Until they arrived, the Eighth Air Force would not be able to resume its offensive against Germany.

On November 11, Arnold, along with Gens. Laurence Kuter, Haywood Hansell, and Rosie O'Donnell, joined Marshall, King, and their staffs, plus President Roosevelt and his staff, for a trip on the battleship *Iowa* to Cairo, where they were to confer once more with Churchill and his staff.[7] Chiang Kai-shek would also be there, to represent China. After these three powers finished their deliberations, everyone would move on to Tehran for a four-power conference with Russia's dictator, Joseph Stalin, whom the American press now referred to as the "president" of Russia since he had become an ally.

On the afternoon of the third day at sea, while the naval convoy was staging an antiaircraft display for the benefit of the president and the other dignitaries aboard, the *Iowa*, America's newest and largest battleship, suddenly received from an escorting destroyer a very real torpedo alarm.

"The whole character of the maneuver changed instantly," Arnold noticed. "We began to zigzag. All ships started to zigzag. More commands from everywhere. Whistles, flags, code signals. The din aboard the ship was terrific. The wake of the torpedo became quite clear. A depth charge went off, and another, and many more. Guns started shooting, but nothing hit the torpedo."

Everyone on board watched helplessly as the torpedo approached the speeding, swerving battleship. Then everyone sighed with relief as the explosive missile sped past the ship, just twenty yards astern. But where was the German submarine that must have fired it? Eventually it became apparent there was no German submarine in the area. A torpedo tube man in one of the escorting destroyers had pulled his trigger by mistake. It was with some relish that Arnold later told this story. He always enjoyed embarrassing the Navy.

Despite the scare, the president and his entourage reached Cairo on schedule on November 21, after a side trip to Tunis, where Arnold stayed in the huge villa Tooey Spaatz was occupying. The main argument in Cairo began with the question of whether the Allies should launch a January operation against the Japanese in Burma, but behind that argument was the greater question of when or whether they would invade northern France. The British remained cool toward both operations. They wanted to expand the eastern Mediterranean front. On November 23 and 24, the Combined Chiefs of Staff almost came to blows on this issue but were unable to settle it.

From Arnold's viewpoint, only one important matter was settled in Cairo. Roosevelt and Chiang Kai-shek agreed that his B-29s, which he hoped would be ready for combat by June 1944, would be stationed in China and would concentrate their attacks on the Japanese homeland. Already, Kenney (with MacArthur's support) and other air commanders in the Pacific were bidding for B-29s, and Arnold was afraid the Superfortresses might be parceled out piecemeal, like the B-17s, to several fronts, thus diluting their impact. When Chiang agreed in Cairo to provide B-29 bases in China, Arnold made an important step toward concentrating the world's largest bombers against their main target.

On the twenty-seventh, the conference moved to Tehran, where most of the British and Americans met Stalin for the first time. Arnold and Marshall met him later than the others because, under the impression that they had the afternoon to themselves, they took off on a trip into the mountains. It was the next day before Arnold met Stalin, and when he did, he was astonished at the Russian dictator's knowledge of American aircraft. "He knew details of their performance, their characteristics, their armament and their armor much better than many of the senior officers in our own Air Force."[8] When he asked Arnold if Russia could have some American heavy bombers, Arnold indicated it was possible, but Stalin would have to send engineers and crews to the

United States to learn how to fly and maintain them. Or, barring that, Americans could be sent with the planes to teach his men in Russia. Stalin said some such thing should be arranged, but in the event, it never was. Stalin did not encourage familiarity between Russians and non-Russians.

Though Arnold didn't like Stalin's methods or his political views, he was quickly impressed by the man's fearlessness, brilliance, ruthlessness, and rapid repartee. Stalin was "half-humorous, half-scathing" in his remarks to and about the British. At one point, when he made one of his typical remarks, "I know sixty thousand German officers I'm going to shoot," Churchill became so agitated he paced the floor for several minutes, preaching about Christianity and civilization. It was against the laws of civilized warfare, he insisted, to shoot sixty thousand officers. Stalin waited patiently until he finished, then said again through his interpreter, "I know sixty thousand German officers I'm going to shoot when the war is over."[9]

On the question of invading the continent, the Americans received strong support from Stalin. He dismissed with contempt Churchill's argument that an enlargement of the eastern Mediterranean front would be a great help to Russia. What was needed, he said, was the invasion of northern France (code-named Overlord), with a smaller, diversionary landing in southern France.[10]

Whether the British liked it or not, the Americans were now determined to press forward with the invasion. President Roosevelt was so set on the project that he had already decided without argument from Churchill that George Marshall would command it. Marshall had done such a splendid job in Washington, coordinating every aspect of the American war effort throughout the world, that Roosevelt felt he deserved a chance to prove his greatness in the field as well. But opposition to Marshall's removal from Washington had come from surprising sources. The *Army and Navy Journal* and the *Army and Navy Register*, both highly respected within the services, had opposed it on the mistaken understanding that it would be a demotion for Marshall. (Actually, Roosevelt intended that Marshall keep his title as chief of staff.) Then General Pershing wrote to Roosevelt that the transfer of Marshall would be a "very grave error."

To Pershing Roosevelt wrote, "I think it is only fair to give George a chance in the field—and because of the nature of the job we shall still have the benefit of his strategical ability. The best way I can express it is to tell you that I want George to be the Pershing of the Second World War—and he cannot be that if we keep him here."[11]

Roosevelt simply ignored other opponents of the idea. But then opposition came from two people he must have expected to support him—General Arnold and Admiral King. They were against moving Marshall to Europe, not because they begrudged him a chance to show his brilliance in the field, but because they would both miss his brilliance in Washington. While they were in Egypt, Roosevelt and Arnold, on November 24, went out to see the Sphinx together. By this time, the president may have been aware of Arnold's feelings in the matter. As they gazed at the huge stone face, he mentioned the problem of command in the upcoming European operations.

Arnold said he thought it was important to establish a unified command with a single commander. And he thought Marshall was the best man for the job. But in spite of that, he would regret seeing him leave Washington because of his "outstanding ability" in the Combined Chiefs of Staff meetings, and because he was such a "superior adviser" to the president.

From Admiral King, the president had received an even more outspoken reaction. "We have the winning combination here in Washington," King had said. "Why break it up?"[12] In his opinion, no one who might replace Marshall would have his knowledge and balanced judgment of the needs of global war.

To these arguments, Roosevelt finally bowed. On December 4, after the Americans and British had returned from Tehran to Cairo, the president had lunch with Marshall and told him he would not be commanding the invasion forces. Though Marshall had been counting on this command, even to the point of sending some of his furniture from Fort Myer back to his home in Virginia, there is no indication that he complained about his disappointment. He and Roosevelt decided that Eisenhower would be the supreme commander in Europe.

Arnold left Cairo with Rosie O'Donnell the morning of December 8, and after a short stop in Tunis, flew on to Sicily, where he met Eisenhower and Gen. Walter Bedell Smith, Eisenhower's chief deputy. With Ike planning now to return to London and establish his supreme command headquarters there, the question arose as to who would be his air commander. Without hesitation, both he and Smith said it would have to be Tooey Spaatz. They wouldn't take anyone else.[13] That was all right with Arnold. He had full confidence in his old friend and he was happy to know that Eisenhower shared it. But whoever became air commander in England would be, in effect, the commander of the Eighth Air Force. Where would that leave another old friend of Arnold's, Ira Eaker? Just three days earlier, on December 5, the first group of P-51s to arrive in England had escorted the B-17s on their first mission. Eaker was now finally getting the long-range fighters for which he had been pleading since late 1942. But how much longer would he be in England to enjoy this luxury?

Four days later, the answer to this question came. On the twelfth, Arnold was back in Tunis, where he spent two hours with Eisenhower. He soon learned that Ike not only wanted Spaatz as Strategic Air Forces commander, but he wanted his other Mediterranean air commander, Gen. Jimmy Doolittle, as commander of the Eighth Air Force.[14] He had worked with both of these men for more than a year. At first he had been unimpressed by Doolittle, but now he had the firmest confidence in both of them, and he wanted them with him when he went to London. As for Eaker, he might be disappointed at having to relinquish the Eighth Air Force, which he had virtually created, but there was a big job waiting for him. He would be the new commander of Allied Air Forces in the Mediterranean.

Before Arnold's December 12 meeting with Eisenhower in Tunis, he had flown with Tooey Spaatz to Foggia on December 8 to see his son Hank, who was now an Artillery major with an infantry division in the thick of the fighting around Monte Cassino.[15] Unsatisfied with his secure position as one of the youngest members of Eisenhower's staff, Hank had asked for action and he was getting it. He was at the front, near the foot of Cassino, watching the Germans lob shells his way, when an order came directing him to report to Gen. Mark Clark's headquarters in the rear. He arrived there in a mud-splattered uniform to learn that his father was coming into Foggia, across the leg of Italy from Naples, and wanted to see him.

An hour later, Hank, still in his muddy uniform, was on a C-47 to Foggia, where he was waiting when his father, with Spaatz and Rosie O'Donnell, landed at 5:15 in the afternoon. Arnold had some good news from home with which to greet him. As Hank knew, Arnold had wanted for many years to own a ranch in California where he could live out his retirement. No one took his dream seriously because, thanks to their Depression losses and family emergencies, he and Bee had been able to accumulate only a few thousand dollars in savings during his long military career. But there were still some beautiful parts of California where land prices were low. Before he left Washington on this trip, Bee had also left, for San Francisco, where Lois had taken an apartment to wait out her husband's latest tour of sea duty. Arnold had asked Bee to look, while she was out there, for a place they might be able to afford. In Cairo, on December 4, he received a cable from her announcing that she had bought "a ranch." In his diary that day, he had written with evident elation, "I own a ranch."

He was still elated when he announced to Hank, "I own a ranch." But unfortunately he couldn't describe it. The only thing he knew about it was that he owned it—he and whatever bank Bee had found to carry the mortgage.

Though Hank had expected to have just time enough with his father to say hello and goodbye, General Arnold planned to stay a few days and he had arranged temporary duty for Hank as his aide. They drove through the bombed-out city of Foggia to the house Spaatz occupied when he was there—another large, sumptuous establishment. This one had been the home of a prominent Fascist who quickly absented himself just before the capture of Foggia by the British. Spaatz, who knew how to live graciously, provided an excellent dinner and so much liquor that before the evening was over, he and Hank were trading uncomplimentary observations about the ground forces and the air forces. The usually silent Spaatz said, "We don't need the Army to win this war. All we need you for is to capture air fields. You wouldn't even get your mail if it weren't for the Air Force."

Though the needling started lightheartedly, it became heated as the hours passed. Hank told Spaatz in no uncertain terms what he thought of the Air Forces and by the time they went to bed they were not amused by each other.

Arnold, however, was evidently quite amused. At breakfast the next morning he asked Hank, "How do you feel?"

"Lousy."

"I thought you might feel better," he said, "after getting all that off your chest."

While Arnold was in Italy, Mark Clark invited him and his entourage to visit the front. The procession of cars and jeeps stopped near the foot of Monte Cassino; then Clark led the party, mostly generals, up an open road, bringing them even closer to the German-held mountain. Hank and Rosie O'Donnell, who had ridden together in a rear jeep, followed the others reluctantly because Hank, who had been fighting in this area, realized that Clark was leading them into very dangerous territory. They were on a road so exposed that the Germans could look directly down at them and, if they used their field glasses, could even read the stars on the collars. Suddenly an 88-millimeter gun fired and the shell landed to their right.

"The next one will be on our left," Hank said to Rosie. "Then they'll have us bracketed."

The next one was indeed on their left, whereupon both Hank and O'Donnell dove into the nearest ditch. The third shell came right at them but luckily landed beyond them.

A few moments later General Arnold saw them in the ditch and said, "What are you two doing down there? You look like a couple of damned fools."

O'Donnell, an outspoken Irishman and one of the few men around Arnold who didn't hesitate to say what he pleased to him, spoke sharply. "We look a hell of a lot better than you'd have looked if that thing had hit you."

Before that day ended, Hap Arnold got a good look at war in all its gory horror. And the description he wrote in his diary that night showed vividly the chilling impression it made upon him:

> Aircraft fighting overhead. . . . Bombs and shells bursting on the German positions a scant 1,800 yards away. Men crouching behind walls in the mud. Tents under bushes and trees. . . . AA guns opening up at FW-190s and 109s overhead. Spitfires coming into the fight. . . . Infantrymen crouching behind any kind of cover. German observers watching our movements up the road from the hill beyond. A tank blown to bits from running over a mine. Five bodies lying in small pieces on the ground. . . . Jeeps and mud, trucks and tanks, more mud . . . bridges and culverts blown out by bombs. . . . Villages and towns demolished. . . . Hospitals . . . operating room. Removing bomb and shell splinters from [a] soldier's head, pulling a mangled hand together, tying a body together after a shell fragment tore loose a hip and almost all of a buttock . . . holes in back and abdomen the size of a football. . . . A man with only half his innards, dying, but still smiling and saying, "I'm all right."

Though he was now a four-star general and one of the nation's most distinguished soldiers, this was the first time in his life Arnold had been in the midst of an actual battle.

Three days after his return to Washington, Arnold had to undertake, on December 18, the unpleasant duty of informing Ira Eaker that he was no longer commander of the Eighth Air Force. Because Eaker was a friend of such long standing, Arnold tried to break the news gently by announcing his new job first and emphasizing its importance, but once again he was a victim of his notorious inability to convey bad news gracefully. His cable to Eaker said:

It has been decided that an American will take over command of the Allied Air Force in the Mediterranean. . . . As a result of your long period of successful operations and the exceptional results of your endeavors as Commander of the Air Force in England, you have been recommended for this position. . . .

Eaker's shock at this totally unexpected news was followed by fury. Having accepted Arnold's impatient insistence on more action during all the months when his bombers were being diverted elsewhere and his pleas for long-range fighters were going unanswered, he couldn't conceive of the Eighth Air Force being taken from him now that his B-17 fleet was beginning to expand and the P-51s were arriving to defend it. On the nineteenth, he fired off a cable to Arnold that gave notice of his intention to fight for his job:

Believe war interest best served by my retention command 8th Air Force: otherwise experience this theater for nearly two years wasted. If I am to be allowed any personal preference, having started with the Eighth and seen it organized for major task in this theater it would be heart-breaking to leave just before climax. If my services satisfactory to seniors, request I be allowed to retain command 8th Air Force.

He then sent similar cables to Eisenhower and Spaatz and inspired Gen. Jacob Devers, European theater commander at the time, to send one to Arnold, requesting that Eaker be retained in England. Arnold's answer to Devers, on December 20, was firm: "For retaining Eaker in command of the 8th Air Force, all the reasons that you have given are those that have been advanced as reasons why he should go down and be commander of the Allied Mediterranean Air Forces." He followed this with another cable to Eaker, on December 21, which settled the matter:

The dictates of world-wide air operations necessitate major changes being made. This affects you personally, and while from your point of view it is unfortunate that you cannot, repeat, not stay and retain command of the organization that you have so carefully and successfully built up, the broader viewpoint of the world-wide war effort indicates the necessity for a change. I extend to you my heart-felt thanks for the splendid cooperation and loyalty that you have given me thus far and for the wonderful success of your organization, but I cannot, repeat, not see my way clear to make any change in the decisions already reached.

Knowing Arnold, Eaker decided it was pointless to continue the battle. On Christmas Eve, he wrote to his old friend a less than friendly cable of compliance: "Orders received. Will be carried out promptly

January one." But he was not a happy man as he took off for the Mediterranean. He would need time to overcome his resentment against Arnold. He wasn't aware that it was Eisenhower, rather than Arnold, who had made the decision which sent him south. And Arnold never explained it to him. In Arnold's old Army view, it would be improper for a senior officer to blame someone else for an order he gave to a subordinate.

The Arnolds had a quiet and lonely Christmas that year. Only Dave was at home, and he was growing up so fast he wasn't there very much. But Bee was more congenial than she had been lately, and they both had the ranch to celebrate. It was a hilly, forty-acre "spread" with an old house and barn in the beautiful Valley of the Moon near Sonoma, about forty-five miles north of San Francisco. Bee loved it and Hap expected to love it as soon as he could get to California to see it. He was planning a trip to the coast in early January but meanwhile, he needed to sit down someplace and rest. He decided on Florida for a few days after Christmas and Bee agreed to go with him. That was as good a Christmas present as the ranch. They sat in the sun together and got along the way they used to in the old days.

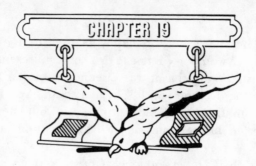

Since the American entry into the war, Hap Arnold had been counting on the B-29 Superfortress to play the major Air Forces role in the defeat of Japan. He hoped, in fact, that by itself it would force Japan's surrender. An aircraft half again as large as any heavy bomber then in operation, the B-29 could carry twice the weight a B-17 could, and carry it twice as far. Its wingspan was 141 feet, its fuselage 99 feet long, and it stood 28 feet, almost three stories, high. Thanks to Arnold's persuasion of the president and the Congress, the U.S. government had already spent more than $1 billion on it before the end of 1943 and was destined to spend $3 billion on it before the end of the war. But the project was in deep trouble as 1944 began, and so, therefore, was Arnold, who had bet so heavily on it.

The aircraft was still plagued by engine problems. The new, 2,200-horsepower Wright Duplex Cyclone that propelled it had been subjected to 2,000 engineering changes but it continued to overheat. Since the engine fire that caused the fatal crash of test pilot Eddie Allen in February 1943, several other B-29 engines had caught fire, though few fatalities had resulted. In addition, the fire-control and pressurization systems weren't yet functioning reliably. One man had been blown out of a gun blister by excess pressure at 25,000 feet. The radar bombing system was complicated to operate and often inaccurate. And the electrically controlled bomb-bay doors seemed to open and close at their own convenience.[1]

Arnold had once promised the president he would have the plane in combat by the beginning of 1944, but the bewildering succession of problems had forced him to renege on that promise. After waiting as long as possible, he had written a (for him) humiliating memorandum to Roosevelt on October 11, 1943:

> In connection with the bombing of Japan from China by B-29s, I regret exceedingly to have to inform you that there has been a holdup in production of engines. It looks now as if it will be impossible to get the required number of B-29s together in China to start bombing before the first of March, and with the possibility of

not getting them there before the first of April. At this writing I expect to have 150 B-29s in China by March 1st, of which 100 can be used against Japan.

Roosevelt had been deeply offended by this news. "The worst thing," he wrote in an October 15 letter to Marshall, "is that we are falling down on our promises to China every single time. We have not fulfilled one of them yet. I do not see why we have to use B-29s. We have several other types of bombing planes."

The president should have known why no other bomber would do. Only the B-29 would be able to reach Japan from the nearest bases China could possibly supply. His annoyance at their delayed arrival gave Arnold further incentive to hasten their delivery. In a memo to Gen. K. B. Wolfe, who was coordinating the project, he said, "I have told the President that this will be started on March 1. See that it is done."

Unfortunately, the job hadn't been that simple. In November 1943, Arnold had tried to get war production schedules changed to give the B-29 "over-riding priority over all other aircraft,"[2] but the Navy stopped him at a November 9 meeting of the Joint Chiefs. Admiral King said he didn't want to delay the B-29 (the Navy had put in a request for some of them to use in submarine patrol) but he felt an overriding priority might retard other essential programs, including, presumably, some of his own. It was a reasonable argument.

Arnold had then tried to hurry up the production line by the sheer force of his personality—his usual method—but that hadn't worked because, as he admitted in a November 12 memo to General Echols at Wright Field, "it is not priority in the strict sense of the word that is required to bring the engine production up to the aircraft production; it is more a matter of adjustment of labor and management in the shops."

There was some labor trouble in the factories, to be sure. And the kinds of skills needed to produce such a complex machine were in short supply. But the basic problems still resided in the machine itself. Every new airplane has bugs. This one had more than usual, first, because it was so big and had so many revolutionary features; second, because it was developed under wartime pressure and many of its component parts, which in peacetime would have been subjected separately to thorough testing, were now being tested on the airplane.

The result of all this was that in January 1944, ninety-seven B-29s had come off the assembly lines but only sixteen of them were flyable. And the shortage of planes had delayed the training of their crews. Blondie Saunders, now back from the Pacific and promoted to brigadier general (after a B-17 crash that almost took his life), was in charge of training, and he had embarked on a plan to prepare 452 crews. But with so few B-29s in which to train anyone, he had managed to check out only sixty-seven first pilots by the beginning of 1944.[3]

At the Cairo Conference, after Chiang Kai-shek agreed to build B-29 bases in time for their expected April 15 arrival (two months before they were scheduled to go into combat), Arnold thought he had at least taken care of that aspect of the operation. But on his return home, he learned from his own sources in China that Chiang, while acknowledging his promise, couldn't get excited about the time element involved. The days were passing and no one in China was recruiting coolies to work on the runways, which would have to be built entirely by hand labor.[4] Someone would have to go over there and get things moving. The logical choice for the task was K. B. Wolfe, who now knew more about the needs of B-29s than anyone else. So Arnold sent him. But unfortunately, Wolfe was also needed in Kansas, where the new B-29s were being prepared for operations and the crews were being trained.

Arnold must have been getting tired of the very mention of B-29s when, one day in January, Rosie O'Donnell, now chief of Arnold's council, came in and told him he wanted to fly one of them. Arnold needed him in Washington and didn't want to let him go. O'Donnell had already had combat experience in the Philippines in the early days of the war, but he wanted more, and he was not afraid to talk back to the boss. Arnold admired him for that. On this occasion, O'Donnell went even further. As the argument became heated, Arnold picked up a paperweight and threw it at him. Rosie, an ex-football star and good athlete, caught it and threw it back to him.

When Arnold went home that night he had a gash on his forehead. "Oh, that Rosie!" he exclaimed to his son David, who asked him what had happened.[5] But shortly thereafter, Rosie O'Donnell got his wish. He took command of the 73rd Wing of what would soon become the Twentieth Air Force, and headed for Kansas to learn how to fly the Superfortress.

Arnold found time in January to fly to California for his first look at his ranch, and he liked what he saw. Lois drove up from San Francisco to inspect it with him, and he enjoyed that, too. He was still indulgent to his daughter. Though he knew she drank too much, she usually managed to control it in his presence so that it seldom became a serious problem between them.

He found that the ranch needed "a little bit of work and quite a lot of improvements," but he decided the family would have "a nice place there . . . if and when we ever raise enough cash to get the job done."[6]

In Sonoma he also saw Bruce, who was stationed in California but expected to be sent overseas. He had some pleasing news. He intended to marry Barbara Douglas, whom his father had always liked. They were already engaged but didn't intend to announce it until Bruce managed to buy a ring. His father wondered "why it should take so darn long to get a ring." It was not because Bruce was strapped for money. He had never forgotten the demand his father made that day in West Point, two years earlier: "You will not get married until you've been out of West Point a year and you've saved a thousand dollars." It was less than a year since Bruce had been graduated from West Point, but he was well on his way to saving the thousand dollars.[7]

Now that Spaatz and Doolittle were running the air show in England, Arnold began giving them the impatient nudges he used to give Eaker. In late January, he wrote to Spaatz: "Can't we, some day and not too far distant, send out a big number—and I mean a big number—of bombers to hit something in the nature of an aircraft factory and lay it flat?"[8]

The Eighth Air Force had expanded so rapidly in recent months that on February 20, Spaatz and Doolittle were able to send out more than a thousand heavy bombers—a far cry from the 300 or so Eaker had been able to put together for his biggest raids the previous year. On that day, Spaatz and Doolittle from England, followed by Eaker in the Mediterranean, began a concentrated six-day assault, which the newspapers at the time called "the Big Week." They sent over Germany an average of almost a thousand bombers a day during that week, escorted by 17 fighter groups, many of them flying P-51s. The losses were heavy—226 bombers and 28 fighters—but not prohibitive for such a large force: roughly six percent compared to the 20 percent Eaker had often lost the previous year, when he was forced to send his bombers unescorted. And aerial photos showed that the damage, especially to German aircraft factories, had been enormous. With the British battering German cities at night and the Americans hitting selected military-industrial targets in the daytime, the air battle over Europe was now definitely in favor of the Allies. And there was no more talk from the British about putting an end to daylight bombing. With the addition of long-range fighter escorts, the American strategy of daylight precision bombing was beginning to prove sound.

Arnold could now almost relax about the air war in Europe, but his worries about the B-29, China, and Japan were intensifying. First he had to settle the question of who would control the B-29s and how they would be used when they were ready. Then he had to figure out how to get them ready and make sure they were worth what they cost. His reputation, perhaps his whole career, was riding on the Superfortress and its contribution to the war effort.

Though no one yet knew whether this giant bomber was worth having, everyone involved in the Pacific war was asking for it. MacArthur and Kenney in Australia fully expected to get their share; so did Nimitz and the Navy. And Chiang Kai-shek, who had agreed to play host to the B-29s, wanted, therefore, to control or at least influence the decision on how they would be used. None of these people intended to use the plane the way Arnold thought it should be used. MacArthur would use it to soften up the Dutch East Indies, and then the Philippines, in preparation for his triumphant return there. Nimitz would use it against submarines. And no one could be sure how Chiang would use it—presumably against Japanese forces in China.

If all these people got their share, the B-29 force would be fractured and the net effect would be to dilute its total impact. To Arnold, Japan was the main target. If the B-29 had any message to carry, he wanted it carried to the Japanese homeland. The way to make that happen, he decided, was to retain control of it himself. With Marshall's help, he managed to put through the Joint Chiefs a directive creating the Twentieth Air Force, comprising the 20th and 21st bomber commands, which would get virtually all the B-29s, and would be commanded by the Joint Chiefs, with himself acting as their executive agent. On February 19, he secured President Roosevelt's approval of this plan. Since the Joint Chiefs had already approved it, Nimitz could hardly put up much of a fight. And Chiang wouldn't be able to stop it. But MacArthur, who sometimes seemed to be running his own private war, and who had strong conservative political support at home, might cause problems. Accordingly, Arnold sent a personal representative, Larry Kuter, to Australia to break the news to him.

Tell MacArthur, Arnold instructed Kuter, that he won't be getting even one B-29, that they're going to be centrally directed and controlled, and that they're going to be used for the defeat of Japan. If any of them become available for such targets as the (Japanese-held) oil fields in Sumatra (targets for which MacArthur might conceivably want to use them), Arnold said, he or one of his deputies would send them there. He wanted Kuter to make sure MacArthur understood and accepted this.

Kuter said, "I'll do my best to tell him, and I'll do my best to make him understand. But I'm not going to make him like it."[9]

When Kuter arrived in Australia, he saw Kenney first and, over a couple of bottles of whisky, spent a whole night explaining the situation. Kenney "blew his top." He had assumed he would get the first batch of Superfortresses. He argued with Kuter for hours, "first bullying, then begging, always trying to force me to change my story, go back and tell Arnold he was wrong."

The next day, Kuter went to the office of Gen. Richard K. Sutherland, MacArthur's chief of staff, and spent four hours explaining the decision to him. He also asked and expected to see MacArthur himself, but after Sutherland heard the whole story, he told Kuter MacArthur was too busy to see him.

Since Kuter was there as Arnold's representative, he was amazed at this. It would be two or three days before he left for home, he said, and he offered to make himself available at MacArthur's convenience.

Sutherland said he was sorry but MacArthur wouldn't be able to work him in. However, since he and Kenney had heard the story, that was sufficient.

After Kuter returned to Washington, he found that Arnold was furious at him. Arnold had received a cablegram from MacArthur stating that Kuter hadn't had the courtesy to call on him when he visited his headquarters. Arnold had already drafted a cable to MacArthur apologizing "for the rudeness shown by my Deputy Chief of Staff."

Kuter erupted when he saw this cable. "You don't apologize," he said to Arnold. "And you don't send that message. You either fire me or you send some other kind of message." He then told Arnold the whole story and that was the end of it.

Arnold received some bad news on February 24 about the airlift operations over the Hump from India to China. Since his promise to Chiang Kai-shek a year earlier, the A.T.C. had been gradually increasing its tonnage over the Hump, but the airlift hadn't quite kept pace with Arnold's expectations. Now he learned that during January and the first twenty-three days of February, forty-seven cargo planes had been lost. (Sixteen of them had simply vanished into the mountains.)

"Unless something is done very soon," he wrote in a memo to Barney Giles, "the morale of the pilots cannot help but be materially affected."

Since it was not possible to cancel operations over this perilous mountain route, some other solution had to be found. Arnold's immediate suggestion to Giles was cosmetic but shockingly unsubstantial:

> a. Double the number of crews but retain the same number of operating missions so that the attrition will be distributed over double the number of people.
> b. Increase the number of airplanes so that we will always have a standard number of about 250 in operation and in that way our losses will not become so noticeable.[10]

If Arnold had done no more than make this suggestion, his solution to the problem would have deserved a high place in the annals of cynicism. But in fact, he was simply proposing a stopgap measure. To find a more substantial remedy, he immediately sent C. R. Smith to India.[11]

Smith found the commanding officer of the Hump operation, Brig. Gen. Earl Hoag, in a New Delhi hotel, about a thousand miles from the air route into China. "How are things going over the Hump?" Smith asked.

Hoag said they were going pretty well.

"When were you over there last?"

He hadn't actually been over the Hump as yet, he said, but he got written reports on it.

When Smith flew the Hump for the first time, he could see why neither Hoag nor anyone else might like the experience. Smith, who had virtually covered the globe during his years as an airline executive, found the Himalayas "the toughest flying place in the world. . . . You could be flying at 25,000 feet and look up at mountains." The monsoon rains were so severe that one A.T.C. station had been soaked with 244 inches in a year. The C-46s and C-47s that flew the route couldn't get above the mountains. They had to fly through the saddles, dodging clouds as well as peaks because inside any cloud there could be a peak. Since the Himalayas sloped toward sea level on the south and east, a more southerly route would have been easier, but there was one important deterrent. It would take the unarmed cargo planes over

Burma, Indochina, and southern China, which were held by the Japanese.

At the makeshift A.T.C. bases in India, there was such a housing shortage that hundreds of men had to live in tents, which increased the danger of malaria. During the monsoon seasons, twenty percent of all personnel became malaria victims. On days when it was not raining, temperatures reached 130 degrees, making the aircraft metal so hot the mechanics couldn't work on it. Much of the maintenance had to be done at night, which was when most of the rain fell.

The heavy losses, due mostly to the mountains and the weather, had brought morale as low as Arnold had feared, and Smith realized something substantial would have to be done soon. Housing would have to be improved. And the two-engine C-47s and C-46s would have to be replaced with four-engine C-54s. But that would take time. What Smith suggested immediately in messages back to Washington was the appointment of a commander who would stay on the spot and even fly the route himself. He recommended Brig. Gen. Thomas Hardin, a pilot who once worked for him at American Airlines. Hardin took command March 15 and the tonnage went up immediately. At the end of 1943 it had been 12,000 monthly. By the summer of 1944 it was up to 23,000, and still climbing. He didn't exactly cure all the morale problems—he couldn't cure the heat or the malaria, and he couldn't make the men who flew the Hump enjoy it—but he did manage to keep them so busy they didn't quite realize how miserable they were.

In late February, Arnold received separate letters from Stilwell and Stratemeyer in the China-Burma-India theater expressing doubts about the plan to bomb Japan with B-29s from bases in China. Arnold, in a February 28 memo to Gen. Hoyt Vandenberg of his staff, said, "Both of these letters are on the 'can't be done' side, and I am not ready to accept either one. I cannot see my way clear to send these B-29s out there to carry on a series of bombardment operations against Hongkong, Formosa, Indochina and Siam, as B-24s can perform these missions. The B-29s are built for long-range missions and our plans should be prepared accordingly."

Yet he himself was beginning to wonder at this time whether the B-29 would ever be able to do the job for which it was designed. "It is highly possible and maybe even probable," he concluded in the memo to Vandenberg, "that we are expecting too much from these operations."

The prospects were not good. The B-29 Wright engine was still undergoing so many modifications that it was considered still in the development stage. As of early February, the entire 20th Bomber Command had flown a mere 9,000 hours in training, testing, and so forth, and "only a negligible number of these hours had been flown over 20,000 feet, due to power plant limitations."[12] (The B-29 was supposed to be a high-altitude bomber.) And the fire-control system had not yet been fully tested in operation. As of March 1, 1944, even the "trained" crews had been able to fly only two-thirds of the B-29 hours required, and very few of them had received more than a fraction of the fire-control practice they would need. Only two aircraft so far were equipped with a complete central fire-control system.

Because the crews were being trained at several bases in Kansas, the modification program was centered there, which meant that a whole cadre of Air Force officers, plus representatives of Boeing and other companies now involved in B-29 production, were swarming over the state, trying to keep up with developments. The situation was chaotic and the Kansas winter was making it worse. The snow in many places was eighteen inches deep and temperatures were below zero. Mechanics were working on airplanes in unheated hangars or even on the runways.[13] Tempers were boiling but hands were freezing.

On March 8, Arnold dropped out of the sky from Washington and into the mess at a place called Pratt, Kansas. "I was appalled at what I found," he later said. "There were shortages in all kinds and classes of equipment. The engines were not fitted with the latest gadgets; the planes were not ready to go. It would be impossible for them to be anywhere near China by the 15th of April unless some drastic measures were taken."[14]

On the ninth, he flew to Salina and found the situation just as distressing. There he met a Technical Service Command officer, Col. I. W. Stephenson, who had the misfortune of being in the wrong place at the right time. Would he please explain all these shortages?

Colonel Stephenson could not explain them.

Was he running this place?

No, he wasn't.

Well, who was running it, then? "If no one else is," Arnold said, "I will."

He ordered Stephenson to prepare, by the following morning, a list of all shortages. Though it wasn't exactly his job, he and his staff worked all night preparing such a list.[15] When Arnold received it, he handed it over to Maj. Gen. Bennett E. Meyers, who was accompanying him.

Meyers, who found himself in trouble after the war for irregularities in the Air Forces procurement program, had always been known to fellow air officers as a dynamic and effective taskmaster. Arnold said of him, "He got things done."[16]

Arnold informed him that he was now the coordinator of the B-29 modification program. By the fifteenth of April, 150 of the big bombers were supposed to be in Asia, and it was his job to make sure they got there.

Meyers and his men examined plane after plane, listed their shortages, then called the factories responsible for each needed part and had them flown to Kansas. Whenever necessary, he even sent planes to get the parts. Since he needed more men to install these parts in a hurry, he called the Boeing factory and arranged the loan of a small army of experienced production people, even though their temporary loss to the company might slow up the assembly lines. Despite another snowstorm and the threat of a labor walkout, he had one group, the 40th, ready to go overseas by April 9.

Two planes, the first one flown by Blondie Saunders, had preceded this group. Saunders arrived at Chakulia, India, on April 7, and was followed within the next ten days by several other planes.[17] But toward the end of April, five of the newly arrived bombers crashed near Karachi on the Arabian Sea, owing to overheated engines. Two planes were demolished and five men were killed. K. B. Wolfe, who was on the scene, grounded all the surviving planes and told Arnold in an urgent message that some method would have to be found to cool the engines.

Arnold had managed by force of will to get at least a few B-29s to Asia in time to keep his promise to President Roosevelt. But he hadn't yet solved the plane's crucial engine problem. It would be a heavy burden for him to carry in the days ahead.

Finally, after ten days in May, the burden became too heavy and Arnold fell victim to his third heart attack in fourteen months.[18] This one was not so severe as the first but it was serious enough to worry Dr. Russell Lee. When Arnold had sufficiently recovered, Lee again prescribed Florida and went with him to Coral Gables. This time Bee also went with him, but she was little comfort. Though she was still working, perhaps too hard, on Air Forces relief projects, she was not well. She had become acutely nervous. She wasn't eating enough and had lost weight. In addition to worrying about his own health, Arnold now worried about hers. And Dr. Lee was not as helpful as he would have liked to be about this problem because he and Bee didn't get along very well. She felt he ignored her and didn't keep her fully informed about Hap's condition.

Unable to cope with all this, Arnold phoned Mary Streett, who had been for years one of Bee's close friends. Mary's husband, Bill, one of Hap's close friends, was now commanding general of the Thirteenth Air Force in the Pacific, and Mary was alone at their Bethesda home. Arnold asked her to come down to Florida and she did so.[19]

Arnold was sufficiently recovered now to go for rides, so Bruce Simmons drove him to the Miami airport to meet her. But they didn't drive directly back to the Arnolds' quarters. Instead they went out into the country, where he talked to her about Bee for a half hour. Simmons, who could hear the entire conversation, was impressed by Arnold's apparent concern about his wife.[20]

Mary Streett was not surprised that he had called upon her for help because he often talked with her about family matters and problems that bothered him. He had confided in her his regret, for instance, that he had been able to spend so little time with his children when they were growing. She had always liked him and thought of him as a convivial man, the life of any party; and she had noticed happily that he hadn't been changed by the importance of his wartime job. He was undoubtedly attractive and had an engaging personality, but she felt he did not know or understand women very well. Though he talked to her earnestly and seriously about Bee, she sensed that it was difficult for him to do so. He was bewildered about Bee's recent behavior, but also deeply concerned for her and he wanted to know what he could do. Should he get someone to be with her when he was away? David, the only one of the children still at home, was too young for such a heavy responsibility.

Mary Streett, hoping Bee would open up to her and talk about her troubles, stayed in Florida for several days, but there was no exchange of confidences between them. Bee seemed to be as cool to her as she was to Hap. The Arnolds' daily life together was less than pleasant. And as if there weren't already enough friction between them, she was now accusing him of seeing other women. She had decided he was having an affair with one of her friends, and all the arguments in the world couldn't convince her otherwise.

Hap thought her Air Forces relief work might be responsible for her condition. She had, after all, attacked the job with all her energy; perhaps it was too much for her. But when he suggested she discontinue it, she would flare up at him. The staff doctors attending him, worried about his condition and anxious for him to get more rest, would encourage her to take afternoon rides with Simmons, and sometimes she did so. But even with him she was irritable now. He would start to say something and she would cut him off in mid-sentence. It was the sort of thing her husband might do to Simmons but it was completely unlike her. After such an outburst, they would travel in silence for a mile or two; then she would say, "Simmons, I'm sorry."

Though these were difficult circumstances under which to recover from a heart attack, Arnold showed gradual improvement. The two of them moved from the hospital to the estate of Gilbert Grosvenor, the publisher of *National Geographic* magazine, who had made the place available for wartime uses. There they had a house to themselves. Arnold, completely back on his feet now, played golf or cruised off the Florida coast on the Air Forces crash boat, a fast 160-footer. One day when he and Simmons were on it, a Navy P-T boat came up beside it, between Coral Gables and Catcaid Island, and challenged it to a race.

Arnold said to the crash boat captain, "Can you whip 'em?"

The captain said, "Yeah, I can whip 'em."

"Don't start anything you can't finish," Arnold warned. "I don't want the Navy to beat me."

With the captain's assurance, Arnold fired a gun and the race was on. The P-T boat got away so fast it seemed about to put the crash boat out of sight. Then the crash boat captain, having given the sailors a sense of false security, began pouring on power. When he passed the P-T boat, it seemed to be standing still.

Arnold said to Simmons, "This fellow knows how to handle a boat."

Simmons, who had been talking to the crew, said, "Yes, sir, he ought to. He used to be a rum-runner."

By early June, Arnold was impatient to get back to work. On the fifth, he learned that 98 Superforts had taken off from India on the first-ever B-29 mission. The 20th Bomber Command had been forced to stage the mission from India because there wasn't yet enough gasoline at the advance bases in China. The B-29s, with the help of the A.T.C., were carrying their own gasoline into China over the Hump, and it was a slow process. From India, the big bombers couldn't reach Japan, so rail yards in Japanese-held Bangkok were the target. Partly because the day was overcast, and partly because neither the airplanes nor the crews were quite ready, the mission was less than successful. Though the yards were virtually undefended, only 77 planes were able to drop bombs and only 18 of those bombs came close to their targets.

It was not a reassuring start but Arnold was unwilling to pull back.

He insisted that the 20th's commander, K. B. Wolfe, get on with the bombing of Japan, and he wanted the first raid against the mainland to coincide with the invasion of Saipan, which the Navy was planning for mid-June.[21] Because of the gas shortage at the China bases, Wolfe doubted he could make that deadline, but he agreed to try.

In early June, Arnold was also aware of the big event scheduled to begin the sixth on the Normandy beaches. He couldn't be there for that, but the Combined Chiefs of Staff had scheduled a meeting in London on June 10, and he intended to go to that.

On the seventh, the day after the Normandy invasion, he flew back into Washington and attended a formal dinner at the White House, but without Bee. On the eighth, he and George Marshall, with their aides, boarded a C-54 for London. This was the first chance the two generals had had in more than a month to exchange confidences, and they took advantage of it for several hours on their way to England. In Arnold's words, they talked about everything "from mice and men to cabbages and kings."

Their personal relationship had deepened continuously during the last five years. Though Marshall outranked Arnold, Laurence Kuter noticed he never "pulled his rank" on him. In air matters, he had given Arnold virtual autonomy. Arnold, for his part, had developed such respect for Marshall that he once told Ira Eaker, "If George Marshall ever took a position contrary to mine, I would know I was wrong."[22]

Robert Lovett felt that Arnold recognized in Marshall "one of the truly great figures that this country has produced," and that Marshall recognized in Arnold "a dedicated officer in a field in which he, General Marshall, was not specialized, and at the same time . . . a human being, this warm-hearted, loyal, mercurial, flamboyant belligerent fellow who didn't care who he took on in battle."[23]

Marshall undoubtedly saw in Arnold the great big, bubbling, energetic, and clumsy boy who would be dangerous in a china shop, but he also was aware of Arnold's genius as a builder, a motivator, a synthesizer. And he so appreciated Arnold's genius that he was tolerant of, and perhaps amused by, the boy in him.

He even tolerated Arnold's outrageously boyish practical jokes. One day, earlier in the year, Arnold, on a mischievous impulse, had sent an old friend, comedian Vince Barnett, into Marshall's office, pretending to be a wealthy European immigrant. In a thick accent, he told the dignified general he wanted to get into the flying business.

Marshall, bewildered at the sudden appearance of this odd-looking stranger, said, "Who are you? How did you get in here?"

"You know what I want," Barnett said in his musical-comedy accent. "You can fix it for me." Thereupon he pulled out a wad of currency and dropped it on Marshall's desk.

Marshall, in a fury, was shouting, "Get out! Get out!" when Arnold, who had been listening outside the door, came in, laughing.[24]

When Marshall and Arnold reached London they were welcomed by British Army commander Sir Alan Brooke, Portal, Spaatz, and several other high officers. Spaatz drove Arnold to the country house at which he was billeted, but Arnold was so tired he fell asleep in the car during their conversation. "Two and a half hours sleep does not go very well any more," he noted in his diary. The house in which he was ensconced, sitting on two hundred manicured acres, had been built by Henry VIII as a hunting lodge.[25]

Arnold didn't spend much time there. He was up at 7:30 the next morning and off to Eisenhower's headquarters for a briefing on the invasion, which was progressing as well as had been expected. He found Ike "very optimistic" and was pleased to hear from Ike's staff that the German Air Force over Normandy was "not so hot." He had doubted British intelligence reports that indicated German air strength was still formidable. Now he learned that no German planes had tried to bomb the ships concentrated in ports in the south of England before the invasion, or to hit the invasion forces during the Channel crossing, or to attack the congested beachhead after the landings. To Arnold this was the ultimate proof that American daylight operations had been effective. The Germans were short of planes because the B-17s had knocked out their aircraft factories and, with the help of the long-range fighters, had shot down the bulk of their fighter force.

On the tenth, the Combined Chiefs of Staff met in the cabinet war office and, after discussing the invasion progress, turned their attention to the Pacific war. The British wanted to know how they could help. Then the question arose as to why MacArthur should be allowed to pursue his personally satisfying plan to invade the Philippines. Why not bypass the Philippines and move directly toward Japan or Formosa?[26] Admiral King, speaking for the Navy, argued for this Central Pacific course of action, and Arnold agreed with him because the Air Forces would need bases for their B-29 strikes against Japan. Until such island bases were available, he would pursue his intention of hitting Japan from China, but if he could establish bases on Saipan, Tinian, or Guam, for instance, he would eliminate the almost insurmountable supply problem he faced in China. There was general sentiment among the Combined Chiefs in favor of the U.S. Navy's Central Pacific path to Japan; but Marshall, keenly aware of MacArthur's rabid political following in the United States, realized it would not be easy to override the popular general's insistence on his return to the Philippines. The Combined Chiefs ended their discussion by voting to solicit opinions from Mac-Arthur and Nimitz on the matter.

On June 12, Marshall, Arnold, King, Eisenhower, and their aides boarded the destroyer *Thompson* in Portsmouth harbor for a trip across the Channel to the beachhead that had been established six days earlier. As they left the harbor at a speed of thirty knots, they passed "hundreds of ships of all kinds." Arnold had never before seen "such a mass, uninterrupted and unimpeded." And off the French coast, there were hundreds more at anchor, waiting to be unloaded. "What a field day for the G.A.F. [German Air Force]," Arnold noted in his diary, "if there is a G.A.F."

After transferring to a landing craft, Ike and his party of dignitaries went ashore at Omaha Beach, where Gen. Omar Bradley and staff met them, and Arnold got a chance to say hello to Pete Quesada, who was Bradley's air commander. After lunch and a briefing at Bradley's headquarters, Arnold, with Quesada and Larry Kuter, toured the Air Forces installations, which included one landing strip already in operation, a second one due to be ready for use that night, a third and fourth to be ready in two days, and a fifth to be ready in three days. Quesada had managed all this in just six days. The air above them was swarming with American and British planes. Quesada told Arnold the Allies had 4,000 planes in the air that day. As far as Arnold could see, the Germans had none. Four P-51s and three Spitfires had been shot down, but not by the Germans. Quick-trigger Navy gunners had hit them. "Our own Navy," Arnold commented in his diary, "[is] far more dangerous than the G.A.F."

The trip to the beachhead was short and well organized. By 6:00 p.m. the same day, the generals and admirals were back in London, where, after a bath, Arnold found himself feeling fine. "A drink and I will feel no pain," he noted. Since his heart attacks, his doctors had suggested he take a drink or two each day.

From England, Marshall and Arnold traveled to Italy and the Mediterranean, inspecting all the fronts, before heading for home June 21. The trip was entirely without ill effect for Arnold, despite an uneasy moment when one of DeGaulle's French pilots in a P-39 almost collided with their C-54 as it was landing at Casablanca. By the time they reached Washington, Arnold's third heart attack was so far behind him that he went back to work as if it hadn't happened. But the incoming details of the first B-29 raid on the Japanese homeland were almost sufficient to bring on a fourth attack.

Led by Blondie Saunders, seventy-five Superforts had taken off from their Chinese bases in the late afternoon of June 18 for the 3,200-mile round trip to Yawata, on the island of Kyushu.[27] They intended to destroy the Imperial Iron and Steel Works, which produced, according to intelligence reports, twenty-four percent of Japan's rolled steel. Because formation flying used too much fuel, Wolfe and Saunders, with Arnold's concurrence, decided to make it a night mission, with the planes following each other and bombing individually.

One bomber crashed on takeoff and four others had to turn back because of mechanical problems. Saunders dropped his bombs at 11:38 p.m., Tokyo time, and having lit the target for those behind him, headed for home. But only forty-seven of those behind him were able to find Yawata. Of the sixty-eight planes that dropped bombs, twenty-one unloaded on what were euphemistically called "other targets." Though Japanese antiaircraft fire was able to destroy only one plane, seven were lost because of various malfunctions. And after these melancholy statistics had been compiled, the most disheartening of all had now become apparent. Aerial photos showed that only one bomb had hit what might be called a significant target—a power house—and it was three-quarters of a mile away from the coke ovens that were the primary targets.

The B-29 hadn't yet come close to proving it was worth the money it had cost. It was only fair to admit, though, that its attempt to do so from bases deep in China had been a handicap almost impossible to overcome. It would soon get a better chance to show what it could do. On June 30, the Navy and Marines had captured enough of Saipan so that construction could begin on the first B-29 installations there. From Saipan, the heart of Japan was only 1,200 miles away, and as soon as the B-29s were based there, the problem of supplying them would be almost eliminated. Arnold could only hope that by then the plane's other problems would also be eliminated. The engines were still overheating, blowing out their cylinder heads, leaking oil, and catching fire. And if the Bangkok and Yawata results were a fair indication, either the radar-controlled bombing system or the crews using it needed improvement.

In mid-August, Arnold suggested to Marshall that they sneak away from Washington together for a week of fishing in the high Sierras.[28] Since it was evident that both of them could use a rest, Marshall agreed. But since they shared between them so much command responsibility, they couldn't simply disappear and forget the war. Consequently, they landed at Bishop Air Force Base on the eastern slope of the Sierras on August 22 with an entourage of aides and communication specialists. When they headed up into the mountains, by car and then by horseback, it looked more like a military expedition than a fishing trip. Besides guards, guides, forest rangers, radio operators, code experts, and staff men, they even had a Signal Corps officer assigned to them. The Pentagon Message Center had arranged for a portable code machine to be set up at the air base, and Arnold had arranged that an airplane, each morning, fly over their camp, which was marked by flares, and drop a pouch of mail. Each day, when they got through running the war, they would ride for several hours through spectacular mountain country, then settle down by a mountain stream and cast their rods. They got more fish than rest, but on August 30, they returned to Washington refreshed.

Though Arnold was still worried about the B-29 as the autumn of 1944 approached, neither he nor anyone else on the Allied side was any longer worried about the outcome of the war. Throughout the Pacific, the Japanese were in general retreat. Though their troops still fought fiercely against one American island invasion after another, they had not been able to hold any island the Americans wanted. And their navy had been reduced to impotence, clearing the way for American advances ever closer to their homeland. In Europe, the Germans were falling back on all fronts. Paris was liberated on August 25. On September 11, the first American patrols crossed the German border from newly liberated Belgium. At the same time, Allied forces in Italy had advanced north of Florence. And on the eastern front, the Russians had pushed the Germans back to the Vistula and Narev rivers and the East Prussian border. Though Germany might still be capable of local victories, it couldn't possibly win the war.

Arnold began thinking, therefore, about the postwar era, how the Air Forces should prepare for it, and how the Air Forces could best maintain a state of readiness during peacetime. In September, he again hired California Institute of Technology scientist Dr. Theodor von Kármán, this time to head a committee that would work out some answers to long-range problems. He made it clear to von Kármán that he didn't want the Air Forces ever again to be caught unprepared, as it had been in 1939 and 1940.

"We have won this war," he told von Kármán, "and I am no longer interested in it. I do not think we should spend time debating whether we obtained the victory by sheer power or by some qualitative superiority. Only one thing should concern us. What is the future of air power and aerial warfare? What is the bearing of the new inventions such as jet propulsion, rockets, radar and other electronic devices?"[29]

The jet fighter plane, plans for which he had brought back from England early in the war, had been manufactured by Bell Aircraft and was now undergoing extensive testing. It was America's first jet airplane. Arnold had also directed Gen. Grandison Gardner at the Eglin Field, Florida, proving grounds to build a prototype of an American version of the rocket-powered buzz bomb with which the Germans were terrorizing London.[30] And though he didn't mention it to von Kármán, he was aware that the United States at that moment was engaged in the development of an atomic weapon that, if completed on time, might be used against Japan. Never before had it been so evident that a small country with advanced technology could defeat a larger, wealthier country that had allowed itself to become complacent. "I want you to come to the Pentagon and gather a group of scientists who will work out a blueprint for air research for the next twenty, thirty, perhaps fifty years," he told von Kármán.

Arnold had always entertained ambivalent feelings about scientists. He didn't know their language, seemed never to be quite at ease in their presence, and enjoyed making fun of them. In a September 12, 1944, letter to Tooey Spaatz, he wrote: "These long-haired scientists have a hard time getting together. They are about as jealous as Brigham Young's seventeenth and eighteenth wives were, so that there is a lot of throat-cutting going on between the scientists in the various agencies connected with the War Department and other branches of the government." But despite such remarks, Arnold never hesitated to call on scientists if he thought they might be useful to aviation. His engagement of von Kármán began a science-oriented military era which would soon revolutionize the Air Forces.

☆ ☆ ☆

Because Bee's hay fever was even more severe than usual in 1944, she and David were spending the summer at Kezar Lake in Maine. Hap, with Bill and Mary Streett (Bill was back from the Pacific), drove up there on September 10 to celebrate the Arnolds' wedding anniversary. They found Bee in better condition than they expected. Hap's brother Cliff, who was a doctor, had given her a new medicine that had proved marvelously helpful. "I have no idea what's in it," Arnold said in a letter to Hank,[31] "but there must be lots of dope." In any case, it put her on her feet and raised her spirits. The Streetts and the Arnolds had "a big time" marking the anniversary, even though Arnold had calculated the year incorrectly. He thought it was their thirtieth; actually it was their thirty-first.

From Kezar Lake, Arnold continued on to Quebec, where, on the twelfth, another meeting between Roosevelt and Churchill, the Octagon Conference, began. There were a few important matters to discuss. Would the British Navy be needed in the Pacific? Admiral King, feeling confident, and perhaps unwilling to share authority, said no. What could be done about the situation in Warsaw, Poland, where the advancing Russians were apparently standing by and allowing the Germans to slaughter Polish resistance fighters? Virtually nothing. But aside from such questions, the debates in Quebec were centered mostly on details of command structure in Europe, where Allied armies, having broken through German defenses in France, were moving inexorably toward the Rhine.

When Arnold returned from Quebec, he began concentrating on a new phase of his Air Forces responsibility—cutbacks in production and personnel. The flow of men, planes and supplies (except B-29s) to all theaters was now so plentiful that Arnold and Lovett felt it had to be restrained to prevent waste.[32] Arnold said to his staff one day, "Just because I turned all the spigots on, isn't there someone around here who knows enough to turn them off?"

There were now almost 2.4 million men and women in the Air Forces, and pilots were graduating at the rate of 105,000 per year. About 4,000 airplanes per month were coming off the assembly lines. Arnold ordered a gradual cutback all the way down the line. Then he flew to California in early October to study the effects of diminishing production in the aircraft industry. With the war moving toward a resolution, the aircraft companies would have to be curtailed sharply, but he thought it would be dangerous to the country's security if they were allowed to return to the skeletal condition from which they had begun war preparations in 1939.

While in California, he had dinner with his son Bruce, now a second lieutenant with an automatic-weapons unit, and Bruce's bride, Donald Douglas's daughter, Barbara. Arnold had missed their June wedding because he was in England. Bruce's unit was training for an amphibious operation and still anticipating shipment overseas. Arnold said in a letter to Hank, "Ultimately he will get his assignment in some theater —probably not the same one you are in." With one son at the front in Europe, Arnold was almost certain he would soon have another at the front in the Pacific.

Lois's husband, Ernie Snowden, now a commander in the Navy, was back in San Francisco with her, at least for a while. In her spare time, Lois was busy trying to get some work done on the family ranch near Sonoma. Arnold had hired a retired soldier to look after it, but before the man got any work done, he broke his ankle and had to return to the Soldiers' Home. The ranch would need a lot of work, but that didn't bother Arnold. It would give him something to do during his own retirement.

Arnold's one continuing worry about the progress of the war was the performance of the B-29, in which he had invested so much of the taxpayers' money. Its first few missions from China had been so unimpressive that he had relieved General Wolfe, a great engineer but without combat experience, and replaced him with Maj. Gen. Curtis LeMay. Though he scarcely knew LeMay, he was well acquainted with the man's combat record, his fierce determination, and his resourcefulness. In two years with the Eighth Air Force, he had risen quickly from group to division commander. He believed if he was tough on his men, they would be tough on the enemy and thereby increase the likelihood of their own survival. If he couldn't get the B-29s moving, nobody could.

When LeMay reached India in September, Blondie Saunders, who was scheduled to return to the States to form a new B-29 wing, volunteered to stay with him two more weeks and help him get acquainted. Saunders's helpfulness almost cost him his life. He took off in a B-25 the night of September 18 on a routine flight from an Indian base and crashed into the jungle, unnoticed, three or four miles from the end of the runway. Late the next day, when LeMay and an aide found the wreckage of his plane, Saunders was pinned beneath one of the engines with a shattered leg and several other broken bones. But he was not about to die. The first thing he did, as LeMay recalled, was to "give us hell for taking so long to get there." Saunders survived, after months of surgery, but his combat career was at an end, and his removal to hospital deprived LeMay of an important source of advice about B-29 problems in China and India.[33]

Fortunately, the plane itself was now showing signs of improvement. A new baffling system had cut down the excessive engine heat, and several less critical bugs had been eliminated, especially in the latest models. But LeMay still had some big decisions to make about the operation and he didn't have much time to make them. Chiang Kai-shek, using Claire Chennault as his spokesman, was demanding that the B-29s in China either be turned over to him or be moved to another theater. Though Arnold was ignoring this demand, he knew he had to get some action out of the Superforts against Japan soon, or Chiang, MacArthur, the Navy, and others who wanted them for local actions would have legitimate arguments for taking them from him.

LeMay was aware of the pressures upon Arnold, and he was also, even more keenly, aware of the pressures Arnold was already putting upon him. In a September 22 letter to him, Arnold pointed out that "we have not as yet obtained the bomb loads which originally were envisaged for the B-29." And in the next paragraph, he said, "Pilots that are weak must either be replaced or trained to a point where they can obtain the maximum from their airplane. I wish you would drive home to your crews and commanders the necessity for carrying maximum weight of bombs on all missions and the fact that every bomb that is carried on each B-29 will contribute to the overall air effort against Japan."

LeMay began by going on a mission, then telling his crews how unimpressed he was with the quality of the Japanese opposition, compared to what he had faced in Germany. He grounded all the planes until he was satisfied with their condition, and began retraining the crews in accordance with what he had learned in the skies over Europe. He also announced that henceforth, instead of bombing individually to save gas, the planes were to fly in formations and drop their bombs on their leader's cue. By this time he was fairly unpopular with his men, but at least he had them fighting mad and that was what he wanted. On September 26 he staged his first mission, with seventy-three B-29s hitting a Japanese steel plant at Anshan, Manchuria. Because the sky was overcast and his men weren't yet sufficiently skilled in radar bombing, the raid had little effect. No planes were lost, however, and that was an encouraging change.

Meanwhile, Maj. Gen. Haywood Hansell, one of the chief architects of the Air Forces' overall war plan (AWPD-1), had taken charge, on August 28, of the 21st Bomber Command, which was then at its headquarters in Colorado Springs.³⁴ It consisted of one B-29 wing already trained for night bombing but due to be retrained for day bombing, plus three more wings as yet untrained. The trained wing, the 73rd, was under the command of Arnold's friend and former aide Rosie O'Donnell.

In early October, when the crews of the 21st seemed sufficiently trained, Hansell staged a shakedown "mission" from Salina, Kansas, to Havana, Cuba, in formation. The purpose of this cruise was to find out if the 21st was ready for the more arduous trip from Saipan to Tokyo. Hansell discovered it was not quite ready. The B-29s made forced landings "all over the gulf states."

Hansell and O'Donnell knew Arnold too well to use that as an excuse for delay. On October 12, the vanguard of O'Donnell's 73rd Wing took off for Saipan. On landing they found a morass of disorganization. The fields were still under construction, and at the other end of the island, the Marines were still fighting the Japanese. But within a week, Saipan was home to Hansell's 21st Bomber Command. Despite bad weather, the confusion and fighting around them, the inexperience of the crews, and some last-minute doubts about feasibility, O'Donnell, followed by 110 B-29s, took off from Saipan for Tokyo on the morning of November 24. The Japanese capital was overcast and the bombing was poor, but by late afternoon, Hap Arnold could say at last that his B-29s had attacked Tokyo. And only two of them had been lost.

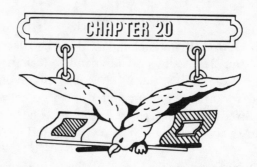

CHAPTER 20

I n 1944 and early 1945, Hap Arnold was receiving frequent visits from an Army officer the rest of his staff did not know. His name was Groves, Maj. Gen. Leslie R. Groves. The first time he came to visit, Arnold said to the new chief of his advisory council, Col. Fred Dean, "always let that fellow in. He's an old pal of mine."

Thereafter, Dean would quickly usher Groves into Arnold's office, but he was never invited to stay and listen to their conversations. "You won't need to sit in," Arnold would say, and Dean would discreetly retire, pleased that Arnold had this old friend with whom he could relax for a few minutes.

Not until August 6, 1945, did Dean find out what Groves and Arnold had been discussing.[1] It wasn't until the beginning of 1945 that Arnold's chief of staff, Lt. Gen. Barney Giles, was let in on the secret.

One morning, Arnold called Giles into his office and said, "We're going to meet with General Marshall."

When they entered Marshall's office, Marshall dismissed his secretary and an aide who happened to be there. Then he carefully closed all the doors and turned to his visitors.

"Giles," he said, "we're going to let you in on a very close-top-secret project."

But first Giles had to raise his hand and take an oath that he would not divulge anything said in that room, or ever discuss anything about the project, except to people who were connected with it.

This was the first time in Giles's entire military career that he had been asked to take such an oath. After he was sworn, Marshall proceeded to explain to him the Manhattan project and the atomic bomb that was in the process of development. Back in Arnold's office a few minutes later, Arnold said, "Now, Giles, I want you to take this thing from here and start a program of training crews to drop this bomb—if and when we make it and drop it."[2]

Because Giles would have to know something about the weapon if he was to decide whether an airplane could carry it, he was allowed to have lunch with Dr. Vannevar Bush, who was involved in the project.

When Giles asked him how big the bomb would be, Bush said, "Actually, the bomb itself you could hold in the palm of your hand, but the bomb ready to be dropped will weigh in the neighborhood of six or seven thousand pounds." (Most of this weight went into the mechanism which made the bomb explode.) Since it was evident that only the B-29 could deliver such a bomb, Giles began the process of selecting B-29 crews to train for the momentous mission.

There were now two hundred B-29s in the Marianas (the Navy, Marines, and Army had conquered Tinian and Guam as well as Saipan), and eight to ten new Superforts were arriving each day. But Arnold was not yet satisfied with the performance of Haywood Hansell's 21st Bomber Command because it was sending out an average of only about seventy planes per mission.[3] He knew about Hansell's difficulties. The maintenance depot hadn't yet been built, which meant that a lot of planes were grounded awaiting repairs. And he was convinced that Hansell had done an excellent job of pioneering, planning, and organizing his units.[4] But Arnold's key consideration now was the operation of the force. Curt LeMay was doing an excellent job in China. Though he was averaging only four missions a month, it was a miracle that he could manage more than one or two. And his accomplishments with the Eighth Air Force in Europe had impressed everyone. LeMay, he decided, would be the new commander of the 21st. To announce this change, he sent to Hansell's Guam headquarters Brig. Gen. Lauris Norstad, another of his former council members, who was now chief of staff of the 20th Air Force.

Norstad arrived in Guam on January 7 and broke the news to both Hansell and LeMay, who had been summoned there from China for this meeting.[5] Norstad made it clear to them, as if they didn't already know it, that Arnold was absolutely determined to get results out of the B-29. LeMay was to stay in Guam and speed up the operations of the 21st as quickly as possible. Brig. Gen. Roger M. Ramey, Hansell's chief of staff, was to take over LeMay's 20th Bomber Command in China, but only for the purpose of phasing it out. Now that there were enough bases in the Marianas, it would be pointless to continue hauling gasoline over the Hump into China.

Arnold's deep concern about the B-29 operations did not abate simply because he had changed commanders. Norstad had barely returned to Washington when, on January 14, Arnold wrote him an anxious and impatient memorandum:

> I am still worried—we have built up ideas in the Army, the Navy, and among civilians of what we can do with our B-29s. We had all

realized that in order to do considerable damage, large numbers of B-29s would have to deliver their loads of bombs against Japan continuously and consistently, and yet in spite of the above, really and truly, our average daily delivery rate against Japan is very, very small. . . . Unless something drastic is done to change this condition soon, it will not be long before the B-29 is just another tactical airplane. . . . These airplanes are quite expensive and carry with them a crew of 12 men, and yet our results are far from what we expected and what everyone else expects.

Three days after he wrote this memo, Arnold suffered his fourth serious coronary in less than two years. Though it is impossible to say whether there was any connection between this heart attack and his B-29 problems, it is apparent that he felt intensely and perhaps beyond reason his obligation to deliver on his B-29 promises.

When this attack hit him, Bee was in California, planning to attend a Los Angeles meeting of the National Association of Air Force Women. Arnold was planning a quiet dinner at their Fort Myer quarters with Harry Hopkins, and in Bee's absence, had asked Mary Streett to act as his hostess. But before Bruce Simmons left to get Mrs. Streett, Arnold had felt a sudden, sharp pain, so severe he could just barely manage to get over to the bed and lie down. When Simmons picked up Mrs. Streett, he announced that the general was sick again. She arrived to find him still in bed. While he seemed comfortable, she thought he looked frightened, even when he pounded his chest to show her how healthy he was. She stayed only ten minutes, feeling he should get some rest.[6]

Three days later, Gene Beebe, who had recently returned from China as a brigadier general, was called into Arnold's office. Dave Grant, the Air Forces' chief flight surgeon, was there with Suzy Adkins and they were both worried. Arnold hadn't come to work for three days, and when Grant tried to visit him, he had refused to let the doctor into his quarters. He had told his orderly not to admit anyone. Would Beebe please go over and find out what was wrong?[7]

When Beebe arrived, the orderly, afraid to disobey Arnold, tried to turn him away, but Beebe shouted through the door loud enough to be heard upstairs, "It's Gene!"

Arnold shouted back, "Come up here."

Beebe found him still in bed. "I guess I had an attack of some kind," he admitted.

Beebe, who had been in the Orient when the earlier attacks occurred, may not have known, since Arnold was so secretive about his health, that he had suffered three coronaries, and that this was probably another. "What do you want to do about it?" he asked.

There can be no doubt that Arnold knew what was wrong. After a man has had three heart attacks, he recognizes the fourth one. And after lying in bed with it for three days, he had apparently decided at last that he needed help, even if the disclosure of his condition did end up costing him his job. "I want to do something to get over it," he said.

On Sunday, the twenty-first, Arnold flew again to Coral Gables, with Beebe and Bruce Simmons. Claiming he felt perfectly all right, he refused to sit in the rear of his comfortable, upholstered C-47. He took his usual place in the copilot's seat. To Simmons, he appeared healthy, but when they reached Coral Gables, Col. Gilbert Marquardt, the physician in charge there, placed him immediately under intensive care, with nurses around him twenty-four hours a day. For nine days, until Bee's arrival from California on the thirtieth, only Beebe and the hospital staff were allowed to see him. He was more severely stricken this time than ever before.

Beebe felt that for the first few days, Arnold was shocked and frightened by the reaction of the doctors to his illness. Unimpressed by his protestations of good health, they made it clear to him that his condition was serious. He was also afraid that Marshall, learning he had suffered still another attack, would finally become impatient and choose someone to replace him. But Beebe, after talking to Marshall, was able to assure him no such thing was in the wind. This news in itself seemed to help him relax.

When Bee arrived, she occupied the room Beebe had been using, adjacent to her husband's room. She soon found, however, that Dr. Marquardt had no intention of letting her walk in on him any time she pleased. The doctor, quickly perceiving that Arnold and his wife were having problems, and convinced that her presence unduly agitated his patient, asked her not to disturb him.

To Bee, any exclusion from her husband's room was like an exclusion from her own home. The suggestion that she might disturb him angered her. She wasn't there to disturb him, she was there to comfort him. She argued with Dr. Marquardt, but her vehemence further convinced him that she might needlessly agitate and thereby endanger his patient. For two days there was an unpleasant standoff between Bee and Dr. Marquardt. Then, still angry, she went home to Washington.

Beebe continued to act as Arnold's liaison with his office, from which Barney Giles sent memoranda every other day, summarizing developments that might cheer the boss but omitting matters that might excite or agitate him. On the fifth of February, for instance, Giles had some good news to forward. The A.T.C. (now flying C-54s) had carried 44,000 tons of materiel over the Hump to China in January. And "over a hundred" B-29s had hit Kobe with incendiaries the day before, starting great fires. Only one plane was lost, and it ditched in the water so near Saipan that only one man was missing.

This news didn't cheer Arnold as much as Giles may have expected. Arnold's reaction was, "Grand, but why not 150 or 200 [B-29s]?"[8]

By February 16, his health was apparently improving because his usual impatience had returned. On that day he sent Giles a letter devoted to his old theme: get more B-29s in the air against Japan. He was concerned about two newspaper stories he had seen:

> One talked of the one thousandth B-29 being produced at Wichita. The other . . . told of the Navy's fifteen hundred airplanes hitting Japan proper.
>
> As you know, if Boeing-Wichita produced one thousand B-29s, there must be at least another one thousand produced by Boeing-Seattle and Bell-Atlanta. . . . if sixty or eighty is a maximum we can put over the Japanese mainland, a change in management is certainly in order. Nimitz, for instance, has every right to say, "Give me command of these heavy bombers and I will get three hundred over Japan at a time." And I would be the one who would be bound to support him. MacArthur could very rightly say (with Kenney's backing), "I could certainly get more airplanes over Japan than that, were I using the 20th Air Force." . . .
>
> I know that you are going to be told that they must have X-number of these planes for training. I know that you will also be told that it is difficult to get them in the air from their bases in the Pacific. And I know that there are one thousand other reasons for not getting two, three, or four hundred B-29s over Japan every other day. But all of these reasons must be pushed to one side with a grim determination.

In late February, Arnold received a letter from Chiang Kai-shek that must have amused him, especially in light of his own low regard for Chiang and Joe Stilwell's difficulties in getting Chiang's army to fight the Japanese:

> The help and inspiration we have received from you in our hard times are beyond estimate. Fighting shoulder to shoulder, the Chinese and American airmen have developed ties of friendship and comradeship that are destined to last for generations to come. I assure you, my dear General Arnold, that I shall exhort the officers and men of the Chinese air force to redouble their efforts so that they may not fall short of the high standard of morale and heroism set by their American comrades-in-arms.
>
> I here also wish to thank you heartily for the plane which you have kindly made available for my personal use.[9]

By this time Arnold was back on his feet, playing golf and making jokes about his illness. In a February 22 letter to Lois he wrote, "Apparently, one of my cylinders blew a gasket and I had to get down here to have an overhaul job done." But while he was making light of his own health problems, he was still concerned about Bee, whose nervous condition had been kept from him by his doctors. "I just heard that your mother had not been too well," he told Lois. "She had an excellent doctor at Fort Myer [Dr. Lee Martin] and I think she is much improved now, although I am still waiting for further information."

Happily, Bee was back in Florida two weeks later, much more relaxed than when she left, and the two of them were again getting along quite well. "We have nothing to do," he wrote Lois on March 7, "but sit in the sun and enjoy the Florida climate."

Arnold had never learned to sit very long in the sun, however, without becoming restless. Three days later he was plotting his escape from Florida. In a March 10 letter to Bruce in San Francisco, he wrote, "Don't even breathe a word about it, but it may not be too long before I see you. . . . In my opinion, I will recuperate a darn sight faster going places and seeing things, with enough rest in between, than I will trying to ride the bucking bronco back in the Pentagon building."

His doctors had been telling him he would have to learn to take it easy, and now, with the outcome of the war no longer in doubt, there was no reason why he shouldn't do so. Travel would be more relaxing for him than a return to his office routine, but instead of going west, he decided to go east, to Europe, where he had been planning to go (for the Yalta Conference) when he was stricken. Larry Kuter had substituted ably for him at Yalta, but there were other matters that still needed attention in Europe. Some of his best senior officers were there and it was time for all of them to start thinking about the future of the Air Forces. They ought to be getting ready to resume the long-dormant campaign for a separate air force. He would also have to choose one of these men to come home and run the Air Forces as his deputy because his doctors forbade him to resume a full schedule. And he was going to have to send Barney Giles to the Pacific to replace Miff Harmon, whose plane had just disappeared on a routine flight. Barney hadn't yet been given his tour of duty in the field, and it was unfair to deprive him of it.

Arnold gathered his small personal staff together on March 31 (including Dr. Marquardt this time, as well as Beebe and Clair Peterson) for a flight to Bermuda en route to Paris. They landed the second of April,[10] and Arnold was ushered into the suite at the Ritz that Goering had occupied on his triumphant trips to Paris. All the rooms were large and the bathtub, like Goering himself, was huge. "Goering must have sat down with a thud," Arnold observed, "for the porcelain is cracked."

Arnold was in bed by 9:30 the night he arrived, because Dr. Marquardt was determined that he get plenty of sleep—as was George Marshall back in Washington. Marshall had reacted favorably to Arnold's travel plan because it would get him out of Washington, where he was seldom able to relax, but Marshall did not want him to go to Europe and act as if he were still in Washington. The two men had talked earnestly about this before Arnold left for Europe, and Arnold had promised he would take it easy.

He did, at least, get up "late" his first morning in Paris. "The doctor must have given me a slug, for I didn't awaken until 8:15." Then with Tooey Spaatz, Marquardt, and others, he took a drive through Paris ("a sorry city [with] scars from street battles") to the airport, where they took off for Rheims and a long lunch with Eisenhower at his headquarters. After a visit to Spaatz's headquarters, he flew back to Paris in time for drinks with his staff, then dinner and gin rummy. Summing up this "lazy" day, he claimed to have had two hours of bed rest at some time or other, plus a forty-five-minute nap. Dr. Marquardt was already finding that Hap Arnold was a difficult man to restrain.

On April 5 he was up at 7:30 and off to the airport for a tour of bombed-out and occupied Germany—Aachen, Bonn, Cologne, Coblenz, Frankfurt, and Darmstadt, where, at Gen. Alexander M. Patch's headquarters, he found his son Hank awaiting him. He had brought two boxes of gifts for Hank, now a lieutenant colonel and combat veteran, but one of these gifts—liquor—turned out to be superfluous. Hank had just captured a German warehouse full of Scotch and brandy. When Arnold returned to Paris that evening, he took Hank with him.

From the moment of Arnold's arrival in Europe, American war correspondents had been following him, and his statements, mostly about the effectiveness of the American aerial bombardment of Germany, were being reported daily in the newspapers back home. As a result, he received on April 9 a terse cable from Marshall:

> I read of your presence and statements with various active commands. Where is the Bermuda rest, the lazy days at Cannes, the period of retirement at Capri? You are riding for a fall, doctor or no doctor.

Arnold insisted in his reply that "my doctor has been taking care of me. . . . There has not been a single night since I left the U.S. that I went to bed later than 9:30. . . . I am feeling fine and have shown no symptoms of any kind."[11] His visit had done much, he wrote, toward stopping "the many current rumors concerning my being an invalid for life."

A few minutes after he sent this cable, he was off on another trip. This time to the Riviera, where he stayed put for almost three weeks, in another "grand" villa Spaatz had found for himself. This one was "right on the shore of the bay looking across to Cannes." He was there on the thirteenth when Dr. Marquardt came into his room and told him President Roosevelt had died. At this news, Arnold felt the same kind of shock that hit most Americans (Roosevelt had been president for twelve years), followed by personal loss and concern for the Air Forces. While Arnold, like many Army and Navy officers, entertained political beliefs more conservative than Roosevelt's, he had developed a deep admiration and fondness for the president.

"Franklin Roosevelt was not only a personal friend," he wrote later in his memoirs, "but one of the best friends the Air Force ever had. He had supported me in the development of the Air Force and in its global operations to an extent that I little dreamed of a few years before, when I was in the doghouse."[12]

Arnold also said in his memoirs he then had "high hopes of President Truman's support" for the Air Forces, but in fact those hopes were mixed with deep concern because Truman's previous contact with the Air Forces had been less than cordial. As a senator from Missouri, he had chaired a committee investigating wartime waste, and had inevitably found some instances of it in the aircraft procurement program. When Arnold was visiting China in 1943, the senator had even paid a visit to his office, demanding certain files, and when Arnold's secretary, Suzy Adkins, refused to hand them over, pointing out that she had no authorization to do so, Truman had walked out indignantly. The new president had been an Artillery captain in World War I. Would he be sympathetic to the Air Forces, or to the concept of a separate air force? It was something that should not be left to chance.

Spaatz suggested to Arnold that he go right back to Washington because he was the man to lead the campaign for a separate air force, and with the advent of a new administration, this was the time to lay the foundation for it. Even working part-time, Spaatz believed, Arnold could do the job better than anyone else.[13]

Arnold reacted to this with a surprising show of self-preservation. Earlier that day he had announced to Ira Eaker that he would have to come home and run the Air Forces for him, and that he was to bring along Fred Anderson, Doolittle, Cabell, Kuter, and Vandenberg, all of whom were then in Europe. He was thus acknowledging that he could no longer handle the kind of burden to which he had been accustomed. His response to Spaatz's suggestion indicated that he hadn't yet lost respect for his most recent heart attack. "I am of the opinion that I would only make an invalid of myself if I returned before Eaker and the men whom I am getting from Spaatz. I realize that there is much spade-work to be done right now—with a new President, and the war in Germany coming to a close. I cannot see my way clear to deliberately ruin myself again physically, when there is so little chance of permanent change in Air Force activities."

He seemed also, in that observation, to lack confidence that a campaign for a separate air force would succeed. But he wanted his men to fight for it anyway.

By this time, Arnold was tentatively planning to continue on to the Pacific instead of returning home from Europe, but when Marshall learned about this plan, he sent a cable, on April 17, objecting to it:

> I am rather depressed at seeing you start on another of your strenuous trips, this time carrying you around the world. It may demonstrate to the Army and to the public that you certainly are not on the retired list but also it may result in your landing there. I will have to trust your judgment though I have little hope that you can curtail your wasteful expenditure of physical strength and nervous energy.

After reading this, Arnold observed that it didn't "show much confidence in my judgment as to taking care of myself." It did, however, show that Marshall knew his man well, and in the event, Marshall prevailed. Arnold decided to go only as far as Italy, observe the situation there, then return home via South America.

Before he left Cannes, he talked to Spaatz and Eaker about what Eaker would have to do when he got to Washington. Differences arose among these old friends and the discussion became so heated that Eaker said, "I didn't ask to go to Washington."[14]

Whether he knew it or not, he had touched a sore spot. He had reminded Arnold of one of the great frustrations of his life—the fact that although his career as a soldier had spanned two world wars, he had never commanded troops under fire.

"Who in the hell ever did ask to go to Washington?" Arnold shouted. "Do you think I asked to go there and stay there for ten years? Someone has to run the Army Air Forces. We can't all be in command of combat air forces all around the world."

Spaatz quickly stepped in and restored calm, but as usual, Arnold prevailed and Eaker prepared to return home, while Arnold crossed the Alps to Florence, Pisa, Bologna, Foggia, and Naples, then crossed the Mediterranean to Marrakesh and Dakar, and then the Atlantic to Rio. On May 7, when he learned that the Germans had finally surrendered, he was airborne over South America between Santa Cruz and Borinquen, en route to Miami.[15] Awaiting him there was a letter from the new president, Harry Truman. "You have my entire confidence," Truman wrote. It helped to counteract a newspaper clipping also awaiting him which said Truman was going to ask for his resignation.

After several days in Miami for a physical checkup (he could now climb steps and was doing without his daily medicine) he returned to Washington, where he found another letter that must have pleased and perhaps slightly amused him. It was from Henry Morgenthau, his prewar adversary, who now wrote: "I thank you and congratulate you on your great part in getting the machines and men and training and directing our glorious army of the air."[16]

There was also some good news about that "glorious army of the air." His 20th Air Force now had 700 B-29s in the Pacific. The previous June, the 20th was able to manage only 68 sorties over Japan. This June it was expecting to make 5,900. The previous June it had dropped 92 tons of bombs over Japan. This June it would be capable of dropping 59,000 tons.[17] The B-29 was finally doing the job Arnold had demanded of it. And the Pacific air operation was so big that he decided, with the approval of the Joint Chiefs, to send Tooey Spaatz to command it.

The Air Transport Command was now very much on Arnold's mind because, in becoming the largest airline the world had ever seen, it had made him realize the enormous role airlines would play in the postwar world. In 1944, the A.T.C. had carried 1,200,000 passengers and 400,000 tons of cargo all over the world. It now had 3,000 planes operating on worldwide routes. Its success, under Hal George and C. R. Smith, had proven the practicality of airline operations on a massive scale. And the prospects of even larger, jet-propelled planes made Arnold aware that his long-held dreams of an age of flight were soon to become reality. How could the United States protect its national interests in the expanding airline industry, and what role could the Air Forces properly play?

These were not new questions in Arnold's mind. A year earlier, on March 25, 1944, he had written a memorandum to President Roosevelt on the subject, in which he pointed out that air power, now vital to the nation, would depend on the peacetime existence of a strong aircraft-manufacturing industry; that a strong, American-owned international air transport system would be important because it could readily be adapted to military use; and that, therefore, the national policy should include "maximum encouragement of regulated private competitive enterprise in United States international air transport operation."

With the war almost won, he was approaching the problem on a more immediate basis in May of 1945. He had already arranged to sell A.T.C. transport planes to the airlines as soon as they were no longer needed for military use. (He thought, incidentally, that his friend, and his son's father-in-law, Donald Douglas, was planning to charge too much for converting Army transports to civilian standards.) He was encouraging the airlines to hire discharged Air Forces pilots. And he was suggesting that, to avoid delay, the airlines work out a plan to take over from the Air Forces contracts for new but unneeded transport planes.

In a May 28 memo to C. R. Smith (now a major general), who would soon be returning to his civilian post as president of American Airlines, he offered advice on the best way to hasten the expansion of the entire airline industry:

> I am convinced that now more than ever before it is essential that the airlines have one man who can bring them together and who can think out ways and means of increasing their efficiency, taking advantage in every way possible of any aid that the government can give them.

Arnold was still, at heart, as much a dreamer and builder now as he had been before the war. He had realized his own ambition and built his own edifice—the U.S. Army Air Forces. And with his health uncertain, he understood—sadly, no doubt—that he himself would do no more building. But he couldn't resist the urge to hurry others, in this case the airline people, toward their goals.

After a month in Washington, during which he had some pleasant and reassuring visits with President Truman, Arnold once again exercised his option to get out of town and see what his men were doing in the theaters of action. He took off June 6 for California en route to the Pacific.[18] After landing at Hamilton Field north of San Francisco, he spent two days at his ranch near Sonoma, where he took pictures, bought feed for the few animals on hand, put men to work on various

Arnold looked him in the eye and said, "If Stalin could hear you say that, he'd hang you up by the balls."[21]

Did that mean Arnold favored or disfavored the use of the great new bomb? Stone couldn't tell.

While Arnold was in the Philippines he drove out to Fort McKinley, where he had been stationed in the early days of his career, and tried to find the house he and Bee had occupied. All he could find was the concrete steps leading up to the porch.

From Manila, he flew directly to Okinawa, where, after a welcome by several generals and admirals, he met his son Bruce, who, like his son Hank in Europe, was now a combat veteran.[22] Bruce and his artillery unit had waded ashore with the initial wave of American troops the day Okinawa was invaded—the first of April—and they were still seeing sporadic action. Arnold took Bruce to dinner at Tenth Army headquarters, and afterward they had some time to themselves.

Like any father whose son is in a battle situation, Arnold was worried about Bruce and wanted to give him some advice based on information he had picked up in Guam. He had been told that Japanese troops there, after killing some American guards, had committed atrocities upon them.

Visibly uncomfortable, he said to Bruce, "They cut off their . . ." He hesitated as if he didn't know how to continue. He had never found it easy to use vulgar language. He might do so, on a rare occasion, in front of a man like Chuck Stone, whom he had known for a long time, but he had never talked that way in front of his own sons. Flustered but determined, he said finally, "their 'peters.'"

Bruce was momentarily surprised by his father's evident embarrassment, but when he reflected upon it, he realized that within the Arnold family, "we had never talked about our bodies." His father was still so Victorian in his sexual attitudes that "he couldn't even talk Army talk with me." But as Bruce realized how difficult it had been for his father to tell him that story, he also realized why his father had done so. Arnold obviously believed the danger that such a thing could happen to his son was very real, and he was therefore obliged to warn Bruce despite his own embarrassment.

During his inspections on Okinawa, Arnold concluded that more airfields would have to be built immediately for the B-29s he was planning to send there, as well as more ports and post facilities. It seemed to him there was a logjam in the existing ports, which were crowded with ships waiting to be unloaded. Concerned about this, he flew back to Guam for more conferences with Nimitz, who graciously promised him that everything would move along on schedule. Thus reassured, he flew back to San Francisco (via Eniwetok, Johnson Island, and Hawaii), arriving there on June 25, his birthday.

Bee and Lois were both on hand to greet him with birthday celebration plans all set, but alas for Bee, her husband's career foiled her again as it had done so often through the years.[23] It was understandable that she should lose her patience. It was not always easy to live with Hap and his Air Forces. This time it was the president of the United States who foreclosed his birthday celebration. Harry Truman also arrived in San Francisco on June 25, and Arnold had to attend an official dinner that night. By the following evening he was out of the family doghouse and the celebration of his fifty-ninth birthday took place at the ranch, one day late. After a few days there together, he and Bee flew home to Washington in time to see Dave off for West Point the following Sunday.

Arnold stayed less than two weeks in Washington this time before flying to Europe on July 11, for the Potsdam Conference. After a day's fishing in Canada and a short stop in Paris, he and his party, which included Fred Dean and Lauris Norstad, arrived in Berchtesgaden on the fourteenth, where Arnold occupied Himmler's hotel suite and rode around in an open touring car that had belonged to the late Adolf Hitler.[24] Arnold had come there primarily to find Hank, whose unit was supposed to be stationed nearby, and eventually they did make connections. With the permission of his commanding officer, Hank joined their party the next day when they took off for Berlin.

On the morning of the sixteenth, the American Joint Chiefs met to discuss the coming conference, but spent much of the time discussing instead what should be done with the powerful new weapon that was due to be tested any day now. If it worked, should it be used against Japan? Arnold said he was certain that B-29s with conventional bombs could force the Japanese to surrender. Admiral King said his naval blockade would eventually starve them into surrender. Marshall said the Japanese ought to be warned about the bomb before it was dropped, in the hope that they would be persuaded to surrender.

Later that day, the Joint Chiefs assembled with their British counterparts for a pleasant meeting, unaware that, even as they talked, something far more earthshaking than any item on the conference agenda was taking place near Alamogordo, New Mexico. That evening, President Truman would learn about it from a cable received by Secretary of War Stimson. But Marshall and Arnold were not to learn about it until the following day. At lunch on the seventeenth they were told that Stimson wanted to see them. When they reached his villa, he showed them the now-famous cable from Washington that informed him that the first atomic bomb had been successfully detonated in the New Mexico desert:

> Operated on this morning. Diagnosis not yet complete but results seem satisfactory and already exceed expectations. Local press release necessary as interest extends great distance.

Stimson, Marshall, and Arnold sat down immediately to discuss the possible use of the astonishing new weapon against Japan. It has been suggested that because Arnold believed his Air Forces could defeat Japan without the bomb, he therefore opposed the use of it. The evidence disproves this. As he himself described the meeting with Stimson and Marshall, it was not a debate over whether the bomb should be used; the questions were when and where. Arnold pointed out that Spaatz had planes and carefully trained crews in the Pacific, awaiting the arrival of the bomb, and suggested that the question of the targets should be turned over to him.

The next day at Potsdam passed quietly, with nothing substantial happening as yet. Arnold and Marshall were chatting together when Arnold suggested that with the war coming to an end, both of them should consider retirement. Neither of them could continue to work as they had for the last four years, he said, "with our necks up in the collars." Arnold was as concerned about Marshall's health as Marshall was about his. Marshall said he agreed, but Arnold didn't believe him. He offered to bet five dollars that Marshall would still be on the job six months after Japan surrendered, and Marshall took the bet.

The same afternoon, Arnold ran into Dwight Eisenhower, who would almost certainly become Army chief of staff when Marshall did retire, and asked him whom he would like to have as Arnold's successor in the Air Forces. Ike needed no time for discussion. He wanted Spaatz, and Arnold agreed with him.

The Potsdam Conference, attended by Truman, Stalin, and Churchill, with Clement Attlee replacing Churchill as British prime minister while the meetings were in progress, settled certain important questions about postwar Europe. But the talks were conducted in a strange, tentative atmosphere, not only because of the change of power in England, but also because the meetings were overshadowed by the one item that was not discussed—the atomic bomb. On the twenty-fourth, Truman and Churchill met with their combined chiefs and approved the step-by-step military strategy the chiefs recommended for the final stages of the war against Japan. These steps included the invasion contemplated for late 1945, the efforts to get Russia into the Pacific war, and the use of the British fleet in the assault upon Japan. But Truman said nothing to his British allies that day about the atomic bomb. (He did, however, mention it privately to Churchill.)

Later on the twenty-fourth, Truman, Stimson, Marshall, and Arnold met privately to discuss possible targets for the bomb and the matter of timing. The president accepted Arnold's suggestion that Spaatz, whose planes would deliver the bomb, be given a list of four targets—Hiroshima, Kokura, Niigata, and Nagasaki—and he should then be offered "some latitude as to when and on which of the four targets the bomb would be dropped." Thus the decision was made, and Arnold was part of it.

While he was in Potsdam, Arnold wrote to Bee almost daily—warm and loving "My darling Beetle" letters, solicitous about her health. He was especially worried about her weight, which had been much too low for some time. "I haven't heard from you and hope that you are putting on those 25 pounds," he wrote on July 22. "I want a couple of more curves. How about it? I miss you a lot." And two days later, he repeated the same theme: "Hope to see you soon with the additional 25 pounds."

As a result of her Air Forces relief work, for which she had earned universal praise, the Royal Air Force had invited her to England to inspect its benevolent fund and suggest ways to improve it in accordance with what she had helped to accomplish at home. The U.S. Army Air Forces was in the process of creating an agency to take care of the widows and orphans of airmen. Sir Charles Portal spoke to Arnold several times in Potsdam about her proposed trip and how eager he was to have her come, but the plans had developed a snag she couldn't circumvent. The Army had a wartime regulation prohibiting the wife of any officer or enlisted man from visiting the theater in which he was stationed. The purpose of the regulation was obvious. Since it would be impossible and insane to have all servicemen take their wives into the war zones, there had to be a rule forbidding any of them to do so. Because Arnold was now on duty in Europe, both Robert Lovett and Ira Eaker believed they would be violating that regulation if they approved her trip.[25] They may also have feared that if they allowed the commanding general's wife to disregard the regulation, they would be flooded with travel requests from the wives of other generals. In any case, Eaker did not authorize the trip, and though Arnold, as he said to Portal in Potsdam, thought that "Eaker and Lovett are getting too cautious," he did not countermand Eaker's action.

None of this improved Bee's disposition. When Arnold and his son Hank returned to Washington on July 30, Hank was alarmed at his mother's condition. "She wasn't well at all—hysteria, screaming, throwing things."[26] But Hank was impressed by his father's kindness to her. "My father was actually a saint with her. He wouldn't put up with that from me."

One day, after they had been back in Washington about a month, Arnold turned to his son and in his usual blunt manner said, "You know, your mother is sick."

Bee's emotional episodes continued to bewilder her husband. He told Hank that after one of them he had given her a watch as a present, and she had thrown it back at him. If she had been a man, Hap Arnold could have coped with that. He would probably have thought no more of it than the incident during which he and Rosie O'Donnell had exchanged a paperweight at point-blank range. But he still suffered from his lifelong inability to cope with women and their emotions.

"I just don't understand these things about women," he said to Hank. "I guess I never will."

Hank couldn't help feeling sorry for both of his parents. He knew his father loved his mother deeply—that was evident in his patience with her. It was equally evident that Bee returned his love. He wasn't the easiest man in the world to get along with, yet she had done so for more than thirty years. But she was now fifty-eight years old. She had raised her children and they were gone; her husband had suffered four serious heart attacks, would soon have to retire, and might drop dead at any moment. The fabric of her life was changing drastically. The story seemed to be coming to an end and she was understandably deeply disturbed by it.

Not knowing what result to expect from the atomic bomb, Arnold went to work at the beginning of August on the redeployment of more air strength to the Pacific. But on the fifth, this effort began to appear superfluous. Aware of what was scheduled that day (it was August 6 in the Far East), Arnold waited at home, hoping to get the first news of it on the private White House wire that had been installed in his quarters. He assumed that even though President Truman was still in mid-Atlantic on the cruiser *Augusta,* en route home from Potsdam, the White House would get the news before it became public, or even before it was transmitted by Spaatz's headquarters. It was early evening when the cable came:

> Hiroshima bombed visually with one tenth [cloud] cover at 052315A [August 5, 7:15 p.m. in Washington]. There was no fighter opposition and no flak. Parsons [weaponer aboard the *Enola Gay*] reports 15 minutes after bomb as follows: "Results clear-cut successful in all respects. Visible effects greater than in any test. Condition normal in airplane following delivery.

The days passed thereafter with everyone in Washington wondering why Japan refused to surrender. The devastation at Hiroshima was only a small part of the destruction Arnold's B-29s had visited upon Japan. With high-explosive bombs alone, the 20th Air Force had levelled 2,333,000 homes in Japan, and most of the business and industry in sixty of its cities. These conventional bombings had killed at least 240,000 people and wounded more than 300,000. The nation lay in ruins even before the ultimate bomb fell on Hiroshima. On the ninth, since there was no word from Tokyo, another atomic bomb fell—this one at Nagasaki, but still there was no surrender. On the eleventh, Arnold sent an order instructing Spaatz to drop leaflets over what was left of Japan's bombed-out and burned-out cities, telling the people what was happening and urging them to come to terms.

Finally, on August 15, official word arrived. The Japanese government of Prime Minister Kantaro Suzuki had accepted the unconditional surrender terms agreed upon at the Potsdam Conference.

The Arnolds had finished their evening meal when the news arrived.[27] That afternoon they had entertained British Air Marshal Arthur Harris at a small reception, and a few of the guests were still there, including Hank and his wife, Kaye. There was no loud outcry when the news became official, perhaps because, for several hours, everyone in the house had known it was coming. Within a few minutes, however, old friends began dropping in and soon the house was crowded. Hank took over the bartending duties while his father shook hands with each new arrival.

After a while, George Marshall, who lived only a few doors down the street, walked in quietly. As usual, his presence commanded attention and he thanked the officers in the room for their help in the war effort. Then he and Arnold shook hands and congratulated each other. That was all.

T he end of World War II marked, in effect, the end of Hap Arnold's active career. Though it was not until six months later, on February 9, 1946, that he resigned as commanding general, Army Air Forces, the dynamic drive for which he had become famous began to diminish soon after Germany and Japan surrendered. He was a tired man, his energy drained by seven years of unremitting effort to build the Air Forces, his personal life upset by his bewildering difficulties with his wife, and his very existence threatened by the four heart attacks he had suffered. By any reasonable measurement, he was a casualty of the war.

He continued to preside over the Air Forces. He directed the effort toward unification of the armed services and parity among the Army, Navy, and Air Force, but other men (notably Carl Spaatz) carried the heavy burden in that campaign. He steered the Air Forces toward a continuing program of scientific research and technological development. He watched his staff reduce the size of the forces from 2,400,000 people and 72,000 airplanes to a half million people and 10,000 planes. But he insisted that the relatively new Air Transport Command survive the demobilization. It would be needed, he said, as a link between installations around the world, and as a means of deploying troops quickly in case of an emergency.[1] At the same time, he suggested that surplus aircraft be melted down and the metal be salvaged. His advice about the A.T.C. prevailed but his effort to save metals was ignored.

During much of September, Bee was in California, which left him alone in Washington. He had now shortened his work day, coming home usually in the early afternoon to write to her, rest for an hour or so, and walk the dogs. His letters showed his continuing concern about her health: "All my love—get some curves, eat well, be your own sweet self and come home to your Hap."[2]

In October he wrote a remarkable article entitled "Our Power to Destroy War," in which he argued for a continuing national research and development program, but to the surprise of those who knew him, not necessarily for an endless commitment to military aircraft:

If the nations of the world find that they cannot act in concert, our possession of power will be our only resource. Therefore we must at all cost maintain it.

What do we need to maintain it?

I will start by emphasizing that I am not holding any brief for a permanent air force in terms of the mighty air forces we built up during the war. What we will need is an adequate, well-trained, fully equipped force of whatever kind is necessary to use the new weapons and devices properly.

This was the man who, more than any other, had brought the airplane and the U.S. Air Forces to the ultimate moment of power. In 1945, only an airplane could have delivered the atomic bombs to Hiroshima and Nagasaki. The release of those bombs was the culmination of the campaign Billy Mitchell, Arnold, and others had waged in favor of air power since the end of World War I. On the day of the Hiroshima cataclysm, the Air Forces Arnold had built were capable of dominating the entire world. But now, only two months later, he was telling the airmen who would follow him that if something better came along, they must be ready ruthlessly to discard the airplane.

In late October, he flew to Mexico as President Truman's representative to try to build up that country's air strength. And on November 8, he wrote a memorandum to George Marshall recommending his own retirement from active duty. But he was still on active duty later that month when Marshall resigned as chief of staff to become ambassador to China. Did this mean Marshall had won their five-dollar bet as to which of them would retire first? Arnold didn't think so, because Marshall's China job could hardly be considered a retirement. At Christmastime he exchanged letters with Bob Lovett, who had already retired and was sitting in the Florida sun, dreadfully missing the Air Forces.[3]

In early January, with Bee and Lois, Arnold embarked on a trip to South America representing the president in hemisphere aviation matters. He intended to visit Colombia, Peru, Chile, Brazil, and Argentina, but the high altitude in Bogotá affected his heart and by the time he reached Lima he had developed a flutter severe enough to make him call off the rest of the trip and return to the hospital in Coral Gables. When he flew from there to Washington in early February, it was only for his retirement ceremony.

One of his last acts, as part of the retirement process, was to gather his headquarters personnel in the Pentagon auditorium and talk to them about what they had been through, what they were going through, and what kind of future they might expect. He talked about the infancy and growth of the Air Forces, the huge wartime expansion, and the current contraction. He talked about supersonic aircraft, rockets, and the exploration of space. He described a world of the future, a world he could envision but would probably never see. He warned them to be ready for this world, to anticipate the changes to come, to be willing to discard the obsolete, however sentimentally attached to it they might be, and to examine new ideas, however outlandish they might appear at first glance. Only by making the maximum use of science, technology, and imagination could the Air Forces hope to maintain the strength necessary for the defense of the nation.

At the end of his speech he paused and looked down at all the familiar faces in front of him. "I know you people think the old man has lost his marbles and ought to retire," he told them. "But I hope you'll all remember what I said here today."[4]

The Arnolds spent the rest of February closing out their Fort Myer quarters, and to the extent Hap's health would allow, attending farewell parties in their honor. Since Hap was physically limited, the heavy burden fell on Bee, and she worked too hard, not only on the arrangements for their move from Washington, but on the Air Forces relief problems that still engrossed her. She seemed unable to relax and control her own moods. She might act quite normally one minute, then a minute later explode emotionally. Like her husband, though to a lesser degree, she too was a casualty of the war.

At one of the parties they attended, a National Press Club luncheon, a correspondent asked Arnold what he intended to do in retirement.

"I'm going out to my ranch in the Valley of the Moon," he said, "to sit under an oak tree. From there I'll look across the valley at the white-faced cattle. And if one of them even moves too fast, I'll look the other way."

Did this mean he was all through with airplanes? "Yes!" he cried. "If one dares to fly low over my ranch house, I'll grab a rifle or something and shoot it down."[5]

He and Bee set out for California in their fully loaded new Packard Clipper on the first of March, but not with the intention of settling immediately into their ranch. Their new house wasn't quite finished and the road up to it was in the process of improvement. But they did stop and inspect the progress before continuing on to San Francisco, where Lois and Ernie had offered them the use of their apartment for as long as they might need it.[6]

It was the summer of 1946 before the Arnolds were able to move into their ranch house in the Valley of the Moon. There was nothing the least bit pretentious about the place. The house had three bedrooms, a tiny kitchen, and a modest living room, which looked out upon the grandeur of the lovely hills and valleys surrounding it. They hoped eventually to build a larger house and use this one for guests, but that would have to wait until they had more money and building materials became easier to get. In 1946, the country was still feeling the pinch of wartime scarcities, just as Arnold was feeling the pinch of retirement on limited funds. Though the property had cost only $7,500, he did not have, after forty-two years in the service, enough cash to pay for it in full. Both the land and the new house were under heavy mortgages. Aside from his two $10,000 insurance policies and a few hundred dollars in the bank, his only financial asset was his pension, about $12,000 a year. He and Bee could live on that, but not in the style to which he had become accustomed as a five-star general. His lack of funds was eloquent testimony to his honesty in handling billions of dollars worth of government contracts, but it would hardly facilitate the happy retirement he had been looking forward to.

He had never fully recovered from his last heart attack, but his medical problems were somewhat alleviated when Dr. Russell Lee began coming up to see him every two weeks, out of simple friendship. Lee had returned to civilian life and to his clinic at Palo Alto (he was also a Stanford Medical School professor), but his association with the Air Forces had made him such an aviation enthusiast he now owned a plane, a little Aercoupe. He would fly it to Sonoma and set it down in a field, where Arnold would be waiting to greet him and guide him with hand signals. It amused Lee to think of himself, an amateur pilot, with "a five-star general shagging me in to land in a pasture."[7]

At the doctor's suggestion, Arnold began to increase his liquor allotment. He had been drinking two Old Fashioneds a day, and he continued to drink only two, but he began serving himself from a larger glass which naturally called for larger amounts. Lee's visits also reminded him to watch his diet, and gave him someone to whom he could talk about his active years. Yet these visits were dampened to some degree by the fact that Bee and the doctor unmistakably disliked each other. To her, he was one of those medical men who had tried to keep her away from Hap after the heart attacks. She felt he was not as compassionate as he might have been.[8] She also seemed to think he had arranged for Hap to meet other women, and there was no way to convince her this was untrue.

Arnold spent a lot of time on the land with M. Sgt. Bruce Simmons, who had been assigned to him as an aide. Simmons thought of him almost as a father now, and his affection for Simmons was obvious, though he would never admit it. Simmons and his wife occupied a house near the gate of the ranch and helped the Arnolds in every way they could. The two men would drive to Sonoma together and Arnold, still addicted to sweets, would buy pastries at the local bakery shop to augment the bowl of soup or the salad that had been his entire meal at home.[9]

Simmons preferred to do the driving on the excursions, but Arnold would insist he was quite capable of it. One day he slammed into the rear of a bricklayer's car and turned it over. Immediately he began cussing his victim.

"Get that car out of the way!" he demanded. "Get it out of there!"

"But, General, it was your fault," Simmons suggested.

"Don't tell me it was my fault!" he cried, and forgetting the bricklayer, he began cussing Simmons. He never did admit his blame, but Simmons took the bricklayer's name and Bee sent the man a check to cover the damage.

Such incidents at least brought back a bit of his old spark, but they were not frequent. In the fall of 1946, Gov. Earl Warren appointed him a California fish and game commissioner, which pleased him but hardly kept him busy. Since he couldn't keep up with Simmons in serious work projects, he would sit in the sun and gaze at the far-off hills. Or he would write letters. He kept up his correspondence with old associates like Bob Lovett, who was back with the Wall Street brokerage house of Brown Brothers Harriman; and George Marshall, who was in China until the end of 1946, then in Washington as secretary of state. "It is a great relief not to be burdened with War Department responsibilities," Marshall wrote, "but my troubles have merely been transferred to another issue and other surroundings while you fish and shoot, dammit."[10]

Arnold did fish and shoot on occasion, but he lacked the stamina to do it often. He traveled infrequently now. At home he puttered in his woodworking shop, where he had made the redwood furniture for the patio. He watched his livestock grow—a flock of chickens, several ornery geese, which chased people out of the yard, a few white-faced Hereford calves, which Simmons was fattening. And when his papers and documents arrived from Washington (through Hamilton Field, where the Air Forces still maintained an office for him), he got to work on his memoirs. To this project he devoted himself seriously. Several friends had told him he could make a lot of money by publishing the story of his wartime experiences, and he badly needed money. He was worried about leaving his wife destitute. He was well aware that when he died, his pension would stop, and thereafter she would receive only a token monthly sum. And the proceeds of his insurance policies wouldn't last very long. He signed a book contract with Harper and Brothers, then, after completing to his satisfaction the enormous task of organizing his letters and official papers, sat down at his typewriter to begin his story. He wasted no time getting to the dominant theme of his life: "The first airplane I ever saw was . . ."

When, at the time of his retirement, he told an audience of Washington newsmen he wanted to have nothing more to do with airplanes, he had been speaking in jest. But at his ranch one day, he had occasion to feel that way seriously. Two AT-6 training planes, staging a mock dogfight in the sky above his property, collided, sending one of them into a careening dive toward his house. After the pilot bailed out, the damaged craft plummeted directly toward Arnold's roof, and he could do nothing but stand by helplessly, waiting to see the house smashed by the impact, then burned to the ground by exploding airplane gas. But at the moment of apparent disaster, as the plane seemed certain to hit the roof, it made one last lurch and missed by inches, bursting into flames at the edge of a pasture, just a few yards away.

In November 1947, Arnold had to return to Washington to testify before a Senate subcommittee investigating one of his former officers, Gen. Bennett Meyers. The senators were accusing Meyers of using his position as an Air Forces procurement officer to enhance the value of stock he secretly held in manufacturing companies. Though Arnold was in no way involved in Meyers's dealings, the revelations about Meyers were a source of embarrassment, pain, perhaps even anguish to him.

"If, to our regret, we of the Air Force did not find a rotten apple in our barrel," he told the subcommittee, "we are grateful that others have done so. If we were at fault in not finding it, we must admit our fault. . . . We thought we had reason to rely on the integrity as well as ability of men entrusted with high responsibility."[11]

Less than two months later, in January 1948, Arnold was in bed again with another heart attack, this one so serious it kept him down for three months. It was Dr. Lee who put him to bed (at that time bedrest rather than regulated exercise was considered the best therapy for heart patients), but it was Bee who made him stay there, and while he didn't always appreciate her insistence, he acknowledged, after he was on his feet again, that it was she who "put me on the road to recovery."[12]

Bruce Arnold, who often spent weekends and leave time at the ranch, felt that his parents were "completely compatible and extremely loving to each other" during this period.[13] He never heard his mother raise her voice or show anger toward anyone. He found her as warm-hearted, loving, and protective of her husband as she had always been.

Henry Arnold, Jr., has conceded that there may have been "a certain amount of strain" between his parents, but he also pointed out that, if so, it was understandable. "Mother was working [during the war] as much as 14–16 hours a day at her duties as head of the Air Force Relief Society, frequently to the point of total exhaustion. . . . And to complicate matters, so much of my father's work was classified, even the trips that he took, that he could not discuss any of it with my mother, as he had always done throughout their life previous to the war." As for any difficulties there might have been between them during their retirement years, Hank made an observation no one could deny: "Their complete devotion to each other, to the day my father died, was a fact of life in our immediate family, and absolutely legendary among friends who knew them intimately."

David Arnold, like his brothers, saw very little tension between his parents. While acknowledging that "they naturally had their off moments," he too recalled that "Mother was working a 12-to-16-hour day plus all her travels and Dad was gone a large amount of the time. When they were together they were a loving and friendly couple."

If there was stress between the Arnolds, it was, indeed, understandable. A lifetime with a man as professionally dedicated and personally tumultuous as Hap Arnold could not have left Bee Arnold totally unaffected.

While Hap lay in bed trying to regain his strength, he also became more conscious than ever of a long-standing concern about his daughter, Lois, and her husband, Ernie Snowden, now a commander in the peacetime Navy. Arnold had known for a long time that they both drank excessively. One day, deciding he should no longer remain silent about it, he wrote them a letter, which came as close to being tactful as Hap Arnold could get:

> This must be read as one of those father to son and daughter letters. These letters are not easy to write, but I believe necessary. . . . For some time I have been convinced that you are both drinking more than people of your age should—more than does you any good—so much that it may be detrimental to your future. Won't you both think this over carefully? . . . Everyone in the services that I have met who knows you has you spotted as real outstanding people.
>
> I am not preaching—for God knows I am not that kind—but where you have so much ahead of you, why spoil it?[14]

In mid-May 1948, Bee traveled east to see her aging mother. Arnold had recovered sufficiently to be left alone with the two dogs, but without his wife, he wrote the Snowdens, "the house seems sort of empty."[15] He kept as busy as possible dictating his autobiography, in which he had reached the year 1940, but he wasn't able to work full days on the book.

"It seems like years since they put me to bed," he wrote to Lois and Ernie on May 23. "Now I am allowed to go around the farm but there are all kinds of restrictions placed upon me that keep me under control. I cannot go to town, San Francisco, as yet, but they tell me I can sometime soon. I cannot climb hills. I must not get tired. However, when you have two strikes on you, I guess that a fellow can't be too choosey."

In June, indications came from West Point that David, finishing his third year there, was likely to encounter the same difficulty as Hank and Bruce had in passing the eye examination for flight training. It looked as if Hap Arnold would never have a son in the Air Force. One day he called Bruce, now stationed at Point Mugu in southern California, and asked him urgently to come up to Sonoma for a visit.

When Bruce arrived, his father sat him at a table, then settled down across from him and put a full bottle of bourbon between them.

"If necessary, we're going to sit here and finish this bottle," he said, "while you convince me why you can't transfer to the Air Force."

They talked for a long time and Bruce explained the basic problem. In the Air Force, the highest ranks and the best jobs were reserved almost exclusively for flying officers. But he was not and could not become a pilot. Arnold, unable to deny that this had always been so, insisted that times were changing because of new technology, and that henceforth, a nonflying officer would be able to go all the way to the top if he had the ability. Bruce was not convinced. It seemed to him that a career officer in the Air Force who couldn't fly would feel "like a eunuch in a harem."

Finally Arnold looked across at Bruce and said plaintively, "God-dammit, can't I have at least one son in the Air Force?"

It was the first time in Bruce's life that his father had ever pleaded with him for anything. They had never been close. Bruce had always felt his father was not interested in his choice of a career. From childhood he remembered his father saying that Hank would go to West Point, whereas Bruce could go to school wherever he pleased. He had been convinced, even at that early age, that his father didn't care about him. At the same time, he hadn't exactly envied Hank, who suffered the first-born's fate of seeing his freedom of choice foreclosed. Now, as Bruce faced his father across the bottle of whiskey and all of these memories flooded through him, he felt the rules were suddenly being changed and he was getting a "dose of Hank's medicine." He didn't like it. Yet his understanding of his father had deepened in recent years, and as he gazed at this once strong but now wasted man who had dominated his life, he was overcome with sympathy for him.

"Sure, Pop," he said.

Bruce stayed several days, well aware of his father's deteriorating condition. It was during this visit Hap said to him, "It's hell to be sick. They want to keep me alive by wrapping me in cotton and placing me in a glass case, but I'll be goddamned if I'll let them." As soon as Bruce returned to Point Mugu, he began arranging for his transfer to the Air Force.

Bee returned from Philadelphia the seventeenth of June[16] and she was not in the best of moods. There were difficult moments between them during the rest of that summer. Near the end of June, Hank arrived with his wife, Kaye, their young son, Hankie, and Kaye's mother. Though they stayed at a cottage on Dillon's Beach, about twenty-five miles away, they spent much of their time at the ranch, which made the days there somewhat hectic but also produced an unexpected benefit. Hank put up several tons of hay for his father.

Though Arnold was pleased with the progress of his book, Harper and Brothers, apparently deciding that what they had seen of the manuscript would need work, sent a professional writer, William R. Laidlaw, to help him with it. Laidlaw, who had been a lieutenant colonel in the Eighth Air Force during the war, was familiar with much of Arnold's story, which proved to be an advantage in their collaboration, but there were also disadvantages. Arnold could be a difficult man under the best conditions. Now his health was a factor in everything he tried to do. He may also have resented the publisher's presumption that he needed help. And he quickly formed the impression that Laidlaw wanted to overemphasize the role of the Eighth Air Force in winning the war. The two men did find a way to work together, but they got into some loud and ludicrous arguments about it.

One day, after a raucous blowout between them, Arnold threw the manuscript on the ground in front of the guest house near Sonoma where Laidlaw and his wife, Helen, were staying.

Laidlaw said, "You pick that up or we're through."

Arnold finally did so, then drove away. Two days later, he gathered up great bunches of vegetables from his garden, drove back to the Laidlaws' and presented them to Helen. Bill Laidlaw shook hands with

him and all differences seemed to have been forgotten. When Arnold
left, Laidlaw walked out to the car with him.

As Arnold started the car, Laidlaw happened to be standing behind
it in the gravel driveway. "Stay where you are," Arnold called out to him.
"I've got something else for you!"

Thereupon, he shoved the gas pedal all the way to the floor and
showered Laidlaw with gravel from his spinning wheels as he sped
away.[17]

Despite such incidents, they managed to finish the book together
and it was scheduled for publication in the fall of 1949. Arnold waited
with great expectations. The memoirs of several famous World War II
figures had already been published and had done well. Arnold's
publisher was anticipating a sale of between 60,000 and 80,000 copies;
Arnold himself, improving on that, envisioned a sale of 100,000.[18]

When the book was finished, Arnold had very little to do. He helped
edit a piece he had written for the *National Geographic* magazine entitled,
"My Life in the Valley of the Moon." He made his life there appear to be
much more idyllic than it actually was. Why, he asked, had he chosen to
retire in the Valley of the Moon. First of all, because it was one of three
places in the country where his wife didn't suffer from hay fever. But
apart from that:

> Does one need further reason than a family of unafraid deer not
> more than a few hundred feet away from his back door; or three
> coveys of quail that come to the house to get feed and water morning
> and night; or the dozens of humming birds, and many other species
> of birds, that come daily to the bird baths. . . . ?
> Could one ask more than expansive horizons of softly rolling
> wooded hills stretching away to blue-misted mountains; or the
> fascination of the valley itself—the colorful woof and warp of its
> history, its serene indifference to the driving, restless tempo of
> today, its charming devotion to the gracious living, the leisureliness,
> the romance of a yesteryear?[19]

It was more than a dream. The charm of the Valley of the Moon was
there, just as Arnold, and Jack London before him, described it. But
Arnold was no longer steeping himself in the charm and beauty of the
place as much as he pretended. His strength and vitality were diminishing almost daily. He had struck up a friendship with a Sonoma
physician, Dr. Robert Mollenhauer, whom Dr. Lee had recommended to
him. When he would become short of breath, or when his ankles would
swell, indicating he had retained too much fluid, he would go to
Mollenhauer, who would give him digitalis or whatever medication was

indicated. At this time, Mollenhauer happened to be building a new house, and Arnold, limited now in what he could do to occupy his time, would come, not for treatment, but to sit and watch the carpenters at work. His gradual debilitation was obvious to Dr. Mollenhauer. At each visit, he would be slightly thinner.[20]

To while away his hours, Arnold used also to visit some neighbors he had met through Bill Laidlaw, Gordon and Josephine Tevis, but they seldom visited the Arnolds because Mrs. Tevis didn't like Bee. Since Hap had been told by the doctors not to walk any more than necessary, he would ride to the Tevis ranch on a scooter and sit for an hour or so, making small talk. It seemed to Josephine Tevis that the man was completely at loose ends. She would invite him to dinner when Bee was out of town.[21]

During one of Bee's trips, Lois came to the ranch so there would be someone in the house with her father, but her drinking had begun to affect her nerves, and it was not easy even for him to get along with her. She was in the kitchen one day with her back to the glass door when Simmons came and knocked. She jumped in fright, then accused him of sneaking up on her. Arnold came into the kitchen and sided with her, as he often did, but the next day he took Simmons to Sonoma and bought him an ice cream cone. It was as close as he could come to apologizing.[22]

Arnold, having always been soft with Lois, could hardly change now when her condition seemed almost as hopeless as his own. Her attachment to him had become so obsessive that she tended to become hostile to anyone else who was attached to him. She hadn't been able to get along very well with her mother for several years. At one time she had been cordial to Simmons, but that cordiality had faded as the comradeship between Simmons and her father deepened.

Arnold still heard from old friends. Dwight Eisenhower wrote to him in March 1949,[23] about the soon-to-be successful struggle to unite the services and make the Air Force equal to the Army and Navy. Charles Portal wrote to him about his quiet life in peacetime England.[24] Charles Lindbergh wrote to tell him how much he had enjoyed their association.[25] And there was a letter from the White House, dated May 27, which pleased him mightily. President Truman wrote to say he had just signed a bill making Arnold the first (and still the only) permanent five-star general of the Air Force.

It became an occasion for a family celebration. Hap summoned Dr. Lee and another friend, one-time aide Harry Chesley, then arranged for a B-17 to fly them east, stopping to pick up Bruce at Point Mugu and Hank at Camp Carson, Colorado. After a White House ceremony during which President Truman bestowed a permanent five-star insignia, the entire party flew to West Point where Bee met them. She had been visiting her mother and sister Lois on Long Island. The Arnolds then attended David's graduation, followed by his marriage to a beautiful young New Yorker, Miss Jean Simmons. Bee returned to Long Island after the celebration and the rest of the party flew west.

Several days later, David and his bride came to California on leave. Hap's pride in his youngest son was increased by the fact that David was also entering the Air Force, as a ground officer. Hap would now have two sons in the service he loved.

David couldn't help noticing the pleasure his father took in the hilly land that was his home.[26] It was the only land Hap Arnold had ever owned. Since childhood David had heard him talk about retiring on the West Coast, in beautiful country with a trout stream running through it. He had all of that except the trout stream, but David wondered sadly how much longer he would be there to enjoy it. Hap was pitifully thin and much of his strength was gone.

In the autumn of 1949, Bob Lovett came to the ranch for a visit.[27] He was making periodic trips to California because he was once again on the board of directors and the executive committee of the Union Pacific Railroad. He found his old friend Hap noticeably thin and "slowed up," but with good skin color. They talked about the Air Force, old and new—matters Arnold couldn't discuss with anyone else he was now seeing. It seemed to bring back some of his lifelong passion for the air.

By this time he had begun work on the article *Encyclopaedia Britannica* wanted him to write about military aviation. Though he no longer found it as easy as it once had been to marshal his thoughts on the subject, he eventually finished a first draft and put it in the mail.

At the end of September, his autobiographical book, *Global Mission,* was published and received good reviews, though he himself was not happy with it. Sizable sections of his original manuscript had been deleted. He was eager for its success, however, because he was more than ever conscious of the need to build an estate for Bee. He went to San Francisco to help promote the book, and in one afternoon at the City of Paris department store, helped sell six hundred copies by autographing them. Nevertheless, despite this good start, he knew by the end of the year that his high hopes for the book were not to be realized. The people at Harpers who had once talked about selling 60,000 or 80,000 copies were then expecting to sell only 6,000 to 8,000.[28]

Bruce and Barbara came for Christmas and found him cheerful despite his dismal prospects. He no longer had the strength to make his traditional Christmas cookies, but he supervised as the others baked.[29] From Barbara's father, Donald Douglas, they brought Hap a gag present—a shower curtain depicting Ulysses as he passed the Sirens, one of whom had tatooed on her anatomy the famous grafitto that American servicemen had written on countless walls all over the world during World War II—"Kilroy was here." Arnold loved it. He put it up immediately and made all of his visitors go into the bathroom to see it.

Bruce and Barbara themselves brought him a four-light bar to use with his home movie camera. They realized how sick he was when he proved to be too weak to hold up the bar.

On Christmas Day, Bruce decided to play for his father all the Army bugle calls in their proper order from morning to night. He had already embarked on this nostalgic program when it dawned on him how his father might interpret the last one. When evening came and it was time for Taps, Bruce let the hour pass. No one mentioned it.

A few days after Christmas, Bruce and Barbara left Sonoma for Cape Canaveral, Florida. Hap and Bee went together to Gordon and Josephine Tevis's New Year's Eve party, but they didn't stay long. Mrs. Tevis noticed that he looked even less well than usual. He was so thin his collar hung loose around his neck.[30]

After the holidays, he went to work on the revision of his military aviation article for the *Britannica,* but day by day he became more aware that he was not up to the task. Bee, whose devotion to him had never faded, watched over him more closely than ever now, and made sure that Simmons did likewise. Hap and Bee both knew that the happy retirement of which they dreamed had somehow escaped them. They had never learned how to accept the joys of leisure. And now, because of his health, they were deprived even of such simple joys as a walk through their land. But they still had the shared memories of a long and for many years happy life together, of endless struggles, monumental events, and great accomplishments. And they still had each other. Through the best and the worst of times they had clung together.

It was on the thirteenth of January that Hap Arnold wrote his last bewildered, impatient and tragically prophetic telegram to the *Britannica*: "... am all at sea. ... What's the score before I strike out ... ?" Two days later, he was dead.

T he sixty-two lengthy interviews by the author and other research-
ers listed below provide many of the anecdotes and details that
help to make General Arnold an understandable, human personality.
But the materials that verify the interviews, the primary sources on
which the book is based, also listed below, are the voluminous documents, correspondence, records, and reports still extant which pinpoint
the important issues, relationships, and events of Arnold's life. These
materials, together with reminiscences and other memorabilia, reside in
several depositories, including the Library of Congress; the National
Archives; the Albert F. Simpson Historical Research Center at the Air
University, Maxwell Air Force Base, Alabama; the Air Force Academy,
Colorado Springs, Colorado; the British Public Records Office, the Air
Historical Branch, and the Imperial War Museum, all in London. Much
of the personal correspondence is in the possession of the surviving
members of Arnold's immediate family—his sons Henry, Jr., William
Bruce, and David Lee Arnold, all three of whom have been wonderfully
generous, cooperative, and helpful to the author.

Among the other people who have been exceptionally helpful are:
Dr. Paul Heffner and C.F.W. Coker of the Library of Congress; Maj.
Gen. John Huston, David Schoen, William Heimdahl, and Ms. Margaret
Peters of the Office of Air Force History; Mrs. Elizabeth B. Mason of the
Columbia University Oral History Research Office; Lloyd H. Cornett,
Luther E. Lee, Mrs. Judy Endicott, and Pressley Bickerstaff of the
Simpson Historical Research Center at the Air University; Col. Alfred
Hurley, Lt. Col. Benjamin C. Glidden, Lt. Col. John Reynolds, Lt. Aaron
Byerley, Donald Barrett, Duane Reed, and Robert Burke of the Air
Force Academy; John Taylor, William Cunliffe, Gloria Wheeler, and
James Hastings of the National Archives; Bruce Callander and John
Hickerson of the *Air Force Times;* Dr. Noble Frankland of the Imperial
War Museum; Jeffrey Ede of the British Public Records Office; Group
Cap. Edward B. Haslam of the Air Historical Branch; Lt. Gen. John B.
McPherson, Ret., and Col. James L. Cannell, Ret., of the Air Force

Historical Foundation, which has given full and generous support to this project.

Interviewed by the Author
Anderson, Gen. Samuel E., Ret., Aug. 31, 1978
Arnold, Col. David Lee, Ret., Sept. 12, 1978; Jan. 27, 1979
Arnold, Col. Henry H., Jr., Ret., Sept. 28 & 29, 1978; Jan. 27, 1979
Arnold, Col. William Bruce, Ret., Oct. 13 & Nov. 13, 1978; Jan. 27, 1979
Beebe, Brig. Gen. Eugene, Ret., Aug. 14, 1978; Aug. 11, 1979
Cook, Gen. Orval, Ret., Nov. 2, 1978
Dean, Lt. Gen. Fred M., Ret., Nov. 21, 1978
Devers, Gen. Jacob, Ret., April 25, 1975
Douglas, Donald, Sr., Aug. 25 & Aug. 30, 1978
Eaker, Lt. Gen. Ira C., Ret., Oct. 27, 1978; June 22, 1979; Oct. 30, 1979
Giles, Lt. Gen. Barney, Ret., Nov. 27, 1978
Hansell, Maj. Gen. Haywood S., Jr., Ret., Nov. 21, 1978
Harris, Marshal of the Royal Air Force Sir Arthur T., Oct. 3, 1974; May 31, 1975
Kuter, Gen. Laurence S., Ret., on undated tape in reply to author's letter of June
    12, 1979, which included an extensive series of questions
Laidlaw, William R., Nov. 8, 1978
Lay, Lt. Col. Beirne, Jr., Ret., Dec. 30, 1974; Jan. 6, 1975; Aug. 19, 1979
Lee, Dr. Russell V., Feb. 6, 1979
LeMay, Gen. Curtis E., Ret., Dec. 7, 1973
Lovett, Robert A., Nov. 6, 1978
McKee, Gen. W. F., Ret., Nov. 1, 1978
Martin, Dr. Lee B., Sr., Apr. 3, 1980
Mollenhauer, Dr. Robert, Jan. 27, 1979
Parton, James, Oct. 27, 1978
Peterson, Col. Clair, Ret., Nov. 29, 1978
Pogue, Dr. Forrest C., Nov. 30, 1978
Putt, Gen. Donald L., Ret., Sept. 7, 1978
Rusk, Dr. Howard, Nov. 8, 1978
Saunders, Brig. Gen. Laverne, Ret., Sept. 30 & Oct. 1, 1978
Simmons, M/Sgt. Bruce, Ret., June 24, 1979
Smith, Maj. Gen. C.R., Ret., June 19, 1979
Spaatz, Mrs. Ruth, June 22, 1979
Stone, Lt. Gen. Charles, Ret., Aug. 10, 1978
Streett, Mrs. Mary, June 27, 1979
Tevis, Mrs. Josephine, Jan. 6, 1980
Weyland, Gen. O. P., Ret., Nov. 27, 1978

Interviewed by Dr. Murray Green
Knerr, Maj. Gen. Hugh J., Ret., Aug. 27, 1969

Interviewed by John F. Loosbrock
Beebe, Brig. Gen. Eugene, Ret., Oct. 2, 1969

Interviewed by Dr. Donald Shaughnessy in 1959 as part of a project to record the
    reminiscences of friends of acquaintances of General Arnold for the Columbia
    University Oral History Research Office
Anderson, Gen. Orvil A.
Arnold, Mrs. Eleanor

Atwood, J.L.
Beebe, Brig. Gen. Eugene, Ret.
Burns, Col. James H., Ret.
Cabell, Gen. Charles P.
Castle, Col. Benjamin, Ret.
Conant, F. W.
Douglas, Donald, Sr.
Eaker, Lt. Gen. Ira C., Ret.
Gardner, Gen. Grandison, Ret.
Gross, Robert
Kindelberger, J. H.
Lahm, Gen. Frank P., Ret.
Lovett, Robert A.
Lutes, Gen. L. T., Ret.
Milling, Gen. Thomas DeWitt, Ret.
Peterson, Col. Clair, Ret.
Quesada, Lt. Gen. E.P., Ret.
Raymond, Arthur E.
Self, Sir Henry
Spaatz, Gen. Carl A., Ret.
Strangman, H.
Wagner, Col. Hayden
Wolfe, Lt. Gen. K. B., Ret.

Library of Congress
Most useful to the author were the papers and correspondence of the following:
    Lt. Gen. Frank M. Andrews (the bulk of whose papers are in the library of Tennessee State University, Nashville)
    Gen. H. H. Arnold
    Gen. Ira C. Eaker
    Maj. Gen. Benjamin D. Foulois
    Gen. Hugh Knerr
    Gen. Frank P. Lahm
    Robert P. Patterson
    Gen. E. P. Quesada
    Gen. Carl A. Spaatz
    Gen. Hoyt S. Vandenberg

National Archives, Washington, D.C.
Records of the United States Joint Chiefs
Records of the Office of the Secretary of Wars
Records of the Adjutant General's Office

Air University, Maxwell Air Force Base, Alabama
Correspondence, records, documents, reports, and interviews of the following:
    Gen. Orvil Anderson
    Gen. H. H. Arnold (some miscellaneous letters, especially concerning motion pictures and the Air Force song)
    Gen. Charles P. Cabell
    Lt. Gen. William E. Kepner
    Gen. Laurence S. Kuter

Maj. Gen. Walter Reed Weaver
Gen. K. B. Wolfe
Oral History interviews with the following:
  Mrs. Eleanor Arnold
  Gen. Mark E. Bradley
  Gen. Orval Cook
  Gen. Fred M. Dean
  Gen. James H. Doolittle
  Gen. Ira C. Eaker
  Gen. Benjamin D. Foulois
  Gen. Barney Giles
  Gen. Haywood S. Hansell, Jr.
  Gen. George C. Kenney
  Gen. Hugh Knerr
  Gen. Frank P. Lahm
  Gen. Donald L. Putt
  Gen. Carl A. Spaatz
  Gen. K. B. Wolfe

Air Force Academy
Gen. Carl A. Spaatz, interviewed at the academy by a panel of three unnamed
  officers, Sept. 27, 1968
Lt. Gen. Harold Lee George and Gen. Haywood S. Hansell, Jr., interviewed
  jointly at the academy by Capt. Robert S. Bartanowicz, Oct. 23, 1970
  Selected papers and memorabilia of:
  Gen. Frank M. Andrews
  Gen. H. H. Arnold
  Brig. Gen. John B. Williams
  Gen. Hugh Knerr
  Gen. Laurence S. Kuter
  Gen. Haywood S. Hansell, Jr.
  Gen. Emmett O'Donnell, Jr.
  James Parton
  Theodor von Kármán

Public Records Office, London
Selected letters and memoranda between Prime Minister Winston Churchill and
  his air advisers, 1941–43
Chief of Air Staff papers
R.A.F. Bomber Command records

Books
Allen, H. R. *The Legacy of Lord Trenchard.* London, Cassell, 1972.
Andrews, Allen. *The Air Marshals.* New York: Morrow, 1970.
Arnold, H. H., and Eaker, Ira C. *Army Flyer.* New York: Harper & Bros., 1942.
Arnold, H. H. *Bill Bruce and the Pioneer Aviators. Bill Bruce the Flying Cadet. Bill
  Bruce Becomes an Ace. Bill Bruce on Border Patrol.* New York: A. L. Burt Co.,
  1928.
————. *Global Mission.* New York: Harper & Bros., 1949.
Arnold, William Bruce. "Pop Raced the Pigeons." Unpublished manuscript.
Butcher, Harry C. *Three Years With Eisenhower.* London: Heinemann, 1946.
Caidin, Martin. *Flying Forts.* New York: Ballantine, 1969.

Campbell, James. *The Bombing of Nuremberg*. Garden City, N.Y.: Doubleday, 1974.

Catton, Bruce. *The War Lords of Washington*. New York: Harcourt Brace, 1948.

Churchill, Winston. *The Second World War*. Boston: Houghton Mifflin, 1948–53.

Clark, Mark W. *Calculated Risk*. New York: Harper, 1950.

Coffey, Thomas M. *Imperial Tragedy*. New York: World, 1970.

––––––. *Decision Over Schweinfurt*. New York: McKay, 1977.

Craig, William. *The Fall of Japan*. New York: Dial, 1967.

Craven. W. E., and Cate, J. L. *The Army Air Forces in World War II*. Chicago: University of Chicago Press, 1948–51.

Current, Richard W. *Secretary Stimson: A Study in Statecraft*. New Brunswick, N. J.: Rutgers University Press, 1954.

Davis, Vincent. *The Admirals' Lobby*. Chapel Hill: University of North Carolina Press, 1967.

Eliot, George Fielding. *The Ramparts We Watch*. New York: Reynal & Hitchcock, 1938.

Farrago, Ladislas. *Patton: Ordeal and Triumph*. New York: Dell, 1963.

Foulois, Benjamin D. *From the Wright Brothers to the Astronauts*. New York: McGraw-Hill, 1968.

Frankland, Noble. *Bomber Offensive*. London: Macdonald, 1970.

Freeman, Roger. *Mustang at War*. London: Ian Allan, 1974.

Goddard, George. *Overview*. Garden City, N.Y.: Doubleday, 1969.

Goldberg, Alfred. *History of the United States Air Force—1907–1957*. New York: Van Nostrand, 1957

Gauvreau, Emile. *The Wild Blue Yonder*. New York: Dutton, 1944.

Hansell, Haywood S., Jr. *The Air Plan That Defeated Hitler*. Atlanta, Ga.: MacArthur/Longino & Porter, 1972.

––––––."Strategic Air War Against Japan—A Memoir 30 Years Later." Unpublished manuscript.

Hastings, Max. *Bomber Command*. New York: Dial Press/James Wade, 1979.

Hess, William. *P-51 Mustang*. New York: Ballantine, 1971.

––––––. *B-17 Flying Fortress*. New York: Ballantine, 1974.

Huie, William Bradford. *The Fight for Air Power*. New York: L. B. Fischer, 1942.

––––––. *The Case Against the Admirals*. New York: Dutton, 1946.

Hurley, Alfred F. *Billy Mitchell, Crusader for Air Power*. New York: Franklin Watts, Inc., 1964.

Jablonski, Edward. *Air War*. Garden City, N.Y.: Doubleday, 1971.

––––––. *Flying Fortress*. Garden City, N.Y.: Doubleday, 1974.

King, Ernest J., and Whitehill, Walter Muir. *A Naval Record*. New York: Norton, 1952.

Knerr, Hugh J., "The Vital Era." Unpublished manuscript.

La Farge, Oliver. *The Eagle in the Egg*. Boston: Houghton Mifflin, 1949.

Lay, Beirne, Jr. *I Wanted Wings*. New York: Grosset & Dunlap, 1937.

––––––. Unpublished diary: May 26 to June 7, 1942.

LeMay, Curtis E., and Kantor, MacKinlay. *Mission With LeMay*. Garden City, N.Y.: Doubleday, 1965.

Levine, Isaac Don. *Mitchell—Pioneer of Air Power*. Cleveland & New York: World, 1943.

Lindbergh, Charles A. *The Wartime Journals of Charles A. Lindbergh*. New York: Harcourt Brace Jovanovich, 1970.

Lukas, Richard C. *Eagles Nest—The Army Air Forces and the Soviet Union: 1941–45*. Tallahassee: Florida State University Press, 1970.

Lyall, Gavin. *The War in the Air*. London: Hutchinson, 1968.

Mee, Charles L., Jr. *Meeting at Potsdam*. New York: Evans, 1975.

Middleton, Drew. *The Sky Suspended*. London: Secker & Warburg, 1960.

Milward, Alan S. *The German Economy at War*. London: University of London, Athlone Press, 1965.

Morgenthau, Henry, Jr. *From the Diaries of Henry Morgenthau, Jr.*, ed. John M. Blum. Boston: Houghton Mifflin, 1959–67.

Morrison, Wilbur H. *Point of No Return*. New York: Times Books, 1979.

Pogue, Forrest C. *George C. Marshall, Ordeal and Hope: 1939–1942*. New York: Viking Press, 1966.

———. *George C. Marshall: Organizer of Victory, 1943–45*. New York: Viking Press, 1973.

Pogue, Forrest C., and Harrison, Gordon. *George C. Marshall: Education of a General*. New York: Viking Press, 1963.

Revie, Alastair. *The Bomber Command*. New York: Ballantine, 1971.

Roosevelt, Elliott. *As He Saw It*. New York: Duell, Sloan & Pearce, 1946.

Rusk, Howard A. *A World to Care For*. New York: Random House/Reader's Digest Press, 1972.

Saundby, Robert. *Air Bombardment*. New York: Harper & Bros., 1961.

Sherwood, Robert E. *Roosevelt and Hopkins*. New York: Harper & Bros., 1948.

Shirer, William L. *The Rise and Fall of the Third Reich*. New York: Simon & Schuster, 1960.

Stilwell, Joseph W. *The Stilwell Papers*, ed. Theodore H. White. New York: William Sloane Assoc., 1948.

Thomas, Gordon, and Witts, Max M. *Enola Gay*. New York: Stein & Day, 1977.

Thomas, Lowell, and Jablonski, Edward. *Doolittle—A Biography*. Garden City, N.Y.: Doubleday, 1976.

Toland, John. *The Rising Sun*. New York, Random House, 1970.

Tubbs, D.B. *Lancaster Bomber*. New York: Ballantine, 1972.

Tuchman, Barbara. *Stilwell and the American Experience in China, 1911–45*. New York: Macmillan, 1970.

Vader, John. *Spitfire*. New York: Ballantine, 1969.

Verrier, Anthony. *The Bomber Offensive*. London: Batsford, 1968.

von Kármán, Theodor. *The Wind and Beyond*. Boston: Little, Brown, 1967.

Webster, Charles, and Frankland, Noble. *The Strategic Air Offensive Against Germany, 1939–45*. 4 Vols. London: Her Majesty's Stationery Office, 1961.

Winterbotham, F. W. *The Ultra Secret*. New York: Dell, 1975.

Newspapers and Periodicals
  Aerospace Historian
  Air Force Magazine
  Air Force Times
  Literary Digest
  Long Beach Morning Sun
  Long Beach Press-Telegram
  Los Angeles Examiner
  Los Angeles Times
  National Geographic
  New York Times
  Time

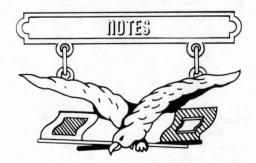

NOTES

Chapter One

1. Telegram, Gen. H. H. Arnold to *Britannica* editor Walter Yast, Jan. 13, 1950.
2. M. Sgt. Bruce Simmons to author, Jan. 24, 1979.
3. Col. William Bruce Arnold to author, Jan. 27, 1979.
4. Edwin S. Pillsbury, letter to Robert Proctor, Jan. 3, 1950.
5. Undated statement by Capt. H. A. Cargue to investigators regarding the Bishop-Robertson flight, Jan. 10, 1917.
6. Statement by Arnold to investigators, Jan. 27, 1917.
7. Gen. Frank P. Lahm, Columbia transcript, p. 20.
8. Ibid., p. 28.
9. H.H. Arnold, *Global Mission*, pp. 114–16, 122.
10. Gen. Ira C. Eaker to author, Jan. 22, 1978.
11. Mrs. Eleanor Arnold, Columbia transcript, p. 55.
12. Reprimand of Maj. H. H. Arnold, Mar. 2, 1926.
13. W. B. Arnold to author, Oct. 13, 1978; Mrs. Arnold, Columbia transcript, pp. 53–54.
14. Col. David Lee Arnold to author, Sept. 12, 1978.
15. *New York Times, Los Angeles Times, Long Beach Morning Sun, Long Beach Press-Telegram*, Mar. 11–23, 1933.
16. Mrs. Arnold, Columbia transcript, p. 98.
17. Gen. Eaker to author, Oct. 27, 1978; Eaker, Columbia transcript, p. 44.
18. *Long Beach Morning Sun*, Mar. 14, 1933.
19. Gen. Carl A. Spaatz, Columbia transcript, p. 60.
20. Mrs. Arnold, Columbia transcript, p. 98.
21. *From the Diaries of Henry Morgenthau, Jr.,* vol. 2, p. 46.
22. *New York Times*, Mar. 6 & 13, 1940.
23. Morgenthau, *Diaries*, vol. 2, p. 117. Also, Arnold memorandum of record, Mar. 13, 1940. Arnold in his memoirs indicated this incident occurred in 1939, and other authors have accepted that date, but his memorandum of record and Morgenthau's diary both show it occurred Mar. 12, 1940.

Chapter Two

1. Col. H. H. Arnold, Jr., to author, Sept 28, 1978.
2. *Main Line Daily Times* (Pa.), Oct. 27, 1933.
3. Mrs. Eleanor Arnold, Columbia transcript, pp. 18ff.
4. Ibid., p. 22.
5. H. H. Arnold, Jr., to author, Sept 28, 1978; W. B. Arnold to author, Oct. 13, 1978.
6. H. H. Arnold, *Global Mission*, p. 6.
7. For the following account of a plebe's life at West Point during this period:

the Columbia transcripts of Col. Benjamin Castle, Col. Hayden Wagner, and Gen. Thomas Milling.

8. W. B. Arnold to author, Sept 27, 1979.
9. *Global Mission,* p. 8.
10. Arnold to his mother, Feb. 1906 (exact date obscure).
11. *Global Mission,* pp. 7ff.
12. Gen. Ira C. Eaker to author, Sept. 27, 1979.
13. Arnold to his mother, letter tentatively dated Sept. 1905.
14. The following account of Arnold's activities as a member of the "Black Hand" comes from *Global Mission,* pp. 7ff., and from the Columbia transcripts of Colonels Castle and Wagner.
15. Mrs. Arnold, Columbia transcript, p. 1.
16. W. B. Arnold, "Pop Raced the Pigeons," p. 15.
17. Mrs. Arnold, Columbia transcript, pp. 1, 5.
18. *Global Mission,* p. 8.
19. Col. Castle, Columbia transcript, p. 36.
20. *Global Mission,* p. 8.

Chapter Three
1. Col. Benjamin Castle, Columbia transcript, p. 30.
2. Mrs. Eleanor Arnold, Columbia transcript, p. 1.
3. Col. Castle, Columbia transcript, p. 30.
4. H. H. Arnold, *Global Mission,* p. 9.
5. Ibid., p. 10; Col. Castle, Columbia transcript, p. 31; Gen. Eugene Beebe, interviewed by John Loosbrock, Oct. 2, 1969.
6. *Global Mission,* p. 10.
7. Col. Castle, Columbia transcript, p. 34.
8. *Global Mission,* p. 10.
9. Col. Castle, Columbia transcript, p. 55.
10. Col. Charles M. Gandy to Dr. Herbert Arnold, Feb. 8, 1909.
11. Col. Castle, Columbia transcript, pp. 39, 55.
12. *Global Mission,* pp. 1ff.
13. *Global Mission,* pp. 2–3.
14. Mrs. Arnold, notes on her tape at Air University.
15. *Global Mission,* p. 2.
16. Ibid., p. 12.
17. Gen. Beebe, Loosbrock interview.
18. Mrs. Arnold, Columbia transcript, pp. 1–2; Air University tape.
19. *Global Mission,* p. 13.
20. Arnold to adjutant general, Apr. 7, 1911.

Chapter Four
1. Gen. Thomas DeW. Milling, Columbia transcript, pp. 44ff.; Air University tape 767, transcript, p. 41ff.
2. H. H. Arnold, *Global Mission,* p. 28.
3. Gen. Milling, Columbia transcript, p. 12.
4. *Global Mission,* p. 16.
5. Arnold flight log, May 3–13, 1911.
6. *Global Mission,* p. 20.
7. Gen. Milling, Air University transcript, p. 45.
8. Ibid., p. 42; Gen. Milling, Columbia transcript, p. 22.
9. *Global Mission,* pp. 24–25.
10. W. B. Arnold, "Pop Raced the Pigeons," p. 20.

11. Arnold to his father, July 2, 1911.
12. *Global Mission,* p. 31.
13. Gen. Benjamin D. Foulois, *From the Wright Brothers to the Astronauts,* p. 95.
14. Gen. Milling, Air University transcript, p. 48.
15. *Global Mission,* pp. 33–34.
16. Arnold's Air Force biographical outline, p. 5.
17. Mrs. Eleanor Arnold, Columbia transcript, p. 2.
18. *Global Mission,* p. 39.
19. Letter signed by Lt. Col. Fred S. Foltz, General Staff, Oct. 9, 1912.
20. Office, Chief of Air Corps, memorandum dated Mar. 26, 1937.
21. Gen. Milling, in roundtable discussion of early aviation, Maxwell Field, June 29, 1954.
22. Arnold's reports to his commanding officer, Nov. 6 & 7, 1912; *Global Mission,* p. 41; Gen. Milling, Air University transcript, pp. 50–52; his Columbia transcript, p. 57; Gen. Frank P. Lahm, Columbia transcript, p. 4; Dr. Russell V. Lee to author, Feb. 6, 1979.

Chapter Five
1. Mrs. Eleanor Arnold, Columbia transcript, pp. 2–3; W.B. Arnold to author, Oct. 13, 1978.
2. Mrs. Arnold, notes on her Air University tape.
3. Orville Wright to Arnold, Mar. 22, 1913.
4. Orville Wright to Arnold, Jan. 30, 1913.
5. Hearings of the House of Representatives, Military Affairs Committee, Aug. 16, 1913.
6. Mrs. Arnold, Columbia transcript, pp. 3, 9–10; notes on her Air University tape.
7. Mrs. Ruth Spaatz to author, June 22, 1975.
8. H. H. Arnold, Jr., to author, Sept. 29, 1978.
9. Adjutant general to Arnold, July 14, 1913.
10. Military Affairs Committee hearing, Aug. 16, 1913.
11. H. H. Arnold, *Global Mission,* p. 43.
12. Mrs. Arnold, Columbia transcript, pp. 19–20.

Chapter Six
1. Mrs. Eleanor Arnold, Columbia transcript, pp. 23ff.
2. Arnold to Mrs. Arnold, Jan. 25, 1914.
3. Forrest Pogue and Gordon Harrison, *George C. Marshall: Education of a General,* pp. 121ff.
4. Arnold to Mrs. Arnold, Jan. 31, 1914.
5. Mrs. Arnold, Columbia transcript, p. 28.
6. Arnold to Mrs. Arnold, Feb. 25, 1914.
7. H. H. Arnold, *Global Mission,* p. 44.
8. Mrs. Arnold, Columbia transcript, p. 32.
9. Ibid., p. 20.
10. Entry in Arnold's efficiency record, June 9, 1915.
11. Mrs. Arnold, Columbia transcript, p. 28–29.
12. The account of Mrs. Arnold's illness was drawn from her Columbia transcript, p. 43; from a phone conversation between W. B. Arnold and the author, Dec. 6, 1979; and from several conversations with all three of her sons.
13. Mrs. Arnold, Columbia transcript, p. 33.
14. *Global Mission,* p. 45.

15. Mrs. Arnold, Columbia transcript, p. 33.
16. Ibid., pp. 34–35.
17. Arnold flight log, Oct.–Dec. 1916.
18. Mrs. Arnold, Columbia transcript, p. 35.
19. Dr. Russell V. Lee to author, Feb. 6, 1979. Arnold, late in life, spoke to Dr. Lee about the personal crisis that resulted from his near-crash in November 1912.
20. The account of Arnold's involvement in the Bishop-Robertson controversy comes from Arnold's statement to Army investigators, Jan. 27, 1917; Dargue's undated statement to Army investigators; *New York Times*, Jan. 20, 1917; and *Global Mission*, pp. 45–47.
21. Arnold, in *Global Mission*, p. 46, recalled that he left San Diego on Jan. 30, 1917. His journal at the time put the date at Feb. 6. Later correspondence indicates his book is correct.
22. Arnold to Mrs. Arnold, Jan. 31, 1917.
23. Arnold to Mrs. Arnold, Feb. 15, 1917.
24. Arnold memorandum (undated) listing his assignments during 1917–18.
25. Mrs. Arnold, Columbia transcript, p. 40.
26. *Global Mission*, p. 50.
27. Mrs. Arnold, Columbia transcript, p. 42–43.
28. *Global Mission*, p. 83.
29. Ibid., pp. 74–76, 83.
30. The three Arnold brothers to the author, quoting their mother, Jan. 27, 1979.
31. Mrs. Arnold, Columbia transcript, p. 41.
32. This account of Arnold's 1918 mission to Europe comes from his diary of the trip, and, to a lesser extent, from *Global Mission*, pp. 83–86.

Chapter Seven
1. Gen. Ira C. Eaker in an address at the Industrial War College, Washington, Apr. 14, 1977.
2. Donald Douglas, Sr., Columbia transcript, pp. 22–23.
3. Gen. Eaker, Columbia transcript, pp. 10, 11.
4. H. H. Arnold, *Global Mission*, p. 88.
5. Ibid., p. 81.
6. Ibid., p. 86.
7. Ibid., p. 91.
8. Gen. Eaker to author, Oct. 27, 1978.
9. *Global Mission*, p. 91.
10. Ibid., pp. 106–107; W. B. Arnold to author, Oct. 13, 1978; Arnold to his father, Aug. 23, 1922.
11. Isaac Don Levine, *Mitchell—Pioneer of Air Power*, pp. 183ff.
12. Mrs. Ruth Spaatz to author, June 22, 1979; *Global Mission*, p. 99.
13. H. H. Arnold, Jr., to author, Sept. 28, 1978.
14. W. B. Arnold, "Pop Raced the Pigeons," p. 57.
15. *Global Mission*, pp. 106–107.
16. "Pop Raced the Pigeons," pp. 71ff.
17. H. H. Arnold, Jr., to author, Sept. 28, 1978; the three Arnold brothers to author, Jan. 27, 1979.
18. H. H. Arnold, Jr., to author, Sept. 28, 1978; W. B. Arnold to author, Oct. 13, 1978.
19. "Pop Raced the Pigeons," pp. 58ff.
20. Mrs. Eleanor Arnold, Columbia transcript, p. 48.

21. Donald Douglas, Sr., Columbia transcript, pp. 59ff.
22. Lt. Col. Beirne Lay, Jr., to author, Aug. 10, 1979.
23. Mrs. Arnold, Columbia transcript, pp. 51ff.; Arnold to Mrs. Arnold, Jan. 14, 1924.
24. "Pop Raced the Pigeons," p. 37.
25. Ibid., pp. 73, 125ff.

Chapter Eight
1. Isaac Don Levine, *Mitchell—Pioneer of Air Power,* p. 309.
2. W. B. Arnold to author, Oct. 13, 1978.
3. H. H. Arnold, *Global Mission,* pp. 116–17.
4. Gen. Ira C. Eaker, Columbia transcript, p. 24.
5. *Los Angeles Examiner,* Oct. 17, 1925; W. B. Arnold to author, Oct. 13, 1978, and Nov. 13, 1978.
6. Gen. Eaker to author, Apr. 8, 1975.
7. *Global Mission,* p. 122.
8. Gen. Eaker to author, June 22, 1979.
9. H. H. Arnold, Jr., to author, Sept. 28, 1978; W. B. Arnold to author, Oct. 13, 1978.
10. W. B. Arnold, "Pop Raced the Pigeons," p. 148; Mrs. Eleanor Arnold, Columbia transcript, pp. 52, 60, 63; *Global Mission,* pp. 122ff.
11. W. B. Arnold to author, Nov. 1, 1978; Mrs. Arnold, Columbia transcript, pp. 76–77.
12. H. H. Arnold, Jr., to author, Sept. 28, 1978.
13. W. B. Arnold to author, Oct. 13, 1978.
14. W. B. Arnold to author, Nov. 1, 1978.
15. W. B. Arnold to author, Oct. 13, 1978.
16. *Global Mission,* pp. 125–26; commendations to Arnold from assistant secretary of war, Nov. 28, 1928.
17. "Pop Raced the Pigeons," p. 209.
18. Mrs. Arnold, Columbia transcript, pp. 61–62, 65.
19. Gen. Orval Cook to author, Nov. 2, 1978.

Chapter Nine
1. W. B. Arnold, "Pop Raced the Pigeons," p. 299.
2. This account of the destruction of the Barling Bomber was compiled from H. H. Arnold's *Global Mission,* p. 128; W. B. Arnold to author, Nov. 1, 1978; "Pop Raced the Pigeons," p. 265; and "The Short, Unhappy Life of the Barling Bomber" by Capt. Earl H. Telford, *Air Force Magazine* (Feb. 1978), p. 70.
3. W. B. Arnold to author, Nov. 1, 1978.
4. Arnold to Mrs. Arnold, Jan. 21, 1930.
5. Crissy Field accident report, Apr. 17, 1930.
6. Gen. Orval Cook to author, Nov. 2, 1978.
7. Gen. Grandison Gardner, Columbia transcript, p. 10.
8. H. H. Arnold, Jr., to author, Sept. 28, 1978.
9. The details of this water fight were related to the author by H. H. Arnold, Jr., Sept. 28, 1978, and were confirmed by him and his two brothers, Jan. 27, 1979.
10. *Global Mission,* p. 130.
11. Mrs. Eleanor Arnold, Columbia transcript, p. 79.
12. D. L. Arnold to author, Sept. 12, 1978; Mrs. Ruth Spaatz to author, June 22, 1979.

13. Gen. Ira C. Eaker to author, Apr. 18, 1975; Eaker, Columbia transcript, p. 39.
14. The account of Dr. Arnold's last days was compiled from the author's conversations with the three Arnold brothers, and from Mrs. Arnold's Columbia transcript, p. 79.
15. W. B. Arnold to author, Nov. 1, 1978.
16. Ibid., Oct. 13, 1978.
17. Donald Douglas, Sr., Columbia transcript, p. 52.
18. *Global Mission,* p. 139.
19. The account of Arnold's actions and difficulties as a result of the Long Beach earthquake was compiled from the author's conversations with D. L. Arnold, Sept. 12, 1978; H. H. Arnold, Jr., Sept. 28, 1978; Gen. Eaker, Oct. 27, 1978; Gen. Eugene Beebe, Aug. 11, 1979; also from Mrs. Arnold's Columbia transcript, pp. 98ff., and the Beebe-Loosbrock tape, foot 216.
20. Gen. Beebe's 1933 flight logs.
21. H. H. Arnold, Jr., to author, Sept. 28, 1978.

Chapter Ten
1. H. H. Arnold, *Global Mission,* p. 134.
2. Arnold brothers to author, Jan. 27, 1979; H. H. Arnold, Jr., to author, Sept. 28, 1978.
3. "Gen. Benjamin Foulois and the 1934 Air Mail Disaster," *Aerospace Historian* (Dec. 1978).
4. Gen. Ira C. Eaker, Air University tape No. 626, transcript, pp. 30ff.
5. This account of the Alaska flight was compiled from Arnold's letters to his wife; Mrs. Arnold's Columbia transcript; W. B. Arnold to author, Oct. 13, 1978; and Dr. Murray Green's interview with Maj. Gen. Hugh Knerr, Aug. 27, 1969.

Chapter Eleven
1. Mrs. Eleanor Arnold, Columbia transcript, pp. 69–71, 78.
2. W. B. Arnold to author, Oct. 13, 1978.
3. Lois Arnold to Mrs. Arnold, Oct. 25, 1934; also Lois to her mother a few days earlier, but undated; Arnold to his daughter, Lois, Oct. 10, 1934; W. B. Arnold to author, Oct. 13, 1978; the Arnold brothers to author, Jan. 27, 1979.
4. Maj. Gen. Haywood S. Hansell, Jr., *The Air Plan That Defeated Hitler,* passim.
5. H. H. Arnold, *Global Mission,* p. 149.
6. Arnold letters to Mrs. Arnold between Dec. 1 and Dec. 15, 1935.
7. Gen. Oscar Westover to Mrs. Arnold, Nov. 28, 1933.
8. Gen. Eugene Beebe, Loosbrock interview tape, side one, foot 267.
9. The story of the move to Washington was compiled from Mrs. Arnold's Columbia transcript, pp. 97, 102ff.; D.L. Arnold to author, Sept. 12, 1978; W. B. Arnold to author, Oct. 13, 1978; and W. B. Arnold, "Pop Raced the Pigeons," pp. 383ff.
10. *Global Mission,* p. 153.
11. Mrs. Arnold, Columbia transcript, p. 99.
12. F. W. Conant, Columbia transcript, p. 1.
13. Gen. Donald L. Putt to author, Sept. 6, 1978.
14. "Development of the Big Bombers," *Aerospace Historian* (Dec. 1978), pp. 214ff.
15. Gen. Hugh J. Knerr's interview with Dr. Murray Green.

16. *Global Mission*, p. 163.
17. USAAF memorandum re: Navigational Flight Limit of 100 Miles Seaward —Nov. 20, 1945, by A. M. Miller.
18. W. B. Huie, *The Case Against the Admirals*, pp. 77–78.
19. Mark W. Watson, "The U.S. Army in World War II: The War Department —Chief of Staff: Prewar Plans and Preparations" (Washington: Government Printing Office, 1950), pp. 35–36.
20. D. L. Arnold to author, Jan. 27, 1979.
21. H. H. Arnold, Jr., to author, Sept. 28, 1978; and the three Arnold brothers to author, Jan. 27, 1979.
22. *Global Mission*, pp. 163ff.
23. Col. James H. Burns, Columbia transcript, pp. 22ff.
24. Robert Sherwood, *Roosevelt and Hopkins*, pp. 99–100.
25. Lt. Gen. K. B. Wolfe, Columbia transcript, pp. 10ff.
26. W. B. Arnold to author, Oct. 13, 1978.
27. This meeting, which, according to Arnold (*Global Mission*, p. 177) took place Sept. 28, 1938, has been dated by several historians as having taken place on Nov. 14. Arnold is the only person known to have taken notes of the meeting, and his notes reflect great surprise on the part of other Army and Navy representatives at Roosevelt's sudden advocacy of air power. If the meeting took place on Nov. 14, it is hardly conceivable that these men could have been surprised by Roosevelt's air power advocacy at that time. An Oct. 27, 1938, report by Arnold to the assistant secretary of war shows that he then envisioned aircraft production capacity of 40,000 planes per year, which indicates he was already under the influence of the president's expansion plans. The author therefore accepts Arnold's date.

Chapter Twelve
1. H. H. Arnold, *Global Mission*, p. 171.
2. "Development of the Big Bombers," *Aerospace Historian* (Dec. 1978), pp. 216–17.
3. *From the Diaries of Henry Morgenthau, Jr.*, entry for Oct. 20, 1938.
4. Forrest C. Pogue and Harrison Gordon, *George C. Marshall: Education of a General*, pp. 314ff.
5. *The Wartime Journals of Charles A. Lindbergh*, entries for Oct. 1 & 3, 1938.
6. Arnold to Lois and Ernest Snowden, Oct. 23, 1938.
7. W. B. Arnold to author, Oct. 13, 1978.
8. Morgenthau, *Diaries*, entry for Jan. 16, 1939.
9. *New York Times*, Jan. 25, 1939; Donald Douglas, Sr., Columbia transcript, pp. 89ff.; J. L. Atwood, Columbia transcript, p. 24; Gen. K. B. Wolfe, Columbia transcript, p. 16.
10. *New York Times*, Jan. 27, Feb. 18 & 22, 1939.
11. Gen. Ira C. Eaker to author, Oct. 27, 1978, and Jan. 22, 1979.
12. *Global Mission*, p. 181.
13. Gen. Orvil A. Anderson, Columbia transcript, pp. 6–10.
14. Lindbergh, *Wartime Journals*, entry for Apr. 15, 1939; *Global Mission*, pp. 188ff.
15. Mrs. Eleanor Arnold, Columbia transcript, p. 105.
16. W. B. Arnold to author, June 22, 1979.
17. Lindbergh, *Wartime Journals*, entry for June 12, 1939.
18. Ibid., June 7, 1939.

Chapter Thirteen

1. Gen. George C. Marshall to his biographer, Forrest Pogue, Jan. 22, 1947.
2. Wilbur H. Morrison, *Point of No Return*, pp. 9–10.
3. *The Wartime Journals of Charles A. Lindbergh*, entries for Sept. 14 & 15, 1939; H. H. Arnold, *Global Mission*, p. 359.
4. Gen. Carl A. Spaatz, Columbia transcript, pp. 41ff.
5. *Global Mission*, p. 165–66.
6. Theodore von Kármán, *The Wind and Beyond*, pp. 225–26.
7. Lindbergh, *Wartime Journals*, entry for Sept. 14, 1939.
8. Gen. Laurence S. Kuter, Ret., "George C. Marshall, Architect of Air Power," *Air Force Magazine*, (Aug. 1978).
9. *From the Diaries of Henry Morgenthau, Jr.*, entry for Jan. 8, 1940.
10. Arnold to Woodring, Jan. 12, 1940.
11. Morgenthau, *Diaries*, entry for Mar. 12, 1940.
12. Arnold memorandum of record, Mar. 13, 1940. In *Global Mission*, Arnold indicates he was banished from the White House in 1939. Actually it took place Mar. 12, 1940, as this memo and the Morgenthau diaries clearly show.
13. D. L. Arnold to author, Sept. 12, 1978.
14. Arnold to his son Henry, Oct. 28, 1939; W. B. Arnold to author, June 24, 1979.
15. Sgt. Bruce Simmons to author, June 24, 1979.
16. Gen. Eugene Beebe to author, Aug. 11, 1979.
17. Air Marshal Sir Arthur T. Harris to author, May 31, 1975; J. H. Kindelberger, Columbia transcript, pp. 25, 27.
18. Forrest Pogue, *George C. Marshall: Ordeal and Hope*, p. 49.
19. Gen. Ira C. Eaker to author, Oct. 27, 1978.
20. Arnold memorandum of record, Aug. 14, 1940.
21. Pogue, *Ordeal and Hope*, p. 64.
22. Elliott Roosevelt, *As He Saw It*, p. 9; *Global Mission*, p. 213.
23. *Global Mission*, p. 194.

Chapter Fourteen

1. Gen. Carl A. Spaatz, Columbia transcript, pp. 51–52.
2. Robert Lovett to author, Nov. 6, 1978.
3. H. H. Arnold, *Global Mission*, p. 195.
4. Lovett to author, Nov. 6, 1978.
5. Gen. Grandison Gardner, Columbia transcript, p. 11.
6. Gen. Eugene Beebe, Loosbrock interview tape, side 1, foot 321.
7. F. W. Conant, Columbia transcript, p. 11.
8. Gen. K. B. Wolfe, Columbia transcript, p. 33.
9. J. H. Kindelberger, Columbia transcript, p. 23.
10. *Time* magazine, Nov. 22, 1943, pp. 79–80.
11. Lt. Gen. James H. Doolittle, Air University tape 793, transcript, pp. 37ff.
12. Arnold memorandum of record, Mar. 10, 1941.
13. This account of Arnold's trip to England has been compiled from his diary of the trip, Gen. E. P. Quesada's Columbia transcript, and *Global Mission*, pp. 215–40.
14. Quesada, Columbia transcript, pp. 7ff.
15. Gen. Haywood S. Hansell, Jr., to author, Nov. 21, 1978; Allen Andrews, *The Air Marshals*, pp. 189ff.; and *Global Mission*, p. 245.
16. This account of Gen. Knerr's 1941 efforts to return to active duty was compiled from Knerr's letters to Gen. Andrews dated May 14, 1939, June 5

& 18, 1941, and an undated letter late that month; Andrews to Knerr letters of May 28, June 23, July 1 & 28, Sept. 15, 1941; Andrews to Arnold, Aug. 19, 1941; Dr. Murray Green's inverview with Gen. Knerr, Aug. 27, 1969; and "Maj. Gen. Hugh J. Knerr, Hard Campaigner for Air Power," *Air Force Magazine* (Oct. 1978).

17. Office of the Chief of Staff, record of phone conversation, Marshall and Arnold, Sept, 25, 1941.
18. Memorandum, Arnold to Lovett, Oct. 8, 1941.
19. *Global Mission*, pp. 259–60.
20. Sgt. Bruce Simmons to author, June 24, 1979.
21. W. B. Arnold to author, Oct. 13, 1978.
22. The account of this Arnold trip to California was compiled from the author's interviews with Gen. Beebe, Aug. 14, 1978, and Aug. 11, 1979; *Global Mission*, pp. 266ff.; the author's conversation with Donald Douglas, Sr., Aug. 30, 1978; the Douglas Columbia transcript, pp. 84ff., and the Gen. Beebe—Loosbrock tape, side one, foot 460.

Chapter Fifteen
1. Gen. Eugene Beebe to author, Aug. 11, 1979.
2. H. H. Arnold, *Global Mission*, p. 271.
3. Mrs. Eleanor Arnold, Columbia transcript, p. 73.
4. Gen. Laurence S. Kuter, Air University tape 810, foot 160.
5. Gen. James H. Doolittle, Air University tape 793, transcript, pp. 40ff.; Lowell Thomas and Edward Jablonski, *Doolittle—A Biography*, pp. 155–56.
6. *Global Mission*, pp. 274ff.
7. Cypher telegram, Air Marshal Arthur T. Harris to Air Chief Marshal Sir Charles Portal, Jan. 29, 1942, which reports Arnold's reaction to the request.
8. Ibid.
9. Air Marshal Harris to author, May 31, 1975.
10. Gen. Carl A. Spaatz, Columbia transcript, p. 59.
11. Mrs. Ruth Spaatz to author, June 22, 1979.
12. Gen. Ira C. Eaker to author, Apr. 8, 1975.
13. Gen. Kuter in his article "George C. Marshall, Architect of Air Power," *Air Force Magazine* (Aug. 1978).
14. Forrest C. Pogue, *George C. Marshall: Ordeal and Hope*, pp. 290–91.
15. Gen. Kuter's taped responses to the author's questions of Jan. 12, 1979.
16. Gen. Charles P. Cabell, Columbia transcript, pp. 4ff.
17. Gen. Orvil A. Anderson, Columbia transcript, p. 35.
18. Gen. Kuter in his article "The General vs. the Establishment," *Aerospace Historian* (Dec. 1974).
19. D. L. Arnold to author, Sept. 12, 1978; *Global Mission*, pp. 292–93.
20. Gen. Barney Giles to author, Nov. 27, 1978; Giles, Air University tape 814, transcript, pp. 59ff.
21. W. B. Arnold to author, Nov. 13, 1978.
22. Donald Douglas, Sr., Columbia transcript, pp. 99ff.; Gen. Eaker to author, Oct. 27, 1978.
23. Pogue, *Ordeal and Hope*, pp. 372–73.
24. Gen. Dwight Eisenhower, private diary, as reported in *The New York Times*, Sept. 19, 1979.
25. Gen. Anderson, Columbia transcript, pp. 29–30.
26. *Global Mission*, pp. 362–63.
27. Ibid., p. 304.

28. Robert A. Lovett to author, Nov. 6, 1978; Kuter, "The General vs. the Establishment"; Kuter, Air University tape 810, foot 259.
29. D. L. Arnold to author, Sept. 18, 1978.

Chapter Sixteen
1. D. L. Arnold to author, Sept. 12, 1978.
2. Irving Berlin to Arnold, Jan. 27, 1942.
3. H. H. Arnold, Jr., to author, Sept. 29, 1978.
4. Gen. Grandison Gardner, Columbia transcript, pp. 12ff.
5. H. H. Arnold, *Global Mission*, p. 340.
6. Ibid., p. 298.
7. Gen. James H. Doolittle, Air University tape 793, transcript p. 40.
8. Gen. Eugene Beebe, Columbia transcript, pp. 15–16.
9. Arnold diary, May 23, 1942.
10. Diary of Col. Beirne Lay, Jr., May 26–30, 1942; Gen. Ira C. Eaker to author, Apr. 8, 1975.
11. Arnold diary, May 26, 1942.
12. Air Marshal Arthur T. Harris to author, May 31, 1975.
13. Harris to Arnold, Apr. 22, 1942.
14. *Global Mission*, p. 316.
15. Col. Lay to author, Aug. 10, 1979; Lay diary, June 12, 1942.
16. Dr. Howard Rusk to author, Nov. 8, 1978; Dr. Rusk's *A World to Care For*, pp. 72–73.
17. *Global Mission*, p. 379.
18. Gen. Orvil A. Anderson, Columbia transcript, pp. 97–105; *Global Mission*, pp. 314, 328.
19. Forrest C. Pogue, *George C. Marshall: Ordeal and Hope*, pp. 379–80.
20. Gen. Samuel Anderson to author, Oct. 31, 1978.
21. Mrs. Ruth Spaatz to author, June 22, 1979.
22. Gen. Beebe to author, Aug. 11, 1979; Beebe, Columbia transcript, pp. 51ff.
23. Arnold to Cabell and Norstad, Jan. 29, 1942.
24. *The Wartime Journals of Charles A. Lindbergh*, pp. 684, 687, 690, 694, 709.
25. Gen. C. R. Smith to author, June 19, 1979.
26. *Global Mission*, p. 357.
27. Col. Clair Peterson to author, Nov. 29, 1978; Gen. Smith to author, June 19, 1979; Peterson, Columbia transcript, pp. 8ff.
28. Mrs. Eleanor Arnold, Air University tape notes.
29. Arnold to Spaatz, Aug. 14, 1942.
20. Pogue, *Ordeal and Hope*, p. 380.
31. Henry L. Stimson diary, Sept. 3, 1942.
32. Joint Chiefs of Staff meeting summary, Sept. 15, 1942.
33. Arnold diary, Sept. 16, 1942.
34. The account of Arnold's Sept. 1942 trip to the Pacific was compiled from *Global Mission*, Arnold's diary, and Gen. Charles P. Cabell's Columbia transcript, pp. 43ff.
35. Gen. Laverne Saunders to author, Oct. 1, 1978.
36. *Global Mission*, p. 350.
37. Ibid., p. 354.

Chapter Seventeen
1. Gen. Ira C. Eaker's work paper, "Why Have U.S. Bombers Not Bombed Germany?," written in Casablanca, Jan. 16, 1943.
2. Arnold to Lovett, Dec. 11, 1942.

3. Gen. C. R. Smith to author, June 19, 1979.
4. Arnold's diary, Jan. 9 to 24, 1943, was one of the main sources of this account of the Casablanca Conference. Other sources were the author's book, *Decision Over Schweinfurt*, pp. 183–89, and the author's interviews with Gen. Eaker in April 1975 and on June 22, 1979.
5. Arnold's diary, Jan. 29, 1943; H. H. Arnold, *Global Mission*, pp. 407–408.
6. This account of the flight into China was compiled from Arnold's diary, Feb. 4, 1943, and the author's interview of Nov. 29, 1978, with Col. Clair Peterson, Arnold's pilot on the flight.
7. This account of Arnold's meetings with Chiang Kai-shek is based on Arnold's diary, Feb. 6–8, 1943.
8. Col. Peterson to author, Nov. 29, 1978; *Global Mission*, p. 430; Arnold's diary, Feb. 17, 1943.
9. Gen. K. B. Wolfe, Air University tape 694, transcript, p. 1; tape 788, transcript, pp. 9ff.; Wilbur H. Morrison, *Point of No Return*, pp. 18–19. (In *Global Mission* Gen. Arnold inadvertently dated this crash a year earlier than it happened.)
10. Gen. Frank M. Andrews to Arnold, Feb. 26, 1943.
11. Gen. Smith to author, June 19, 1979.
12. The account of Arnold's Feb. 1943 heart attack is based on the author's interviews with D. L. Arnold, Sept. 12, 1978; Dr. Russell V. Lee, Feb. 6, 1979; Dr. Lee B. Martin, Sr., Apr. 3, 1980; Robert A. Lovett, Nov. 6, 1978; and Sgt. Bruce Simmons, June 24, 1979.
13. Arnold to W. B. Arnold, Mar. 28, 1943.
14. Arnold to Lois Snowden, Mar. 15, 1943.
15. Arnold to H. H. Arnold, Jr., Apr. 1, 1943.
16. Gen. Eaker to author, April 1975.
17. Gen. Barney Giles to author, Nov. 27, 1978; Giles, Air University tape 779, transcript, pp. 2ff.
18. Dr. Martin to author, Apr. 3, 1980.
19. Dr. Lee to author, Feb. 6, 1979.
20. Gen. W. F. McKee to author, Nov. 1, 1978.
21. *Global Mission*, p. 440.
22. Arnold to Andrews, Apr. 26, 1943.
23. Arnold to Beebe, June 10, 1943.
24. Lovett to author, Nov. 6, 1978; Gen. Eaker to author, April 1975.

Chapter Eighteen
1. Arnold to Beebe, July 23, 1943.
2. Lt. Gen. Fred M. Dean to author, Nov. 21, 1978; Dean, Air University tape 834, transcript, pp. 49ff.
3. Dr. Rusk told this story to the author in 1971, and retold it to him Nov. 8, 1978.
4. Sgt. Bruce Simmons to author, June 24, 1979.
5. Gen. Ira C. Eaker to author, April 1975.
6. H. H. Arnold, *Global Mission*, p. 376.
7. This account of the Cairo and Tehran Conferences is based mainly on Arnold's diary, Nov. 11 to Dec. 15, 1943.
8. *Global Mission*, p. 467.
9. Ibid., p. 466; Arnold's diary, Nov. 30, 1943.
10. Forrest C. Pogue, *George C. Marshall: Organizer of Victory*, p. 311.
11. Robert E. Sherwood, *Roosevelt and Hopkins*, p. 760.
12. Ibid., p. 759.

13. Arnold's diary, Dec. 8, 1943.
14. Ibid., Dec. 12, 1943.
15. The account of the remainder of Arnold's stay in Italy is based on Arnold's diary and the author's conversations with his son H. H. Arnold, Jr., who was with his father at the time.

Chapter Nineteen
 1. Gen. Orval Cook to author, Nov. 2, 1978; Gen. K. B. Wolfe, Air University tape 788, transcript, pp. 13ff.; Wolfe to Arnold, Nov. 10, 1943.
 2. Arnold to Joint Chiefs of Staff, Nov. 2, 1943.
 3. Gen. Emmett O'Donnell memorandum to Arnold, Feb. 7, 1944; Wilbur H. Morrison, *Point of No Return*, p. 39.
 4. Arnold to Gen. Hoyt S. Vandenberg, Feb. 28, 1944.
 5. D. L. Arnold to author, Sept. 12, 1978. His brothers were unfamiliar with this incident, perhaps because they were both in service in 1944. David was the only one at home at the time and he remembers the incident vividly.
 6. Arnold to H. H. Arnold, Jr., Jan. 15, 1944.
 7. W. B. Arnold to author, Oct. 13, 1978.
 8. Lowell Thomas, *Doolittle—A Biography*, p. 269.
 9. This account of Gen. Kuter's trip to the Pacific is based on the tape he made for the author in Jan. 1979.
10. Arnold to Giles, Feb. 28, 1944.
11. This account of Gen. Smith's trip to India is based on the author's conversation with him, June 19, 1979.
12. O'Donnell to Arnold, Feb. 7, 1944.
13. Gen. Cook to author, Nov. 2, 1978.
14. H. H. Arnold, *Global Mission*, p. 479.
15. Morrison, *Point of No Return*, p. 43.
16. *Global Mission*, p. 43.
17. Gen. Laverne Saunders to author, Oct. 1, 1978.
18. Arnold, in *Global Mission*, confuses this heart attack with a later one.
19. Mrs. Mary Streett to author, June 27, 1979.
20. Sgt. Bruce Simmons to author, June 24, 1979.
21. Gen. Wolfe, Air University tape 788, transcript, p. 4; Morrison, *Point of No Return*, pp. 59–60.
22. Gen. Ira C. Eaker to author, Apr. 18, 1975.
23. Robert A. Lovett to author, Nov. 6, 1978.
24. W. B. Arnold to author, Oct. 13, 1978.
25. Much of the information about this trip to Europe came from Arnold's diary.
26. Forrest C. Pogue, *George C. Marshall: Organizer of Victory*, pp. 443–44, 447.
27. Gen. Saunders to author, Oct. 1, 1978; Gen. Wolfe, Air University tape 788, transcript, p. 4.
28. Arnold to H. H. Arnold, Jr., Oct. 15, 1944; *Global Mission*, p. 522; Pogue, *Organizer of Victory*, p. 432.
29. Theodor von Kármán, *The Wind and Beyond*, pp. 267ff.
30. Gen. Grandison Gardner, Columbia transcript, pp. 22ff.
31. Arnold to his son Henry, Oct. 15, 1944.
32. Lovett to author, Nov. 6, 1978; Gen. Fred M. Dean, Air University tape 834, transcript, p. 115.
33. Gen. Saunders to author, Oct. 1, 1978; Gen. Curtis LeMay and MacKinlay Kantor, *Mission with LeMay*, p. 326.
34. Gen. Haywood S. Hansell, Jr., to author, Nov. 21, 1978.

Chapter Twenty
1. Gen. Fred M. Dean to author, Nov. 21, 1978; Dean, Air University tape 834, transcript, pp. 121ff.
2. Gen. Barney Giles to author, Nov. 27, 1978; Giles, Air University tape 779, transcript, p. 22.
3. Arnold to Norstad, Jan. 14, 1945.
4. Arnold to Hansell, Feb. 1, 1945.
5. Gen. Curtis LeMay and MacKinlay Kantor, *Mission with LeMay*, pp. 338–39.
6. Mrs. Mary Streett to author, June 27, 1979; Sgt. Bruce Simmons to author, June 24, 1979.
7. Gen. Eugene Beebe to author, Aug. 14, 1978.
8. Arnold to Giles, Feb. 7, 1945.
9. Chiang Kai-shek to Arnold, Feb. 17, 1945.
10. Arnold's diary, Mar. 31 to May 8, 1945, was the main source of information about this trip to Europe.
11. Arnold to Marshall, Apr. 19, 1945.
12. H. H. Arnold, *Global Mission*, pp. 548–49.
13. Arnold's diary, Apr. 13, 1945.
14. Ibid., Apr. 19, 1945; Gen. Ira C. Eaker to author, Apr. 18, 1975, and Oct. 27, 1978.
15. *Global Mission*, p. 560.
16. Henry Morgenthau to Arnold, May 8, 1945.
17. Arnold memorandum to Joint Chiefs of Staff, May 26, 1945.
18. Much of the information about Arnold's trip to the Pacific, June 6 to 24, 1945, came from his letters to his wife, and from *Global Mission*, pp. 561ff.
19. Arnold to Mrs. Arnold, June 18, 1945.
20. Ibid., June 17, 1945.
21. Gen. Charles Stone to author, Aug. 10, 1978.
22. Arnold to W. B. Arnold, July 6, 1945; W. B. Arnold to author, Nov. 1, 1978; *Global Mission*, p. 571.
23. Arnold to W. B. Arnold, July 6, 1945.
24. Arnold to Mrs. Arnold, July 14, 1945.
25. Ibid., July 22, 1945.
26. H. H. Arnold, Jr., to author, Jan. 27, 1979.
27. H. H. Arnold, Jr., to author, Sept. 28, 1978.

Chapter Twenty-one
1. Arnold to Gen. Carl A. Spaatz, Jan. 7, 1946.
2. Arnold to Mrs. Arnold, Sept. 17, 23 & 25, 1945.
3. Robert A. Lovett to Arnold, Jan. 1, 1946.
4. Gen. W. F. McKee to author, Nov. 1, 1978.
5. H. H. Arnold, *Global Mission*, p. 608.
6. Arnold to Ernest Snowden, Mar. 10, 1946.
7. Dr. Russell V. Lee to author, Feb. 6, 1979.
8. W. B. Arnold in a letter to the author, July 29, 1980.
9. Sgt. Bruce Simmons to author, June 24, 1979.
10. Gen. George C. Marshall to Arnold, Oct. 17, 1946.
11. Statement by Arnold before a subcommittee of the Special U.S. Senate Committee Investigating the National Defense Program, Nov. 22, 1947.
12. Arnold to the Snowdens, May 23, 1948.
13. W. B. Arnold in his letter to the author, July 29, 1980.
14. Arnold to the Snowdens, Mar. 18, 1948.
15. Ibid., May 23, 1945.

16. Ibid., June 17, 1948.
17. William Laidlaw to author, Nov. 6, 1978, July 5, 1979; Sgt. Simmons to author, June 24, 1979.
18. Arnold to the Snowdens, Sept. 30, 1949.
19. *National Geographic* magazine, Dec. 1948.
20. Dr. Robert Mollenhauer to author, Jan. 27, 1979.
21. Mrs. Josephine Tevis to author, Jan. 6, 1980.
22. Sgt. Simmons to author, June 24, 1979.
23. Gen. Dwight Eisenhower to Arnold, Mar. 5 & 14, 1949.
24. Charles Portal to Arnold, May 18, 1949.
25. Charles A. Lindbergh to Arnold, June 7, 1949.
26. D. L. Arnold to author, Sept. 12, 1978.
27. Lovett to Arnold, July 11, 1949; Lovett to author, Nov. 6, 1978.
28. Arnold to the Snowdens, Jan. 9, 1950.
29. W. B. Arnold to author, Nov. 1, 1978.
30. Mrs. Tevis to author, Jan. 6, 1980.

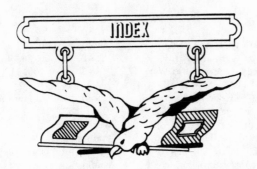